LEAD MINING IN DERBYSHIRE
HISTORY, DEVELOPMENT & DRAINAGE
1. CASTLETON TO THE RIVER WYE

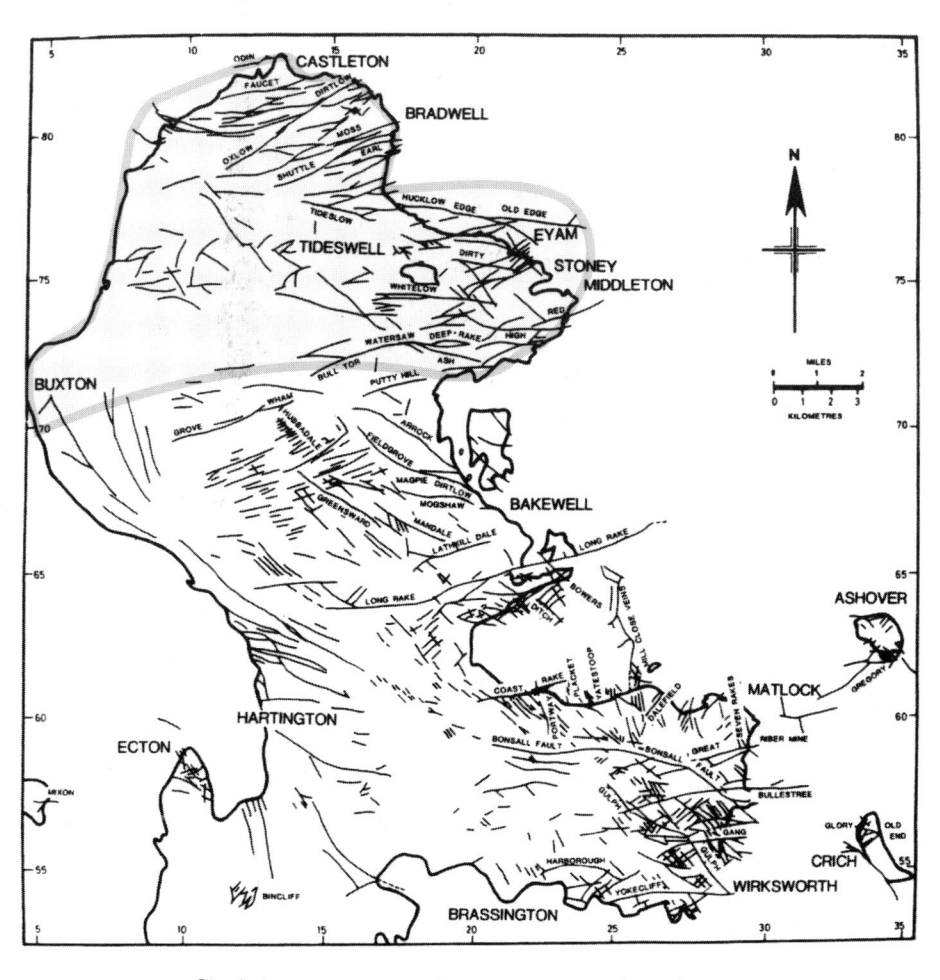

Shaded area represents the mines, veins and soughs discussed in volume 1.

Published by

Ashbourne Hall, Cokayne Ave
Ashbourne, Derbyshire, DE6 1EJ England
Tel: (01335) 347349 Fax: (01335) 347303
e-mail: landmark@clara.net

1st Edition

13 ISBN: 978-1-84306-343-8

© J.H. Rieuwerts 2007

The right of J.H. Rieuwerts as author of this work has been asserted by him in accordance with the Copyright, Design and Patents Act, 1993.

All rights reserved. No part of this publication may be reproduced, stored in a retrieval system or transmitted in any form or by any means, electronic, mechanical, photocopying, recording or otherwise without the prior permission of Landmark Publishing Ltd.

British Library Cataloguing in Publication Data: a catalogue record for this book is available from the British Library.

Dedication

To Paul Deakin, F.R.P.S. in recognition of his unique contribution to the photographic recording of mining history.

Print: Cromwell Press Ltd
Design by: Mark Titterton
Edited by: Ian Howe

Front Cover: A mine behind Hagg Tors, Matlock Bath, from a watercolour by William Day.
Back Cover: Moorwood Sough, Stoney Middleton.
Page 3: The 'Leviathian' in James Hall's Mine, New Rake, Castleton.

LEAD MINING IN DERBYSHIRE
HISTORY, DEVELOPMENT & DRAINAGE
1. CASTLETON TO THE RIVER WYE

Landmark Publishing

CONTENTS

	Preface	6
1	**Introduction**	7
	Summary of technological advances (table)	14-15
2	**astleton Liberty**	21
	Oden Mine	24
	Dirtlow Rake & Pindale	41
	Hazard & Hollandtwine	47
	Speedwell and others	49
3	**The Liberties of Bradwell, Hazlebadge and part of Great Hucklow**	50
	Pindale & Smalldale area	50
	The Drainage of Moss Rake, Bradwell	54
	Hazlebadge Mines & Pic-Tor-End Sough	62
	The southern end of Hazlebadge Lordship & part of Great Hucklow Liberty	70
4	**Coalpithole Rake and drainage on the western edge of Peak Forest Liberty**	73
5	**Tideslow Rake and Hucklow Edge Rake**	81
	Workings within limestone	83
	Tideswell Liberty	83
	Little Hucklow Liberty	88
	Great Hucklow Liberty	92
	Workings beneath the shale cover	96
	Great Hucklow Liberty	96
	Grindlow Liberty	98

	Eyam Liberty	100
6	**Eyam Edge Mines, Stoke Sough & Magclough Sough**	110
	Stoke Sough	110
	Magclough Sough	117
7	**Watergrove and soughs in Upper Middleton Dale**	120
8	**Veins and mines between Foolow and Eyam**	130
9	**Eyam and the north side of Middleton Dale**	134
10	**The south side of Middleton Dale**	145
11	**Calver, Hassop and Rowland**	149
12	**Longstone Edge and adjacent workings**	160
	south side	160
	north side	164
13	**The north side of Coombs Dale**	166
14	**Veins and mines draining into Cressbrook Dale**	170
	east side	170
	west side	172
15	**Edge Rake and Brandy Bottle mines, Wheston**	175
16	**Lead mining at Burbage and Chrome Hill, near Buxton**	177
	Bibliography	181
	Acknowledgements	190
	Subscribers	191

PREFACE

More than thirty years ago the author began a compilation of the history and technology of drainage levels (known locally as soughs) serving the Derbyshire lead orefield. The object was publication of a book that would combine into one volume all the basic elements contained in his previously published lists and extended articles dating back to the 1960s. The majority of the above works are to be found in several issues of the Bulletin of the Peak District Mines Historical Society.

The book was subsequently published in 1987 and was restricted to a print-run of only two hundred copies. The contents were in effect a gazetteer containing a much abridged history of each of the 300 or so soughs then known. The publication, though well received by mining historians, experienced delays and production difficulties due to the serious ill-health of the printer. The unfortunate train of events resulted in a less than satisfactory publication, although good fortune prevailed in that the factual information reproduced from the manuscript remained unaltered and accurate within the limits of the author`s research. There was however a rapid realisation that a far more substantial work was a necessity. This significantly expanded new work is different in content and format to the first edition.

Semi-retirement in 1991 allowed immediate access to archives previously unseen. Research in the National Archive, initially at Chancery Lane, later at the Public Record Office, Kew, has already revealed a staggering one thousand six hundred manuscripts relating to Derbyshire lead mining; research is on-going. Many other sources include the Guildhall Library, London; the British Library; the Duchy of Lancaster Office, London; Imperial College, London and the archive of the Duke of Rutland, Belvoir Castle.

The new publication will extend to three volumes. Each will cover a far wider scope than the first edition (1987). The historical and technological development of each area will be discussed in substantial detail, relying on much of the above mentioned previously unseen and unpublished evidence, most of which can be intimately related to the overall geological context. The intensive research alluded to above has allowed identification of more than one hundred extra drainage levels, and of significant importance, details of many 16th to 18th century `engines` and water raising devices.

The volumes are illustrated by area maps, vertical sections demonstrating mining and geological details, all enhanced by a series of magnificent photographs, the work of Paul Deakin, FRPS.

1. INTRODUCTION

The main text will be found to contain extended discussion of the relevant geology and the history and chronological development of mining and mine drainage within all individual districts of the Derbyshire lead orefield. Nevertheless, in order to aid understanding, a brief resume of these themes until the end of 18th century is necessary here in order to set them into an overall context. Thereafter, developments became intense, were influenced more than ever by outside sources and are so well documented that a summary is not relevant, they are fully discussed within the main body of this book. However, as an aid, an extended table listing the principal technological developments involved is included. The table is an up-dated version of that to be found in Rieuwerts [1998].

The word sough (suff, sow, sufe) in Derbyshire lead mining terminology refers to a near horizontal passageway (there were steeper gradient exceptions) constructed for the purpose of draining waterlogged mine workings in order to allow operations to proceed to deeper levels.

Several articles compiled by the author during a period in excess of forty years have listed and provided limited additional comment concerning the dozens of soughs or drainage levels that served the mines. None of these articles, or indeed the rather slender first edition of this book, devoted much attention to the earlier history of the orefield. Although a short geological and historical introduction was given for each drainage `compartment` or district group of mines, nevertheless discussion was brief. This approach, though dictated by financial constraints and thus the available space, was completely inadequate. Comments relating to important contributions made by a large number of pre-1650 drainage `Engines` were similarly inadequate. The machines were driven by a variety of forms of motive power including men, horse(s) and water.

This second edition seeks to rectify these omissions. The format adopted in the first edition, whereby the orefield was divided into well defined districts or `drainage compartments` has been retained, but with accompanying explanations greatly expanded.

GENERAL OBSERVATIONS

The early history of Derbyshire lead mining, occupying the period from the Roman domination of this country, up to and including the 14th century, has been discussed by many authors, but its content is almost wholly outwith the scope of this publication. There are a few exceptions. During the 12th to 14th centuries, documentary evidence points to the existence of eleven and possibly twelve mining sites each containing more than one individual working. Five sites were situated in the northern area (the High Peak), the remainder in the central, western and southern parts. Most, if not all would have been worked opencast, though a mine at *Rotherlowe*, location un-traced, but near Bradwell, was closed in 1247 because of flooding [Lander and Vellacott, 1907]. The Rotherlowe mine might have been an opencast trench excavated along the strike of a vein, or a shallow underground working.

The earliest laws and customs, written in 1288, record the illegal practice of *underbeating*, that is mining at depth by one party of miners, trespassing beneath the higher workings of another group who were in lawfull possession of the same part of the vein [Rieuwerts, 1998].

The fragmentary ore production figures available for the 12th-13th centuries record substantial output from the Tideslow mines (1215–1251) and from mines at *Wardlow Copp*, very probably that section of Cop Rake lying within Peak Forest [Rieuwerts, 1994: Ford and Rieuwerts, 2000].

The historical development of the orefield after about 1450 was governed by a number of factors, some, though not all, were interrelated and thus mutually dependant on each other. The miners` ability to work the ore deposits relied on a gradual awakening and understanding of their geological environment. During early times this basic knowledge was derived by working miners, but before the mid 18th century and before geology became a science, the knowledge began to become concentrated in the minds of mine agents and overseers, many of whom possessed an intimate comprehension of the succession of rocks in their own neighbourhood and hence the position of ore bearing beds.

The first sections illustrating geology date from the mid 18th century and are due to Samuel Heyward, George Heyward, George Tissington and Joseph Cook, all agents at a number of mines. Their sections depicting the succession of strata at Hubbadale and Highlow mines, near Taddington; Basrobin Sough, Wensley; High Rake Mine, Hucklow and Burfoot Mine, Millers Dale are all very localised. Later, significant observations on Derbyshire strata in and adjacent to the orefield were made by geologists such as John Whitehurst [1778, 1786], John Mawe [1802], John Farey [1811], White Watson [1811, 1813 and many manuscripts] and William Hopkins [1834]. An important contribution, often overlooked by commentators, was that made by Thomas Short in his treatise on mineral waters published in 1734. Short, a medical practitioner based in Sheffield made many astute observations in addition to recording the succession of strata in different parts of Derbyshire.

The principal elements to occupy the minds of mine owners and working miners alike concerned the diverse forms of mineralisation, ranging in shape from the vertical and near vertical rakes and scrins to essentially horizontal cavernous pipes and strata bound flats; recognition that limestones were the predominant rock-types likely to host ore deposits, and similarly the occurrence of beds of igneous rock, usually basalts and tuffs interlayered within the limestones. These latter rocks, visually different to the limestones, acquired a variety of local names, the most common being *toadstone, channel, blackstone*, their weathered equivalents as *clay*. The miners realised too that these `toadstones` were virtually barren, but had important functions in acting as aquicludes to ground water and as cap rocks or basement rocks controlling mineralisation. The discovery during the mid 16th century that the mineralised limestones passed beneath the covering of shale and newer rocks was a major revelation. Faulting, inclination of the strata, expansion and contraction of the ore-bodies and the presence of natural cave systems were all of major significance to mining operations. All the above features are discussed in detail at appropriate points in the main text. The spatial relationships between shale, limestone and igneous rocks became important, not least in predicting what rocks might be passed through in both shaft sinking and sough construction.

The major soughs in the orefield such as Meerbrook, Hillcarr, Cromford, Yatestoop and Stoke took upwards of 30 to 50 years or even 100 years for completion and were major feats of mining engineering. A legal agreement was often drawn up between mine owners and the `soughers` or adventurers, detailing composition payments due on lead ore obtained below the standing water level before drainage was achieved. Agreements were also made with land owners, there being no legal right to drive a level through barren rock, the owners permission to do so being required.

The earliest list of soughs is that compiled by Farey [1811] who also noted the strata through which they passed. Stokes [1880–1881] published a similar list, though both include but a small proportion of the known soughs. Nellie Kirkham (the late Mrs. J.H.D. Myatt) stimulated the interest of mining historians in the old soughs and she published much detail about them in different journals. An article published by her in 1954 referred to her knowing of over 70 lead mine soughs in the orefield. More recently detailed research has been published by Flindall, Willies and the author.

THE 15TH CENTURY
GEOLOGY

The written versions of the laws and customs of the mines compiled between 1288 and 1525 demonstrate that the basic concept of a vertical/hading vein containing a rib of lead ore, bounded by walls of country rock or gangue mineral, was by then well understood, indeed the laws are founded on that premise. The term rake was taken to mean only that part of the mineralised structure containing discrete ribs of galena, and clearly did not refer to the entire contents within the width of a great rake such as Dirtlow Rake, Tideslow Rake or Dovegang Rake. `Hole` in Derbyshire lead mining terminology usually referred to a natural cave or to a pipe-cum-flat deposit. Therefore the meers of ground set in 1470 at the *Breakholes* north of Nestalls Rake (now part of the Masson Show Cave), demonstrates the miners understanding of this different form of mineralisation.

MINING TECHNIQUES; ROCK BREAKAGE, VENTILATION

The physical process of mining at ever greater depths was reliant upon rock breakage, haulage, improved methods of ventilation and not least, adequate drainage

1. introduction

A swarm of parallel scrins at Bonsall Lees. Mining at *Bontysalleys* was taking place by 1541 at least (J.H. Rieuwerts).

Shallow opencuts on Tideslow Rake. Lead ore was worked in this vicinity, no doubt from surface excavations, in the 12th and 13th centuries (J.H. Rieuwerts).

of the mines. The awakenings of some of the above ideas began about 1450. By 1470 the Nestalls Rake at Matlock had been exploited for a distance of 725 yards from a point close to the river Derwent, westwardly to the boundary with Bonsall Liberty. Numerous cross veins were also being worked, but perhaps most significantly a length of six meers, or 174 yards in *the Breakholes*, ranging north west from Nestalls Rake (known in later times as Bacon Rake). The workings in the Breakholes are characterised by thousands of tiny peckings adorning the walls. The effect is considered to have been created by extraction of *bing ore* by use of a long, very thin pointed *lough chisel* and a very small pick known as a *foudenhead*. The sheer intensity of ore removal using this technology has not been recorded elsewhere, but similar work has been noted very sparingly at pipes in Northern Dale, near Snitterton. Identical methods have been reported from only two European mines, one in eastern France and one in Germany. One of these has been positively dated to the 13th century (Dr. Christoph Bartels, pers comm).

How ventilation was achieved within the complex ramifications of workings at the Breakholes is not clear, but perhaps an air circulation by natural air flow was induced by carefully routing it between shafts on Nestalls Rake through whichever stopes were currently in work and via shafts (at least two are known) communicating with the stopes in the Breakholes.

THE 16TH CENTURY
GEOLOGY

The laws and customs of the mines continued to echo the miners` understanding of the form of a rake. An un-dated document dating from 1553–1558 demonstrates that the nature of wide horizontal deposits was understood, necessitating meers being measured in squares rather than the usual linear measurement along the strike of the vein. The meer was defined as *contayninge xxix yardes everye and yche waye* [PRO, C 1/1422/18-21]. Later in the century the miners realised that the ore bearing limestones continued at depth beneath the shale cover. Shaley Grove at Matlock was producing ore in 1576 and possibly just beneath the shale at Starkholmes by 1520-41.

MINING TECHNIQUES; ROCK BREAKAGE

The sixteenth century witnessed considerable expansion. Many more mines were at work, sixty four are individually named, though as the work by Kiernan [1989] has shown, many groups of miners might be at work along a single vein. The first evidence of fireing rock underground, drainage using horse-powered pumps (c.1579–1581) and a long drainage adit all appear in contemporary documentation.

Excavation of rock and hard veinstone was assisted at many mines by use of fireing or `fire-setting`. There are many underground sites were the remains of these operations can be seen, but unfortunately few can be dated by documentary evidence until the following century. The Coalpit Rake, Matlock contains abundant evidence of soot covered roofs, the characteristic `onion skin` peeling of wall rock and traces of burnt and unburnt coal. The rake was referred to as *Colpyt Rake* in fragmentary ore accounts dating from c.1528 [PRO, STAC 2/15].

Very small cross section, short levels driven through barren limestone have been seen in workings north of Nestalls Rake and also in the so-called `Old Ash Mine` in Northern Dale. The pickwork visible in the walls and roofs seems to demonstrate that they were cut by repeated hammering and chiselling down individual grooves using slightly larger picks than the foudenhead.

DRAINAGE

A horse operated rag and chain pump was in operation at *Ashbury Crofts* in Matlock c.1579-1581. The site of Ashbury Croft has not been positively identified, but Roger Flindall (pers comm) considers that it may have been at Paddock Torr Rake, part of the Dimple Mine complex, Matlock Bank. The *Engine* was installed by Sir Francis Willoughby of Wollaton Hall, Nottingham, it being the first such machine known at a Derbyshire lead mine. Installed within a quarter of a century of publication of Agricola`s great treatise, Willoughby was aware of *De Re Metallica*, a single page of which survives in the family manuscripts; it is an illustration of a water-lifting machine.

Towards the end of the century there appear a few references to *Waterworks*. The meaning of the term is not always clear from available documentation, but it seems to relate to heavily watered mines where concentrated pumping was necessary. `Engines` are sometimes noted at the Waterworks and these engines were likely to have been large, hand operated pumps using maybe four men in tandem. Six sites are known from documentary evidence.

One reference to a late 16th century-early 17th century drainage adit is even more enigmatic. Sir Richard Fleetwood claimed that his father and he had constructed a drain, 1½ miles in length to the Staffordshire and Derbyshire mines, which task had occupied them from 1594 to 1634 [BL, Loan ms 16]. No location has yet been verified, but a route close to the valley of the river Dove, anywhere between Snelston in the south and the Carder Low mines in the north might be appropriate. Fleetwood`s adit was the forerunner of more than four hundred soughs driven during the following three hundred years.

Carving of 'T'owd Man' in Wirksworth Church. The basket or; wisket', was used for carrying ore (J.H.Rieuwerts).

ORE DRESSING

The introduction of a fine meshed wire sieve and a water-filled vat *(ffatt)* by William Humphrey and Christopher Schutz, under license from the Society of Mineral and Battery Works, permitted discarded *bouse* originally thrown onto the hillocks as waste to be re-dressed. Humphrey claimed that two thousand poor people earned a living by this method.

17TH CENTURY
GEOLOGY

This century witnessed rapid expansion in both geological knowledge and technological advance. That the miners were well aware of the essential differences between a rake, a pipe and a flatwork has been noted already in a previous section. A definition of Dovegang Rake in 1633 stated that it was only 5 or 6 feet in width, 240 feet in depth and a quarter of a mile in length [Rieuwerts, 1998]. The width must refer to the composite width of the galena ribs, it cannot relate to the much greater total width of the rake. Hopkinson [1644] considered that there was no limitation to the depth of a rake. The earliest specific record of a *pipe* dates from 1635 at the *Nohole Rake Veyne or pipe* [PRO, E134, 11th Chas I, Mich. 20].

Before 1640 the miners were perfectly well aware that the shales and gritstones occurring above the limestones did not contain payable ore-shoots and considered that the weathered basalts and tuffs, known as clay beds, terminated mineralisation downwards. At Gentlewomans Grove, Matlock it was noted in 1637 that *Scrins, breaks, vaynes - - are all - - cut of - - by the Clay-bed* [PRO, DL 1/352].

These references also hint that there was by then a realisation that certain bearing horizons existed, these acting as more favourable host rocks to mineralisation. A document written c.1603, but harking back to the dissolution of the monasteries, speaks of mines in Newton Grange, owned in former times by Combermere Abbey, and *of leade oare growinge and being there* [PRO, E 112, 75(160). The belief that metallic ores possessed a `vegetable power` and were regenerated in the veins was a belief widespread throughout European mining regions at that time.

Displacement of strata due to both vertical and horizontal movement began to be appreciated at least by the mid century. Before 1652 the miners believed that the horizontal continuity of Dovegang Rake was cut-off by Sliding Pitts Vein, whilst the following year Manlove [1653] referred to *break-offs* in his well known poem, *The Rhymed Chronicle*. A plan of Ratchwood Mine drawn in 1699 illustrated horizontal displacement of a vein by a *slip*.

ROCK BREAKAGE, HAULAGE AND VENTILATION

Improvements in smelting technology made during the last quarter of the 16th century allowed smaller sized ore to be used in the new ore-hearth furnaces introduced by William Humphrey and Christopher Schutz. A direct consequence of this was economic removal of large quantities of galena disseminated within other gangue minerals. Thus many large scale opencast workings were developed, enlarged from the original slits created when only rich ribs were mined; spectacular examples yet remain for example at Oden Mine and Dirtlow Rake, Castleton; Cop Rake, Bradwell Moor, Tideslow Rake and along Hard Rake (or Bacon Rake) at High Tor, Matlock Bath.

The major development in rock breakage in the 17th century involved the use of gunpowder blasting. Definitely in use in 1672 at the nearby Ecton mines, Staffordshire and shortly afterwards in the Earl of Rutland`s Haddon mines [Belvoir], there is very strong circumstantial evidence for its use a decade earlier during 1662–1663 in driving Longe Sough, or Cromford Sough [Rieuwerts, 1983; 1998]. Ralph Greatorex, a Derbyshire-born engineer and scientist appears to allude to the boring of shot holes in limestone and *churt* in the mid to late 1660s, possibly those at Longe Sough, where his brother John was a partner [Royal Society, Boyle Papers].

Concurrent with the introduction of gunpowder, the old technique of cutting levels through solid rock by means of chisel, gad and hammer and plug and feathers still persisted and was to do so well into the following century and even later. Almost all examples of these *old man`s cross cuts* within the Derbyshire orefield can be dated to post 1650, a remarkable fact, because by then the technique had been extensively used in European metal mining for at least two centuries. None of the few soughs driven through limestone that pre-date 1650, for example Vermuyden`s and that at Tearsall Mine, have been entered in recent times and construction methods are not known.

Fireing (or fire setting) was also used on a wide scale. Articles regulating its use were only introduced into the laws and customs throughout much of the orefield in the 17th century.

Mines were being worked to greater depths; workings 300 feet in depth were recorded at Wirksworth and at Mandale Mine, Over Haddon. Two shafts, each 240 feet in depth, served by horse gins, were sunk at Dovegang Mine in 1615; a shaft 170 feet in depth served Tearsall Mine, Wensley in 1634–1635.

These technologies dictated that far more efficient methods of ventilation were necessary. Records of miners being *damped* i.e. suffocated by gas, begin to occur in the late 16th century. Methods of alleviating the problem included sinking air shafts (wind shafts) at regular spaced intervals into the deeper workings and into drainage soughs. Extra benefits were to be had by using *fangs* (wooden box air ducting with clay sealed joints), a *lamp turn* (creation of an upward draught by hanging a basket of burning coals at the shaft top), and parallel air gates connected by *thurls*, one gate opening into daylight at a lower contour allowing entry of fresh air along it, along the working face, the foul air exiting via the parallel drivage into an upcast shaft with a hanging coal basket, at a higher contour. References to bellows and fans are rare, but both were in use before the end of the century, thurls had been in use in the neighbouring coalfields at least since the 16th century, but they too do not make an appearance in the lead mines until late in the 17th century.

Underground transport still remained primitive in comparison, contrasting with the Lake District mines and those of Central Wales, where wheeled haulage systems with boarded floors acting as rails had been introduced by 16th century Austrian/German miners. Derbyshire mines had to wait another century and a half for such luxury. Carriage of waste rock and ore underground relied on *corves* and/or *wiskets*. Corves were shallow wooden boxes that could be either dragged along the floor or carried, whilst wiskets were small baskets with a curved handle and were carried; both types are described in contemporary documents. The system using *carriers* or *bearers* was described at the Wirksworth mines in 1629 [France, 1951]. Carrying was in use at Hard Rake, Rowland in 1699, when special provisions were made in an agreement allowing miners from two parties: *To have – way gate to carey and ree carey pas and repas without any Let or hindrance* [SCL, Bag 3357]. Corves were recorded at the Westedge Mine, Ashover in 1617, but their construction was not described [Band, 1975-1976]. The Long Drift Vein, an old part of Waterhole Mine, Hassop may have taken its name from a purpose made haulage gate [SCL, Bag 702; Rieuwerts, 2005].

DRAINAGE

Waterworks

References to certain mines being styled as `waterworks` continue throughout the 17th century, and references become sufficiently detailed to provide clear indication of the methods in use. The arrangements at such mines might range from large, man powered rag and chain pumps to horse driven, or even water wheel powered water lifting machines.

Engines

The Dovegang mines suffered acute drainage problems and evidence given by miners stated that the rake had been `drowned` since 1597, or even as early as 1540. Protracted efforts to drain the mines were begun in 1609 and from that date until 1629 at least eight and possibly twelve `engines` had been tried. All appear to have been motivated by horse-power, some were rag and chain pumps, others lifted water in large bags or barrels. Soon after 1615 two engine shafts were each sunk to a depth of 40 fathoms (240 feet). A unique method used only at Dovegang Rake was the installation deep underground of two tread wheels, one in 1651, another in 1657. They lifted water via rag and chain pumps into the newly completed Vermuyden`s Sough.

The utilisation of power derived from water wheels took place a little later. The earliest proven example, the Park Wheel, was sited on Harthill Park Vein (known later as Grime Sough Vein), near Alport. It was in operation by 1665 [Belvoir]. Earlier, but unproven examples may have been sited at Paddock Torr Vein c.1644–1662 and at Ladygate Rake in 1655. Both of these mines were situated at the side of the river Derwent at Matlock. The last two decades of the century saw the focus of water-powered drainage machines shift to the Alport-Youlgreave district, the aptly named Haddon Wheels Rake being the most prominent. During the 17th century at least thirty eight `Engines` were installed at Derbyshire lead mines. Unfortunately, engineering details for most are poorly recorded. The term `engineer` began to appear in the period and some twenty men were named.

The Soughs

The term sough (suff, sugh, sow, sufe) has become synonymous with Derbyshire lead mining, though this claim to fame is slightly unfair as there were many such drainage levels in the adjacent coalfield, many of which pre-date examples at the lead mines. Adits and water-levels are documented at least by the 14th century in others areas of the country too, in Devon, Lancashire, Yorkshire and the Northern Pennines.

Anomalies in identification still exist, as indeed they did during compilation of the author`s first list of Derbyshire lead mine soughs in 1966. The recorded number of these drainage levels now rests in excess of 400. Mining historians believed for many years that the sough made by Sir Cornelius Vermuyden was the first such level to be constructed in the Derbyshire orefield [eg. Kirkham, 1953; Rieuwerts, 1987]. More recent research by this author has revealed that it was preceded by three and possibly four other soughs. They are discussed in rather more detail in the main text, suffice to say that the level made by Sir Richard Fleetwood somewhere along the Derbyshire-Staffordshire border; Wet Sough, Winster; a sough begun by John Bartholomew to drain Dovegang Rake; the first section of Tearsall Sough, Wensley, all pre-date Vermuyden`s Sough.

Some seventy named soughs are known before 1700, of which only twelve were situated in the area north of the river Wye. The largest concentrations were at Alport-Youlgreave where sixteen have been identified, and eight each at Elton-Winster and Wirksworth. No less than six drainage levels were driven into Milnclose (Millclose) Pipe between 1658 and 1688. Before 1700, Tideslow Rake could boast four soughs, three levels served the immensely rich Dovegang mines, and Portaway Pipe at Winster was also served by three soughs.

The principal aim of a sough was to lower the water table at a mine, or at a series of mines to the lowest practicable contour, generally the nearest valley. Sometimes mine water could be turned through old workings, or along a purpose made passage into an underground swallow or cave-system. Such levels were termed *swallow drifts;* one served Tearsall Rake before 1633–1634 after which it was extended as a sough [Wolley, 6680 ff.68-70]. A cave passage was used for drainage at the Seventh Meer, adjacent to Gentlewomans Pipe, Masson Hill, Matlock, in 1641 it being: *A sough or natural watercourse made by nature in the 7th meere* [PRO, DL 1/367].

Many early drainage levels were driven along the sole of a vein and for obvious reasons these were often called `vein-soughs`. Seventeenth century examples include Oden Groves Sough, two soughs excavated along Mawrey Rake, Millers Dale, two soughs driven along Portaway Pipe, Winster and two soughs along Dun Rake, Cromford. At least one long level was driven along Tideslow Rake, the water being conducted into an underground swallow. There were few cross measure drifts driven in the 17th century, the considerable costs incurred, together with time taken for completion were understandable deterrents. Notwithstanding, they were often of considerable length, driven largely through barren rock to a group of mines. The largest of those constructed in

Summary of technological advances

Date	Excavation	Drainage
pre 1300	1. shallow, opencast trenches	
1400	2. removal of rich ribs of ore from veins and scrins	
1500	1. narrow opencuts 2. limited underground developments, depth c. 100 feet 3. small cross section levels, hand picked 4. fire setting 1528 5. excavation beneath shale possibly 1520s-1540s 6. excavation beneath shale 1576	1. horse powered 'engine' lifting water c. 1581 2. Fleetwood's Sough 1594-1634 3. 'water works' 1597
1600	1. workings 200-300 feet deep 2. fire setting with coal pre 1633 3. development of major opencuts 4. large stopes in veins and pipes 5. development of hand-picked levels and adits 6. gunpowder blasting c. 1662	1. water drawn in bags/buckets 2. hand operated pumps c. 1610 3. horse powered pumps 1615 4. sough drainage 1627-32 5. water wheel powered pumps c. 1640-1650 6. shale gates c. 1670-1690
1700	1. fire setting obsolete c. 1725 2. shafts and workings to 700 feet depth 1732 3. shaft 624 feet deep 1749 4. shaft in excess of 900 feet deep 1795	1. first Newcomen engine 1716-1719 2. 40 feet diameter water wheel 1747 3. hydraulic engine or water pressure engine possibly 1765-70 4. tub or water balance 1783
1800	1. shaft 911 feet deep 1811 2. introduction of cast steel borers 1835 3. shaft 936 feet deep 1863 4. introduction of rock drills 1874 5. nitro-glycerine explosives 6. electricity for underground lighting c. 1886	1. water pressure engine 1803-05 2. last Newcomen engine 1824 3. hydraulic 'disc' engine 1830 4. Cornish engine 1837 5. horizontal engine 1852

(based on Rieuwerts, 1987, modified and with additions)

Haulage Access	Ventilation	Dressing Smelting
1. wiskets		1. communal ore washing sites
		2. bole furnaces, small diameter
		3. bole furnaces, larger diameter pre 1470
		4. blackwork ovens for smelting slag
1. hand wound stows		1. ore stamps 1553
		2. Almain furnace 1553
		3. washing troughs at the mines by 1557
		4. wire meshed sieve and water vat 1571-72
		5. ore heath furnace:
		foot blast 1571
		water powered 1572
		6. slag hearth 1572
1. horse-gin 1615	1. wind shafts 1629	1. buddling c. 1600
2. corves 1617	2. fangs 1629	
3. horse-gin 1634	3. bellows 1676	
	4. fan 1694	
1. carrying gate 1706	1. thurls 1706	1. cupola furnace 1737
2. levy 1708	2. fan house 1724	2. ore hearth obsolete 1777
3. horse-gins became common 1710-15	3. fire house (?)1732	
4. cart-gate; plain wheeled wagons 1730	4. fire house 1746	
5. wharle 1747	5. cupola 1766	
6. boatway/ canal 1766	6. water blast 1766	
7. Newcastle road; flanged wheels, wooden rails 1770	7. large fans 1776	
8. horse level 1783	8. wind engine 1783	
9. steam whimsey 1795		
1. iron rails 1820	1. Davy lamp 1819	1. horse powered ore crusher 1817
2. horizontal engine 1844	2. Blow George c. 1820	2. 'washing machine'-hotcher 1825
3. large horse levels c. 1845-50	3. wind machine worked by water wheel 1880-81	3. crushing rollers 1836
		4. steam powered ore crusher 1842
		5. Spanish slag hearth 1849
		6. mechanised dressing floors c. 1868
		7. Scotch hearth c. 1886

An iron-bound, wooden kibble found in Long Rake Mine, Youlgreave (Paul Deakin).

the 17th century was the Longe Sough or Cromford Sough, both it and Bates Sough were driven to unwater Dovegang Rake. The Great Sough was driven to the Crich Cliff mines in mid century.

There were variations to the principal idea. Some levels were driven from a high contour, specifically aimed at a significant geological horizon such as an ore bearing pipe, or above or beneath a bed of toadstone. During the 17th century the best examples were sited at Nether Pitts, Winster and Ash Grove, Snitterton. This category also includes several 18th century high contour soughs in the Via Gellia such as Slaley Sough, Lees Sough and Dunsley Sough.

A number of large and rich veins on the northern and eastern edges of the orefield continue beneath the shale cover. It became the practice in the late 17th and early 18th centuries to drive shale gate soughs searching for the extensions of these veins buried deep in the underlying limestones. The shale gate soughs reputed to have been driven to Old Edge and New Edge groves at Great Hucklow, c. 1670-95 would place them as the earliest examples known in the orefield. The position of the buried vein could be detected by the presence of mineralised leaders visible in the shale. They were known to the miners as *symptoms of the vein*. Shale gates at Oden Vein, Castleton and several sited along the lower slopes of Hucklow Edge and Eyam Edge were driven for the purpose. They were used subsequently for draining water from the shales and also as pumpways.

Slightly earlier, a sough driven entirely through limestone, but apparently designed as a purpose built pumpway rather than a gravity drainage adit, is recorded in 1666 at Humble Dale Sough, Taddington [PRO, DL 1/444].

18TH CENTURY

GEOLOGY

The century witnessed development and refinement of existing ideas. The embryonic notion of a stratigraphic succession in Derbyshire can be traced back to Thomas Short [1734] who gave examples of the succession of strata met in sinking mines and driving soughs, coupled with surface observations, however he made no attempt to correlate strata between his chosen sites. Anthony Tissington, a Fellow of the Royal Society, a mine owner and Barmaster of Matlock Liberty, contributed notes about Derbyshire geology, mines and minerals to Short`s book. Towards the end of the 17th century and into the first half of the 18th century the accumulated knowledge derived from sough driving and shaft sinking would have permitted the basic geological succession to be elucidated, certainly at Winster, Wensley, Matlock, Cromford and Wirksworth, but there is no known documentation discussing such matters. William Hooson [1747] contributed a substantial number of comments relating to differing forms of the veins, a variety of minerals and local arrangement of strata and can therefore be added to the list with some justification.

Several mine owners, mine overseers and some working miners were possessed of a degree of geological knowledge. The most prominent were Samuel Heyward, George Tissington, whilst Joseph Cook of Tideswell possibly should be included. The list of lesser figures includes Adam Dawson, Robert Bateman, George Heyward, (Samuel`s brother), Cornelius Flint, Daniel Rose, several members of the Royse family of Castleton, with their many mining interests in the northern part of the orefield, Francis Drabble and William Mettam. John Roose, prominent at the Winster and Elton mines, reserved his most spectacular work as agent for Charles Roe when he discovered the great copper ore-body at Parys Mountain, Anglesey. Francis Mason, overseer at mines along Eyam Edge and elsewhere, sold mineral specimens to White Watson, not only from Derbyshire, but also from the Anglezark lead mines, near Chorley in Lancashire.

Samuel Heyward`s geological section extending from Hubbadale Pipe to the Highlow mines covers a distance of about 1¼ miles in length and is the first known attempt to correlate the strata between several locations. He recognised different varieties of limestone, together with interleaved clay wayboards. The section is un-dated but can be assigned to around 1766. George Tissington`s section along the line of Basrobin Sough, Wensley, is dated 1767. Though very localised, it introduced the concept of what was to become widely accepted as a regional succession within the orefield of *1st Limestone, Blackstone, 2nd Limestone*, etc. The concept was extended by Whitehurst [1778] to include four limestones, separated by three toadstones (or blackstones). Whitehurst gave grateful acknowledgement to George Tissington for the information the latter had given to him. Joseph Cook, agent at High Rake and Burfoot mines drew sections at both mines in the 1780s illustrating an upper limestone containing clay wayboards and at each mine an underlying very thick stratum of channel (toadstone).

The concept of regularity in extent and thickness of continuous limestone beds seperated by toadstones as proposed by Tissington and elaborated upon by Whitehurst persisted well into 19th century. However, the interplay between beds of lava, impersistent tuff horizons and clay wayboards, and intrusive sills and sill feeders, caused enormous consternation amongst early geologists. The irregular tuffs and clay wayboards were termed *Chance Beds* by Farey [1811] whilst Whitehurst coined the word *troughing* to describe dyke-like masses of weathered toadstone that had fallen into vein fractures, mainly at mines on Bonsall Moor.

Tideswell Moor presented Whitehurst, Farey and others with a far more difficult problem in trying to account for the great variations in thickness of toadstones met in near adjacent mines. Only in the late 20th century did geologists recognise the existence of a sill feeder at both High Rake Mine and Black Hillock Mine, but several beds of basalt lava and layers of tuff and clay wayboards encountered in the Maiden Rake and Chapmaiden Mine, these beds were also met in the workings of a collection of smaller mines west of Chapmaiden [Walters, 1981].

The northern part of the orefield became the focus of attention during the late 18th century and early 19th century disputes between the disciples of Hutton and Werner. Geologists, including the Frenchman, Faujas St. Fond and Hedinger, visited mines and soughs at Castleton, Bradwell, Hucklow and Tideswell seeking evidence for either a sedimentary or an igneous origin of the toadstones. The local `professional` geologists like White Watson, John Mawe, John Farey, Elias Hall of Castleton, more famous for his work in the coalfields, and William Hopkins, followed by William Adam, all belong more rightly to the 19th century. So too lesser figures such as John Milnes, John Alsop, William Wyatt and other men and miners who followed in the footsteps of Heyward, Tissington and Cook.

Many authors refer to a supposed long held belief of the Derbyshire miners that little or no ore would be found within or beneath a toadstone bed. Certainly there is supporting evidence from Gentlewoman's Pipe in the 1630s, from the Dunnington mines at Elton in the 1660s [PRO, DL 1 and DL 4, various] and from Short [1734] suggesting that such a belief did exist. Conversely the miners worked payable ore shoots beneath this rock-type in the late 17th century at Bates Sough, rich ore in Dovegang Vein beneath the *Great Clay* in 1679 and at Tearsall Rake, near Wensley in the 1630s-1650s. Additional evidence can be found from mines in the Via Gellia where by 1705 the miners were working the Sticking, or Stitchen Vein *under the Clay* (Matlock Lower Lava). During the following century mine owners often insisted that documentary proof be entered into Barmaster's books and elsewhere that when leasing the right to work the old, upper levels of their mine to a third party, the owners reserved the ore beneath the blackstone/toadstone. Evidence for this procedure can be traced for example at Gorseydale Mine, Bonsall Moor; Mossey Meer Mine, Winster, and at Leas Sough and Dunsley Sough driven beneath the Matlock Lower Lava at Bonsall Lees. Rich ore was worked in the toadstones/blackstone at Calvestone Mine near Little Hucklow in 1757, Friden Mine on Elton Moor and at Seven Rakes, Matlock.

Notwithstanding the above positive examples it might be that the opposing negative idea, which certainly gained considerable momentum, was due to two principal factors; lateral displacement of many veins beneath lava horizons, known in Derbyshire as *squinting* [Rieuwerts, 1998] and the disastrous, very deep sinkings through great thicknesses of igneous rocks in the Hucklow-Windmill area at Clear-the-Way Mine and High Rake Mine. Soughs were frequently abandoned if toadstone was met in the forefield. Examples occur at Moorwood Sough, Victory Level, Oakenedge Sough, Streaks Sough and Main Rake Sough, all in Middleton Dale, Black Sough and Winchester Level, both at Nether Haddon and the Halliker Wood Level, Via Gellia.

The limited geological contributions made by Ferber and St. Fond merit comment, though as might be expected much of their work relied heavily on local information. Ferber [1776] in discussing the deeper beds beneath Masson Hill, hinted at what might lie beneath the limestones, though it was Adam [1838] who (apparently) first speculated that *the old Red Sandstone is presumed to be the sub-stratum.*

MINING TECHNIQUES

Mining technology advanced rapidly during the 18th century and the various innovations and improvements are fully discussed in the main body of the work. Suffice then at this point to merely summarise these developments.

ROCK BREAKAGE; STOPING

The ancient technique of fireing (fire-setting) became obsolete soon after 1720-1730. Blasting using gunpowder had been around since about 1662-1663 [Rieuwerts, 1983; 1998]. The technique developed slowly, but in the first decades of the 18th century its use became widespread. However, older methods lingered on and hand pickwork used for rock excavation is often seen alongside shotholes in both 18th and even some 19th century mines.

Old tools and equipment found in Hilltop Mine, Great Hucklow.

1. introduction

HAULAGE

The early decades of the century saw the extended use of `carrying gates`, the material being carried in small wooden boxes by relays of boys spaced at suitable intervals along the gate, the box being passed from one to another, each carrying for perhaps twenty to forty yards before handing it on to the next boy. A variation employed a box or container suspended from an overhead rope and pulley system. Known as a *wharle* it was described by Hooson [1747], but only three examples are known, all at the Eyam Edge mines.

The traditional methods of hauling ore/waste rock along passageways in sleds or corves were superseded by the introduction of small, plain wheeled wagons running along two parallel planks laid on the floor of a level known as a *cartgate*. The idea of wheeled transport, so slow to reach Derbyshire, can be traced back to European mines in the 15th-16th centuries. An improvement to the floor planks was provision of an edged board forming an `L` shaped track that helped to prevent slippage of the carts. Edged boards were introduced about 1748. Later still, after around 1760, wooden rails were used in waggon gates, the waggons had flanged wheels. They were followed in the 1770s by large section wooden `joists` acting as substantial rails for larger waggons. These latter were known as a Newcastle Road, but only three examples are known from Derbyshire.

Transportation of waste rock using boats in underground canals was introduced at Hillcarr Sough soon after 1766 and in Speedwell Level during the following decade. Both mines were associated with the engineer John Gilbert who had constructed similar arrangements for the Duke of Bridgewater at his coal mines near Manchester.

Two waggons; that with the plain wooden wheels was found in Ash Nursery Mine, Longstone Edge and ran along the boarded floor of a cartgate. The waggon with the small diameter metal wheels operated on rails made from plain, square section iron bars. It was recovered from Wham Engine, Castleton Moor (H.M.Parker)

Haulage to surface from shallow shafts maintained usage of the traditional stows. Larger versions, probably wound by two or even four men, were known as *Great Stows*. Horse-gins were in common use at most medium sized and large mines, whilst at Gregory Mine, Ashover, a Newcomen engine winder or *Whimsey* was installed in 1795 [Band 1983]. The principal, but not entirely exclusive function of the horse-gin in earlier times had been in winding water, or operating rag and chain pumps, but the focus changed from the 18th century onward, concentrating on ore and waste rock haulage. A gin operated by a single horse was capable of lifting from about 240 feet, but on the deeper shafts, say 600-650 feet on Eyam Edge, four or even six horses were required.

Wooden corve found in the Tearsall workings, Wensley (H.M.Parker)

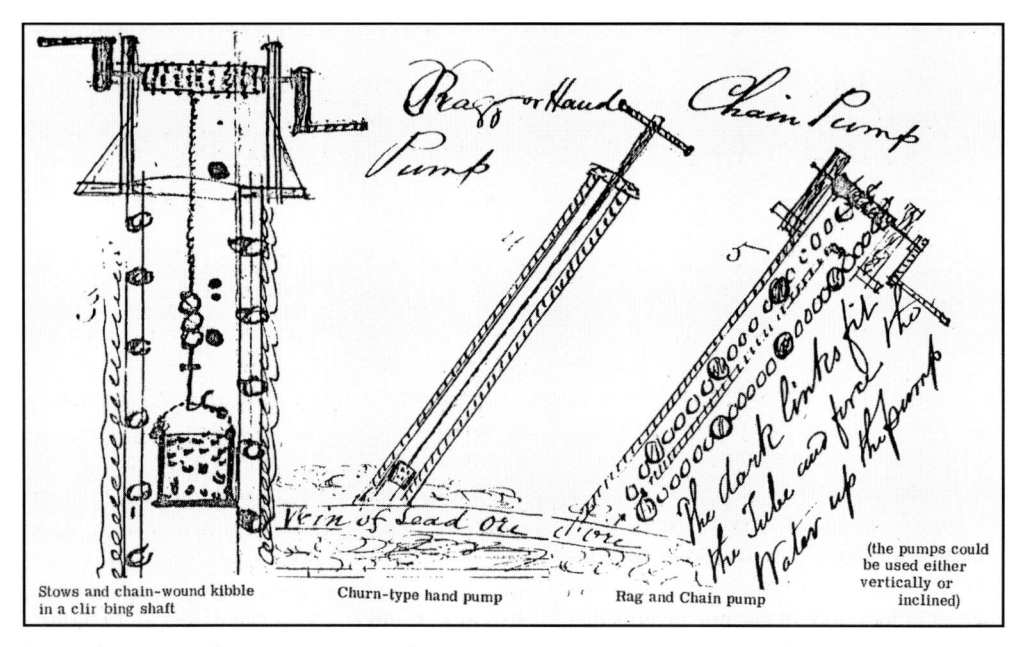

Late 18th or early 19th century equipment found on re-opening a mine in 1880 (DRO Rieuwerts Collection).

Labels on figure: Stows and chain-wound kibble in a clir bing shaft; Churn-type hand pump; Rag and Chain pump; (the pumps could be used either vertically or inclined).

VENTILATION

Shaft sinking reached unprecedented depths in Derbyshire mining. In 1749 a shaft at Ladywash Mine was sunk to 104 fathoms (624 feet). possibly the deepest shaft in Great Britain at the time. In 1769 the New Engine Mine Shaft was sunk 135 fathoms (786 feet).

In addition longer, deep level soughs and deeper mine workings demanded improved methods of ventilation. Excavations within the shales sometimes promoted explosions of methane gas. Provision of a current of fresh air to the working face was achieved by driving double drifts, linked by short connecting passages known as *thurls*, the air current being induced by a furnace covering the `upcast` shaft head, or by a basket of burning coals suspended at the shaft top, but enclosed within a dome or small building termed a *fire-house* or *cupola*. The deep shaft at Ladywash was ventilated in this way. Water-blasts were sometimes installed, but only four mines are known to have used the technique; all date from the period 1766–1790 [Rieuwerts, 1998]. The older, well-tried methods, for example using fans and bellows connected to air-ducting were of course still very much in demand and continued to be widely used.

DRAINAGE

Apart from the continued driving of sough levels, the principal developments in mine drainage in 18th century Derbyshire concerned the introduction of the Newcomen engine in 1716, large diameter water wheels, such as the 40 feet diameter example at Stoney Lee Mine, Stanton, installed in 1747, and the double, vertically placed, overshot wheels at Coalpithole Mine, Peak Forest. A hydraulic water-balance engine possibly operated at Lathkilldale Mine in the mid 1760s and 1770s, but few details are known.

Small diameter, undershot wheels were operational on Lathkilldale Vein by the first decade of the century, somewhat later a concentration of at least eight water wheels powered by the river Derwent served mines between Matlock and Matlock Bath.

The first proven hydraulic, or water pressure engine dates from the early years of the 19th century. The engine was designed by Richard Trevithick, but as noted above it is possible that a Westgarth engine may have been installed c.1765–1770 at the Lathkilldale Mine, for the London Lead Company.

Five soughs, arguably the most important drainage levels serving the orefield, were begun in the 18th century, they being Stoke Sough c.1720, Magclough Sough 1724, Yatestoop Sough 1751, Hillcarr Sough 1766 and Meerbrook Sough 1772.

2. THE MINES OF CASTLETON LIBERTY, WITH PARTS OF HOPE AND PEAK FOREST

Many of the lead mines in the Castleton area benefited from the drainage provided by an extensive and presently incompletely explored series of natural caves and natural watercourses. Surface streams engulfed at the shale-limestone boundary along the lower slopes of Rushup Edge, feed into a series of swallow holes such as Gautries Hole at Perryfoot, P8 and Giants Hole, their flow being then chanelled through the Speedwell – Peak Cavern cave systems to resurge in Castleton village. The caves were encountered directly or indirectly during mining operations. Rumours persist in local lore of gigantic caverns discovered by the lead miners and since lost. There is a solid foundation for these tales because within the last twenty to thirty years enormous caverns have been found by speleologists, several, though not all, bearing traces of t`owd man`s handiwork.

Mines and veins worked on the high limestone ground south of the Hope Valley were worked to depths of 400-650 feet without real hindrance from inflows of ground water. Water percolation from many square miles of this limestone hinterland flows into the Peak Cavern system. Evidence from ore accounts and mine sections demonstrates that the deeper mines, such as Hazard Mine and Hollandtwine Mine became unprofitable due to impoverishment of ore content about 500 feet to 600 feet beneath the surface, coincident with haulage and ventilation difficulties.

Dirtlow Rake is the principal vein in the Castleton district and one of the major veins of the Derbyshire orefield. The vein, a complex fault structure, is a very wide zone of mineralisation that extends for 1½ miles from the foot of Pin Dale to Dirtlow Head near Hollandtwine Mine (now destroyed by fluorspar workings). At Siggate Head Mine near the top of Pin Dale, the north eastern end of the rake splits into three main components, Kytle (or Kitle) End Vein, Pindale Side or Lawyer Vein and Fire Scrin. In the opposite direction, near Hollandtwine Mine the rake divides into two major branches. The northern branch passes through Hazard Mine and the Wham mines into Peak Forest Liberty, passing through Portaway Mine, Jowl Grove, Watts Grove and Hurdlowend Mine to Coalpithole Rake. The southern branch, known as Deasy (Daisy) Rake, then Old Moor Mine, also passes into Peak Forest Liberty, there becoming the wide and well defined Oxlow Rake.

Ore accounts covering Castleton Liberty exist for the years 1726-1736, but are then largely missing until 1752. The inference from the detail contained within them must be that most of the rich ore shoots at mines all along Dirtlow Rake had been extracted from the near surface workings on the vein well before 1750. The large opencast lead workings at and adjacent to Smith Grove or Old Grove, and Ashton`s Mine or Nether Dirtlow Mine are testimony to the work undertaken by pre 18th century miners. From 1752 until mining ceased on the rake in the 1890s, production of lead ore from Siggate Head Mine, Ashton`s Mine (or Nether Dirtlow), Hollandtwine Mine and Hazard Mine was substantial only for very limited periods of time. During these periods the above mines could be classified as `medium` sized ventures, whilst remaining mines on the rake were small scale operations and produced little ore.

Oden Rake was very rich, its history dates from 1600 at least, but possibly back to the 13th century. Artificial drainage was necessary at the Oden mines where the problem was localised but acute, necessitating construction of several drainage levels. Much of the mining along the vein was conducted in the limestones beneath the shale cover, deep beneath the flanks of Mam Tor. Oden Rake was bedevilled by adverse geology. The irregular mid-Carboniferous erosion surface at the shale-limestone interface, together with horizontal faulting along the rake, contributed to difficult working conditions and unpredictable inflows of ground water into the mine. Troughs of shale filling erosion hollows in the former limestone surface caused the vein to be `lost` in the shale, costly driveages through barren rock were then necessary to re-locate it in the limestone. The *Levys* at Oden Mine, (there were at least two at the mine), were driven partly for such exploration purposes, but they certainly served a secondary function as drainage levels and they are therefore included in this account.

Dirtlow opencuts, Castleton (J.H. Rieuwerts).

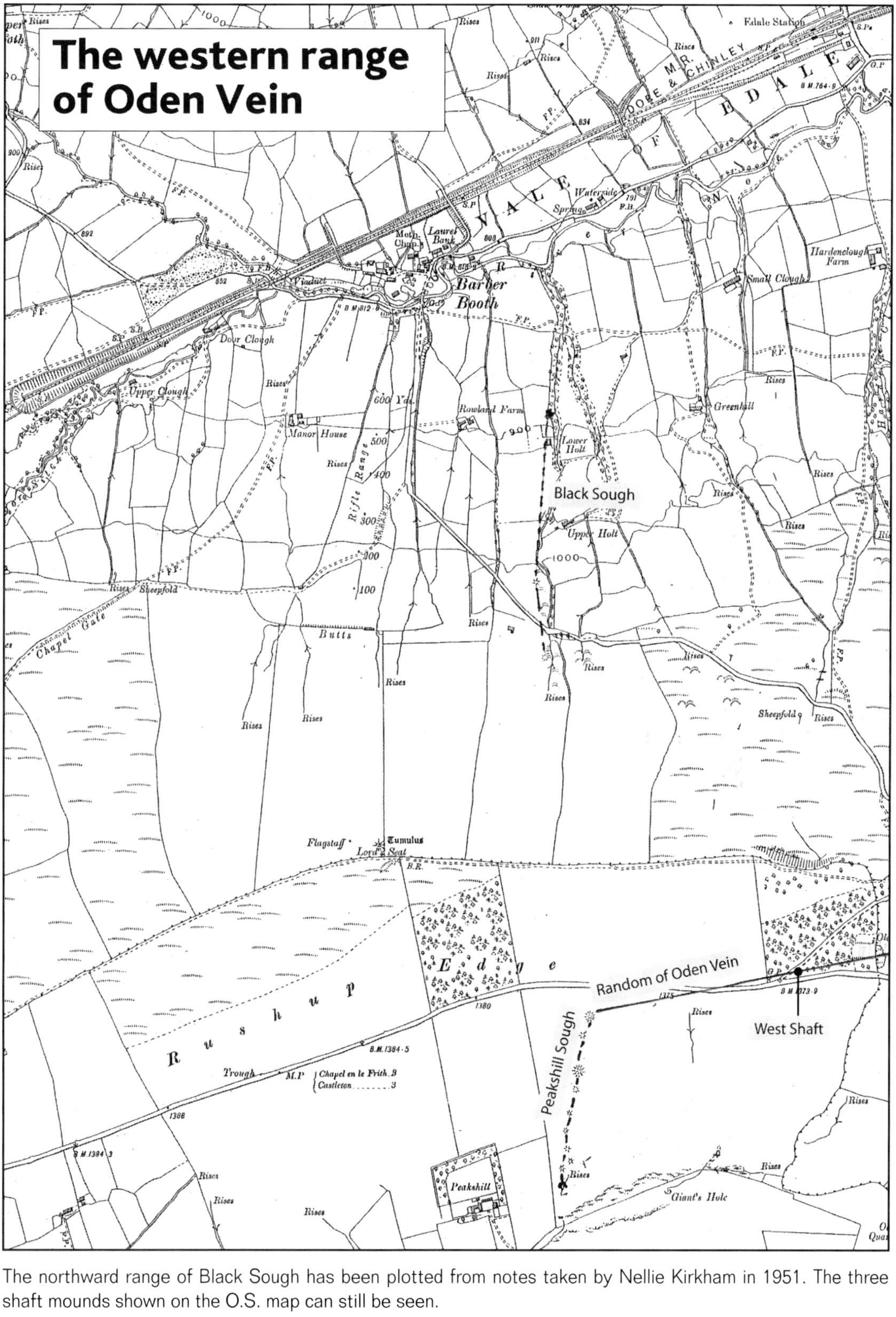

The northward range of Black Sough has been plotted from notes taken by Nellie Kirkham in 1951. The three shaft mounds shown on the O.S. map can still be seen.

A further problem manifested itself, more than one active cave passage was intersected, at times pouring considerable volumes of flood water into the mine.

An explanation for the omission of Speedwell (or Oakden) Level from this book, save for very brief details, is provided in the miscellaneous section at the end of the main Castleton account.

The *Levy* driven into Longcliffe Vein in the first decade of the 18th century was a haulage gate rather than a drainage sough. Some readers may mis-interpret the original function of the Levy as that of a sough, therefore the few details known about it are also included in the miscellaneous section at the end of the main Castleton account.

Peakshole Sough, driven from Peak Cavern gorge toward the Longcliffe mines was a failure and it was abandoned well short of the target area after achieving little success. Pindale Sough was driven to the mines in Pin Dale where, north east from Siggate Head, the great Dirtlow Rake splits into many parallel scrins. Above Siggate Head, mines on Dirtlow Rake lying between there and Hollandtwine Mine were drained by part of the Peak Cavern system. The so-called Hazard Mine – Hollandtwine Mine Sough may not have been constructed; its purpose is obscure.

THE DRAINAGE OF ODEN MINE

Oden Rake or Vein (generally spelled Odin in later documents, both versions are used in this account as appropriate), outcrops at the base of Mam Tor, at the northern end of Treak Cliff, Castleton. Here, the very limited surface expression of this ancient and important vein is confined to the well-known, spectacular, hading opencut. The opencut and the main entrance into the mine are depicted in several late 18th century and 19th century paintings, watercolours and prints. These openworks begin close to the former Castleton to Chapel-en-le- Frith road, at a location known to miners, at least since the early part of the 17th century, as the Gank Mouth. One hundred and thirty yards south west from the Gank Mouth the openworks terminate, and in this direction the vein passes beneath the cover of Edale Shale. From this point it is completely buried beneath the shales as it ranges beneath the flanks of Mam Tor, beyond which it continues as far as the small plantation near the Chapel-en-le-Frith – Edale road junction. The old wall at the eastern end of the modern car park, near the Edale road, forms the boundary between the mineral liberties of Castleton and Peak Forest. This division wall had important implications for working the mine after 1722, Castleton Liberty lying within the jurisdiction of the Duchy of Lancaster, whilst Peak Forest Liberty belongs to the Duke of Devonshire.

The workings within Peak Forest Liberty finally terminated very nearly 1,350 yards beyond the Gank Mouth, where the shale dipped down into the forefield of the mine and the vein was finally lost. The event was expressed in the quaint language of the miners as, *where the vein overdipped the levy,* (and) *a shale drift in ye levy to discover ye vein.* What appears to have been an abortive attempt to re-locate the western extension of Oden Rake beneath Rushop Edge was made by driving a shale gate from near Peakshill Farm, northwards towards the Edge. Despite setting taker meers for over a mile in length along its presumed range, the vein hereabouts is deeply buried beneath the shales and the miners failed to find it.

Beyond the Gank Mouth, in the opposite direction, the north eastern continuation of the vein passes beneath the toe of the Mam Tor landslip and the underlying Edale Shales which form the floor of the upper end of the Hope Valley. The vein was worked in this direction for only about 700 feet. Both a water wheel and a Newcomen-type fire engine were considered for dewatering this section, but surprisingly no mechanical pumping was ever undertaken.

Plans and vertical sections of the mine drawn in the mid 18th century demonstrate that at various intermediate points between the Gank Mouth and the south western forefield in Peak Forest Liberty, the vein was `lost` where shale troughs plunged down to and below the horizon of the contemporary workings. The troughs represent hollows formed on an extremely irregular, eroded limestone surface, subsequently filled with shale. No sections showing geological details along the vein appear to have been drawn, a surprising situation given the irregularity of the geological profile. A curious fact is that Robert How of Castleton, who produced many of the plans and sections of Oden Mine, was responsible for a section, dated 1766 demonstrating the basic geology of Whale Sough and Hubbadale Pipe, Taddington. Published geological maps depict the vein as a simple straight line, but 18th century plans of the workings demonstrate that in reality the vein consisted of a series of parallel and sub-parallel mineralised fractures. For example, old engravings and early 20th century photographs show the prominent rider separating

Oden Vein and its Soughs

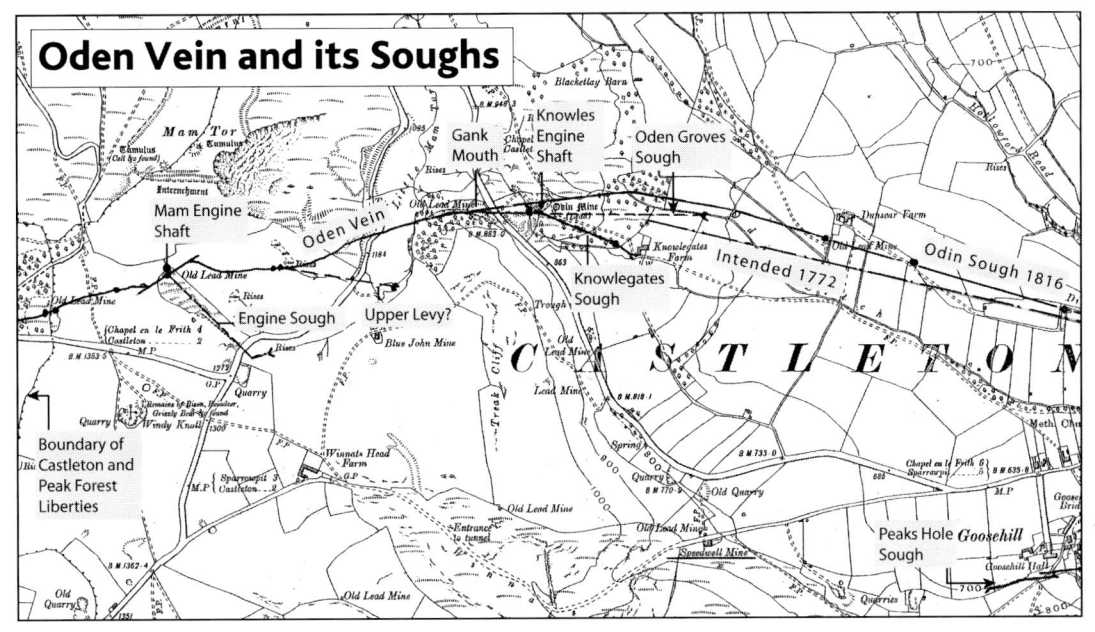

18th century plans of Oden Mine demonstrate the complexity of the workings and the presence of several near parallel mineralised fractures, nevertheless all freed as Oden Vein or Rake. The map provides only an outline indication of the main range of the `vein`.

the Oden North and South Veins; parts of which still remain in-situ.

The combination of deep, shale-filled troughs at the shale/limestone interface, coupled with the irregular nature of the mineralised fault fractures, resulted in exploratory levels being driven to re-locate the `lost` ore bodies. Begun during the first decade of the 18th century, they are amongst the earliest known examples in the Derbyshire orefield, pre-dating the better known shale-gate `soughs` driven for the same purpose to the Eyam Edge mines.

Several words appear to have been peculiar to the miners at Oden Mine. They include *Crooked Knerl*, meaning a wide place in the vein and *stocks*, referring to a narrow part of the vein. The name *jerranite* was applied to shale, and zinc blende was known as *saracole*, both apparently unique to Oden Mine. None of the words have been seen elsewhere in the orefield [Rieuwerts, 1998]. They appear only as part of a handwritten appendix to a copy of Mander`s Miners Glossary [Rieuwerts, 1998]. Old plans also give curious names to parts of the mine, but offer few clues to their meaning. Amongst these might be cited, *Gin Swafe or Gin Sweep,* (probably a stows handle), *Old Garden, Gilbrey Yates, Slatter Bullock, The Safe, the Brass Castle*. Several small pipes were found in the walls of the vein, the largest of which was situated near the Gank Mouth and variously known as the *Jove Hole, Joume Hole,* and *Jouph Hole*. A Jouph-hole, or Lough-hole was a miners` term for a mineral lined cavity (vugh) [Rieuwerts, 1998].

The mine was well-known to 18th century geologists and mineralogists and indeed ordinary visitors were taken into the mine to view the workings, as described by Hedinger [c. 1795]:

The traveller who wishes to gratify his curiosity, by going through the works of this mine, so instructive in natural history from its situation, will reap much information by enquiring ... for a miner who works in it and whose name is Samuel Needham. For his attention and civility I mention his name in hopes that it may be of service to him.

Reports began to appear by the early years of the 19th century that the galena obtained from Odin Mine contained up to 3ozs of silver/ton of ore (the old spelling Oden seems to have been abandoned during the period 1800-1820). Robert How Ashton journeyed to Sheffield in September, 1827 *trying ore as it was reported that it contained a large proportion of silver* [Rieuwerts and Ford, 1976]. Unfortunately, the result of this analysis has not been seen, neither do the reckoning books record the sale of silver bearing lead ore. The numerous 18th century reckoning books and records of smelting trials using Oden ore are also silent on the matter. The variety of galena known as `potters ore` did occur.

Zinc blende (sphalerite) was found, but again there is no evidence that it was exploited commercially. During late 1828 Robert How Ashton again visited Sheffield, on this occasion, *to try if I could sell (Black) Jack ore* [Rieuwerts and Ford, 1976]. No doubt he was trying the market with the Sheffield brass-founders.

The mineral elaterite was described by Lister [1673] who commented on a *Subterraneous Fungus* found:

> *about two miles from Castleton 15 or 16 yards deep in the Old Man, as they call a mine formerly wrought, and now stopped up, covered with earth, that had either fallen or was thrown in. This fungus is much like peat or turf (but) does not dry – some is very soft, and like jelly.*

Lister was uncertain whether it was a vegetable substance or a mineral, but was inclined to the view that it probably had grown from the old birch props used in the workings. Though he did not name the precise locality, it has long been presumed that he was referring to the deposits in Oden Vein. Pilkington [1789] also discussed elaterite which he called *bitumen, exceedingly elastic* and also *Hardened rock oil*, both occurring at Oden Mine. Jameson [1820] described *Elastic Mineral Pitch* being found in the cavities of a vein in the lead mine called Odin. It was, according to Jameson, accompanied by the usual gangue minerals and also *slaggy mineral pitch*. Greg and Lettsom [1858] refer to it occurring *plentifully at the great Odin mine*.

Pilkington [1789] seems to have been the first to notice sulphur at Odin Mine, where it was of nearly equal purity with that found at the Virgin Mine, Hazlebadge and in the mines on Tideswell Moor, at which places it would take flame with a candle. Britton and Brayley [1802] were slightly contradictory. They repeated that it would burn with a candle, but added:

> *Veins of pyrites, which the miners have commonly, but improperly, called sulphur, have been found in the virgin mines near Bradwell, and in the Odin Mine at Castleton.*

Hedinger [c. 1795] noted cerussite and the rare mineral lead molybdate [wulfenite] at the mine. Contrary to many recent geological and mineralogical works, Mawe [1802] did not record the occurrence of native sulphur, or elaterite, or lead molybdate at Oden Mine. Explosive slickensides of the type found in Haycliffe Mine, Eyam; Gang Mine, Cromford and elsewhere were encountered. A level called *Slicken Drift* is marked on many of the 18th century plans.

What may be the earliest reference to the mine occurs in an un-dated document, written not later than 1280. A fugitive detained in the Royal Forest of the Peak appeared before justices accused of poaching `in the wood at the entrance to Odin` [SCL, Brooksbank]. It is difficult to conclude that the `entrance to Odin` can refer to any feature other the mine.

At least some lead ore obtained from Oden Rake and no doubt from other mines in Castleton, before about 1575-1600, was probably smelted at the Hollins Cross bole, on the ridge between Mam Tor and Back Tor.

Recorded lead mining within the Oden title lasted for a period of at least 235 years and probably much longer. The geological structure associated with the vein dictated that the workings were developed in a somewhat irregular pattern and at this point it is perhaps appropriate to set out a brief synopsis of events during the 17th century. This, along with the accompanying general section along the vein, provides a ready check on chronological events.

1575pre   The richer ribs of ore on the south side of the Oden Rake were probably worked during the period before ore hearth smelting appeared.

1600c.   The mine was definitely at work.

1630   The vein had been worked opencast adjacent to the *Gank Mouth*.

1638pre   Nine meers of ground extending west from the Gank Mouth were in part possession of Robert Hallom and Robert Dakin. Some contemporary documents refer to them as *the Ancient Meers of ground*.

1638pre   The workings were already troubled by water inflows and lack of ventilation. These difficulties must refer to workings beyond the openworks and beneath the shale cover.

1638pre	Ore was smelted at *Norlees* (North Lees) Mill and Highlow Mill, both at Hathersage and at Mousehole Mill, Sheffield.
1638	*Deepe Shafte Meer,* the second meer southwest from Gank Hole was the only part of Oden Rake then at work.
1659pre	Considerable sums of money had been spent in developing the mine and a short, and probably ineffectual sough had been driven.
1659pre	Trial borings were made along the line of a proposed sough to be begun from a lower contour. The sough was begun in 1659.
1659	The first major sough level, Oden Groves Sough, was commenced from a point about 1100 feet north east from the Gank Mouth.
1659	Richard Torre took possession of meers northeast from the Gank Mouth.
1662c.	The *Gank Door* was made.
1663	Five partners at the mine above the Gank Mouth reached an agreement with Torre regarding the driving and financing of the sough.
1667-68	The sough reached Oden Vein.
1669	The sough reached the Gank Mouth in September.
1669	Legal arguments about the interpretation of the 1663 agreement.
1673	The sough was still under construction, being driven along the vein.
1673-4	The mine was probably abandoned. The sough forefield was probably in the 6th meer.

The openworks at Gank Mouth were at least partially open by 1630 [SCL, Bag 702], but work had been in progress for several years before that date. Evidence given during the course of a great lawsuit held in the late 1660s and early 1670s, and which passed from the Barmote Court into the Court of the Duchy of Lancaster, was that a continuous link in partnership and possession of the mine had existed from at least 1603. During the first half of the 17th century exploitation of the mine was confined to nine meers of ground extending west from the Gank Mouth. Later, they were referred to as the *Ancient Meers of ground – of (Robert) Hallom.* and that title was retained until 1709 at least. The Nine Meers were defined as *Deepe Shaft meer* and one meer east and seven meers west. The five meers at the west end were buried beneath the shale cover. Some of these meers beneath the shale were definitely worked before 1638, because Robert Dakin, a sixty six years old Castleton miner, deposed in 1669 that *about thirty one years ago the meers of ground in Oden were troubled by abundance of water and want of winde* [PRO, DL 4 112/10].

Unfortunately, it is not known if all of the five meers beneath the shale were developed. The workings beneath the shale at Oden Mine are pre-dated in that particular technique only by those at Shaley Grove, Matlock in 1576, Gurdall Mine, Wensley in 1599 and at the Hamber Grove and Miln Close Groves, Wensley, by 1617, but there exists a strong probability that workings of a similar nature were in operation at or adjacent to Hard Rake at Starkholmes, Matlock as early as 1520. Exploitation beneath the shale east of the Gank Mouth does not appear to have been tried before 1658. Some limited stoping was undertaken in this direction, this part of the mine below the Gank Mouth becoming known as Nether Oden Grove, and later as the Sough Grove, the workings above the Gank Mouth were known as Over Oden Groves. The existence of at least part of the openworks by 1630 is consistent with the hypothesis that very early workings at Oden would have been confined to exploitation of rich ribs of ore from very narrow stopes, perhaps 30 to 40 feet in depth. Opencast removal of smaller sized ore became viable in the Derbyshire orefield after about 1570 – 1600, after the introduction of the ore hearth method of smelting.

Oden Groves Sough reached the vein in c.1667-1668, but immediately afterwards extensive litigation concerning ownership and drainage arrangements dictated that continuity of 17th century exploitation seems to have been abandoned in about 1673-1674, the end of a seventy year stint.

The eastern portion of Oden Vein was drained by at least three soughs, which between 1659 and 1822 progressively lowered the water table in the vein to approximately the contour of the valley floor at Castleton village. There is some evidence to suggest that the earliest of these soughs, begun in 1659, was pre-dated by a yet older level, referred to herein as Oden `Old` Sough. Unfortunately, it proved to be ineffectual and was soon abandoned.

Trial smeltings of ore from Oden Mine were carried out in 1704-1705 and might signify the onset of

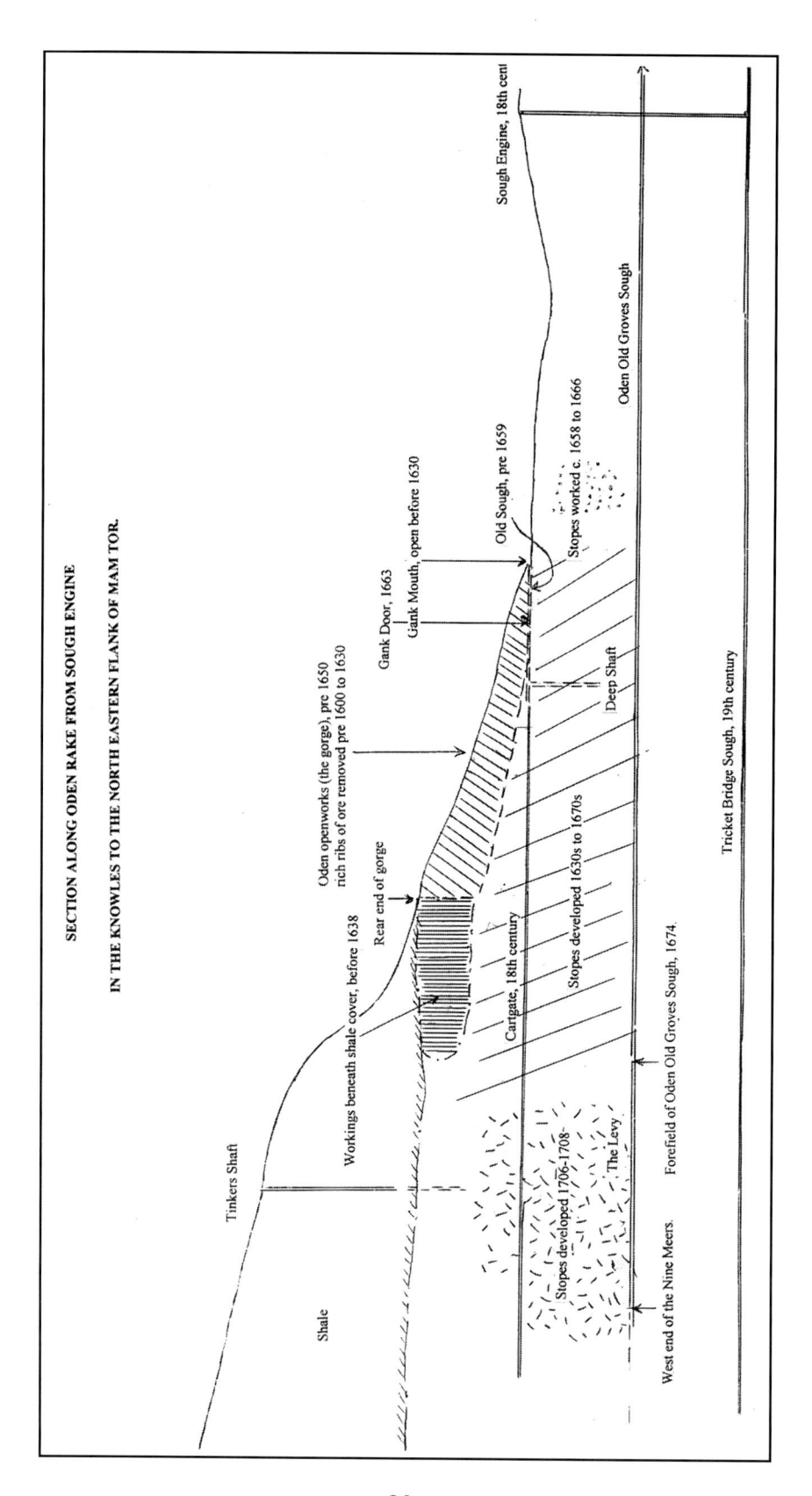

SECTION ALONG ODEN RAKE FROM SOUGH ENGINE IN THE KNOWLES TO THE NORTH EASTERN FLANK OF MAM TOR.

Sough Engine, 18th cent

Oden Old Groves Sough

Old Sough, pre 1659

Stopes worked c. 1658 to 1666

Gank Mouth, open before 1630

Gank Door, 1663

Oden openworks (the gorge), pre 1650
rich ribs of ore removed pre 1600 to 1630

Rear end of gorge

Workings beneath shale cover, before 1638

Tinkers Shaft

Shale

Cartgate, 18th century

Deep Shaft

Stopes developed 1630s to 1670s

Tricket Bridge Sough, 19th century

Forefield of Oden Old Groves Sough, 1674.

The Levy

Stopes developed 1706-1708

West end of the Nine Meers.

the next phase of mining [Lawson, 1968]. The recussitation consisted of three elements; stoping at *Oden fforefield,* i.e. mining ore from the vein beyond the areas developed by the 17th century miners, continuing the Oden Groves Sough, but by now re-named as *The Levy,* hereafter (*lower) Levy and, perhaps more importantly, proving the range and continuity of the vein south westwards beneath the flanks of Mam Tor.

Beyond the Nine Meers the random of the vein at a higher horizon was proved by driving two crosscut levels, an (*upper) Levy, begun about 1708 and slightly later, about 1711, the Engine Sough, both at about the anticipated contour of the vein-head, i.e. at the shale/limestone interface. The location of the former entrance to the (upper) Levy is not known, but logically it must have been situated fairly close to where a small stream gully is crossed by the Blue John Mine access track. The absence of a hillock of driveage waste is baffling, but it might form part of the access embankment to the Mine. The level was no doubt also intended to act as a pumpway, taking off water from the shale, as a ventilation gate and also as a high level haulage gate. [(*lower) Levy and (*upper) Levy titled by author to avoid confusion].

The existence of two levels, each called `The Levy`, but physically unconnected, has caused immense difficulties in historical interpretation. The author now considers that it was the c1708 (upper) Levy that reached the Castleton-Peak Forest Liberty boundary in 1722, rather than a Levy, postulated to have been driven from the back of the Oden openworks, to which interpretation the author does not now subscribe. References to *Shale Drifts* and a *Shale Sough* within Peak Forest Liberty, draining water eastwards from the taker meers, through the Lord`s Meer and founder meers, were probably extensions to the (upper) Levy.

Unfortunately, none of the many extant plans and sections of the mine explain the position and relationship of these levels, or the contours of any other features in the workings above the level of the mid 18th century Cartgate. From other internal evidence, it can be concluded that from the Gank Mouth to Crooked Knerl rither point the horizontal plans were all drawn at the contour of the Cartgate; beyond the 14th taker meer west of the Gank Mouth, reaching to the western extremity of the mine in Peak Forest Liberty, the plans must have been drawn to represent a higher horizon corresponding to the contour of the c1708 (upper) Levy. The second high contour level, known as the Engine Sough, was probably begun about 1711. No doubt useful in locating the continuation of the vein towards Peak Forest, it afterwards acted as a pumpway for intensive hand-pumping arrangements used at the Mam Engine Shaft.

A summary chronology of the above events is as follows:

1704	Trial smelting of Oden ore probably signifies an intention to re-open the mine.
1704-1705	Oden Mine re-opened after standing idle for about thirty years.
1704-1705	The (lower) Levy begun. It was a continuation of the Oden Groves Sough, previously abandoned about 1673-74. The late 17th century forefield stopes were re-started.
1707	The Levy had been driven beyond the Nine Meers.
1708c	The higher contour (upper) Levy was begun.
1711c	The Engine Sough was begun.
1716c	The upper Levy reached Mam Engine Shaft.
1722	The upper Levy may have reached Peak Forest Liberty.

Intensive work was carried out in Oden Vein from a little east of Mam Engine shaft, through into Peak Forest Liberty. Ore production was very significant and the Duke of Devonshire, who worked the Lord`s Meer in that liberty on his own account, obtained 4,462 loads of ore from it between 1726 and 1736 [Chats, Dev Coll]. The old partners, despite nearly thirty years interruption to their activities, traced ownership back to the early years of the 17th century, and mined extensively and profitably both within Castleton Liberty and Peak Forest Liberty. What may have been the earliest cartgate in a Derbyshire lead mine is recorded in the Lord`s Meer in Peak Forest Liberty in 1730 [Chats, Dev Coll]. Two plans, dated 1751 and 1757 respectively, show an *Engine cart drift* running west from Mam Engine Shaft [DRO, BSA Coll LP3 and LP11].

At later periods during the 18th century deeper exploitation of Oden Vein from the eastern end was achieved by means of a major haulage level, the

The Cartgate in Oden Mine.

Cartgate. This was begun from the Gank Mouth in 1755 and driven through to Peak Forest Liberty, whilst drainage was achieved by Knowlegates Sough, begun in 1711. The sough, after being abandoned for over forty years, was then recussitated and also continued to Peak Forest Liberty, reaching there about 1790-1800. The Cartgate became a well known feature at Oden Mine; it was served by four-wheeled waggons, pushed by manpower along wooden planks. Numerous 18th and 19th century guide books comment on it and the entrance is depicted on several drawings, paintings and woodcuts. At various periods the mine gave employment to over 150 people and throughout the 18th century ore output was large. The mine was regularly visited by tourists, a fact recorded in many contemporary guide books. A miner named Samuel Needham was the guide there around 1790 and the early years of the following century.

The ultimate gravity drainage available to Oden Rake or Vein was achieved by driving a deep sough from Trickett Bridge in Castleton village. The sough was planned in 1772, but for reasons unknown it was not commenced until 1816. The sough intersected Oden Vein in 1821 and eventually reached the liberty boundary at Peak Forest about 1850 [Chats, Bar Coll]. Oden Mine was finally abandoned in 1867, but hillocking took place in the early 20th century around Mam Engine and elsewhere in the Second World War. The tips around Knowlegates Engine Shaft, east of the Gank Mouth, were worked as a source of roadstone in the 19th century.

ODEN `OLD` SOUGH

The workings at Oden Groves were troubled by water at least by 1638 [PRO, DL 4 112/10]. Before 1638, the year in which Robert Hallom died, he owned a 1/4th part of Oden Rake. Nicholas How, a sixty six year old Castleton miner, confirmed that

> *during Halloms lifetime the charge was increased by reason of the drawinge of the water ... hee and others esteemed it to be An Hard beatinge work – (and) looked upon the worke to be of noe great value.*

Drawing water refers to either hand winding of water filled bags, or lifting it by means of hand operated pumping devices. Until about 1668, Oden Rake was said to have been *surrounded, drowned and overflowed with water – the oare therein lying very low – and not to be got but by sinking through hard Stone which was very difficult* [PRO, DL 1/425].

The existence of the `Old Sough` is, to say the least, very hypothetical and is based on only two rather tenuous references. During 1673 the partners stated that they had been in possession of Oden since 1603 *haveinge been at greate and vast charges in Digging, Soughing and working of the same and searching for lead oare – at at last found great Store of lead oare* [PRO, DL 1/426]. The document continues by describing the driving of the Oden Groves Sough, commenced about 1659, and thus by implication, their *Digging and Soughing* must represent earlier efforts at drainage. Richard Torre, who later became a partner in the Oden Groves Sough, recited that about 1658-1659, he took possessions of eight meers in the vein east from the Gank Mouth, at which time *there was noe Sough then begunne or at least none That was, or was likely to bee effectual for the unwatering of the said Oden Groves* [PRO, DL 1/426].

Again the implication must be that the original partners in the mine, had, sometime before 1658-59, attempted to drive a sough into the vein. It is not known where this level, (if it ever existed), was situated, but a tail or outfall adjacent to the Gank Mouth would be consistent with a site for any very early drainage arrangements. The *vast charges,* were presumably incurred in working the vein beyond the back of the openworks, sinking and working beneath the shale and resultant trouble with lack of wind and heavy water inflows. No further references occur to this, the earliest drainage level at Oden mines, and it must be presumed that it was a very short and ineffectual trial level.

ODEN GROVES SOUGH or THE (LOWER) LEVY or THE OLD MAN`S LEVEL

Nicholas Stones of Hemsworth, now a suburb of Sheffield, had after Hallom`s death gradually obtained a 1/4th share during the years between 1638 and 1641. Robert Dakin of Castleton owned a 1/4th share and Rowland Eyre of Bradway may also have held a 1/4th part. At that period *eastwards from the Ancient Meers of ground – of Hallom – was without possession.* Richard Torre giving evidence some fourteen years later, claimed that before Oden Groves Sough was commenced he had taken eight meers of ground below the Gank Mouth, but had not freed them according to mineral custom. Subsequently Eyre and partners took four of Torre`s meers, those immediately north east from the Gank Mouth and at some time shortly afterwards began to consider the possibility of driving a deep sough beginning from a point well to the east of these meers. Torre then took the remaining four meers and claimed he had obtained good ore from them. This seems unlikely, given the steep dip of the limestone beneath the shale covering.

Eyre and partners made exploratory borings along the proposed route of their sough and work began about 1659. They

did provide workemen and make ready for the Soughing thereof and were begun to sett upon the same – the partners had begun their Sough a great distance from the said Workes and farr from any part of any Myne – to procure the greater fall for the Water to bring itt to the Levell they aymed att – Richard Torre – a Myner then living – neare unto the same Workes – set stows – neare unto the said Sough pretending that hee would sincke there for to find a Myne [PRO, DL 1/419].

There was thus a conflict of interests with Torre and he threatened to sue the sough partners for trespass if they drove through his ground. Afterwards, Torre denied that this was a ploy to stop Eyre and partners, but eventually he obtained a 1/6th share in the meers above the Gank Mouth and a half share in the meers below it. The costs of carrying on the works and driving the sough were to be shared equally.

Before 1670 the partners at Oden Vein had taken title to many other taker meers. They included possessions beyond the Nine Meers, in the random of the vein ranging toward Peak Forest Liberty; eighteen taker meers north eastwardly from the Gank Mouth and they also held shorter lengths on two runs adjacent to the eighteen meers. All these additional meers were concealed beneath the shale cover.

The eighteen meers below the Gank Mouth terminated at a field known as the Fens. The Oden Groves Sough was begun from this point, well beyond the toe of the unstable, Mam Tor landslip. The position of the sough tail was well chosen because to obtain any additional depth of gravity drainage would have involved a long driveage through barren ground. The sough began as a bolt, the underground section beginning at the foot of the landslip, but very probably at sufficient depth to avoid the very disturbed shale within the slip. The level was then driven through shale for 1,100 feet before it reached limestone some 300 feet east of Gank Mouth. The latter was eventually reached in September, 1669 [PRO, DL 4 112/10]. The agreement for continuing the sough was made in July, 1663 [SCL, Bag 702]. One clause stipulated that the sough should be completed into Oden Rake within seven years, otherwise Torre would have to pay back one half of any clear profits he had received and relinquish a half of his sixth share in the meers above the Gank Mouth. It was then to be carried forward in the vein from meer to meer, each partner paying his proportionable charges.

The major part of the total expenditure on it took place between June, 1666 and September, 1669, suggesting that the original dispute with Richard Torre continued and may have initially hindered driving. The cost of the operation amounted to £1,259, of which £640 was expended before any ore was found, but most of the total sum (over 90%) was incurred between June, 1666 and September, 1669, when £1,152-13-6 was spent [PRO, DL 4 112/10]. These figures must represent the total charges, including materials, because any attempt to calculate driveage bargain rates proves to be un-realistic. Ore mined from the sough amounted to 1,578 loads and 4 dishes, which sold for about 20/- per load so that the sough was soon recording profits.

During yet another legal suit, Eyre and partners claimed that Torre had not completed the sough within the stipulated time. The argument hinged on whether in the Agreement of 1663 the point of completion for Torre was at the Gank Mouth or the Gank Door; the two places were 24 yards apart. Several actions were heard in the Barmote Court [SCL, Bag 702]. They also stated that Torre had lost the level of the sough. Torre denied these allegations, the position in 1673 being that:

> *the said Sough hath beene endeavoured to be carryed on from meere to meere and soe is now driveinge on by the doinge of two dayes worke in one day – he doth deny that he hath lost the leavell of the Sough* [PRO, DL1/426].

Torre also said that the sough was at a lower level than any of the current workings in Oden Mine. The sough was carried along the vein until at least late 1673, when the mine was possibly abandoned. Assuming a realistic driveage rate for the sough forefield of 1½ inches per shift, then for a three shift day (*doinge of two dayes worke in one day*) by 1673-1674 the forefield would have reached into the 6th meer beyond the Gank Mouth. The implications of this are discussed immediately below.

ODEN GROVES SOUGH or THE (LOWER) LEVY

The term Levy, meaning a level, appears to be confined to the extreme northern part of the orefield, but then only sparsely. The word has been found at Oden Mine, Longcliffe Mine, May Sough, Stoke Sough and in some of the Eyam mines [Rieuwerts, 1998]. It is an obvious corruption of the word `level`, but seems to signify a haulage, exploratory or ventilation adit, rather than one used for drainage purposes, though no doubt some drainage was also effected. Determining the nature, location and extent of *The Levy(s)* at Oden Mine proved especially problematical during compilation of the original PDMHS Special Publication, [Rieuwerts and Ford, 1976]. Since that time, despite additional information, unresolved questions still remain and this present account does not lay claim to be completely and positively correct in all details.

The situation is complicated by references to a Levy, (1705-1707) associated with the Nine Meers and, that part of the vein immediately beyond the Nine Meers, and what the author now believes to have been a separate Levy. This was driven at a higher contour during the first quarter of the 18th century (see below). A postulated position for a Levy beginning at the head of the Oden openworks and continued throughout the mine into Peak Forest Liberty, has now been discounted by the writer.

References to the Levy first appear in late 1704 and early 1705. Payment in the reckoning book dated January, 1706 recording *Ale when ye Levy was stricken through - 6/-* [SCL, OD 1495] possibly refers to an event when, after driving along what later plans call the *Slicken Drift* and the *Crooked Drift*, the miners encountered, or re-discovered what they believed to be the old Oden Vein. This position, within the 8th meer west of the Gank Mouth, is consistent with a continued forefield driveage rate of 4½ inches per day. Tinkers Shaft was sunk in the 8th meer and references to ore measured at *Oden hillock* in this period most probably refer to this shaft.

Ore was mined from the Levy, both within the Nine Meers in 1705-1706 and beyond them during 1706-1707 [SCL, OD 1149]. The workforce was of considerable size and in 1706, 41 men and 8 women were at work at Oden Mine. Ore production from the Levy ceased in August, 1707 and likely the forefield, by then very probably driven into the 11th meer, had encountered shale in the form of a sunken trough and work was abandoned. Ore production from the whole mine in the period 1709-1715 was between 1,000 to 1,250 loads/annum, exclusive of lot ore. Profits during these years amounted to £2,459 [Rylands, Bag 12/1/60].

THE (UPPER) LEVY: SHALE DRIFT IN PEAK FOREST LIBERTY

None of the many detailed plans of the mine give any indication of the position of the entrance into the (upper) Levy, but a plan dating from about 1751-1752 [DRO, BSA] strongly implies that the vein-head was reached in the 14th or 15th taker meer west from the Gank Mouth. The Swine Hole was located here; Swine Hole Pipe had been discovered by 1709 [SCL, OD 1149]. Field work has failed to locate the position of the level tail, but the likeliest position would be where the access trackway to the Blue John Mine crosses over the small stream that was diverted across the back of the Oden openworks. It was probably driven primarily as an exploration gate seeking the vein-head buried beneath the shale cover. The two small hillocks, named on some mid 18th century plans as *Blew Hillocks* may have served as air-shafts for it.

A starting date of about 1708 would be consistent with cessation of work in the western forefield of the lower Levy in the previous autumn. Considerable sections of the upper Levy were driven through shale so that an overall driveage rate of 6½ inches/day is consistent with the level reaching Mam Engine Shaft about 1716 and the Peak Forest boundary in December, 1722. The latter date is significant because in March, 1723 the vein was freed in Peak Forest Liberty and is therefore consistent with the postulated driveage rate. The vein was eventually worked for seven meers in that liberty (the fifth taker meer was not freed), beneath an ever increasing thickness of shale, before it plunged down too deep for further exploitation.

A lengthy dispute ensued between the partners in the mine and the Duke of Devonshire. He claimed that the vein should have been freed as a *New Thing* because it was a new working within Peak Forest. The partners complained, stating that they had been in possession of the mine for over a century, therefore it could not possibly be new, therefore they were not obliged to free two founder meers and negotiate for the Lord`s Meer. Eventually agreement was reached, the Duke working the Lord`s Meer on his own account. The various legal documents submitted by both sides enable a good deal of information to be obtained. Several of them refer to what must be extensions to the upper Levy.

An agreement was reached on the 29th October, 1726 whereby *the partners – to have Liberty at their own cost and Charges to carry on a Drift or Levell thro` ye Shale in ye Lord`s Meer to their next Taker Meer.*

Three taker meers beyond the Lord`s Meer had been freed by February, 1729. [Chats, Dev Coll]. But misfortune struck, for in March, 1729 a note states that:

at Oden we have lately struck to a Spring on our deepest soles or works wch at pr`sent is very Expensive and troublesome and am afraid it will soe continue the intended new Shaft there goes very slowly forward the Sough going up to it being hard shale [DRO, Grant Papers 345/824; microfilm].

Two months later almost identical comments were made: *As to the Sough going up in order to sink a new Shaft it is very hard and difficult to be got forward but hope time will perfect it.* The `new Shaft` presumably was the West Shaft in the 4th taker meer.

The miners were dogged by ill-fortune and there is an air of desperation in a letter dated 1731:

The forfield of Oden is very expensive in pumping Water wch cannot be avoided till the Partners are Satisfied whether the vein will rise again or no; we are Driving forward for that purpose and making all tryals possible; for if the Water be ever suffered to fill those works at the forfield it will

Scarce ever be seen again in our tyme But if a few months do not produce an Alteration for the better it will then be tyme to consider if not necessary to leave the forfield and work backwards in the old works for w`ch purpose we are proposing to Sink an Engin upon the old works to Land Oare cheaper than by hand [DRO, Grant Papers 345/824, microfilm].

The 5th taker meer was never freed and it was hereabouts that the shale cut off the vein and it was lost completely. There is an intriguing remark in a questionnaire sent to `Mr. Bagshawe` about Oden Mine, dated March, 1744, *State of Oden and level brought up to take off the pumps* [DRO, Grant Papers 345/753, microfilm]. Although dated eight years after the forefield in Peak Forest had been abandoned, this question appears to relate to the shale gate extension of the upper Levy. The Lord`s Meer ceased work in 1736; between 1726 and 1736 the Duke of Devonshire had raised 4,462 loads of lead ore. Work in the remainder of the mine within Peak Forest Liberty also terminated at the same time. Ore production there was also considerable, during the period 1727-1730, 8,900 loads were mined, exclusive of duty ore. Output peaked in 1728-1729, when over 5,900 loads were mined.

ENGINE SOUGH

Information about the Engine Sough is extremely scanty. The only positive written record occurs on a plan of the mine drawn by Robert How and dated 1757:

> the Swine Hole – an open Place not cut but Selfly Open from whence at a flood cometh a great Quantity of water from a Place at the Day called Round Hill, very near the Engine Sough tail [DRO, BSA LP3].

This limited information seems to fit if the floodwater was engulfed into Mam Tor Swallet, with the sough tail being located in the upper part of the Blue John gully at about 1,250 feet OD. Again the surface evidence is puzzling because no trace of any mining activity is visible at this point. Two run-in shafts lie in the enclosure above the road, almost in direct line with the Mam Engine Shaft and were probably air shafts on the sough. The level, driven throughout in shale, was thus at least 1,100 feet in length.

The Engine Sough may have been commenced about 1711, originally as an exploratory gate seeking signs of the vein buried beneath the shale cover.

SOUGH NEAR PEAKSHILL FARM

A shale gate sough driven from a small stream gully about 200 yards east of Peakshill Farm. From the tail it was driven slightly east of north for 1,300 feet. Ventilation must have been a major problem because there were at least ten air shafts and the level probably terminated at a shaft, long since run-in and now represented by a large mound of sinking dirt. The shaft is directly along the line of Oden Rake, here deeply buried beneath the shale cover. The shale gate was almost certainly made seeking the vein-head, but its location was set at a far too high contour, the miners being optimistic of the vein rising again. Certainly in 1727 fifty pairs of possessions and slightly later, sixty six pairs of possessions were booked by the Barmaster on the random of Oden Rake in Peak Forest Liberty. No details of the history of the sough appear to have survived, but it was presumably driven in the 1720s-1730s. Miss Kirkham [1962] mistakenly attributed references to the shale gates in the Lord`s Meer to the `Peakshill Sough`.

KNOWLEGATES SOUGH

Construction of the Engine Sough discussed above, was aimed at proving the continuation of the vein beyond the meers worked by the early 18th century Levy. The next logical step for the mine proprietors was yet deeper exploitation from the eastern end of the vein. Oden Groves Sough and its continuation had lost a good deal of level and a new sough was required to correct this situation.

Reckonings for Knowlegates Sough begin in July, 1711, when it was referred to as *ye Sough below Ganck Mouth* [SCL, OD 1149]. The tail was a low bolt issuing from the north bank of Odin Sitch, a few yards west of Knowlegates Farm. Unfortunately, it was destroyed by the farmer during cleaning and widening operations in the sitch. From here the sough was driven through shale for a distance of just over 370 yards to the *Sough fforemost Shaft,* situated a little beyond a later shaft known as *Sough Engine Shaft, or Knowles Engine Shaft.* Here, the forefield met limestone and the veinhead, both rising towards the south west from beneath the shale cover. James Hall`s plan dated c1751-1752 marks this as the Sough Vein, dis-

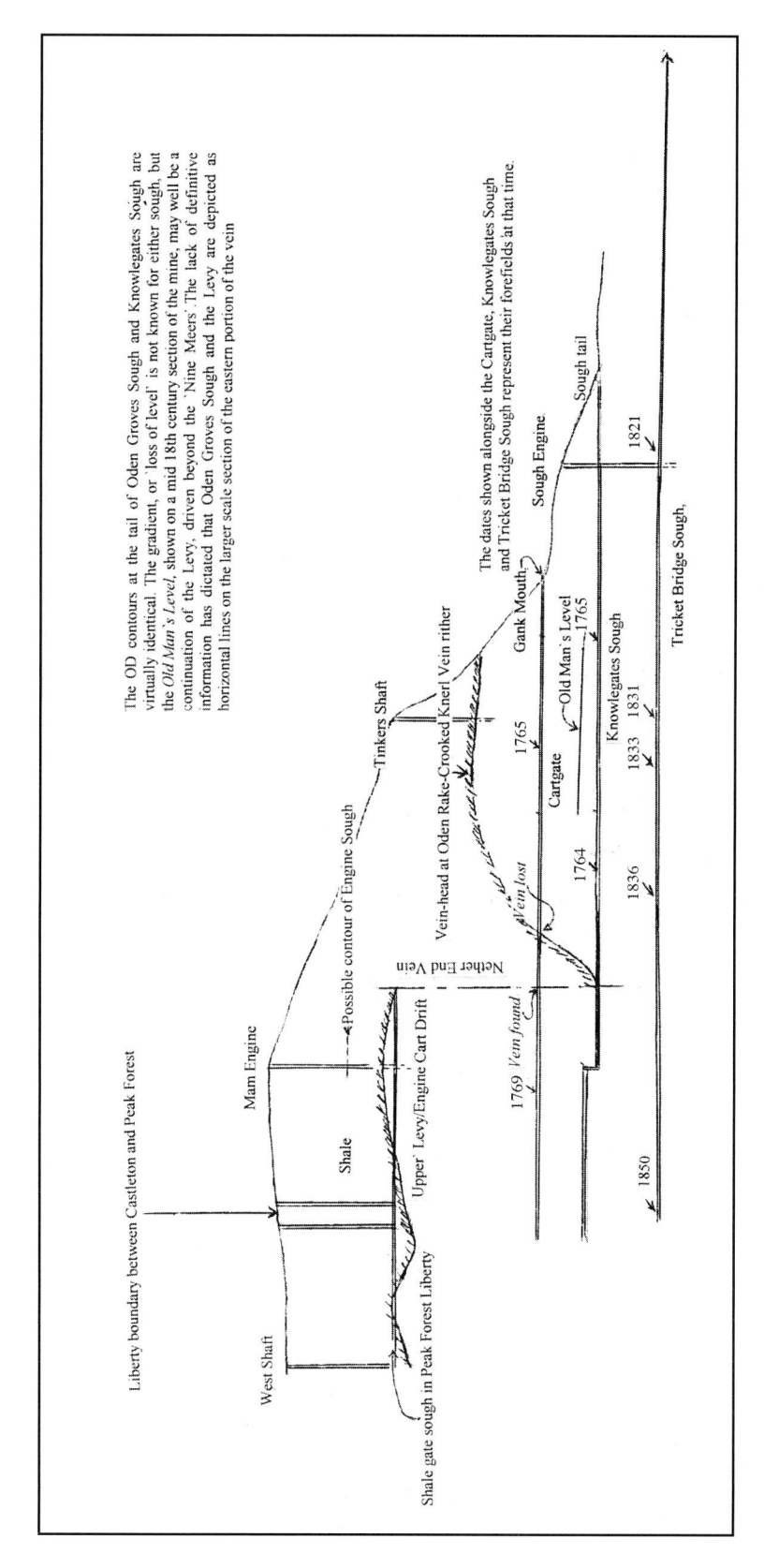

2. The Mines of Castleton Liberty, with parts of Hope and Peak Forest

The OD contours at the tail of Oden Groves Sough and Knowlegates Sough are virtually identical. The gradient, or 'loss of level' is not known for either sough, but the *Old Man's Level*, shown on a mid 18th century section of the mine, may well be a continuation of the Levy, driven beyond the 'Nine Meers'. The lack of definitive information has dictated that Oden Groves Sough and the Levy are depicted as horizontal lines on the larger scale section of the eastern portion of the vein

The dates shown alongside the Cartgate, Knowlegates Sough and Tricket Bridge Sough represent their forefields at that time.

Liberty boundary between Castleton and Peak Forest

West Shaft
Shale
Mam Engine
Possible contour of Engine Sough
Tinkers Shaft
Vein-head at Oden Rake-Crooked Knerl Vein rither
Nether End Vein
Upper' Levy/Engine Cart Drift
Shale gate sough in Peak Forest Liberty
1769 Vein found
Vein lost
1765
Gank Mouth
Old Man's Level
1765
Cartgate
1764
Knowlegates Sough
1836 1833 1831
Sough Engine
Sough tail
1821
1850
Tricket Bridge Sough,

35

tinct from the main Oden Vein, but closely parallel [DRO, BSA]. Later plans demonstrate that the two merged and that it was not a separate vein.

The vein was met in May, 1712 and the sough was not extended beyond here for another forty years. The cost of driveage through 373 yards of shale was £40-10-8, bargain payments to the miners being 3/6d and 5/6d per fathom. The rate of forefield advance was 4 feet per day, reflecting the ease of driving. At least four, possibly five ventilation shafts were sunk onto the sough, finally the *Sough fforemost shaft* was sunk to the sough, here 19 fathoms deep [SCL, OD 1149]. The site of this shaft has been completely obliterated by the 18th and 19th century dressing floors and waste hillocks. Ore began to be measured from the *Sough in Nether Oden* in September, 1713 and was still being obtained from the title in 1717.

Activities within Peak Forest Liberty came to an end in 1736-1737 due to a combination of drainage problems and the vein dipping ever deeper beneath the shale cover as it was pursued westwards. Isolated reckonings made during the 1740s refer to the *Brass Castle*, a part of the vein lying west of Mam Engine Shaft and back-working through old stopes seems to have been carried on hereabouts for a few years. The mine owners soon realised that deeper exploitation of the vein was inevitable, the immediate response being to re-start the old *Sough below the Gank Mouth, or Sough in Nether Oden,* from its point of abandonment in 1713 at the *Sough fforemost shaft.*

By 1750 references again appear for the level, but by then it was referred to as Knowlegates Sough [SCL, OD 1150(a)]. An undated document written by Robert How about 1752, is titled `A Valuation of the Sough Level at Oden from the fforefield shaft to the Gank Torrs`. In fact it is an estimate of the costs of re-starting the sough and carrying it forward for 50 fathoms, with provision of associated boards, timber, *slidges*, ropes, kibbles and *Trogues to carry the Water down ye Level.* How`s estimate was £56-17-6 [SCL, OD 1504].

Deepening of the Sough Engine Shaft was started in late 1750, the miners locating the vein in late 1751. By 1752 the shaft was at least 101 feet in depth. Ore began to be measured at Oden Sough in 1751 and so continued until 1756. A total of 2,535 loads were measured, exclusive of duty ore, the value from 1754 to 1756 amounting to £3,451. Working below the level of Knowlegates Sough was a huge problem. Early in 1757 the owners of Oden Sough had considered the installation of a `Fire-Engine`, but by the autumn of the same year:

The partners of Oden Sough by reason of the prodigious expense of drawing water there have declined working and are now upon a scheme of erecting a water wheel to draw it. They have had a person at the mine skilled in such work to make an estimate. 26th September, 1757 [DRO, Grant Papers 345/832, microfilm].

A year later nothing had been done but Richard Bagshawe writing to Sir Archibald Grant observed:

It is an Engine worked by Water Proposed to be Erected at Oden it will be completed and worked Infinitely at a less Expense than one by ffire and in all Probability Answr ye (Intent?) as well Several Experienced Mechanics have viewed ye Mine made Estimates of necessary Expenses and all Agree it is to be Effected with Success – Application - is to be made to a Person who hath the Reputation of being ye most Skillfull Engineer in these parts his Estimate of Erecting etc. Amounts to about £150. 11th August, 1758 [DRO, Grant Papers 345/832, microfilm].

There are no further references to the scheme and the proposals do not seem to have been implemented. There is however one curious entry in the reckoning book, dated September, 1760 that refers to *Thomas Southern for his trouble coming to view the engine, 10/6d* [SCL, OD 1150a]. Southern was a well known and respected engineer involved with the installation of Newcomen-type engines and other complex machinery and it is difficult to imagine him visiting Oden Mine to view an ordinary horse-gin.

The later progress of Knowlegates Sough is somewhat fragmentary. A section of the mine demonstrates that in March, 1765 the forefield was at the east end of the 4th taker meer west from Gank Mouth, that is 193 yards beyond the old `fforemost shaft`. Because driving was intermittent during the 1750s it is not possible to realistically calculate a daily advance for the forefield. The forefield had reached a point 544 yards west of the Gank Mouth by late 1769, indicating progress of 12½ inches/day, probably working three shifts. If that was maintained, then the workings in Peak Forest Liberty would have been reached and dewatered by Knowlegates Sough about 1776-1777.

Stoping below sough contour was carried out to depths of 9 to 17 fathoms in some places and to 25 fathoms (150 feet) in the 10th meer, water being lifted up to the sough by rag and chain pumps operating in a series of five internal shafts. Incredibly, at one location around the 19th meer a great `lum` of shale even reached down to the Knowlegates Sough. The combination of deep, shale-filled troughs formed on an eroded limestone surface, coupled with dipping strata and complex faulting, was the perfect recipe for completely unpredictable geology as the workings were pushed westwards along the vein complex. Nevertheless, between the years 1770 and 1777 a total of 12,411 loads of ore were measured, exclusive of hillock ore and belland [C. Heathcote, pers comm.].

Vertical sections of the mine show an internal shaft within the 26th meer west from the Gank Mouth, at which point there is a peculiar loss of 33 feet in level, the sough then being continued at this higher contour. This occurred within what one section refers to as *the Brass Castle - a very hard and barren part of the vein*. Despite the latter comment, it is strange that the soughers chose to lose so much level. The sections show the sough continuing into Peak Forest Liberty, reaching to the west end of the third taker meer, with stoping below sough level to a depth of 20 fathoms in the 1st, 2nd and 3rd taker meers. Nothing is known about the history of the sough after it reached into Peak Forest Liberty, nevertheless these far western workings relied on it for drainage until the arrival of the Trickett Bridge Sough three quarters of a century later.

ODEN SOUGH [FROM NEAR TRICKETT BRIDGE IN CASTLETON VILLAGE]

This sough, driven from the lowest practicable point for gravity drainage in Castleton village, was not begun until June, 1816 [Chats, Bar Coll]. Earlier, proposals had been put forward in 1772 and at that date accurate surveys and levellings were made along the intended course and detailed costings for its construction were drawn up. A long section, dated May 15th, 1772 is accompanied by a document entitled *An Estimate of Driving a Level from Hollow Ford Sitch to the East Forefield of Oden Vein* [DRO, BSA LP8 – LP10]. The

Sough tail from the bolt at Oden (Odin) Sough, Castleton. The sough was begun in 1816 (H.M.Parker).

cost of driving 1552 yards would be £970. The last 530 yards, from a shaft to be sunk in Bull Meadow, south west of Dunscar Farm, to the Knowles Engine was to be made as a cartgate. Planking for the cartgate floor, consisting of three double lengths, each two feet long, at 5d per piece would cost £33-2-6. The total cost was estimated at £1,416-0-0.

One item is worthy of special comment *Unforeseen Expenses perhaps meeting with Blackstone, Boreing etc. £132-12-7*. Driving what effectively was a trial level, deep beneath Mam Tor, dictated that the mine owners could not be sure of geological conditions beneath the hill.

Another long section is very similar to that compiled in 1772, but the sough was driven along a parallel line, slightly further north [DRO, BSA LP13 – LP14].

No work was started on the sough until 1816. The reason for the long delay is not known and no hints are given in any available documentation. A letter dating from May, 1816 observed that money for the scheme was to be advanced by the Estate of Sir William Chambers Bagshawe, letting the interest at 5% accumulate *until the mine shall be able to pay the interest to Sir William* [SCL, OD 1173]. An undated document within the same folder states that the total advanced was £3,237-11-4, but the sale of lead amounted to only £3,032-1-3. The sough was eventually started, *June 12th, 1816 Josh. Eyre, John Clayton and Co Began Odin Levil in foxhill* [Chats, Bar Coll].

The sough tail is a low bolt; modern exploration has proved that it soon increases in size to a stooping height. The walls are lined, the roof slabbed, progress being soon halted by bad gas. Unsubstantiated verbal reports dating from 1974 refer to some 1,000 feet being investigated, much driven through un-lined shale. Progress was halted by a roof fall. This would be beneath the enclosure known as Parsons Field. A shallow ventilation shaft, just by the `Z` bend in Dirty Lane, was descended in the summer of 1953. Kirkham [1954] was one of the party and her description reads:

We descended a shaft 37 feet deep, sunk in shale and beautifully lined with dressed limestone blocks. At the foot of the shaft a small archway in the side led to the sough itself -. (The) sough (had) stone lined sides and an arched roof – the mud – was thigh-deep of bright reddish-yellow ochreish colour – 50 feet up the sough from the shaft carbon dioxide began to be thick.

The report conflicts with the more recent claim of 1,000 feet in un-lined shale, but Kirkham`s account is considered to be more accurate. During 1816 the miners drove 110 fathoms. A letter from Robert How to William Bagshawe, dated February, 1817 provides additional information about the initial portion of the sough: *we are now sinking our first air shaft when done we shall begin to wall the level, we are got about 297 yards* [Rylands, Bag 10/2].

Optimism about eventual success was growing, for in March, 1820 *the Oden level goes on about as expected and towards next Xmas it will be coming near or at the old mine to relieve it from water* [SCL, Bag 654(132)]. Two months afterwards the sough forefield had reached a point 1077 yards from the tail at Trickett Bridge. There is no mention of a cartgate, but driveage costs rose steadily from 10/- to 25/- per fathom in 1816; 22/- to 36/- in 1817; 48/- to 84/- in 1819, then dropped back to 42/- to 45/- between January and May, 1820 [Chats, Bar Coll]. Bellows were fixed in the winter of 1816 and *scowering* (cleaning silt from the sough) a regular feature. Boring preceded air shaft sinking. The cost of the sough and ventilation shafts from June, 1816 until May, 1820 was £1,021-17-4. Two of the proposed air shafts lying west of Dunscar farm do not appear to have been sunk.

William Bagshawe was able to write to Benjamin Wyatt in late October, 1821: *Joseph Cock informs me that they had met with limestone at Oden, 11 yards west of ye Lord`s Meer. Have they found any ore yet?* [SCL, Bag 615(35)]. Renewed activity was signalled with the arrival of the deep sough. Ore dressing arrangements were up-dated with the installation of a horse operated bouse crusher in 1823. The gritstone wheel and circular iron bed survive. The Knowles Engine Shaft was sunk, or considerably deepened at this same period and a horse-gin erected on it. The gin-race and ruined wall also survive, so too the shaft although it has been filled to within about fifteen feet from the surface.

Deep drainage offered renewed hope and in the nine years after the vein was first located in the sough, output averaged about 820 loads per annum, not including hillock ore and belland. Twelve to fifteen companies of miners were getting ore on cope-bargains in early 1828. The year 1831 saw a bonanza of

2,141 loads measured followed by 1,205 loads the next year. Despite the optimism in July, 1827 Robert How Ashton wrote to the Rev. William Bagshawe:

we came to a pipe in the forefield of Odin Mine where we got a little ore, but it is now so barren that we have been under the necessity of giving it up for the present and I have returned to pursuing the vein where I am sorry to say we have not any ore at present. The vein is so much confused at this time that I am almost at a loss in what direction to pursue it, it being very much attended with water courses and cavities and broken and thrown about in every direction [Rylands, Bag Coll 13/3/100].

If the above is absolutely correct, then there is more than a hint of unfair dealing here, considering that output from the mine amounted to 713 loads during that very year. An alternative, and perhaps more satisfactory explanation may lie in a dating error, the correct date being 1837, not 1827. John and Thomas Barber were driving the sough in 1830-1831 at £2 to £4 per fathom. At the end of November, 1831 the forefield reached Aymie Gutter Vein, about 230 yards west of the Gank Mouth, the event celebrated *By ale given to the men when they let the Water out of the Rither point Hole.*

A steady and terminal decline in the fortunes of the mine began in 1834. The four years up to and including 1837 saw only 199 loads of ore obtained. A slightly more optimistic air arose in April, 1836, when it was noted that from 1833 the sough had been driven for 236 yards through the barren part of the vein. One month later the sough level was within 64 yards of the `old man` or bearing part of the vein. A pencil note added to Robert How`s plan and section of the mine drawn in 1769, marks the forefield cut 12 yards into the 18th meer by April, 1836 [DRO, BSA LP7]. Output certainly rose again in 1838, though the decade produced only 5048 loads.

Five men were at work in the deep sough, the level being 7 feet in height and 4 feet in width and advancing at about 1 yard per week [SCL, Bag 654(436)]. This rate of advance is entirely consistent with daily progress of 6 inches in the sough forefield from October, 1821 until April, 1836. A long and detailed description of the mine`s fortunes was penned c1838 in an effort to secure a reduction in payment of tithe ore:

The Oden mine – has cost a very considerable sum in driving up a level to relieve it from the water; cost several thousand pounds and was expected to have been sufficiently rich to have repaid the Proprietors for their outlay, which hitherto has not been the case for after working it for nearly seventeen years since the level got up to the vein, it has but repaid a small proportion of the outlay [Rylands, Bag 13/3/100].

More unease was registered by Sir Archibald Grant in writing to William Bagshawe in September, 1843 *Mr. Ashton mentions that a level is now being carried on which costs nearly £8 a yard and that there is not sufficient ore to meet the expense* [SCL, OD 1150b]. Green [1887] stated that the sough continued westwards along the vein for a distance of 1250 yards from the Knowles Engine Shaft, placing the level forefield just extending into Peak Forest Liberty. The sough must have reached here sometime between 1844 and 1850, probably the latter, for in that year Barmote Court jurymen for both Castleton and Peak Forest liberties, inspected that part of the mine, making the liberty partition mark *on the north side of the Level*. Small quantities of ore were measured in Peak Forest in 1849 and 1850, but continuing failure to discover payable ore-bodies led to the abandonment of the sough.

A further decline in output occurred between 1850 and 1856, only 502 loads being measured. There followed a brief respite in 1857-1860, some 1031 loads of ore being mined, followed by a final measurement in 1865 and closure of this once great mine.

John Royse a descendant from a long line of Castleton lead miners, lead merchants and smelters examined a part of the mine and the main cartgate in the 1920s, when he was moved to write:

I dreamt of lighting it brilliantly with electricity for the public to see its drama, depicting a story in human life and character [Royse, 1943].

BLACK SOUGH [IN EDALE]

Black Sough was freed by Robert How Ashton, Jeremy Royse and partners as a new vein in Edale in August, 1824. A freeing dish of ore was given, so unless the `new vein` was salted,* then some mineralisation must have been found. Unfortunately no precise location was given with the Barmaster's entry of the freeing, but signs of mining adjacent to the Mam Nick – Edale road near Upper Holt Farm are considered to be the possible site. There is a very large mound of sinking dirt immediately on the south side of the road and two mounds on the north side before Upper Holt farm is reached.

Nellie Kirkham [1962] made reference to the level:

> *I was directed to what I was told was the tail – a few hundred feet below Lower Holt Farm. It was a small, shattered opening, high in the west bank and there was an ocherous flow.*

The sough must have been at least 1970 feet in length and is aligned almost along the range of `Peakshill Farm` Sough, but the tail is some 360 feet lower. The level may have been a deep trial, intended to be driven beneath Rushup Edge, seeking the Oden Rake. If so, the reason for its premature abandonment is unclear.

* ore obtained from a different place to deceive the Barmaster.

PEAKS HOLE SOUGH

The original sough was begun in about 1770 with the object of working and draining veins between the Peak Cavern gorge and Cowlow Nick. The company was headed by Richard and William Bagshawe and Messrs. Barker and Co, who each held a 1/6th share. The sough title included 14 meers in the Sough Vein, extending from Peak Cavern gorge and terminating at the northeastern margin of the Speedwell Vent, 21 meers in Foreside Rake from the gorge westwardly to Cowlow Nick and five other veins with up to 20 meers set out [DRO, BSA L8]. Surface indications of mining along the lower slopes of Cowlow are so insignificant it is difficult to imagine how the company thought that anything of value would be found, but they were no doubt hoping to discover and work the largely untried eastern portions of the above mentioned veins.

An un-dated note, probably by Robert How, the Castleton Barmaster, commented:

> *Peaks Hole Sough is a tryal that in the course of mining ought to be carried forward but it will be so expensive and a risk to run that I dare not venture on it at present.*

The original intention was to drive southwards beneath the west side of the gorge, successively intersecting each of the veins in the sough title. Presumably the plan was to drive branch levels in a westwardly direction along the sole of each vein as appropriate. Unfortunately, the sough quickly intersected the *Slop Moll* rising, a resurgence for water from Speedwell and Peak Cavern and work on the southern driveage was abandoned. The southern driveage was blocked and the water from the rising was diverted into Peaks Hole Water via a walled channel. For much of the 20th century the channel had been thought by speleologists to be the open section of the sough tail, and thus became the focus of much abortive trial digging. The tail of Peaks Hole Sough was re-located in the 1980s, whilst a portion of the original sough bolt, a cut and cover drain 4 feet high and 2 feet wide was found to run to the north and disappear beneath the Peak Cavern custodian's house [Penney, 1985].

This realignment of the sough was described in the reckoning book:

> *November 20th, 1771 Spent on 16 men Opening the water Course and Stoping the old Level at 2 ½ d each.*

The attention of the miners then turned to driving westwards along the Sough Vein, the most northwardly vein in the sough title. Work in the Sough Vein occupied the period from the summer of 1771 until the early months of 1774, after which a short cross cut was driven south into the South Vein. The work in the Sough Vein and south cross cut was carried out by a gang under William Walker. The remainder of the driveage in the South Vein was under the direction of Abraham Bradshaw [DRO, BSA L8]. Most of the sough was used as a cartgate and Penney and his team were able to leave a considerable portion of the timberwork consisting of cross beams, planks and boards in-situ and untouched.

A report on the sough prepared in 1782, commented *still carrying on but the prospect not very flattering* [SCL, Bag 634]. The last recorded work in the sough was in September, 1783, the forefield being then situated under the northern slopes of Cowlow (Callow). During the life of the venture a mere 53 loads of ore were sold, this obtained mainly from pipe veins adjacent to the Dales Wall Shaft. Charges totalled nearly £564, the loss to the proprietors being

£471-7-11 [SCL, Bag 431a].

During July, 1783 the titles of Peaks Hole Sough, Longcliffe Mine and Hourdlo Stile Mine were consolidated and all work was concentrated on construction of a deep level cartgate at Longcliffe Mine. The first reference dates from 29th November, 1783, *Jno Barber Driving Cartgate in Long Cliffe in the Clay, 5 fathoms at 8/- £2-0-0*. A further 5 fathoms were driven in the `Clay`, this presumably being the weathered margin of the Speedwell Vent. Longcliffe Vein terminates eastwards at the Vent. After a driveage of 94 feet, they were *Cutting through to the Engine with Cartgate* [DRO, BSA L8].

The Engine cannot be the shaft described by Ford [1962], it is situated too far to the west along the rake. Though there is no conclusive evidence, a much overgrown walled channel which leads to a run-in level near the foot of Cowlow Nick may have been the entrance to the cartgate. An alternative hypothesis that the run-in may be the site of the early 18th century Longcliffe Levy cannot be discounted (see below). The cartgate was only 335 feet in length when work on it ceased in 1786; a peculiar feature concerns the highly variable bargain rates paid for its excavation and their equally rapid fluctuations, ranging from a mere 6/- per fathom to £2-12-6 per fathom.

Toward the end, there occur four references as follows *5 fathoms under the Clay towards Callow; 6 fathoms towards Callow; skirting the limestone, skirting the limestone within Callow.* All the work carried out from November, 1783 in the cartgate and at the four locations referred to above concern a very localised area around the foot of Cowlow Nick. The Longcliffe Vein appears to have been poor in ore hereabouts and the miners began trying the scrins at Little Banks and in the lower parts of Cowlow Nick whilst also endeavouring to explore the boundaries of the Speedwell Vent (= *the Clay*) and any mineralisation on its south and east sides.

DRAINAGE OF THE DIRTLOW RAKE MINES

PINDALE SOUGH AND THE LEVEL IN RED SEATS WOOD

The steep sides of Pin Dale display extensive outcrops of the Bee Low limestones and the equivalent fringing apron-reefs. These rocks dip at 10 to 15 degrees to the north east and pass beneath the overlying Edale Shales at the foot of Pin Dale. An extensive tuff cone, the Pindale Tuff and its lateral extension, the Cave Dale Lava exists beneath this area and they were intersected by many mine shafts and workings. The highly weathered tuff, present in the form of soft, sticky clay containing small, hard pellets was known as *cat-dirt*. The term can be traced back to Hooson [1747] and Whitehurst [1778], but its origin is not known [Rieuwerts, 1998]. The less weathered rock was known by the more usual names of channel or toadstone.

The shale rests directly on the tuff at Pindale Mine (*Ashton`s Mine), there being no intervening limestone [Green, 1887]. At Siggate Head Mine the channel was proved to be 72 feet in thickness and at Dirtlow Mine (presumably Nether Dirtlow Engine Shaft)

The wooden floor construction of the cartgate in Peaks Hole Sough, Castleton. The sough was begun in 1771 and abandoned in 1783 (Paul Deakin).

Lead Mining in Derbyshire: History, Development & Drainage

Castleton (part) and the Pindale Mines (part)

Dirtlow Rake and Pindale Mines

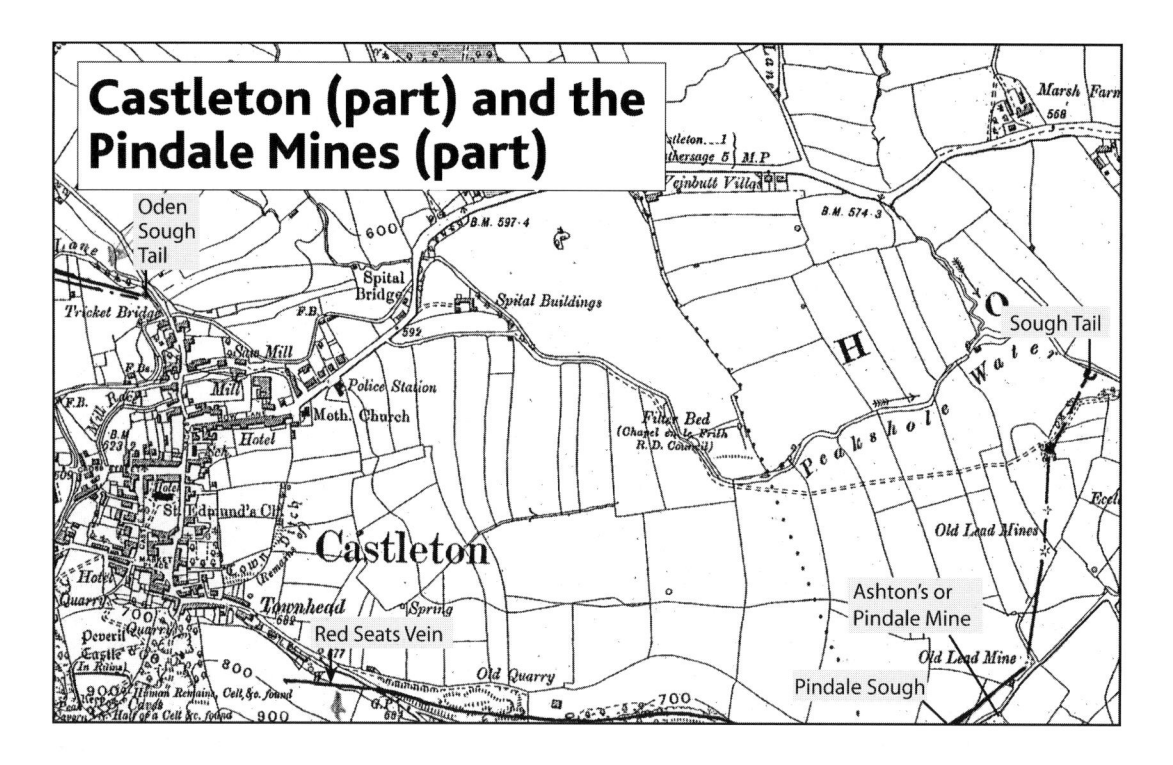

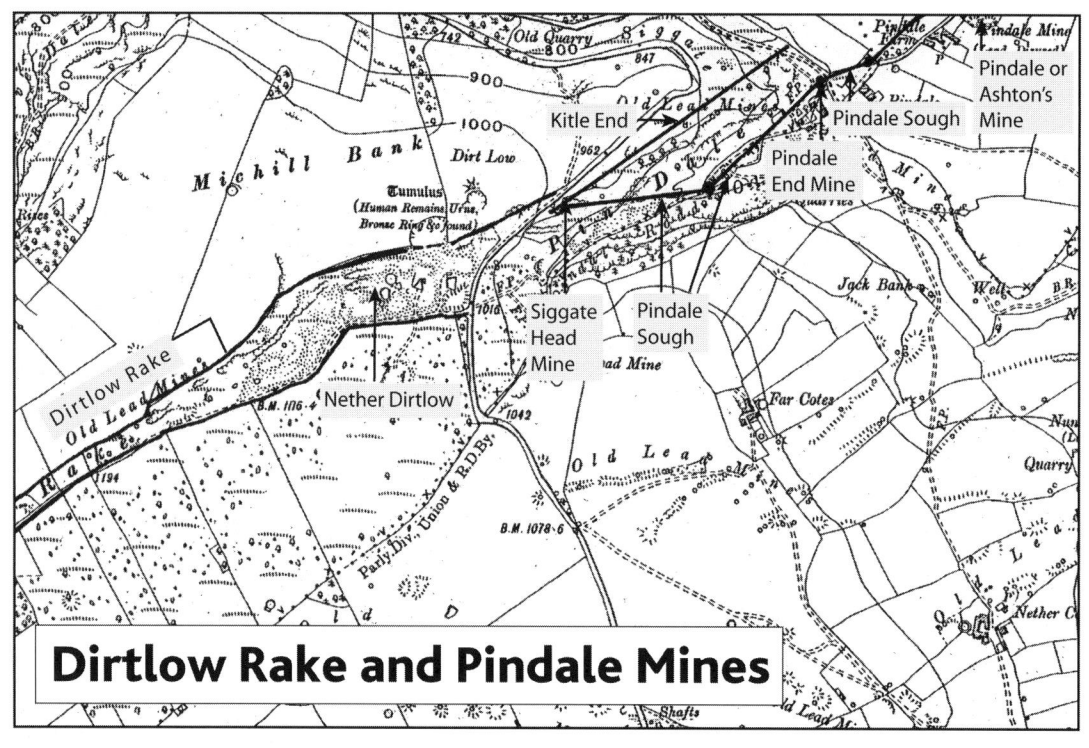

Dirtlow Rake is a major vein complex with many associated scrins and minor veins, these often separated by large riders of rock and gangue mineral. The alignment of the individual veins is impossible to depict on the map, therefore the width of the mineralised zone has been illustrated by highlighting the walls enclosing the surface expression of the vein.

good ore was obtained from within it and from the limestone beneath [Farey, 1811; Green 1887]. Pindale Sough penetrated through the base of the channel at Pindale End Mine, situated at the foot of Pin Dale. A short lived, but significant increase in ore production coincident with the event suggests that workable ore shoots were found in similar circumstances to those met at Dirtlow Mine. Near Pindale (Ashton`s) Mine the veins degenerate into worthless strings in the Pindale Tuff and there is no evidence that they were ever worked or prospected beyond this mine.

Siggate Head Mine and Nether Dirtlow Mine both achieved local celebrity status during the late 18th – early 19th century. The mines were visited by Faujas St Fond, Hedinger and John Mawe who were all interested in the Werner v. Hutton controversy then raging in geological circles, concerning the sedimentary or igneous origin of rocks. These men visited the mines, examined the Pindale Tuff and/or Cave Dale Lava, known to the miners of the day as `channel` or `cat-dirt` and made their pronouncements. Mawe [1802] noted that at Siggate Head Mine:

One side of the vein consisted of what the miners called channel, cat-dirt or toadstone; and a part of the vein was full of that substance. It seemed to me – whether this substance be not a limestone, strongly impregnated with pyrites, which are in a decomposing state; In truth, the miners have applied the same name of toadstone or cat dirt to substances extremely remote

*There is potential for confusion here due to duplication of mine names. Nether Dirtlow Mine was known originally as Ashton`s or Eyre`s Grove, whilst the late 19th century working beyond the foot of Pin Dale was known as Pindale Mine or Ashton`s Mine. They are entirely separate workings.

The first known reference to Dirtlow Rake occurs in 1538 when *Dyrtlo Rake Hed* was noted [Cameron, 1959]. The opencuts must have been begun at a very early date, but no written evidence for this extensive work has yet been found by historians. Isolated documentation, for example disputes heard in the Barmote Court and in the Duchy Court, show that various portions of the rake were being exploited during the late 17th century, but there is little substance in any of them relating to details of the workings. A map of Castleton Enclosures drawn in 1691 demonstrates that by then continuity of the vein had been proved from Pin Dale to the old Castleton to Tideswell road on the Old Moor [SCL, Bag 241].

The next available information covers the period 1727 to 1736 and consists of a series of ore measurements at mines in Castleton Liberty [Chats, Dev Coll]. The 18th and 19th centuries witnessed generally poor levels of production from the Dirtlow mines, only Pindale Mine (Ashton`s) Pindale End, Siggate Head, Nether Dirtlow (Ashton`s), Hollandtwine and Hazard mines achieved the status of medium to large scale mines, and then only for limited periods of time.

Ashton`s or Eyre`s Grove sold a mere 175 loads of ore from 1730 to 1735. The mine was only 30 fathoms (180 feet) in depth in 1739 [Chats, Dev Coll]. These workings must have terminated at the upper surface of the Pindale Tuff. The only exception to the general trend was at Pindale End Grove where 2,789 loads were mined, exclusive of Lot between 1730 and 1736 representing approximately 30% of the total yield from Castleton Liberty. [Chats, Dev Coll; DRO, Br-T L71]. The Pindale End mines were important enough to attract several members of the Derbyshire gentry as shareholders, the most prominent being Henry Thornhill, Nicholas Twigg, Richard Calton and Sir John Statham. There exists the possibility that more than one partnership was exploiting the mines at this time. Before about 1785, none of the mines in Pin Dale, or those along the north eastern portion of Dirtlow Rake had penetrated through the channel.

Construction of Pindale Sough seems to have been the first attempt to work the rake at depth. The agreement to drive Pindale Sough beneath the grounds of several landowners to Pindale Mine, near Pindale End, is dated 1743 [SCL, Bag 2604], but a substantial though short-lived rise in ore production at Pindale End Mine beginning in 1757-1758 hints that the start was delayed until about 1750. Output from 1757 to 1760, excluding Duty ore, amounted to 847 loads [DRO, BSA L7].

The sough tail is a stone lined drain issuing into Peakshole Water a little west of where the branch line to Hope Valley Cement Works crosses the stream. The sough was driven through shale for about 1,750 feet, it then passed into the Pindale Tuff for about 800 feet to the shafts at Pindale End. The sough breached the base of the tuff (channel, cat-dirt) hereabouts.

Calamine (zinc carbonate) was being obtained from Pindale End in 1751-1752 and also from Red Seats Vein. The ore was carted to the Calamine Mill in Dove Dale

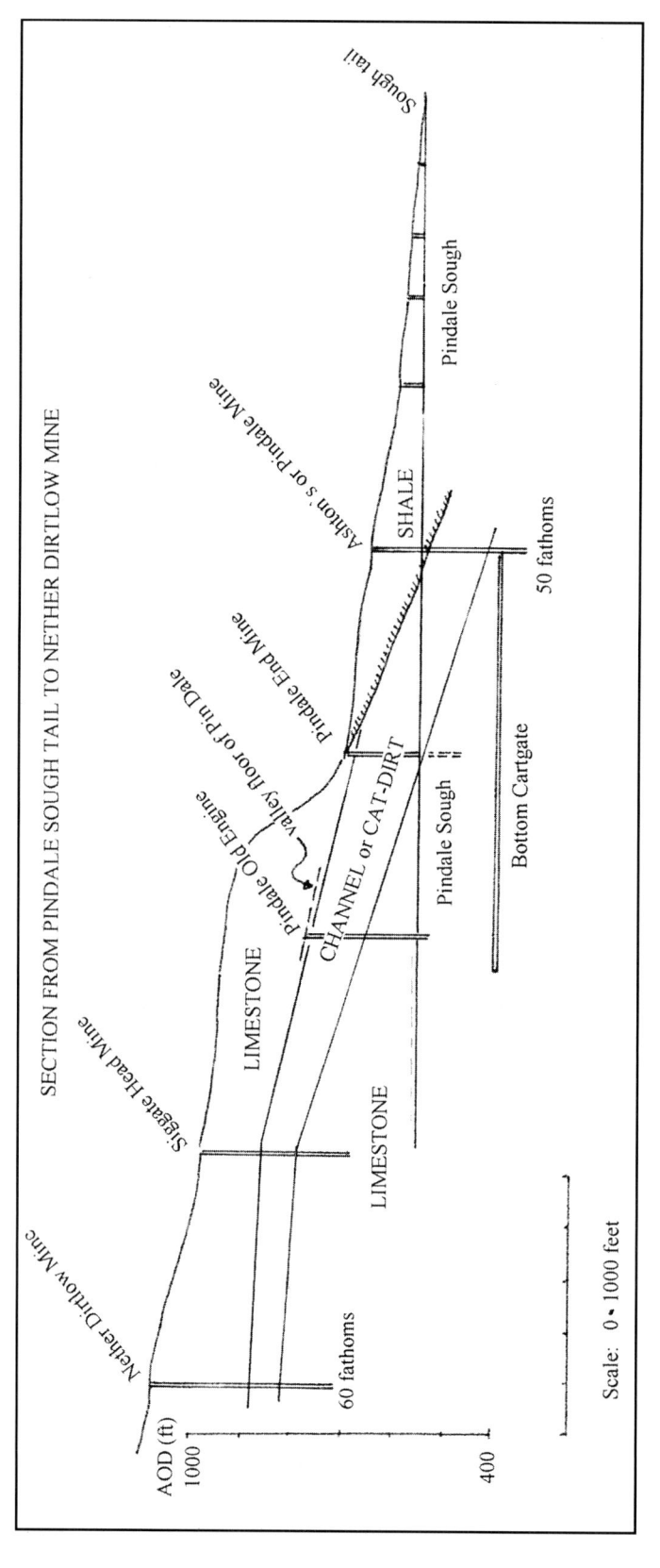

Lead Mining in Derbyshire: History, Development & Drainage

SECTION FROM PINDALE SOUGH TAIL TO NETHER DIRTLOW MINE

Sough tail

Pindale Sough

Ashton's or Pindale Mine

SHALE

50 fathoms

Pindale End Mine

Bottom Cartgate

valley floor of Pin Dale

Pindale Old Engine

CHANNEL or CAT-DIRT

Pindale Sough

LIMESTONE

Siggate Head Mine

LIMESTONE

Nether Dirtlow Mine

60 fathoms

AOD (ft)
1000
400

Scale: 0 — 1000 feet

(Lode Mill). Calamine was also being mined from the same locations at the beginning of the 19th century.

After 1760 output then declined until another burst of activity which lasted from 1786 until 1797 [DRO, BSA L1]. The mine was very active during these years mining 2,421 loads of grove ore. This evidence seems to indicate that the workings had breached the tuff (channel) and entered into the underlying limestone, a locally rich horizon that extended at least as far south west as Siggate Head Mine and Nether Dirtlow Mine. The zone also extended eastwards from Pindale End towards the Pindale (Ashton`s) Mine [DRO, BSA LP 68-69].

A reckoning book for Pindale End Mine covering the period 1784-1795 provides details relating to activities at the mine [DRO, BSA L1]. Throughout 1787 they were refurbishing Pindale Sough, including:

Ditching sough tail, opening the sough by bargain, clearing the Level, repairing West Sough Shaft, walling Middle Shaft foot and *Drawing the shale from Sough West Shaft foot.*

Eleven cope gangs were at work, whilst in August, 1790 Joseph Hall was paid for *Opening the South Vein in the Channel, 6 fathoms at 4/- per fathom*. A haulage gate using waggons with cast metal wheels running on wooden rails was referred to as *the Railway*. It was being driven during 1801-1803, elsewhere in the orefield this level would probably have been referred to as a `Newcastle Road`. A solitary reference in 1802 to *Robert Barber and Co clearing the Level in Red Seats Wood* may indicate the existence of a branch level from the sough along Red Seats Vein.

After 1797 output levels declined, dramatically so after 1817. Saleable ore amounted to 406 loads from 1798 to 1804; from 1805 to 1816, 316 loads, with a mere 24 loads contributed from 1817 to 1831, during this latter period no ore was measured for seven of those years.

Late 19th century plans of Pindale Mine prove that the sough extended at least as far as Siggate Head Mine [DRO, BSA LP 68-69]. The mine had reached a depth of 48 fathoms (288 feet) in 1843, well above sough contour, which fact hints that this portion of the sough was made after mid-century. There is no evidence that it ever reached Nether Dirtlow, despite good ore being found beneath the channel at that mine. Very probably, due to impoverishment of the ore shoots at no great depth beneath the base of the channel, there would have been little incentive to continue the sough in that direction at such a deep contour.

Despite the channel having been reached at the Nether Dirtlow mines by the mid 18th century, if not even earlier, it is surprising that no attempt appears to have been made to explore the ground beneath that stratum until the early 19th century. Jeremy Royse, a lead merchant and smelter and descendant of a long line of Castleton lead miners, began to obtain shares in Ashton`s Grove, Siggate Top Mine (Nether Dirtlow and Siggate Head Mine respectively) and Walker Title in September, 1808. Shortly afterwards Royse obtained the controlling interest in the three mines from Samuel White of Tideswell. Nether Dirtlow Engine Shaft was sunk into the underlying limestones to a total depth of 60 fathoms (360 feet). A reference in 1808 to the *new Engine Shaft on Nether Dirtlow* suggests that the original idea at least came from White. During the first two decades of the 19th century the mine usually yielded 200 to 450 loads per year. In 1809, 557 loads were mined, this being 36% of the total ore mined in Castleton Liberty. Between 1799 and 1821 some 6417 loads of grove ore were sold from Ashton`s Grove. Clearly this ore cannot have been mined as a result of any benefit from Pindale Sough, the date is far too early for the sough to have reached so far west, furthermore, as discussed above there is no evidence that it ever did so.

Pindale End Mine was resuscitated in 1869, the finance provided by Robert How Ashton of Losehill Hall, Castleton. He had been in possession of the mine from 1856, but output was intermittent and small. Attention was turned towards opening the vein further to the north east and to that purpose an engine shaft was sunk nearly 700 feet distant from the old Pindale End Mine. A dual purpose winding and pumping engine made by Walker, Eaton and Co. of Sheffield was installed in the second half of 1870 at a cost of £365. The winding drum and wire rope cost an additional £50-18-9 [DRO, BSA L3]. The Engine House and chimney still stand having been renovated in the 1970s. A report dating from December, 1875 states that 29 men were then at work underground, 8 boys aged 13-16 and 9 men over 18 years of age worked above ground. One female aged 8-13 years was at work on the surface.

The shaft at Pindale Mine was sunk through shale directly into the Pindale Tuff, there being no intervening bed of limestone. Tuff (channel/cat-dirt) was `bottomed` at a depth of 240 feet and a cartgate was then driven south westwards along the sole of the vein

This engine house at Ashton's or Pindale Mine, was restored in the 1970s. The building contained a dual purpose winding and pumping engine made in Sheffield in 1869.

towards Siggate Head Mine. By December, 1875 the forefield was standing close to Pindale End Mine and in 1878 the forefield was 550 yards beyond Pindale Mine Engine Shaft.

The bulk of the production was obtained between 1874 and 1878 and totalled just over 2,700 loads. Most of it was measured in Hope Liberty, confirming that it was mined between Pindale Mine and Pindale End Mine. A section of the mine demonstrates that this ore too came from a limited vertical zone within the limestone beneath the channel. The deeper workings in the cartgate beneath Pin Dale were virtually barren. The last ore was measured in 1879, though locally it is said that the mine continued until 1890, though not necessarily productive of ore, and that Robert How Ashton lost £9,000 on the venture [Thompson, 1969]. Records have been checked up to and including September, 1894; no ore was measured after 1879.

HAZARD – HOLLANDTWINE SOUGH

Hazard Mine, or to give its more usual spelling in mining documents, *Hazzard Mine,* is situated on the Old Moor. The mine worked two veins, the Hazard North and South veins, these diverging westwards as the continuation of the great Dirtlow Rake complex. The Engine Shaft, which is still open, has its *eye* at an altitude of 1,410 feet above sea level, the deepest stopes being 116 fathoms (696 feet) from the surface, i.e. 710 feet OD. The most intense period of work recorded in extant documents, dates from the 1830s and concentrated on exploitation of the South Vein.

The near surface levels and stopes in the veins were worked in the lower beds of the Monsal Dale Limestones, but the major stoping was carried out in the underlying Bee Low and Woo Dale Limestones. The Upper and Lower Millers Dale lavas were met in the higher workings of the mine. So too was an un-named bed of channel met in the 32 fathom cartgate, at a point 600 feet west of the Engine Shaft, noted on a section of the mine, drawn in 1837 as *where the Ore whent out with the Channel* [SCL, Bag 665].

The earliest reference to the mine so far located occurs in a Barmote Court dispute heard in April, 1747 about non-payment of shares at Hazard and Chance [Chats, Dev Coll]. Chance Vein is the continuation of Hazard South Vein through the Wham enclosure.

The large scale development of the mine into a major producer of lead ore began in 1825, though output exceeding 1,000 loads per annum was not achieved until 1834. The years 1825 to 1830 saw 3,040 loads of ore measured, exclusive of duty, this represented 40% - 50% of the total ore obtained in Castleton Liberty. Thomas Hall became mine agent and in 1834 1,150 loads of ore were measured exclusive of duty ore. Output rose steadily and from 1835 to 1838 some 8,544 loads were mined. The year 1835 saw Hazard Mine contributing no less than 93% of the total ore mined in Castleton Liberty; the richest year was 1837 when 2,400 loads were measured. The profit to the mine proprietors amounted to £1,141 in a period of only fourteen weeks in February – April, 1836 [Notebook of Thomas Hall, in private possession].

A detailed section of the mine drawn in June, 1837 illustrates developments along the South Vein. The Engine Shaft was then 60 fathoms (360 feet) in depth, beneath it a series of climbing shafts and sumps gave access to the bottom of the mine 696 feet beneath the surface. Eighteen cope gangs were employed, but the section demonstrates that a great volume of ground had already been stoped-out. If each cope gang had only four members (there were usually six to eight men in a gang), then together with winders and drawers, ore dressers and other surface personnel, the total workforce must have been in excess of one hundred persons.

There were four `Cartgates`, but the terminology is perhaps misleading. Almost certainly these haulage levels were waggon gates, using small, wooden-bodied tubs with flanged metal wheels running on narrow gauge iron rails. The shallow cartgate at the nearby Wham Mine, from where a waggon of the type described above was recovered, is probably identical with those in Hazard Mine, so too the waggon gate in Hollandtwine Mine, photographed by the Pegasus Caving Club many years ago. The 32 fathom Cartgate extended both sides of the Engine Shaft and was 460 yards in length. There was a Middle Cartgate, the *East Cartgate going towards the Twine* (i.e. Hollandtwine Mine) and the Bottom Cartgate.

The year 1839 witnessed the onset of a marked decline in production, although average output between 1839 and 1859 was 435 loads/annum. A second vertical section of the mine was prepared in February, 1844, by then nine cope-gangs were working the western part of the mine *above* the Middle Cartgate, but none had reached the positions of the 1837 forefield stopes. The vein was no doubt being re-worked, taking out poorer quality ore remaining in riders, stalches and pannels. At 85 fathoms deep (510

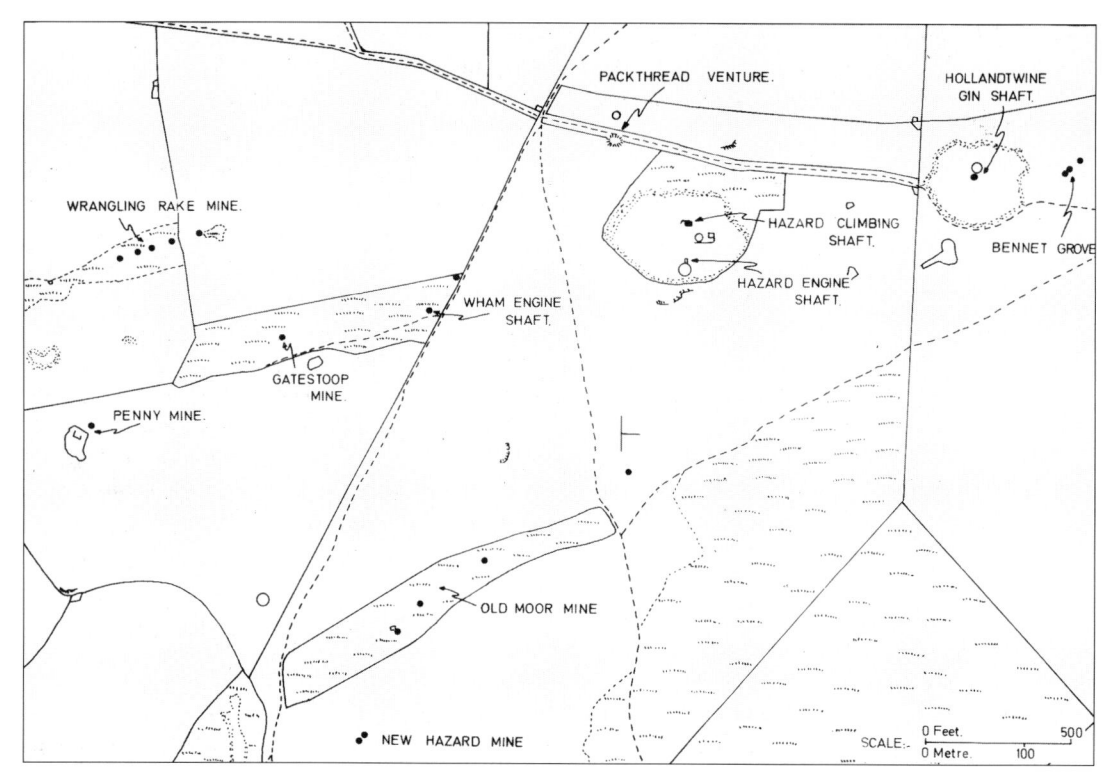

A map of the mines on the south-western section of Dirtlow Rake.

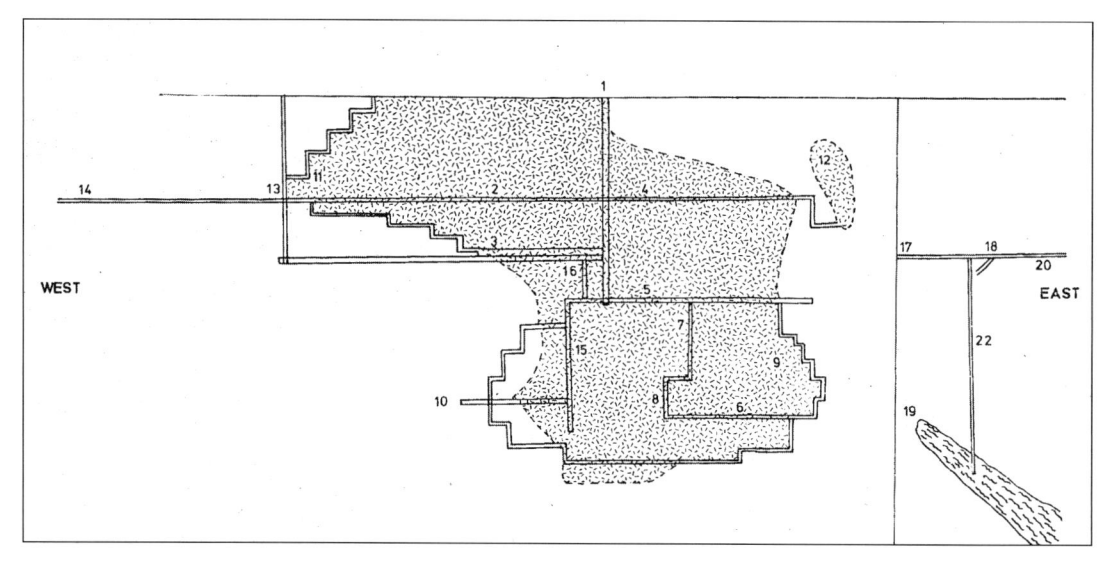

Section of Hazard (or Hazzard) Mine, Castleton Moor. 17th September, 1837. The section is drawn along the Hazard South Vein. 1. The Engine Shaft, 60 fathoms deep. 2. West Cartgate. 3. Middle Cartgate west. 4. East Cartgate. 5. Middle Cartgate east. 6 Botham (bottom) Cartgate to the works. 7. Drawing Sump. 8. Swallow Sump. 9. The present workings. 10. Rodger Forefield west. 11. Where we get so much ore. 12 Gytes in the pipe. 13. Where the ore whent (went) out with the channel. 14. The Cartgate in the Wham. 15 Botham (bottom) Water Sump. 16. Top Water Sump. 17. Twines ground End. 18. Bradshaw Vein. 19. Twine Water Course. 20. Twine Cartgate. 21. Dotted area thus all cut out (the soles of the lowest workings were 690 feet beneath the surface). 22. Twine Sump to the Water Course.

feet) the vein was described as *very poor*. Output continued to fall and the mine was finally abandoned in 1884 having yielded a mere 35 loads in the last fourteen years of its life.

The *Hazard – Hollandtwine* Sough may not have existed. Natural drainage provided by the streamways associated with Peak Cavern enabled the deepest stopes to be developed nearly 700 feet beneath the surface. There is but one reference to the sough, a schedule of deeds and plans formerly held by Hall and Co., solicitors of Castleton, lists an agreement for making a sough between Hazard Mine and Hollandtwine Mine [SCL, Bag 701]. No date is quoted and unfortunately the original document has disappeared.

The mine section dated June, 1837 [SCL, Bag 665] marks *The Great Swallow in the Twine* adjacent to the division line between the two mine titles. An internal shaft 380 feet in depth connects the `Twine Cartgate` with the Swallow. The base of this internal shaft must have been very close to the water table. Speculation suggests that in the 1830s when Hazard Mine was very rich and was already nearly 700 feet in depth, they contemplated cutting a level connecting the lowest soles with the Great Swallow in Hollandtwine Mine. The 1844 section does not mark a level driven in this direction and it is assumed that the rapid decline in the fortunes of the mine after 1838 was not conducive to making the sough.

SOUGHS AND LEVELS within the LIBERTY OF CASTLETON having uncertain provenance or intended function.

LONGCLIFFE MINE LEVY

The Levy was not a sough but a haulage gate, started sometime before December, 1708, because an entry in Richard Bagshawe`s account book begins:

> Agreed with Robert Tym and George Jackson to drive the Levill from the old one up to the New Shaft and are to give `em for workmanship 7/6 ye fathom [SCL, OD 1149].

The agreement indicates that the Levy must already have been driven to an old shaft and was to be extended to a new one. No details of the earlier work have been traced. Payments for the bargain ceased in July, 1709 and amounted to £9-9-0 signifying that 50 yards was the distance driven between the two shafts. A dead charge of £35-17-9 also accrued in 1709 for *Wages at the Levy and Shaft to that Levy* including *shifts for getting shaft through*.

During 1710 an additional £13-17-8 was spent on wages and other items. Ore began to be mined in May, 1710; thirteen miners (named) were engaged on cope at a rate of 1/10d per dish, which price seems to have been applied by Bagshawe at his Castleton mines. By the year end 90 loads 6 dishes had been obtained, but production soon declined. The following whole year realised 49 loads 7 dishes, 18 loads 5 dishes in 1712 and a mere 4 loads 4 dishes by 1713. Only three men were employed in that final year.

SPEEDWELL LEVEL, or OAKDEN LEVEL or NAVIGATION MINE
FAUCET RAKE SOUGH

Readers may consider it a surprise that the Level is not discussed in this book. Speedwell (or Oakden) Level does present a slight problem; few mining historians now consider that it was designed as a sough, for neither documentary evidence nor exploration of the mine support this hypothesis. Articles of Agreement dated 25th March, 1771 refer to permission from the Countess of Masserene to the owners of Faucet Rake Mine: *for soughing through part of Castleton Pastures* [SCL, Bag 702]. However, the agreement covers constraints imposed not only on sough masters, but permission being required from land owners before cutting any major level through barren ground. Additional confusion has arisen in the minds of mining historians by a barmaster`s entry for November, 1774 referring to: *Mr Oakden`s Mine on Foreside Rake with the sough thereunto* [DRO, BSA L5].

Despite the above mentioned documents, the Level was not conceived as a sough, but an underground canal and it was not designed to lower or alter the pre-mining water table in Longcliffe, Faucet (Foreside), or New rakes or the Hurdlow mines. The history and events that prompted creation of the Level have been discussed in detail by Rieuwerts and Ford [1985].

3. DRAINAGE OF THE MINES WITHIN THE LIBERTIES OF BRADWELL AND HAZLEBADGE AND PART OF GREAT HUCKLOW

Drainage of this district can be conveniently discussed under four sub-headings

(i) The mines on Nunlow, Cotes and Long Rake. The area has now been almost obliterated by large scale quarrying operations.

(ii) Veins and rakes draining into Bradwell Brook within Bradwell village. These soughs were driven to unwater Moss Rake and its associated veins and scrins. One sough may have served Moorfurlong Mine.

(iii) Drainage of the mines on Hazlebadge Hill and the east side of Bradwell Dale.

(iv) Further south, shale gates were driven towards mines developed beneath the shale cover, for example at Virgin Mine and May Sough Mine. Back o`th` Edge Mine at the head of Bretton Clough was associated with May Sough.

No references to pre-18th century sough driving have been seen, the earliest known level, Heald Sough is documented only from 1730. An iron plate bearing the date 1683 was found in Cronstat Sough, but does not prove that the adit was in existence at that time.

Steam powered pumping is recorded at only three sites. A Newcomen-type engine made by John Curr of Sheffield was installed at Hills Rake Mine in 1795, whilst Co-op Mine, Moss Rake was served by a horizontal winding and pumping engine made in 1869 by Davy Brothers of Sheffield. Another horizontal engine dating from the same period was placed on Wortley Mine on the eastern end of Moss Rake, but it served only as a winder. A water wheel of unknown size was installed underground at Hills Rake Mine in 1790. The wheel was probably made by John Thompson and Co. of Chesterfield.

Mines along Shuttle Rake and on Hills Rake west of Bradwell Dale drained into the Bagshawe Cavern streamway and artificial drainage from adit levels was not necessary. Briefly discussed below are a number of levels, some identified as soughs by mistake, others for which the evidence is very slight, or is now known to be incorrect.

MINES AND SOUGHS SITUATED BETWEEN PINDALE AND SMALLDALE

The area has been greatly altered since lead mining ceased about 1890-1900. The huge Hope Valley Cement Works dominate the skyline for miles, the result being that most traces of former mining activities have been obliterated by a combination of quarrying, waste tips, the Cement Works and ancillary buildings and even some limited hillocking.

The lower slopes of Nunlow Hill are lapped by Edale Shales lying on the Bee Low Limestones and equivalent apron-reef limestones. The important Pindale Tuff reaches a thickness of some 140 – 150 feet and was encountered in many mines on Nunlow. Walters and Ineson [1981], described it as *a major tuff and volcanic cone*. The rock was met in Nunlowend Sough and Elias Pedley`s Level. When encountered in Pindale Mine it was known to the miners as *cat-dirt*. Near the shale boundary, the dip of the reef limestones increases to 20 degrees, though higher values can also to be found in the literature. This is in sharp contrast to observations made at the time of construction of the Cement Works:

The dip in the limestone steepens gradually, at surface almost to verticality, and underground – as proved by the position of the shale-limestone boundary in the old Kronstadt Mine adit, from which flows the `spring` on the south side of the cement kilns – the shale-limestone boundary is locally overturned. [Fearnsides and Templeman, 1932].

Mines between Pindale and Smalldale

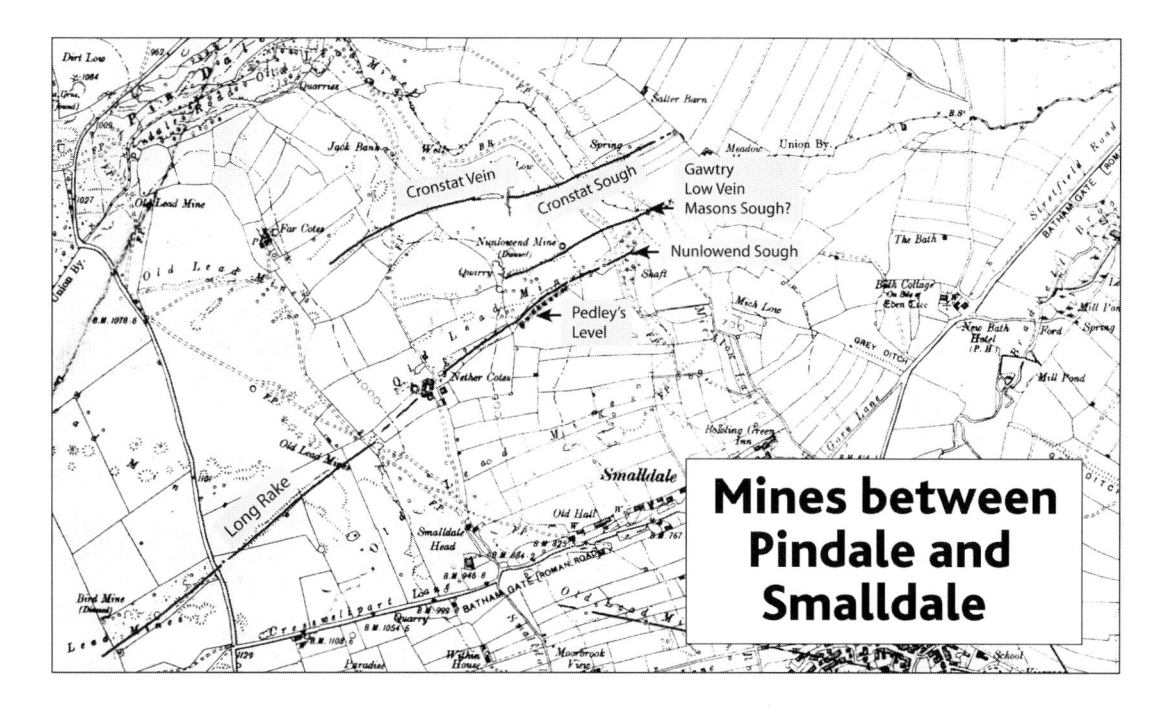

CRONSTAT SOUGH

Cronstat Vein occupied a sinuous course terminating at the limestone-shale boundary at the foot of Nunlow. All surface traces of the vein and sough have been obliterated by the Hope Valley Cement Works. The original tail section of the sough cannot be examined, but a total length of some 550 feet were excavated in shale, of which approximately 350 feet of passage is still accessible beneath the works complex. This was surveyed and photographed by company geologists, the Cement Works being then owned by Blue Circle Ltd. This part of the sough is driven through shale and is of small cross sectional area, about 4 feet in height and 2 feet in width. Parts driven through horizons of very thinly bedded shale are supported by timbers (two *doorstead forks* and one *headtree*), otherwise it is unlined [Dr. D. Jefferson, pers comm.]. The dimensions of the sough suggest a 17th century construction date. Nothing is known of its history, but a cast iron plate bearing the date *1683* and initials *I.T* was found in the workings.

Beyond the surveyed shale section, the underlying limestone was reached. The sough beyond is inaccessible, but an earlier survey made in 1928 when the works was under construction showed that it continued for at least 400 feet through limestone, along the sole of Cronstat Vein to a winding shaft, also now obliterated, on the lower slopes of Nunlow. A branch passage, driven through shale, runs north-west towards Pin Dale, it is not in good condition, exploration was halted by water reaching almost to roof level.

A larger level, some 15 feet higher than the sough, runs parallel to it. The dimensions, six feet in height and more than six feet wide in places, indicate that it was almost certainly a main haulage gate and of later date than the sough. Exploration was halted by a roof fall at the end of an `old man`s` stope, forty feet in length, eight feet wide and more that twenty feet high.

NUNLEY SOUGH (NUNLOWEND SOUGH)

Only one historical reference to Nunley Sough has been located, though it and Nunlowend Sough are identical: *Dispossessed 7 Pairs of Stoces – on Nunley Side all West from Nunley Sough in the Sough Vein belonging to Jno Whitting 5th May, 1790* [Chats, Bar Coll].

The Sough Vein is not marked on any plan or map seen by the author and there are no further references to it in the Barmaster`s Books. An undated plan shows the extent of Nunley End Mine, beginning at the old Bradwell to Castleton footpath, ranging southwest for 670 yards to the lower fence at the long demolished Nether Cotes Farm. Virtually all this ground has been either quarried, covered by waste tips or otherwise

Dirtlow Rake

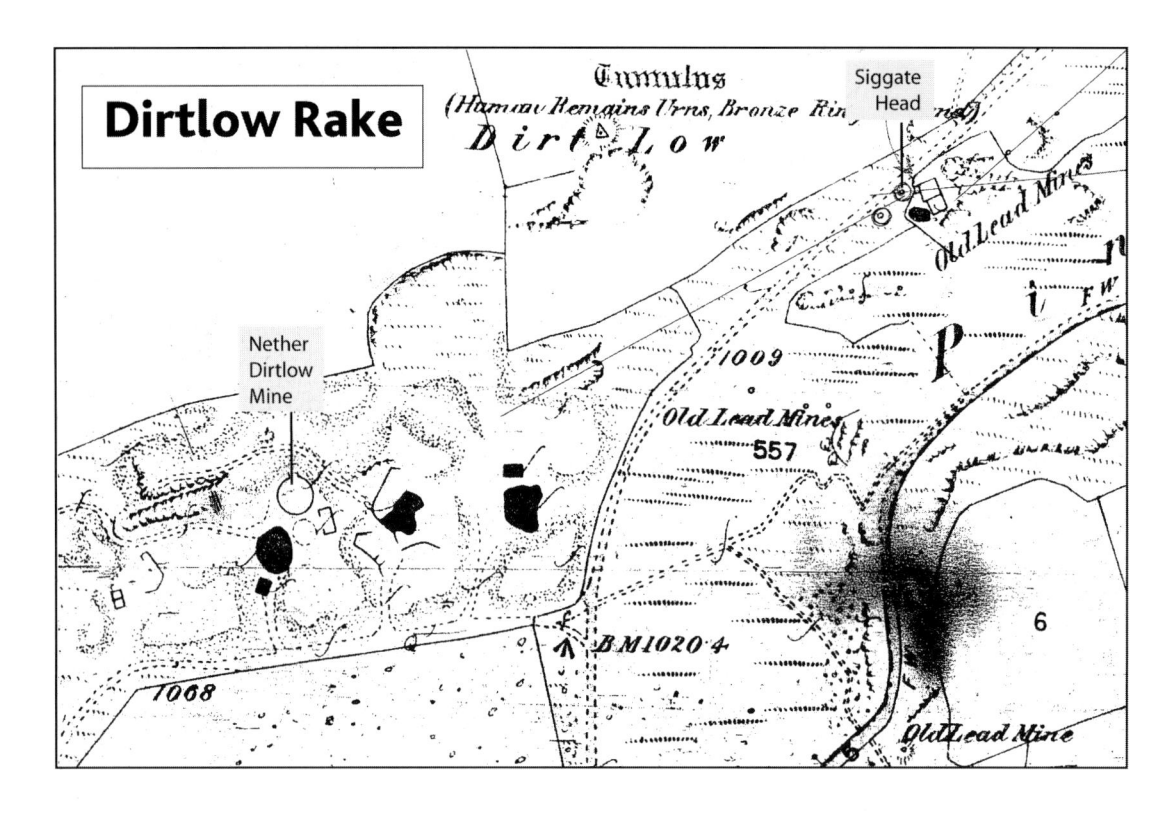

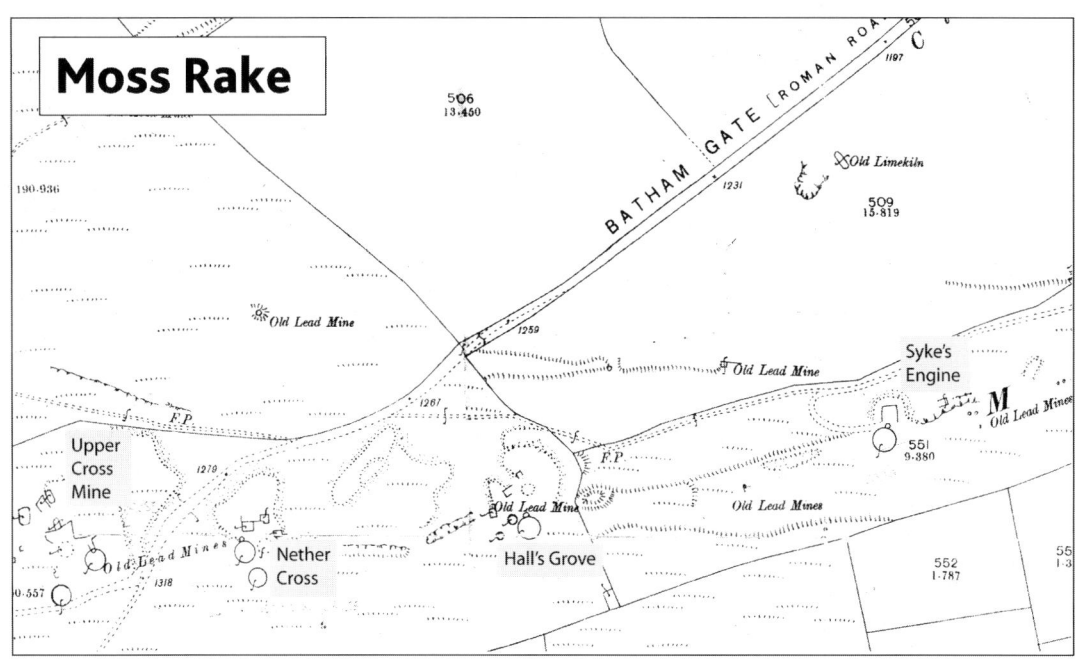

Moss Rake

Moss Rake is a large vein complex and individual veins and scrins are impossible to plot individually.

A lob, a spiral stone stairway in Raddlepitts Mine, Moss Rake, Bradwell Moor (Paul Deakin).

obliterated. The plan also marks a *Water Level and Tunnel* issuing into a surface water course at the foot of the steep hillside. This `Water Level` is Nunlowend Sough. Nunleys Mine, though not named on the plan, was slightly further up the hill and was recorded by Farey [1811] as producing ore in the toadstone. Confusion in identification of Nunlowend Sough and the late 18th century trial level known as Elias Pedley`s Level has been resolved [Rieuwerts, 1993].

Nunlowend Sough has been entered in recent times; after passing through shale for a short distance, the sough reaches limestone where almost immediately it is heavily collapsed in an old stope. The accessible portion is only about 200 feet in length [Dr. D. Jefferson, pers. comm.]. The presence of tuff in the hillock material proves that the sough passed into that stratum [Fearnsides and Templeman, 1932].

MASONS SOUGH

The sough is known only from a Barmaster`s entry dated 16th September, 1796, at which time a first taker meer was freed *west from Olivers Old Founder*, or *Galltree Low Grove*. Possibly the sough drained Gawtry Low Vein, just on the north side of Nunlow End Vein.

THE DRAINAGE OF MOSS RAKE, BRADWELL

Moss Rake is one of the most powerful veins in the Derbyshire orefield. It extends from the Wortley Shaft east of Bradwell village, in a general south westwardly direction for a distance of about three miles, the mineralisation terminating abruptly at the Peak Forest Sill, a dolerite intrusion north east of Peak Forest village.

Modern calcite and fluorspar hillocking and deep trenching operations have destroyed most of the surface remains between Bradwell and Moss Rake Head, but a small site including the gin-circle and winding shaft, together with the gritstone crushing wheel, still remains at Hartledale Bottom Mine. Raddlepits Mine, west of the Batham Gate crossing, contains important underground features, including stone-lined spiral stairways, or *lobbs;* surface remains have disappeared. Modern opencast operations a little east of the mine have revealed old stopes with intricate traceries of pickwork and three `coffin levels` driven into a vein rider. Hugh Grove has been only partially explored, but it also contains important features including a fine, stone arched haulage level. West of Moss Rake Head there are opencuts, shafts, hillocks and dressing floors extending to the termination of the vein at the Peak Forest Sill.

Continuity of the vein must have been established in early times, yet until about 1800 in proceeding south west from the brook in Bradwell village, the vein complex was known as Southfield South and North veins up to Outland Head. Beyond, it was known as Hartlemoor Rake until it crossed the old Castleton – Tideswell road, only beyond the road was it known as Moss Rake. Closely parallel with Southfield South Vein lay Butts Mine or Rake, at least 450 yards in length. Greaves Croft, Marshall and Portaway mines were situated on the North Vein.

A feature of Moss Rake is the presence of thick riders of limestone and calcite, often of very considerable length. Near Hartle Dale there was a rider 10 or 12 yards in thickness, whilst at Southfield a

A typical stope with stacked deads and a stempled climbing route in Hugh Hill Grove (or Moss Rake Head Mine), Bradwell Moor (Paul Deakin).

A fine example of dry-stone arching in the deep working at Hugh Hill Grove, Bradwell Moor (Paul Deakin).

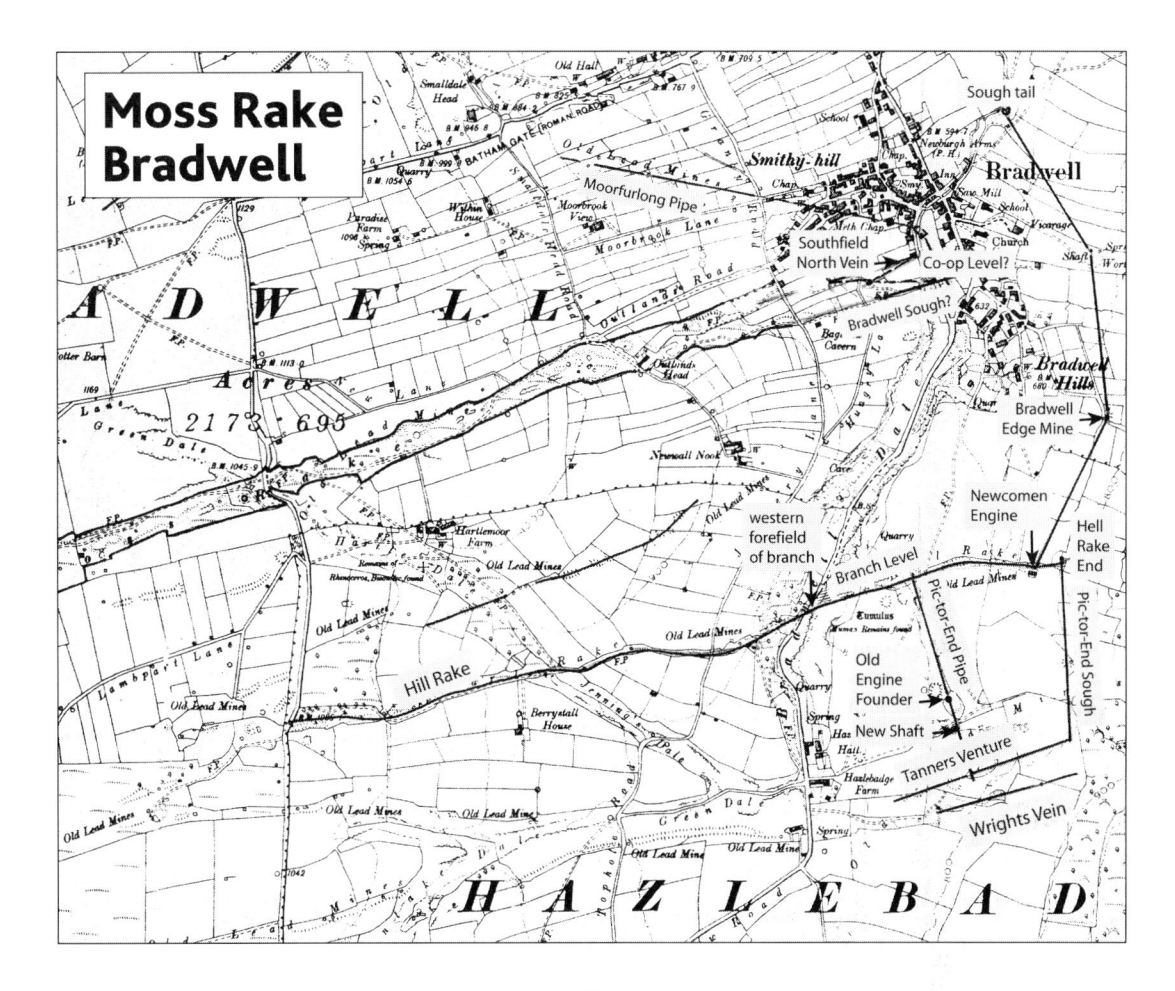

3. Drainage of the Mines within The Liberties of Bradwell & Hazelbadge & part of Great Hucklow

Lime Ryder divided the vein sufficiently to result in an action of title lawsuit being heard at the Barmote Court. Mid 18th century documents refer to both Southfield North and South veins, and a little further west the rider was of sufficient thickness to differentiate between Hartlemoor Vein and *ffrigley Vein* [Chats, Bar Coll].

A dispute heard in the Barmote Court in June 1749 revolved around a rider at a mine on Hartle Dale Rake. The jurymen were asked to descend the mine and give their opinions whether miners upon meeting *Deaf Cavell Riders (had) to prove whether therebe any Lumps of Lyme in them – in such a Strong and powerfull Vein* [Chats, Dev Coll].

The geological succession traversed by the vein consists of a sequence of standard limestones that dip gently to the east and north east across Bradwell Moor, before they disappear beneath the shale capping at Bradwell Brook. Fringing reef limestones occur at Hazlebadge, but the Moss Rake complex lies too far north to intersect them. The shale was penetrated for a depth of 120 feet at Wortley Shaft north east of the Church, before the limestone was encountered. The vein supposedly lay north of Wortley shaft and it was never found [Green, 1887].

South west of Hartle Dale two horizons of basalt lava, the Upper and Lower Millers Dale lavas occur within the limestone. Recent geological research has suggested that the Upper Lava dies out eastwardly around Hartledale Bottom Mine [Walters and Ineson, 1981]. However, investigations by the author indicate that operations at Windy Mine, some 1,200 feet further to the north east, may have terminated on top of the thinning lava, or a clay wayboard at the same horizon. South west from Hartle Dale all the mines as far west as Moss Rake Head reached the Upper Lava and some passed through it to the Lower Lava. At Hugh Grove (sometimes called Rake Head Mine) the Lower Lava was breached [DRO, BSA LP54]. Workable ore was found both in and beneath the Upper Lava:

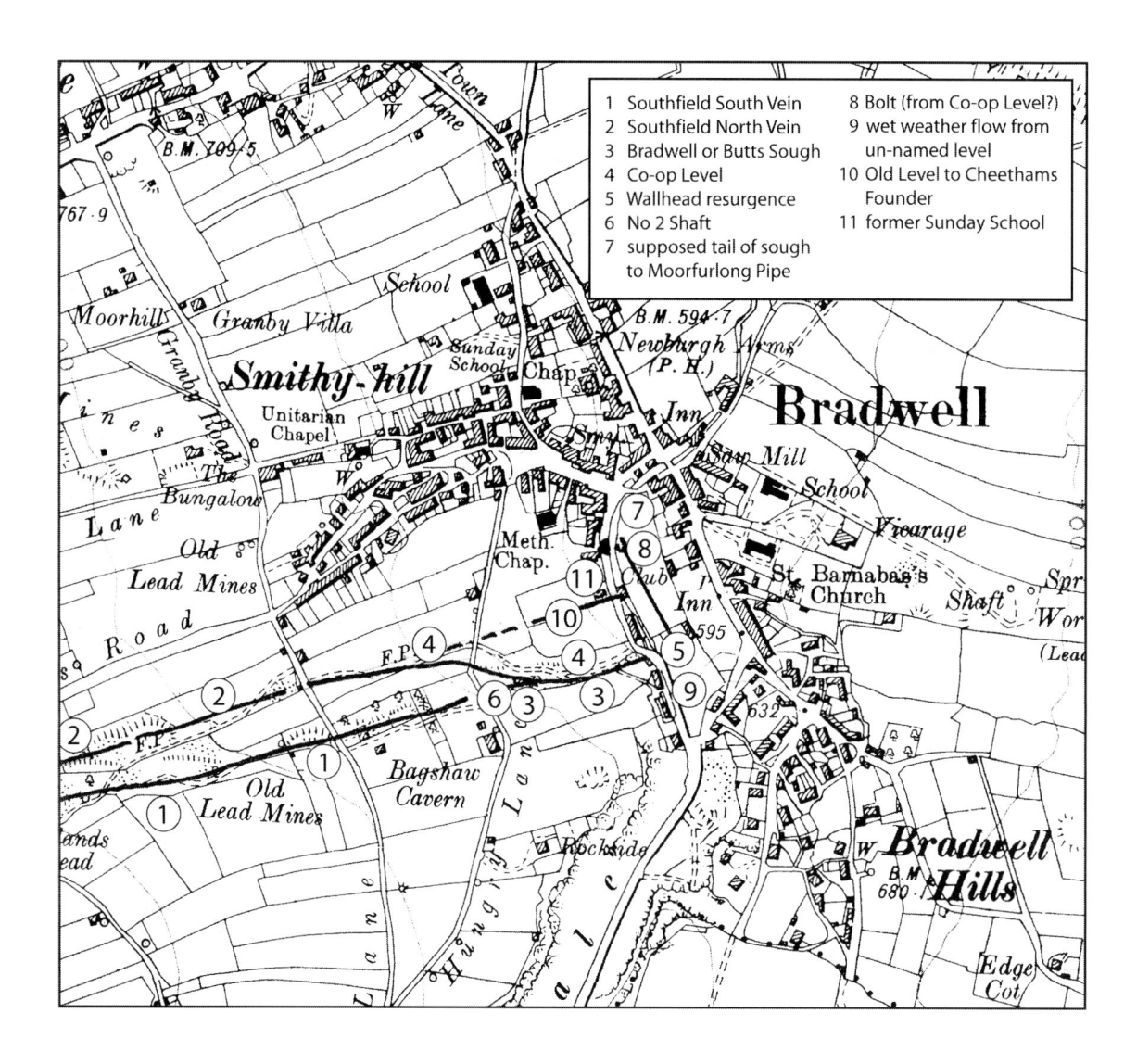

1	Southfield South Vein	8	Bolt (from Co-op Level?)
2	Southfield North Vein	9	wet weather flow from un-named level
3	Bradwell or Butts Sough	10	Old Level to Cheethams Founder
4	Co-op Level		
5	Wallhead resurgence	11	former Sunday School
6	No 2 Shaft		
7	supposed tail of sough to Moorfurlong Pipe		

Toadstone extends from 48 to 50 fathoms and again from 64 to 70 fathoms in this mine, ore being found in and under it [Green, 1887]. Good ore was said to have been worked at Sykes Engine (incorrectly called Silver Cross Mine by Green, 1887); very likely this ore was obtained from beneath the Upper Lava.

The mines on Hartle Moor were worked to depths of 250 feet to 400 feet, but further south west, at Sykes Engine and beyond, 500 feet to 600 feet was more commonplace. The above mentioned wayboard may have persisted as far east as Outland Head Mine, though no documentary evidence has been found to substantiate the claim. If so, then the large volume of water perched above it, derived from Bradwell Moor, would have reached valley contour around Outland Head and thus may have caused abandonment of the late 19th century Co-op Level some 250 yards short of the Outland Head mines. Despite a considerable amount of modern exploration of old mine workings on Moss Rake and also the Bagshawe Cavern system, the precise nature of the underground water flow is not yet fully understood.

The vein is characterised by the large amount of calcite gangue; some of this is nearly pure white and the better quality spar has been actively worked for more than a century for ornamental work and more recently for exposed aggregate concrete finishes.

Calamine (zinc carbonate) was obtained from the Yeld mines and from Mulespinner Mine, the mine being the original entrance into Bagshawe Cavern. The name of an adjacent working called *Brass Venture* is probably significant in that context.

The pre-18th century history of lead mining on Moss Rake is fragmentary. The earliest account dates from 1617 when an agreement was reached between two groups of miners that a piece of ground in dispute on *mosse Racke* should be equally divided. Unfortunately, the document, which is somewhat damaged, does not clarify whether the ground was within Bradwell or Peak Forest liberties [SCL, Bag 702]. Another dispute, dating from 1669-1670, concerned *Beverleys Grove neare Ashenholme pitt,* this working must have been situated at the boundary of the two liberties because two Barmote Court hearings took place, one for Bradwell Liberty, the other for Peak Forest. The mine must have been at Broctor Lane Head [SCL, Bag 702].

Botham Grove at Outland Head was in work in 1673, whilst John Turner had a 1/4th share in a mine on Hartle Rake in 1685. The precise position of Duddens Rake is not known, but from a surviving description contained in a boundary dispute dated 1698, it seems to have been a closely parallel vein lying on the south side of Moss Rake, and running northeastwardly from near Hartledale Bottom Mine [SCL, OD 1345]. Information contained in mid 18th century Barmaster entries and Barmote Court disputes make clear the presence of a well-developed vein hereabouts, seperated from Moss Rake by a thick rider. These few references comprise all that is known about lead mining on Moss Rake before 1700.

There are no extant records of mining along Moss Rake from 1685 until ore accounts for Bradwell Liberty become available for a limited period from midsummer 1727 until March, 1734. Output was very small, for example the most productive year, 1730, saw only 342 loads of grove ore measured, although twenty two mines were at work, of which 23 loads was obtained from Moss Rake Head. From Midsummer, 1732 until March, 1733, thirty three mines measured only 102 loads of ore. The whole period produced only 1832 loads for the entire liberty, exclusive of Lot ore [Chats, Dev Coll].

The location of the outfalls of five named soughs draining the north eastern end of Moss Rake has not been satisfactorily resolved. Details are discussed under individual headings, but the summary below gives an outline of the author`s current thoughts:

Heald Sough, possibly issues into Bradwell Brook from beneath the old Sunday School.

The Old Level to Chethams Mine may also issue into Bradwell Brook from beneath the old Sunday School. Heald Sough may also have been its original name. The Old Level is almost certainly identical with the Level in Southfield North Vein.

Bradwell Sough, or Butts Sough, probably issued into Bradwell Brook from a tail at Wallhead resurgence and which has been completely obliterated due to 19th and 20th century modifications at the resurgence.

The entrance into Co-op Level may have been from within the Wallhead (Bagshawe Cavern) resurgence, or less likely may have been situated a few yards south of Moss Rake and the resurgence, at a point from where considerable quantities of water issue in periods of heavy rain. Water from Co-op Level reputedly flowed through a long bolt issuing into Bradwell

Brook from beneath the Playing Field. An un-substantiated report claims that the main flow now runs in a culvert or bolt parallel to the main road and issues into Bradwell Brook just east of the road bridge in the village.

HEALD SOUGH

The first record of sough drainage from Moss Rake dates only from 1730. At a Barmote Court held in April, 1730:

> *George Berly complains to this Court against Mr.Thomas Marriot, Mr.Robison and the rest of there partners at a sough called heald In ye Libertey of bradwell for not paying ye vallue of a Colt kild in one of there sough shafts* [Chats, Bar Coll].

This brief note constitutes the only known reference to Heald Sough. Marriott`s Grove measured ore in 1727, though no location is given. The Yeld is the area lying uphill and west of Brook Head (Wallhead) and contained several mines on the Southfield North and South veins (i.e. Moss Rake). There can be little doubt that Heald (Yeld) Sough drained the north eastern extremity of the exposed part of Moss Rake before the vein plunges beneath the shale cover.

About 1960-1965 the late Michael Smith, one of the three founders of the Peak District Mines Historical Society, with companions explored a walled, slabbed level issuing into Bradwell Brook from beneath the old Sunday School building at Netherside. The level had run-in within a short distance, but this may be the tail of either Heald Sough, and/or perhaps the `Old Level to Cheethams Founder`.

BRADWELL OR BUTTS SOUGH

In February, 1750 Alexander Barker and partners purchased a quarter share of Southfield Engine Grove on Southfield South Vein, for £30 [SCL, Bag 484]. The mine, which should not be confused with the 19th century Southfield Engine, was situated in the 4th meer west of Bradwell Brook. This action seems to have heralded consideration of deep mining along the north eastern section of the Moss Rake vein complex. Three years later Mr. Richard Keeling was taking possession of three meers east of the Engine, ranging down to the Wallhead (Bagshawe resurgence), two meers for the partnership at the Engine and one meer for himself at Keeling Engine. At the same time he `nicked` six pairs of stows west from Southfield Engine, presumably for the partnership of Alexander Barker and Co., who held 2/3rds and Keeling who held 1/3rd. Eventually the partnership held title to fourteen meers in Butts Mine (sometimes called Butts Rake) on Southfield South Vein, these possessions terminating a little beyond Jeffrey Lane. Richard Keeling of Peak Forest was sometime agent for Bradwell Sough and he held a 1/3rd share in the soughing venture.

The date for the commencement of Bradwell Sough it not documented, but detailed reckonings hint strongly that the event can be dated to the summer of 1755. The reckonings, which sometimes refer to `Butts Mine or Bradwell Sough`, exist only until 1757 during which time just under £217 was expended and some 69 loads of ore were sold. Afterwards, reckonings during 1758 and early 1759 continue only under the Butts Mine title [SCL, Bag 486]. The implication of this is that the sough had reached the end of the four meers at Southfield Engine, about 450 feet from the tail at Wallhead resurgence during the latter part of 1757 after which mining was concentrated along Butts Rake/Southfield South Vein.

Production was disappointingly small; only 160 loads and 2 dishes were sold between 1758 and 1765 [Chats, Bar Coll]. Little wonder then in February, 1774, 2/3rds of Butts Mine were sold to William Howe for 10/6d because *Robert Howe thinks we cannot work on it with any prospect of advantage* [SCL, Bag 431a]. No further references have been found relating to this sough.

LEVEL ALONG SOUTHFIELD NORTH VEIN (LEVEL TO CHEETHAMS MINE)

Only two historical references have been found for the level(s), but it is considered that both may refer to the same feature. The Barmaster`s book of entries records a memorandum made in 1772-73 that:

> *John Hamilton sold to William Marshall a piece or parcel of Ground lying in Southfield North Vein to the roof of the Level being all his right and Tytle lying East from a Spring in the Sole of the Level for the Sum of Three pounds twelve shillings* [Chats, Bar Coll].

Hamilton`s mine was in Greaves Croft. A second memorandum, dated 3rd November, 1810, also entered into the Barmaster`s book, recites details of an agreement between:

Samuel Marshall of Bradwell – Miner – and Thomas Hallam of Bradwell, Miner – that for the sum of ten shillings – Samuel Marshall hath Sold unto the said Thomas Hallam – one half part or share of a Vein Called Mossrake North vein Extending from Cheethams Old Founder Two Mears or More East from the Said Founder the East End being Near Unto Bradwell Brook and it is agreed between the said Parties that the Old Level shall be Driven Up to the Cheethams Old Founder at the Joint and Equal Expenses of the Two parties and Likewise Twelve yards further West of the said Founder at joint and equal expense – Provided the said Level should happen to be run in or filled with Rubbish the said Length of twelve yards. and it is further agreed Between the parties that any Composition Allowance or profit Arising – from Driveing the Level West of the possessions of the parties, Either in the North or Sun Vein shall be Equally and Jointly Devided between the said parties [Chats, Bar Coll].

Thomas Cheetham had freed an old Founder meer in Southfield North Vein in the Heald in May, 1760, which founder is probably identical with Cheethams Old Founder referred to in the agreement. The agreement verifies that the Sough or Level had been driven at least 108 yards before 1810, but perhaps no further, but makes provision for re-driving it entirely. The Southfield South and North veins (= Moss Rake south and north veins) reach Bradwell Brook very close together. Nevertheless the limited historical evidence implies that despite their proximity, due to the existence of different title owners in each, there were two separate drainage soughs, Bradwell or Butts Sough in the South Vein and the level to Cheethams Founder in the North Vein.

CO-OP LEVEL

Activity began in 1862 when John Fairburn, the Sheffield based mining and smelting entrepreneur commenced buying shares in mines at the east end of Moss Rake, including Yeald, Greaves Croft, Marshall and Portway mines. He owned the whole of Greaves Croft Mine by July, 1864, but no ore was measured for Fairburn at any of his mines on Moss Rake. A letter from William Elliott to George Eagle, High Peak Barmaster, confirmed that Fairburn later sold all his titles in the Yeld mines to the Moss Rake Mining Co.[Chats, Bar Coll]. Further southwest on the vein, beyond the Southfield title, Outland Head Mine had proved to be a steady producer during the 1840s and 1850s; it was worked by the Fox family during this time. Whether Fairburn had entertained hopes of buying this mine is not known. Some years earlier, about 1858-1859 he had bought the Bradwell Slag Works [Willies, 1982].

The Moss Rake Mining and Lead Ore Smelting Company was formed in January, 1866. A Prospectus was issued in the Mining Journal which gave details of the share take-up. They advertised for £4000, issued in 4000 shares of £1 each. The aim of the company was to work Moss Rake, about which the usual exaggerations of width, length and depth were given, the purpose being:

to take a level from the east end of the vein, which will give a depth of 100 fathoms per mile. – There are about twenty different mines in the length of this vein or lode and many of the above mines have been given up being wrought for want of the proposed level. [Mining Journal, 21st April, 1866].

According to Evans [1912]: *In the sixties the Bradwell Moss Rake Mining Co. was formed on the Co-operative principle to drive a level and open out the mines, but after some years of unprofitable working the project was abandoned.* The company was also known as the Bradwell Co-operative Mining Company.

The position of Co-op Level is not known with certainty. Information from the late Cyril Evans was that the large bolt issuing into Bradwell Brook from beneath the playing fields was the tail of the sough. The sough bolt then ran southwards for 350 feet to a shaft in the field on the north east side of the Wallhead rising. Some few years ago, c.2000 a large water burst occurred from beneath the eastern boundary wall of the minor brookside road, a few yards south of the Wallhead resurgence. Limited excavation proved the existence of a level running beneath this road, which was also traced as a shallow drain running northwards, parallel with the main Tideswell-Bradwell road, eventually issuing into Bradwell Brook at the bridge in the village [D. Stables, pers. comm]. This description seems to coincide with details in a letter from H.A. Saunders, Steward of the High Peak Barmote Court, to the Barmaster: *There is a very strong head of water running into the Bradwell Brook out of a sough which passes under the main road at Bradwell* [25th January, 1919].

Much of the following discussion concerning the history of the Bradwell Moss Rake Mining and Lead Ore Smelting Co., is taken from a reckoning book and minute book covering the whole period of operations [H.Walker archive, Bradwell].

Co-op Level was begun either from within the Wallhead (Bagshawe) resurgence cave, or as a short crosscut in solid limestone on the south side of Southfield South Vein (Moss Rake). A plan of the Yeld and Greaves Croft mines dated 1907 has a pencilled line running from the resurgence initially along Southfield South Vein, then diverging slightly before crossing Hungry Lane into Greaves Croft. The line is not identified, but almost certainly it marks the course of Co-op Level [Chats, Bar Coll].

Indirect evidence in the reckoning book *suggests* that much of the initial work involved clearing out silt and debris from within the Bagshawe Cavern resurgence. Purchase of at least a dozen pairs of water tight boots provides a hint, whilst in June, 1867 the proprietors: *ordered that the Men who work in the level whilst in the present dirty state shall only require to work six Hours per shift – wages 2/6d.*

The four gangs, each consisting of four miners, were named in the Minute Book on the 8th May, 1867. Some were paid at 2/8d per shift, others at 2/6d per shift.

In September it was:

Ordered – that the level be cut east from No 2 Shaft till they meet the other Parties Going West from No 1 Shaft

Work had commenced by January, 1867 in sinking both No 2 and No 3 shafts, eventually 18 fathoms and 40 fathoms deep respectively [Green, 1887]. Miners were also:

Striping and sinking No 2 Shaft – and Cleaning out the old Level West of No 2 Shaft.

The author considers this *old Level* to be identical with Bradwell or Butts Sough (see above).

Summarising the foregoing, the Level was driven along the South Vein westwards through the Yeld, a short link connecting No 2 Shaft was driven east to meet the west forefield, then as indicated on the plan, the level was continued as a cross cut linking the Southfield South and North veins.

Between September, 1867 and January, 1868 seventy two feet were driven in the Level and fifteen days were spent in April, 1868 in unspecified *work at level Mouth*. At a meeting of the proprietors on the 3rd June, 1868 they ordered: *that the level stand for the Present*. Later evidence confirms that the forefield was by then approaching the top of the Yeld, and in the range of Southfield North Vein. The decision to cease driving the level is confirmed and explained by several reports that appeared in the *Sheffield Morning Telegraph* in 1869-1870. The first report, dated 26th April, 1869 noted that: The Company`s No 3 Shaft, 1500 feet south west of Brook Head (Wallhead) was sunk 40 fathoms.

Efforts were concentrated on sinking at No 3 Shaft and installing a horizontal steam winding and pumping engine at Outland Head Mine. The engine, made by Davy Brothers, Sheffield was rated at 12HP, it had a 12 inches diameter cylinder and cost £518 [H. Walker archive, Bradwell]. Payments were made in October, 1869: *5 times Outland head with two horses with the Engine at 2/6d per time*. The engine house was under construction in the latter months of 1869 and they were *Setting Boiler* in January, 1870. The engine was still not at work in February, however: *Their shaft has been lined with conductors and every exertion made to render it as safe for the men as possible.*

The shaft was to be sunk four to six yards deeper in order to meet the vein which was expected to be uncut at that point.

The Minute Book noted in August, 1868 that: *Two hurys and extra Barrells to be provided for No 3 Shaft to Bring the Stuff to the Engine foot*. A hurrier and hurrying are coal mining terms, in the above context it perhaps means a flat-bed, or shallow sided waggon.

The level stood until April, 1874 when they were:

commencing operations again by driving the Level. That the Level be driven up the north side of Greaves Croft.

Two hundred and fifty six feet were driven to a

forefield in Greaves Croft where the sough was abandoned. The last bargain dates from October, 1875, the bargain rates had differed in dramatic fashion, ranging from £1-12-6 to £5-10-0 per fathom.

Green [1887] commented that the Bradwell Co-operative Mining Co. drove the Level to a point 250 yards west of the Wallhead resurgence, their furthest shaft (No 3) being 500 yards west of the spring; it was 40 fathoms in depth. Ore was found there at 30 fathoms and good ore was left in the vein west of Outland Head *for want of a water level.* The length of the Level quoted by Green fits exactly with the forefield in Greaves Croft as it stood in October, 1875.

The Company was in the process of being wound up in October, 1894. Sale of the Engine House was being arranged in November, 1894 and the plant was sold on 1st January, 1895. A late 19th century guide book states that Sheffield businessmen lost £6,000 at these mines, *the idle, rusty steam engine and plant still standing above Bradwell Brook as a memorial.*

SOUGHS and LEVELS within BRADWELL LIBERTY having uncertain provenance or mistaken function

BARBER SOUGH

The existence of this level is known from only one reference, when in May, 1761 the title was arrested for debt. The location is not known.

BARLOW SOUGH

A 1/4th share in the sough was arrested for debt in July, 1762. Barlow Sough Old Vein was freed in May, 1763 and a small quantity of ore was measured, 6 loads 7 dishes, in 1763-64. Like Barber Sough its location is not known, but the similarity of name may indicate that they are identical.

ELIAS PEDLEY`S LEVEL

Not a sough, but a short level driven by Elias Pedley, a Castleton miner, in the 1770s. The level, situated on the lower slopes of Nunlow, was developed for about ninety feet along a thin scrin. The level was visited by the noted French geologist St. Fond in 1784. He was keen to examine the vein/scrin containing galena occurring within the channel (Pindale Tuff) and which led him to the erroneous conclusion that the stratum could not therefore be of igneous origin [Rieuwerts, 1993].

SUPPOSED SOUGH TO MOORFURLONG PIPE

Moorfurlong Pipe and Stone Hole Pipe range north west – south east aslant the hillside west of Bradwell village. They are not connected with Moss Rake, but their artificial drainage, if it ever existed, possibly discharged into Bradwell Brook a little to the north of the Moss Rake complex.

A local tradition in Bradwell refers to a sough driven from Bradwell Brook at a point between the old Sunday School and the bottom of Smithy Hill. Here, a slabbed level issues into the brook and always seems to carry a strong issue of water. There is said to be a covered shaft in the Methodist Chapel graveyard which is on the sough. Maybe coincidentally, the supposed sough tail and shaft are more or less along the south eastern random of Moorfurlong Pipe.

The shaft descended by modern exploration groups and always referred to as Moorfurlong Mine, appears to fit with the Lord`s Meer Shaft on Stone Hole Pipe, a vein closely parallel with Moorfurlong Pipe. Stone Hole Founder was sunk about 1663-1664, the pipe being discovered shortly afterwards [PRO, DL 4 127/6/1694]. A series of title disputes occurred at these mines during the period 1692-1696; contemporary descriptions of the upper and under levels in the Lord`s meer fit remarkably well with the presently accessible workings in `Moorfurlong Pipe` adjacent to the entrance shaft [Surrey, Bray Papers]. Included in the legal depositions a Peak Forest miner named Robert Jowle stated that he had *set them a ffan to gain Winde,* the first documentary record of this method of ventilation in the Derbyshire orefield [Rieuwerts, 1998], though surely not the first example.

Richard Bagshawe owned shares in Moorfurlong Grove, for which abbreviated reckonings are available from 1709 to 1715, together with the adjacent *Mooloe Torr Grove* and Noger (Noker, Nawger) Hole Grove [Rylands, Bag 12/1/60]. Stone Hole Pipe is not recorded and likely by then it was regarded as part of Moorfurlong.

The workings high on the hillside, west of Bradwell village are fairly shallow and although flowing water was used for ore-washing underground, there are no records of drainage problems. Only at the south eastern end, where the workings are now inaccessible, might such problems have occurred and therefore a sough might have been necessary. The source of the copious flow of water issuing into Bradwell Brook has not been confirmed, the adit being inaccessible due to obstructions beneath the road.

SOUGH IN BURTON PINGLES PIPE

The mine workings are entered from the base of the disused quarry on the west side of Bradwell Dale. They lie approximately on, or slightly south of the random of Bradwell Edge Mine on Hazlebadge Hill, but no discernable surface connection is apparent. A caving trip dating from the 1970s reported a hand picked `sough-like` level in the lower reaches of Burton Pingles Pipe, close to active stream passages in Bagshawe Cavern. More recent explorations have failed to recognise this feature and the original report may have been in error. No historically documented sough is known in the vicinity.

THE HAZLEBADGE MINES AND PIC-TOR-END SOUGH

Hazlebadge (or Haslebadge) is a Private Liberty and belongs to the Duke of Rutland. Lead mining activity and its associated drainage problems within the liberty can be considered in the context of three sub-areas. These are :

(i) The whole of Hazlebadge Hill, situated east of Bradwell Dale, plus the tract of land lying north of the Hill and ranging down to Bradwell Brook, together with the enclosures immediately south of the Hill.

(ii) The large district west and south west of Bradwell Dale, rising westwards up onto Bradwell Moor. The mines within this sub-area such as Shuttle Rake, Intake Dale Mine, Scrin Rake and those on Hill Rake west of Jeffrey Lane, were not drained by soughs, but by the natural streamways flowing through the Bagshawe Cavern system. Present exploration of the cave terminates at a sump close to Hill Rake. Therefore, the district is not discussed in the main text below.

(iii) The extreme southern portion of the liberty which includes workings adjacent to Quarters Farm, Virgin Mine, May Sough and within Hucklow Liberty, Back o`th` Edge Mine.

The geological structure is relatively simple. The limestone beds forming the high ground of Bradwell Moor dip gently toward the east and north east, before passing beneath the overlying Edale Shales of Bradwell Edge. The limestones are sub-divided; the uppermost rocks belong to the Monsal Dale Beds, below which are the Bee Low Limestones. The division between the two is marked by the horizon of the Upper Millers Dale Lava. Reef limestones fringe the perimeter of the limestone outcrop and are developed in Bradwell Dale and the whole of Hazlebadge Hill. The Upper Millers Dale Lava dies out eastwardly, whilst a thick lava found in Shuttle Rake Mine possibly lies at a higher stratigraphic horizon. Neither extend as far east as Bradwell Dale [Walters, 1981] and no evidence has been located to suggest that these lava beds were met in the mines along Hill(s) (Hell, Earl) Rake, or in workings on Hazlebadge Hill.

Hills Rake, Tanners Venture, Shuttle Rake and the veins associated with the Virgin and May Sough mines have all been worked beneath the shale cover. Unlike other districts within the orefield there are no records of 17th century exploitation beneath the shales. Prospecting beneath the shale, but in close proximity to the limestone outcrop, was in progress as late as 1758 at Hills Rake Mine [Chats, Bar Coll].

The mineralisation is contained in rake veins, scrins and pipes, but in the mid 17th century there was a historically important dispute about the definition of pipes, flat-works and flots [SCL, Bag 702; Rieuwerts, 1991]. Fluorite was abundant in Pic-Tor-End Pipe and calamine was obtained from several mines, most notably at Nall Hole Mine on Hills Rake. Specimens of *bone-ore,* and crystalline calamine, sometimes with a delicate yellow colouration, can be picked-up from the hillocks at Nall Hole. Calamine Venture, a nearby mine, was at work by 1763. Black Jack (sphalerite or zinc sulphide) was worked at William Howe`s mine on Hills Rake, on the western side of Bradwell Dale. The mineral was being sold to brass manufacturers for £3-8-0 per ton in 1792.

Pilkington [1789] recorded that a layer of native sulphur, 4 inches in thickness, had been found in Virgin Mine, whilst Farey [1811] stated that it had been found in the toadstone there. Unless some exceptionally deep trials were carried out beneath the shale

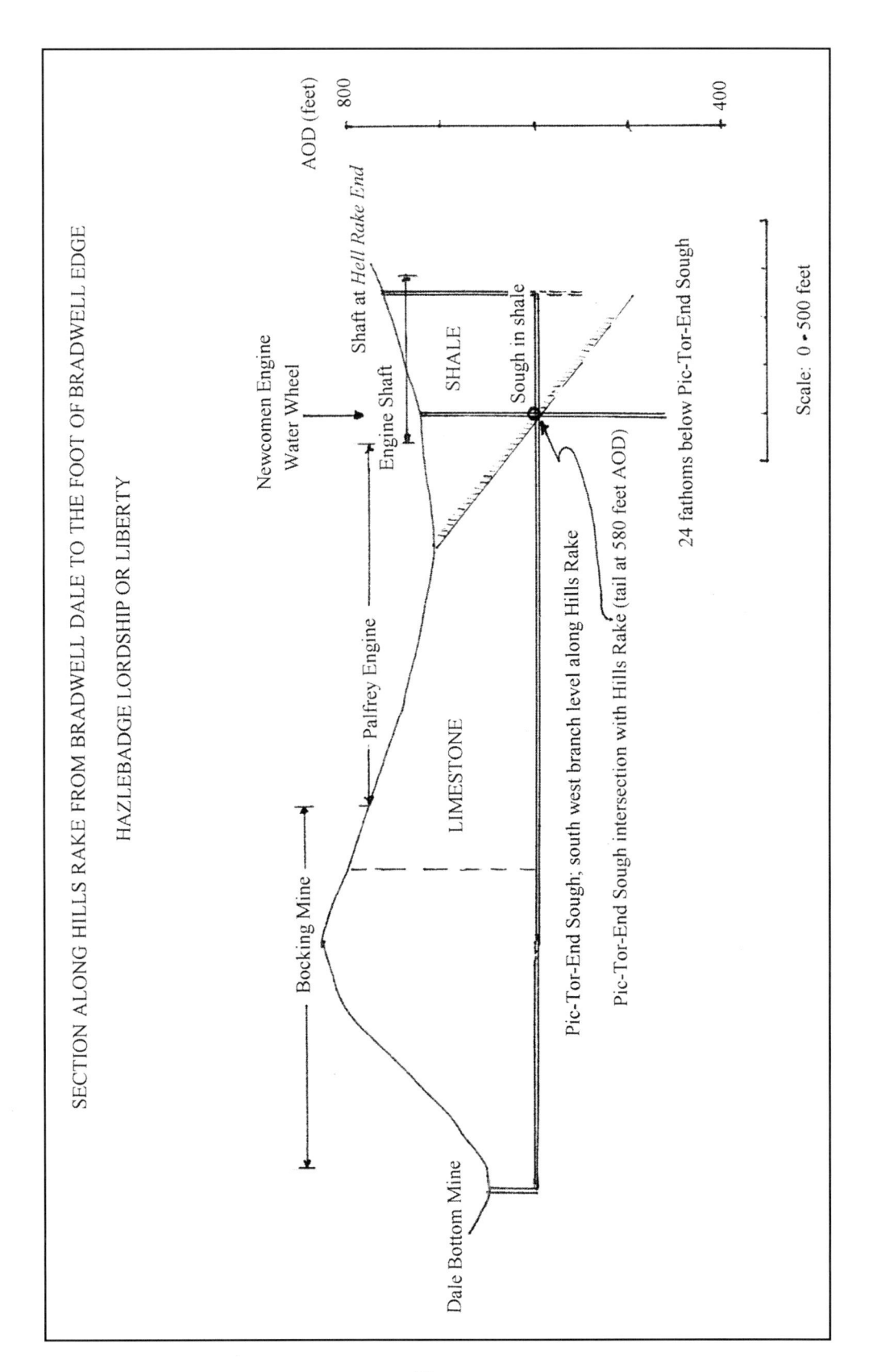

3. Drainage of the Mines within The Liberties of Bradwell & Hazelbadge & part of Great Hucklow

SECTION ALONG HILLS RAKE FROM BRADWELL DALE TO THE FOOT OF BRADWELL EDGE

HAZLEBADGE LORDSHIP OR LIBERTY

AOD (feet)

Shaft at *Hell Rake End*

Newcomen Engine Water Wheel

Engine Shaft

SHALE

Sough in shale

Palfrey Engine

LIMESTONE

Bocking Mine

Pic-Tor-End Sough; south west branch level along Hills Rake

Pic-Tor-End Sough intersection with Hills Rake (tail at 580 feet AOD)

24 fathoms below Pic-Tor-End Sough

Dale Bottom Mine

Scale: 0 – 500 feet

cover, it is difficult to understand the presence of toadstone in Virgin Mine.

George Platt, agent at the Ashford Marble Works, made an agreement in February, 1771 with the partners at Tanners Venture Mine, *for all fossils and putrefactions* to be sold to the Marble Company. In this context `fossils` refers to mineral specimens and `putrefactions` to stalactites, stalagmites and flowstone formations. Several years later, in 1786, White Watson, the Bakewell geologist, purchased `fossils` from Francis Mason of Foolow. Mason was agent at Tanners Venture Mine.

The principal ore deposits worked on and adjacent to Hazlebadge Hill were those at several titles along Hills Rake, at Pic-Tor-End Pipe, Tanners Venture Vein and Wrights Vein. Information spread within several disparate documents can be pieced together from which an idea of the geographical positions of the 18th and 19th century mining titles on Hill, Hills, or Hell Rake can be placed. There may be very slight discrepancies for some locations, but these will not exceed one meer (28 yards) and can be expected to be much less.

Beginning at the extreme eastern end of the vein was Samuel Howe`s Mine, or Ashmore`s Mine. About 200 feet distant from the shaft at Howe`s Mine was Hills Rake Engine, during the mid to late 18th century these mines formed the Barker partnership`s Hell Rake End Mine. Both mines worked the vein beneath the shale cover, as did the first four taker meers of the next title ranging west, Palfrey`s Engine Mine. The four meers extend to the limestone outcrop at the foot of Hazlebadge Hill, the remaining five meers belonging to Palfrey`s Engine reach to the main footpath across the Hill and were worked wholly within the limestone. This last section of Palfrey`s Engine was until recently characterised by untouched hillocks of discarded calcite vein-stuff enclosed within dry-stone walls, known as *belland yard* walls. Unfortunately, all has been removed by recent hillocking operations. From the eastern extremity of the vein at Samuel Howe`s Mine, including Hell Rake End and Palfrey`s Mine contained 13 meers, which in the mid 18th century constituted the Hills Rake title in the possession of Alexander Barker and Co.

Proceeding south west, the next mine was known as Bocking Title. A division stake was placed by the Barmaster in late 1778 parting Hills Rake and Bocking titles. Isaac Morton freed a founder meer and eight taker meers between January, 1779 and December, 1784. Morton`s possessions ranged over the hilltop and down the eastern side of Bradwell Dale. This ground was also known as the *White Hillocks,* an appropriate name, due to the large quantities of white calcite vein-stuff that still covers the eastern side of Bradwell Dale where it is intersected by the rake.

Beyond Bocking Mine and between it and the Bradwell Dale road lay Cobbler Mine, almost certainly identical with Dalebottom Mine, situated in the bottom of Bradwell Dale. There is some evidence to suggest that the south western forefield of the branch sough level driven along the sole of Hill Rake from Pic-Tor-End Sough, was located here.

West of Bradwell Dale lay 9½ meers ranging to Jeffrey Lane, equally divided between two brothers, William and Robert Howe. Then came Providence Mine, west of which was Luck-at-Last terminating in Jennings Dale, or Hartle Dale. On the west side of that dale was the important Nall (or Naw) Hole Mine, beyond there Froghole Mine continued as far as the boundary with Bradwell Liberty in the King`s Field.

Pic-Tor-End Pipe ranges north-north west to south south east, almost along the crest of Hazlebadge Hill. Old miners claimed that the pipe consisted of three distinct levels or horizons, but only two, an upper range, at or very close to the surface, and a lower one some two hundred feet beneath it were seen during 20th century explorations of the workings. The pipe begins from the southern side of Hills Rake and before virtual obliteration by fluorspar hillocking, the upper pipe could be followed for a distance of about 1,050 feet to a shaft covered by a `beehive` and built into a field boundary wall. Here surface indications cease, but a mine plan dated 1800 [Chats, Bar Coll] shows the pipe continuing for another 500 feet to a little beyond Wrights Vein. Local information some fifty years ago (1950s) named the shaft under the wall as Bennetts Mine, but the 1800 plan marks it as New Shaft. Pic-Tor-End Engine Shaft (or *Old Engine Founder*), approximately 200 feet in depth, is situated just over 800 feet south-south east from the Hills Rake boundary wall.

Situated 600 feet north of Hazlebadge Hall Farm on the east side of Bradwell Dale, is a largely natural cavern, still accessible. A phreatic rift, the walls characterised by prominent nodules and lenses of water-resistant black chert, the cave was prospected by lead miners, and in places modified by them, their climbing stemples used for access into the upper reaches of the rift remain in-situ. The prospecting work probably dates from 1777 when the Barmaster gave Daniel Furniss and William Atkinson 7 meers *from the dale belowe Hastlebadge hall house into Hastlebadge hill they expecting to discover a Vein that will range Southeast from the said dale. If no discovery, no grant Joseph Smedley.* [Chats, Bar Coll].

Tanners Venture Vein and Wrights Vein intersect and cross; both are aligned north east – south west, more or less parallel with Hills Rake. They run beneath the shale cover for a short distance and across the flatter ground, south of Hazlebadge Hill, falling into the line of Intake Dale Mine and eventually, at the western end, into Shuttle Rake. Immediately west of Tanners Venture was Lawrence Grove; Old Barn Flatt Vein and the quaintly named *Spice Poke Grove* lay to the south west of Lawrence Grove. The position of the equally strange sounding *Hab nab at a Venture* is not known, but it was recorded in 1776 [SCL, Bag 587(111)]. *Hell Rake*, the earlier spelling for Hill, or Hills Rake, might also lay claim for inclusion with them.

Records of mining within Hazlebadge Liberty before 1700 are very scanty. As early as 1292 the annual value of Lot ore amounted to 10/-, suggesting a yearly output of about 100 loads [Evans, 1912]. No details of the actual mining have emerged. In 1630 twenty eight Articles regulating the working of mines in the Liberty were written down at a Barmote Court held at Hazlebadge [DRO, Rieuwerts L 110]. The Court proceedings may have been the direct result of serious trouble in 1629-1630 when a group of miners took possession of *fower score several meers* in various mines, claimed by them to be unwrought and out of possession. This resulted in seven named miners *and others armed with many weapons and dogs (meeting) in a rebellious manner at the said mines* [PRO, DL 1/323]. In 1636 a grove being sunk on Hell Rake purchased *stoprise*. This term refers to thin timbers and is the earliest reference to the word discovered so far in a Derbyshire lead mining document [Belvoir; Rieuwerts, 1998]. Only one miner, Richard Beversley seems to have been employed, probably assisted by an un-named labourer.

A dispute, apparently unique in the orefield, occurred in 1669. This concerned verifying the definition of rakes, pipes, flats and flots (or *fflotts*) and how meers within such occurrences were to be laid out by the Barmaster [SCL, Bag 702]. The Barmote Court concluded that the custom in Hazlebadge was that:

all the Mynes there except such as were Rakes or Veynes, have beene – freed, staked and layd out as fflotts although most of them do in many places pipe and strike out into pipes – whereupon it is agreed for the preventing of suites that the same and all others of that nature should be wrought and laid out as fflotts whether they were indeed fflotts or pipes unlesse they were apparent Rakes – flotts and pipes measured and layd out after one and the same manner and noe difference in the length and breadth thereof.

Hopkinson [1644] gave the following definitions:

a flot or flatwork which dilateth itself and spreadest in Breadth without any known Bounds is no vein – A fflott or flatwork spreadeth itself all abroad Lying near the Grass – and hath neither Roof nor known skirts to Limit and bound the same.

This definition might apply to alluvial ore, but it could also be applied to the outcrop of a wide, but shallow dipping pipe. Thus at Hazlebadge the flotts were probably the outcrop of the Pic-Tor-End Pipe, which, until destroyed by late 20th century fluorspar working, ranged for some distance along the top of Hazlebadge Hill as a series of mineralised, phreatic cavernous pipes, frequently breaking through to the surface.

The only other pre-18th century account of lead mining in Hazlebadge was an Action of Title, heard in the Barmote Court in April, 1690, concerning a 1/9th part *of a grove or meer of ground lying on Hell Rake in Haslebadge Hills, commonly called Edward Wrights Grove* [SCL, Bag 702]. Godfrey Morten had died about 1676 holding a 1/3rd share in the mine, but it had not been worked since before his death until immediately before the case was heard.

PIC-TOR-END SOUGH
HAZ(S)LEBADGE SOUGH

The enclosure known as Millmeadow is situated on the north side of Hills Rake, and immediately east of the very large area covered by Hazlebadge Hill. During April, 1720 a trial took place in the Barmote Court concerning illegal entry into Millmeadow Rake and removal of 50 loads of lead ore [SCL, OD 1504]. The location of the rake is not known, but presumably it must have been a working situated on the north side of Hill Rake and probably formed a part of that vein complex.

There is little evidence of exploitation of Hill Rake beneath the shale cover until the mid 18th century. An agreement drawn in December, 1758 between Alexander Barker, John Wilkinson and Phillip Sheldon, partners at Hill Rake Mine and Isaac Morton who rented the Lot and Cope from the Duke of Rutland, implies that little exploration had been carried out by then because:

> *that in case in Trying in the shale a new vein should supposed to be found in sinking – Mr. Morton shall leave the appearances to two Indifferent people if it should be judged by all simtoms that it be the old Hill rake Vein, Mr. Morten shall not be intitled to a Lord Meer* [Chats, Bar Coll].

Barker and partners may have carried out limited work on the eastern fringes of the vein before 1758, but the date of their acquisition is not known. Furthermore, no ore is recorded as having been mined anywhere in the liberty between 1740 and 1763 [Belvoir]. The sough agreement refers to Hills Rake Mine being unprofitable because of the large volume of water in it. Five years before Pic-Tor-End Sough was begun, Mr. Joseph Clay, Mr. Allott, Mr Isaac Morton, Mr. William Mettam and other partners were given 62 meers of ground in *Pigtor end pipe*, 52 meers south from the *Old Ingine Founder on the hill end* and 10 meers north. This gift, dated November, 1761, thus included not only the proven length in the pipe from Hill Rake, but over 4,300 feet of purely speculative taker meers lying beneath the shale, ranging to the extent of the Liberty and the King`s Field.

Pic-Tor-End Sough issues into Bradwell Brook a little in excess of 800 feet north east of the bridge carrying the main road over the brook in Bradwell village. The sough, here within Bradwell Liberty, runs in a general south east and south direction, past Wortley Shaft and Bradwell Edge Mine, to a point some 330 feet south of Bradwell Edge Mine. Here it enters into Hazlebadge Liberty, or Lordship, continuing to Hills Rake Engine Shaft situated at the foot of Bradwell Edge, a little to the east of Hazlebadge Hill. The shaft also served as the sough masters Founder Meer at *Hill Rake Old Vein*. Bradwell Edge Mine, the Founder Meer in Hills Rake and the Old Engine at Pic-Tor-End Pipe, are along a straight alignment and presumably the original intention was to continue the sough from Bradwell Edge Mine, through Hills Rake to the Old Engine at Pic-Tor-End.

A branch level was driven south westwards from Hell Rake End, along the sole of Hills Rake at least to the end of Palfrey`s Engine Mine and possibly beyond to Dalebottom Mine, the latter sunk in the floor of Bradwell Dale. The main sough initially turned due east at the Engine (or Founder) Shaft, continuing in shale for a short distance to what later became known as Samuel Howe`s Mine. After a period of quiescence, it was resumed but along a southward alignment towards the eastern random of Tanners Venture Vein, rather than directly towards Pic-Tor-End Old Engine. From the intersection with that vein it was driven south west along the sole until it met Pic-Tor-End Pipe. Here the main sough turned back on itself and was driven north westwards along the bottom horizon of Pic-Tor-End Pipe, finally terminating at the original destination, Old Engine Shaft. Local tradition speaks of a sunken boat in the sough near the foot of New Shaft, or Bennetts Shaft, some 250 feet south of the main Pic-Tor-End Engine Shaft, but this seems highly unlikely.

In the opposite direction, but continuing along the line of the pipe, the 1800 mine plan [Chats, Bar Coll] marks, *The Sough and supposed waterway* connecting through to Wrights Vein whilst a sub-branch from this is called *Wrights supposed waterway.* These notes are not fully understood, but the `waterways` may refer to natural cave passages partly utilised by the miners. The previously mentioned sales of flowstone formations to the marble cutters suggests the presence of a substantial cave-system.

Hills Rake was formerly known as Hell Rake; modern OS maps name it as Earl Rake, but it does not appear under that title in any contemporary mining documents. The rake extends for a total length of approximately 1,930 yards. Eastwards, beyond Hazlebadge Hill it disappears beneath the cover of shale and traces of it are lost 500-600 feet beyond the boundary. The vein-head at this point is 150-200 feet beneath the surface. On the eastern side of Bradwell Dale the vein is exposed as a visually impressive series of open stopes, with hillocks of white calcite trailing down the hillside to the road edge. To the west, beyond the Dale, the vein continues with a markedly sinuous course confined between boundary (belland yard) walls. At least part of this ground belonged to Providence Mine. On the east side of Jennings Dale there are shallow, narrow open stopes of some antiquity; here in the 19th century, if not earlier, was Luck-at-Last Mine. Immediately west of the shallow dale are the hillocks and dressing floors of Nall Hole Mine, worked extensively for calamine in the first half of the 19th century. Few details have survived about this mine. Green [1887] observed that it was the last mine worked on Hill Rake, *many years ago*.

Between the end of Nall Hole title and the upper Castleton road lay Frog Hole Mine. The proprietors of the two mines entered into an agreement in January, 1804 whereby the engine shaft at *Nawhole Mine* was to be deepened to the *Fifty-fathom joint* and ore mined in the Frog Hole title could be drawn at Nall Hole [Chats, Bar Coll]. The reference to the joint perhaps refers to a *bed-joynt,* i.e. a bedding plane, as defined by Hooson [1747; Rieuwerts, 1998].

There are several versions of the Articles of Agreement for making Pic-Tor-End Sough. The earliest dates from October, 1766 at which time Clay and partners at *Pigtorend Pipe,* who were to drive a sough to their mine, agreed with Barker and Co. at Hills Rake that when their sough reached the rake and drained it, the latter company were to pay 1/8th of the ore got above level and 1/16th of the ore got under level as composition. The soughers were to be allowed to drive a gate 6 feet in height, west along Hills Rake to the end of the title. All ore got in the gate and any new veins found in driving it to belong to the soughers.

Three years later in October, 1769, a similar, but not identical agreement was made with the partners at Tanners Venture Mine. The payment of composition ore was different, so too the detail of ore got in driving the sough. The sough masters were to drive a gate 6 feet high and 2 feet wide, westwardly along Tanners Venture Vein to drain Pigtorend Pipe, but they were to launder the water through Tanners Venture Vein so not to hinder the working of that vein.

The sough had reached Bradwell Edge Mine, 2,300 feet from the tail by autumn, 1772. A vein was freed westwardly (6 meers all within Bradwell Liberty) and between 1772 and November, 1779, 96 loads 5 dishes were obtained from it, exclusive of Lot ore. During August, 1774, yet further articles were drawn between the sough masters and the partners at Hills Rake Mine [Chats, Bar Coll]. The sough was to be driven into the rake as soon and as effectively as possible and the soughers were permitted to erect wheels, engines or any other machinery in Hill Rake Mine for drawing water below level. The level continued south westwards, reaching Hills Rake in September, 1775. Expenditure on it had reached £1,571 by that date [SCL, OD 1500]. The total distance from the sough tail to Hills Rake is 3,300 feet, representing average daily progress of 14 inches; nearly 15 inches per day to reach Bradwell Edge Mine, the remaining. 1,000 feet to Hills Rake driven at nearly 13 inches per day. These facts indicate that the level was driven through shale.

A founder was freed at the intersection and the vein was worked both east and west from it:

Gave Mr. Smedley, Barmaster, (one dish) to free a Founder at the Eastmost Shaft in Alice Hawksworth field and gave two dishes more to free the first and second Takers east from the said Founder [DRO, BSA Coll L2].

At the latter end of October, 1775 the third taker east was freed and no further meers were freed in this direction. At least by the 19th century the workings in the third meer became known as Samuel Howe`s Mine, or Ashmores Mine.

The branch level westwards along the sole of the vein was begun almost immediately in October, 1775, 9 taker meers were progressively freed, terminating at the boundary between Palfrey Engine Mine and Bocking Title in June, 1778 [DRO, BSA L2]. The sough forefield had advanced some 11 inches per day. An Engine was purchased from the Cop Mine for £26-5-0 in July, 1776; setting it up was finished by September at a cost of a further £5.

Some six months afterwards Mr. Isaac Morton and partners began to free the ground lying west of the 9 meers owned by Barker and Co., and by December, 1784 they had freed a founder and 8 takers meers, these terminating close to the bottom of the east side of Bradwell Dale. There is no positive evidence that the sough branch was continued along the sole of Hills Rake beyond the nine meers, but there are unsubstantiated reports of a `sough-like` level being entered from the shaft at Dalebottom Mine. The contour of the sough, if it reached this point, would be within a few feet of the contour of the streamways and water table in Bagshawe Cavern.

The branch sough enabled some moderate quantities of ore to be mined in Hills Rake totalling just under 1,670 loads, exclusive of Lot ore from October, 1775 until July, 1780. Comparison with the total ore mined in the liberty during this same period reveals that Hills Rake contributed about 91% of the output. Nearly all the ore was obtained from above the water marks, but the absence of composition payable to the soughers on 1/8th of ore got above the level is not understood. All output was measured for Barker and Co., furthermore, no ore found in driving the gate westwards was measured to the sough masters as per the Agreement made between the parties in 1766.

The best year was 1776 when 652 loads were obtained [DRO, BSA Coll L2]. Six to nine copers were usually employed by Barker and Co. and one gang led by William Marshall earned £47-10-0 in a seven week period in 1775. The reckoning book ceases in July, 1780 and it then records that Mr. Joseph Clay purchased 2/3rds of Hills Rake for £42.

The eastern end of the vein, beneath the shale cover was also receiving attention. The sough had already been driven eastwardly, in shale, whilst in the summer of 1776 the Engine Shaft (or Founder Shaft) was opened from the surface through the shale to the sough, a depth of 135 feet. An accident occurred in this part of the mine in the latter part of 1779 *Dr. Markland Bill attending John Middleton when Burnt in the mine by a Fire Damp*. Middleton must have been badly burnt because at least five months afterwards Dr. Denman was paid for *vigiling John Middleton* [DRO, BSA L2].

Before considering the continuation of the sough southwards towards Tanners Venture Vein and Pic-Tor-End Pipe, it is more convenient to consider the remaining history of mining at the extreme eastern end of Hills Rake. It will be remembered that in 1780 Clay and partners had purchased Alex. Barker and Co`s 2/3rds share of Hills Rake Mine. Nothing is then heard until 1785, when in October they *Began to sink Hell Rake Shaft in ye flashes*. Eventually, in May, 1786 they *got through Hell Rake Shaft to ye Level* (and) *began to draw with ye Engin* (and) *began to drive ye level south* [SCL, OD 1500].

The owners of the mine made two, and possibly three attempts to dewater the workings below the level of Pic-Tor-End Sough, initially using a pump probably worked either by a large team of men, or by horse power, then by water-wheel and finally with a small, Newcomen-type engine. The mine accounts do not accurately distinguish between the first two possibilities and they may be identical. To judge from the total ore mined in the liberty, particularly from 1789 until 1795, the pumping arrangements must have been satisfactory. No less than 6,176 loads were obtained [Belvoir], most no doubt from the deep stopes beneath the shale cover at the eastern end of Hills Rake. The maximum depth of working here reached 24 fathoms (144 feet) beneath the sough level, before a great inrush of water drowned the mine, some time between 1796 and 1800 [SCL, Bag 654 (434)].

The work began in October, 1788 when a *Cast Metal Pump* was bought for £42-12-4, the carriage of it to the mine cost over £5, so clearly it was a considerable piece of machinery. A dam was made at *old Hell Rake* in 1789 and at the end of that year they *pricked*, (i.e. struck) the water in Hell Rake Engine Shaft. However, not until 15th March, 1790 did they begin *to work ye Water Engine at Hell Rake Mine* [SCL, OD 1500]. But a clue about these mysterious engines emerges when, two days later: *at Hills Rake – down to look at a machine J. Thompson had erected to draw the water* [SCL, Bag 655(1)]. John Thompson and Co. engineers of Chesterfield had, between 1783 and 1790, installed various *Machines*, including a *Great Pump*, at Water Grove Mine, Foolow. Mr. Clay and Mr. Winchester were also the principal shareholders at Water Grove and only two days after their inspection at Hills Rake they were *at Water Grove with Thompson fixing of a new engine to draw water* [SCL, Bag 655]. The only definite reference to a water wheel is contained in a letter written in January, 1837 discussing prospects at mines in the northern part of the orefield:

The Hills Rake is low down in the water. Pig-Tor-End Sough was driven up to it but the works soon got under the level. By a water wheel and later by a small steam engine the mine was cut 24 fathoms under Pig-Tor-End Sough, and at last cut a great spring which put an end to our proceeedings [SCL, Bag 654 (434)].

The `small steam engine` was a Newcomen-type engine made by John Curr, the noted Sheffield based mining and mechanical engineer, at his newly established foundry in Sheffield Park [Medlicott, 1999]. The engine, with a cylinder of only 18 inches diameter, was ordered in September, 1795, the total cost being £314-11-10. The engine worked for only a few years and was sold to William Smallwood and Co. for just under £182 [SCL, OD 1500]. This event signalled the end of deep working at Hills Rake, but, as noted above, the sough had already begun to be continued southwards towards Tanners Venture Vein and Pic-Tor-End Pipe.

Clay and Winchester took a ten year lease of Isaac Morton`s 1/4th share of the sough and any new veins discovered in its construction. Hills Rake partners were to bear half the cost in its maintenance. Driving south from Hills Rake began in earnest in September 1787, and the forefield intersected a vein in March, 1794:

Francis Mason of Foolow says that – Haslebadge Sough – has cut into a vein which is supposed to be the vein called Tanners Venture in grant to himself and partners, but as that cannot be proved only by cutting through the same, the said sough partners desire to free the said vein as old and new by two dishes of ore and to cut one meer of ground westwardly – that – the next meer – being the Lord`s Meer (can be valued) *in case the vein proves to be a new one and not the Tanners Venture – leave given to the sough partners to work the said vein by driving their sough therein until they meet in workmanship with the partners at Tanners Venture should this prove to be the Tanners Venture Vein* [Chats, Bar Coll].

Comparison between driveage rates for the sough forefield between Hills Rake and Tanners Venture Vein, 1,000 feet distant and then for 860 feet along the sole of that vein to its intersection with Pic-Tor-End Pipe, corresponds to a forefield advance of 6 inches per day. The intersection was probably reached during the winter of 1799-1800. The mine plan dated 1800 [Chats, Bar Coll] proves that the connection had been made by then. The short driveage back northwards to Pic-Tor-End Mine occupied yet a further two and a half to three years.

The following information relating to Pic-Tor-End Mine and Sough is contained in the same letter that provides detail about Hills Rake Mine during the 1790s:

The Sough was cut into the mine about the year 1802 and for seven years ore was found. Since then many trials in different directions have been made but no ore found. The mine and sough therefore of no value [SCL, Bag 654 (434)].

The assertion that Pic-Tor-End Mine was reached about 1802 is thus consistent with the above facts. Available ore production records for the liberty show a marked increase in output from 1803 to 1808, but unfortunately no individual production is known for the mine [Belvoir]. Thus, Pic-Tor-End Sough took some thirty six years for eventual completion The final cost is not known. The sough had cost £1,571 to construct as far as Hills Rake and by 1788 the net loss to the partnership was £2,440, but this figure does not solely represent the costs of making the sough. By 1837 it was said that Pic-Tor-End Mine and Sough, Tanners Venture, Lawrence Grove and Bradwell Edge Mine were all of no value.

A SOUGH within HAZLEBADGE LORDSHIP OR LIBERTY having uncertain provenance

SOUGH TO MILLDAM MINE

Kirkham [1963] believed that the southern extension of Pic-Tor-End Sough from near Bradwell Edge Mine, through Hills Rake to Tanners Venture Vein, was the first section of a sough intended to drain Milldam Mine, Great Hucklow. She cited a shaft just north of Deadman`s Hollow :

this was the last shaft (and continues) *There is a local tradition that the sough was made by a gentleman from Banner Cross. No date has been confirmed for Mill Dam Sough, which never reached the mine, and is said to have been abandoned because the company went bankrupt.*

Kirkham gave no further information. The section south from Bradwell Edge Mine, and through Hills Rake was of course part of the main sough to Tanners Venture Vein and Pic-Tor-End Pipe and certainly had no intended connection with Milldam Mine. Her `last shaft` is that sunk at the junction of the sough with Tanners Venture Vein. If any work was undertaken towards Milldam Mine, it was very limited in nature. No records of any such driveage have been found and indeed the intended sough would have provided little benefit.

MINING AT THE SOUTHERN END OF HAZLEBADGE LORDSHIP AND PART OF GREAT HUCKLOW LIBERTY

VIRGIN MINE, MAY SOUGH MINES AND BACK O`TH`EDGE MINE

At the extreme southern end of Hazlebadge Liberty or Lordship lie three veins, Maiden Rake, Virgin Vein and Never Fear Vein, or May Sough respectively. The northern boundary of this small mining field is defined by Maiden Rake, seen as a conspicuous openwork at the 20th century fluor-spar mine immediately north of Nether Water Farm. With the exception of this terminal stretch of Maiden Rake adjacent to the farm, the soughing and associated shaft sinking for Virgin Vein and Never Fear Vein took place to the east of the shallow Nether Water valley and was thus carried out within the shale cover before the underlying limestone could be proved at depth.

The principal workings along Maiden Rake were situated within the limestone outcrop beyond Little Hucklow in Hucklow Liberty, and therefore lie outwith the area under consideration. The western section of Maiden Rake and Chapmaiden Mine, together with the adjacent Heath Bush and Calvestones mines became well known locally for the numerous layers of channel, or toadstone encountered in the workings presenting difficulties in interpretation faced by 18th and 19th century geologists. Lead ore was spasmodically worked in these rocks, adding to the confusion.

Virgin Vein and Mine was exploited almost wholly within Hazlebadge Liberty, whilst save for a short section of Never Fear Vein or May Sough in Hazlebadge, this latter was wrought almost entirely within Hucklow Liberty, but as noted above, beneath the shale cover east of the Nether Water hollow. Evans [1912] claimed that a book entitled *Darbyshire*, printed in 1660, contained an account of a large skull, tooth and other bones being found in the Virgin Mine, Hazlebadge, *Near Bradewalle – in sinking a lead-grove – which was worked for lead at least five hundred years.*

The original account seems to have been a document written by William Darbishire in December, 1660 and was given to him by a man named Goodwin, an innkeeper at Tideswell and a former miner:

He and his father had long kept some bones taken out of the same place and time when the Shafte wherein those teeth wear and he and others tooke them out of the heade being found in a hollowe as a Vault as the (they) *sought for leade at a place called Haslebench.*

Why Evans, a noted local historian, equated the find to Virgin Mine, (not discovered until 1773-1774) is not known, unless another mine bearing the same name existed within Hazlebadge Liberty. Farey [1811] stated that native sulphur was found in the toadstone in Virgin Mine, but the occurrence of toadstone there seems unlikely, though Pilkington observed:

Moreover sulphur has been known now and then to occur in it (toadstone). *A layer about an inch thick has been observed in the virgin mines Haslebadge, so pure that it flamed when touched with a candle.*

Elsewhere Pilkington stated that the layer was four inches in thickness.

LEVEL OR SOUGH NEAR QUARTERS FARM, HAZLEBADGE: SOUGH TO VIRGIN MINE

Immediately north of May Sough lies the Virgin Mine, the title to which consists of twenty six meers within Hazlebadge Lordship, all entirely concealed beneath the shale cover. The north eastern random of the vein passes beneath Durham Edge into Hucklow Liberty. The mine was also known as Broomhills Mine. Towards the south west the vein also passes back into Hucklow Liberty, but mining operations there were very small.

At the north eastern extremity of Maiden Rake, nearly 300 feet south of Quarters Farm, is a run-in sough entrance, for which no name is known. It cannot have served Maiden Rake, the workings in the adjacent Nether Water Mine being dry to a depth of 200 feet due to the natural drainage offered by the Bagshawe Cavern water courses, so the level at Quarters Farm must have been driven south eastwards seeking veins beneath the shale cover. Field evidence seems to suggest that this un-named sough was driven entirely through shale, and intended to intersect the random of Virgin Vein, well east of the Founder. The sough would have been 1,300 feet in length, representing about four and a half years work. Very curiously four air shafts along the assumed line of the sough are also directly in line with May Sough Mine. There is a possibility that the level was begun in 1774-1775, contemporary with the freeing of Virgin Vein in Hazlebadge Liberty.

The vein was freed for new in May, 1774 when 6 meers were taken west from the Founder. Two months later, in July, 1774, 15 meers were taken east from the Founder ranging to the end of the Liberty. The operations that took place in 1773-early 1774 of course must have been to the west of the Nether Water valley in Hucklow Liberty. The vein proved very rich, for example from September, 1773 until the end of 1775, 1327 loads of grove ore were sold at a profit of £1,022-16-9 [SCL, Bag 587/26], whilst profits from 1775 to 1777 totalled £1,868-16-0 [SCL, Bag 587/80]. A Barmaster`s entry dated September, 1794 confirmed that William Longsden and partners *have worked it* (ie. Virgin Vein) *to the end of Haslebadge and are to work it in the Kingsfield* [Chats, Bar Coll]. Though not explicity stated, this must mean the eastern boundary of Hazlebadge beneath Durham Edge. No subsequent documentary evidence has appeared to confirm working in this direction, profits of £3,645-13-7 achieved in 1803-1804 can be equated to the freeings of the 5th to 11th meers west of the Founder, all within Hazlebadge Liberty. Sometime between the winter of 1809 and September, 1812 the proprietors purchased an Engine from High Rake Mine for £20 [Goodchild Collection].

MAY SOUGH, MAY SOUGH MINE LEVY

A deep trial shaft near the head of Bretton Clough, was sunk by William Bagshawe and partners, seeking to discover a vein breaking from the Hucklow Edge Vein at Old Grove. Concurrently, a rival company drove an extension from May Sough beneath Burr Tor in Hucklow Liberty, financed by Mr. Clay and partners *who* (were) *driving night and day* to locate the deeply buried break vein before Bagshawe and partners could *expedite the discovery before Clay and Partners*. The Bagshawe partnership worked the mine, and if Green`s [1887] information was correct Clay and company also found the vein, possibly well to the west because, *a vein –* (was) *worked – in the Back o` the Edge Mine and in a level, known as May Sough, on the west side of the grit hill*.

Between Old Grove in Eyam Liberty, Back o` th`Edge Mine and May Sough, the limestone disappears beneath the shale covering, inclining to the north and north east at 5 to 10 degrees. Thus the shaft at Back o` th` Edge was sunk into the bottom of a shallow `synclinal trough`, the limestone being reached only beneath the contour of May Sough. The base of the shale at May Sough tail is 800 feet AOD, placing the top of the limestone at about 580 feet AOD at Back o` th` Edge, wholly compatible with a thickness of 560 to 575 feet for the Edale Shales [IGS, Sheet SK 17]. Reaching the limestone would have entailed a shaft some 475 to 550 feet in depth, though no documentary confirmation has been found.

The shaft known as Back o`th` Edge Mine, or Ritheing Lake Mine was begun about 1758 or 1759. Quite how the mine was given its quaint, peculiar alternative title is not known, the idea of a wave-tossed lake deep beneath Bretton Clough seems very unlikely! The shaft was sunk through a considerable thickness of shale in an attempt to re-discover the north west trending break vein from the Hucklow Edge Vein, first discovered at Old Grove in Eyam Liberty. The break vein was worked in 1749, but it soon passed into Grindlow Liberty, which being a private liberty the usual laws and customs were not applicable and the Lords of the Manor would not permit the miners to trace the course of the vein, or to work it within Grindlow. The deep shaft at Back o`th` Edge Mine was sunk on the random of the break vein, immediately within Hucklow Liberty, which shaft being within the Kingsfield, free mining was permitted. Few financial accounts have survived and as the venture lasted only eight years it must be presumed a failure.

May Sough was begun about 1753 from the eastern side of the Nether Water valley, very nearly 1,000 feet south of Nether Water Farm. A Lord`s Meer was freed there in 1754. The sough was not originally planned to be driven to Back o` th` Edge Mine, but was an exploration drive in the shales along the random of Never Fear Vein, into which it could be connected by means of sumps sunk below sough level into the underlying limestone. The first section of the level, entirely through shale, reached only to May Sough Mine, some 1,650 feet from the tail and was probably completed before 1759.

There is documentary evidence that contemporary with developments at Back o`th`Edge Mine in 1758-1759, either May Sough and/or a Levy begun at a somewhat higher contour, were driven with considerable haste in an effort to establish a connection and thus claim title to the break vein in Hucklow Liberty. The Levy began from the northern side of the May Sough Mine dressing floor at a contour of 1,025 feet AOD. The entrance to the Levy, though now obliterated, still supplies a small water flow, and in the rough, hummocky ground above can be seen the much denuded hillocks from three, closely spaced, run-in shafts. No documentary evidence has been found relating to the May Sough Levy, how far it was driven is not known, no other details seem to have survived.

From the old (1758-1759) forefield of May Sough to Back o`th` Edge Mine is a little over 3250 feet. Within the wooded, landslipped ground at the foot of Burr Tor and directly in line between the two mines, there is a run-in shaft with limestone and vein-stuff in the hillocks. Geological evidence suggests that at this point limestone would have been encountered at about 100 feet beneath the level of May Sough. Contained in a folder of miscellaneous mining documents relating to Hucklow Liberty and dated 1786 is a note that Robert How, the Barmaster *some time ago went to value a Lord`s Meer in a New Vein called Never fear in a place called Hucklow Burrs* [SCL, Bag 671].

Any association between May Sough, driven along the range of Never Fear Vein, the shaft in Burr Wood and the above entry may be coincidental, but ore began to be measured at May Sough in 1785 and again from 1790 to 1806 [SCL, Bag 452]. It is not known if May Sough ever reached Back o`th` Edge Mine, though local tradition recalls another shaft, of which no trace now remains, on the west side of Camphill Road and just within the Gliding Field. The western range of Never Fear Vein was worked along its outcrop within the limestone in Hucklow Liberty.

BACK O`TH`EDGE OR RITHEING LAKE MINE AND SOUGH

At about the same time that Back o`th`Edge Shaft was started, and as explained previously a company of rival miners began to extend May Sough towards Bretton Clough and possibly they also commenced the Levy from May Sough Mine at a contour about 200 feet higher than their sough, very probably as an aid to haulage and ventilation deep beneath Burr Tor.

Financial accounts at *Back of Hucklow Edge Sough called Ritheing Lake Sough* begin in 1759, during a seven month period £288-9-1 was expended. By December at least seventeen men were employed [SCL, Bag 517]. A little later, in April, 1760 the agent George Heyward commented that:

Ritheing Lake Sough Engine Shaft hath been a very wet one as ever I saw down to the Levill. I have gathered the water together at different levels by garland pairs and landers into the Sough Levill and when had done had not so much watter to trouble at first, but when beginning to sink which was April, 14th, when about five feet deep had much watter which I believe was about four gallons a minute [SCl, OD 1504].

The latter part of Heyward`s letter states that below the sough the shaft was sinking through a sequence of interbedded shale and *greetstone,* all being very hard. The above noted *Sough Levill* should not be confused with May Sough; they are not the same. Ritheing Lake Sough probably served as a shallow pumpway, being no more than 100 feet in depth in the shaft. Two run-in air shafts mark the line of the sough between the tail and Back o`th` Edge shaft. No trace of the sough tail remains. The immediate south side of Bretton Brook is occupied by Grindlow Lordship, therefore presumably the water discharged from a tail situated on the north side within Abney Lordship, 200 to 300 yards east from the main shaft. Some form of agreement must have been reached with Mr. Galliard, for permission to drive the sough beneath his land.

During July, 1760 there are brief references to setting up a horse-gin and: *When we fetched spindle; set pit gear up; when we broke great Beam* [SCL, Bag 517]. A vein was found in the late summer of 1761, William Bagshawe, writing from Castleton observed, *Wee have discovered one of ye veins wee were seeking for at ye back of Hucklow Edge* [SCL, OD 1504]. A parallel vein lying south of the main vein was reached via a cross cut from the main shaft, but nothing further is known about it.

The partners wished to drive into Abney Lordship seeking new veins, but they presumed it was not within the Kingsfield and therefore needed to reach agreement with the owner, Mr. Galliard. They were somewhat apprehensive as to whether he owned the lead mining duties, because he claimed the Lordship under a grant from the Crown. Bagshawe proposed Galliard be offered 1/20th of all ore mined, the same duty to that taken at the mines in Grindlow.

The optimism must have been short lived, the mine lost £300 in 1762. The next four years saw further losses of a little over £215, only 2 loads 3 dishes of ore being sold. The reckoning ends with the comment: *This title does not seem worth preserving* [SCL, Bag 431a] endorsing feelings expressed in 1765 that *Writheing Lake Mine is so overloaded with water it will never be of any service.*

4. COALPITHOLE RAKE AND DRAINAGE OF THE MINES ON THE WESTERN EDGE OF PEAK FOREST LIBERTY

The veins and scrins along the western edge of the limestone within Peak Forest Liberty must continue beneath the shale cover, but with the notable exceptions of Oden Vein and Coalpithole Rake, little or no working was ever carried out beneath that formation. For example workings on Foreside (Faucet) Rake, Eldon End and Gautries Rake all terminate abruptly at, or very close to the shale – limestone interface.

Coalpithole Rake was worked in both Peak Forest and Chapel-en-le-Frith liberties, workings in the latter being almost exclusively developed beneath the shale cover. Along Coalpithole Rake within Peak Forest Liberty and before deeper exploitation took place, drainage problems were controlled by a natural streamway flowing partly along the line of that major vein and save for lifting water in large barrels by means of horse gin, no mechanical dewatering was necessary. Mining in Chapel-en-le-Frith Liberty during the second half of the 19th century was pursued to greater depths as the stopes and levels were developed beneath the thickening shale cover, eventually reaching depths of over 600 feet beneath the surface. Two horizontal steam engines were utilised for winding and pumping. During the latter years of operations in the second half of the 19th century several strong springs were found.

The only other mine drainage system within the area was known as Perry Pitts Sough. This level may have been a trial driveage in the shale seeking the south western extension of Foreside Rake, or it may have provided shallow drainage for the Lum and Speedwell titles, from where it discharged into a natural swallow hole known to the miners as `The Lum` and to modern cavers as Jackpot, or P8. A short, partly mined section is visible within the P8 cave and miners also removed a calcite curtain to allow them access to further passages. Deep drainage of the Windle and Rush Vein (Lower Slitherstones Mine) and Birch Hall Mine on the same rake is considered in the miscellaneous section. Limited historical information hints at artificial drainage from these mines into the P8 cave system.

Evidence for pre-18th century mining is very scant. A dispute was heard in the Barmote Court in 1671 about a mine *on the Sun side of Cawthridge*, presumably Gautries Rake [SCL, Bag 702], but nothing further has been found. Richard Bagshawe had a share in Gawtries Grove from at least May, 1709 until the end of December, 1714 during which time only 37 loads 2 dishes of ore were measured for sale, resulting in a loss for the period of £23-5-5 [Rylands, Bag 12/1/60]. Expenditure was very slight, totalling just under £50 for the five and a half years covered.

A notebook belonging to William Bagshawe of Ford Hall, near Chapel-en-le-Frith includes details of small scale lead mining during the years 1707 and 1708 at mines near Perryfoot, none of which can be identified. The mines involved were Perryfoot Grove, Ingolsby`s Grove, Ingolsby`s Vein, Townend Grove, Glover Meers and Upper Grove [SCL, OD 1417]. A shaft at Perryfoot Grove was 20 fathoms in depth, sunk partly through shale into the limestone beneath. Between 14th February and 21st August, 1708 the sum of £20-10-11 was expended on Perryfoot Grove, in the same period 32 loads and 2 dishes of ore were sold for £25-15-6. Miners on wage work were paid 8d/day.

COALPITHOLE RAKE

A major underground watercourse, derived from surface water in the Manifold and Whitelee streams engulphed into a swallow hole at Perryfoot Cave, formerly flowed along the rake before disappearing into an underground swallow near to Perry Dale, the water eventually reappearing in Castleton. Construction by miners of two culverts diverted this flow into Sheepwash Cave, but then away from Coalpithole Rake, northeastwards into Perryfoot Vein and towards Eldon Bent Vein, Linicar Rake, New Rake, and so via the Speedwell Mine – Peak Cavern system to Russet Well. Tradition in Castleton relates that when Coalpithole Mine was at work, the water at Russet Well ran muddy. A reputed swallow hole in Harkforward Mine on the northern side of Perry Dale was sought for by

Coalpithole Mine and the area of Eldon Hill

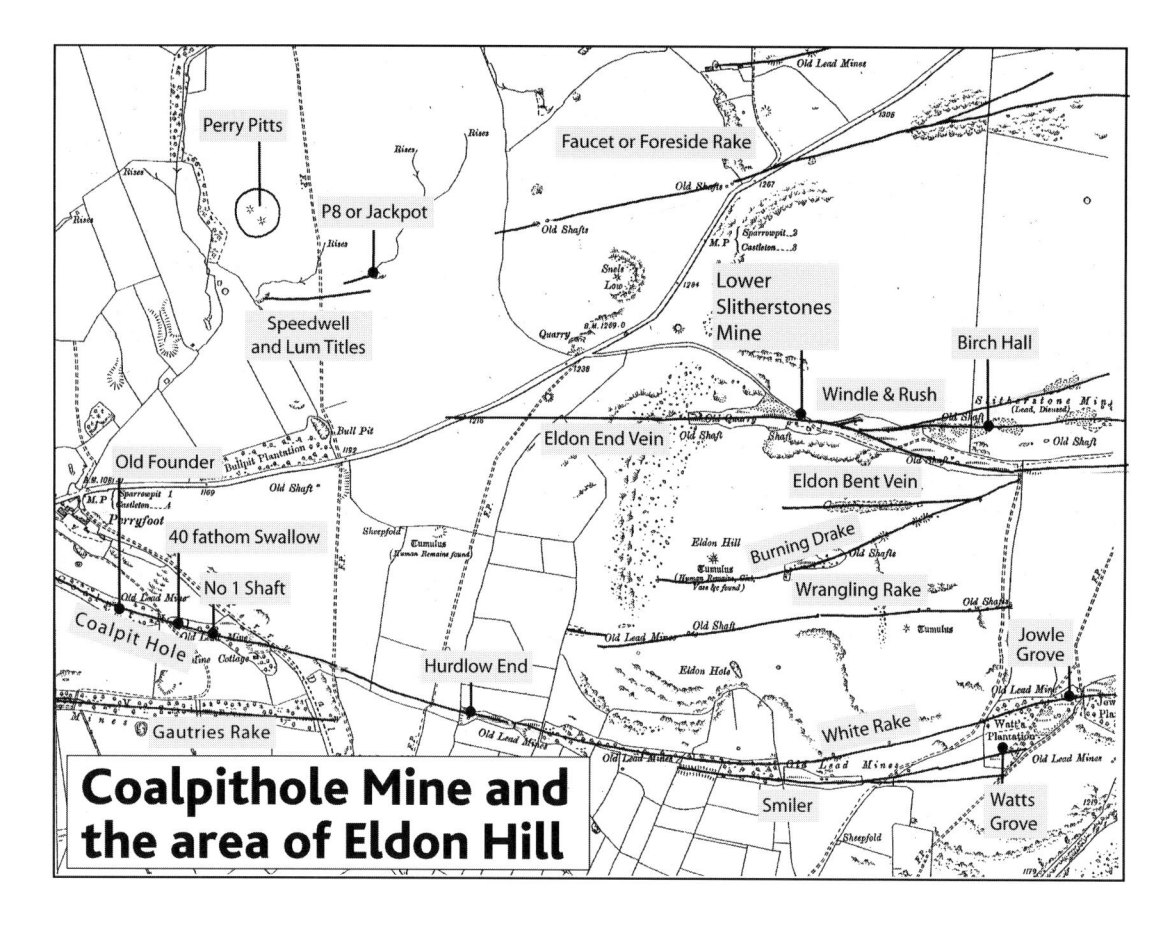

the Peak Forest Mining Co., but it was either at a too high contour, or not located.

The extent of the Coalpithole title in Peak Forest Liberty, embraced the section from the road in Perry Dale, west to the Castleton – Sparrowpit road. Activities before 1760 were mainly within Peak Forest Liberty, but when the vein was freed in Chapel-en-le-Frith Liberty in 1760, it was for old, the absence of a second founder meer and Lord`s meer confirming that earlier development had taken place, though no dates are known. The mine began to be developed beneath the shale cover on a larger scale than hitherto in 1760 and was eventually abandoned in the late 19th century. The westernmost workings, 600 yards west of the Castleton to Sparrowpit road, were then being exploited beneath a cover of some 600 feet of shale. These workings were within Chapel-en-le-Frith Liberty, an *Out Liberty* within the King`s (Queen`s) Field in the High Peak.

Drainage of the mine can be conveniently divided into two sections, a water-level known as *the 40 Fathom Level*, or sometimes as the *Swallow Gate* or *Old Level*, serving that part of the rake on Gautries Hill, whilst the sub-shale workings were also partly served by this level, but more specifically by two water wheels and a Newcomen fire-engine in the latter part of the 18th century and by two horizontal steam engines and deeper water levels during the second half of the 19th century. So far as can be ascertained all the pumped water was delivered into the 40 Fathom Level.

No records of mining activity at Coalpithole have been located before 1705, but mining along the outcrop of such a major rake must have been in progress for many years previously. An isolated reckoning records that in 1705 the sum of £17-11-6 was lost at *Cole Pit Hole* [DRO, Grant, microfilm]. A further isolated reference notes that a small quantity of ore (about 20 loads) was measured at the mine in 1726-1727. A dispute heard in the Peak Forest Barmote Court in October, 1726 lists Mr. Robert Clay, John Nodder and Mr. Cowley as proprietors and they were sued for wages due to Robert Winterbottom for £8-10-5. Between Michaelmas, 1734 and Michaelmas

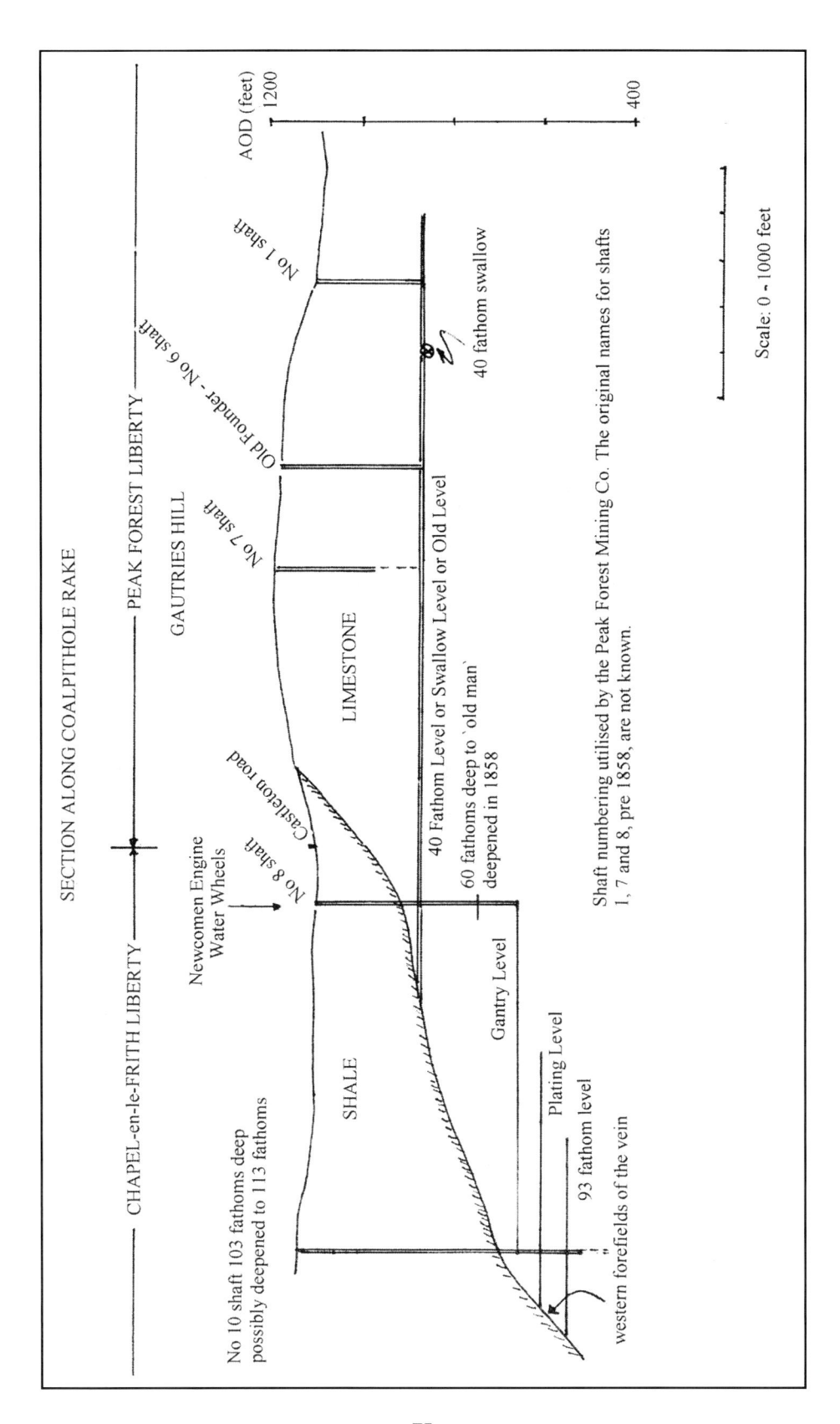

4. Coalpithole Rake and Drainage of the Mines on the Western Edge of Peak Forest Liberty

SECTION ALONG COALPITHOLE RAKE

CHAPEL-en-le-FRITH LIBERTY | PEAK FOREST LIBERTY

GAUTRIES HILL

AOD (feet) 1200 — 400

Scale: 0 - 1000 feet

No 1 shaft
40 fathom swallow
Old Founder - No 6 shaft
No 7 shaft
40 Fathom Level or Swallow Level or Old Level
60 fathoms deep to 'old man' deepened in 1858
Castleton road
No 8 shaft
Newcomen Engine Water Wheels
Gantry Level
Plating Level
93 fathom level
LIMESTONE
SHALE
western forefields of the vein

No 10 shaft 103 fathoms deep possibly deepened to 113 fathoms

Shaft numbering utilised by the Peak Forest Mining Co. The original names for shafts 1, 7 and 8, pre 1858, are not known.

1736 no ore from the mine was recorded in the Peak Forest Barmaster's Book [Chats, Dev Coll].

Charges at *Colepitthole* from 1746 to 1752 amounted to £89-18-0, the highest being in 1749 when £272-8-10 was expended. Ore was sold (76 loads 8 dishes) only in 1752, no other measures being recorded [SCL, Bag 546]. Two miners were owed wages: *For work done at Coalpit Hole at the East End of the Wide Hole* [DRO, Br-T L46]. The position of the `Wide Hole` is not known, but maybe it was part of the 40 Fathom Swallow, the work there marking preparation for beginning the 40 Fathom Level, with subsequent driveage westwards into Chapel Liberty, at least as far as No 8 shaft. No 18th century name for the shaft has survived, the numbering of shafts 1, 6, 8, 9 and 10 being due to the Peak Forest Mining Company after 1858.

Barmasters` books of entry are not available for Peak Forest before 1752, so it is not known when Edward Fletcher, agent to Alexander Barker and Co. freed the founder meer, but in May, 1753 he freed the second and third taker meers west from the founder, whilst in April, 1755 he freed the fourth, fifth and sixth takers east from the founder. Eventually, by March, 1760 all the ground along the vein from the founder meer had been freed (16 meers and a primgap) and the continuation of the vein in that direction lay within Chapel Liberty [DRO, Br-T L31]. The meers lying eastwards from the Founder Shaft extended to the Perry Dale road and must have been freed before 1752. Heathcote [2001] has provided an excellent summary of events, together with a most useful map of the mines on Gautries Hill.

Ore output was never large. During the years 1752 to 1777 average annual production ranged from 54 loads to 240 loads; output exceeded 300 loads only in 1758 when 470 loads were mined. The twenty six year period saw only 3,535 loads of ore taken from the mine, by the author`s definition, a small-medium operation. After 1777 there was a further decline within Peak Forest Liberty. In the seventy eight years to 1855 no output was recorded in twenty eight years, the whole period witnessed a mere 2,436 loads obtained (31 loads/year average).

Progress of the main drainage level, the 40 Fathom Level, or Swallow Gate, driven from the Swallow located east of the Founder Shaft in Peak Forest Liberty, is not documented. However there appears every likelihood that it had been completed as far west as No 8 shaft maybe as early as 1762, almost certainly before 1780.

The vein was pursued beneath the shale cover into Chapel Liberty. Between July, 1760, when the founder meer was freed, until February, 1778, seven taker meers were freed [DRO, BSA L4 and 5]. The 40 Fathom Level terminates seven meers beyond No

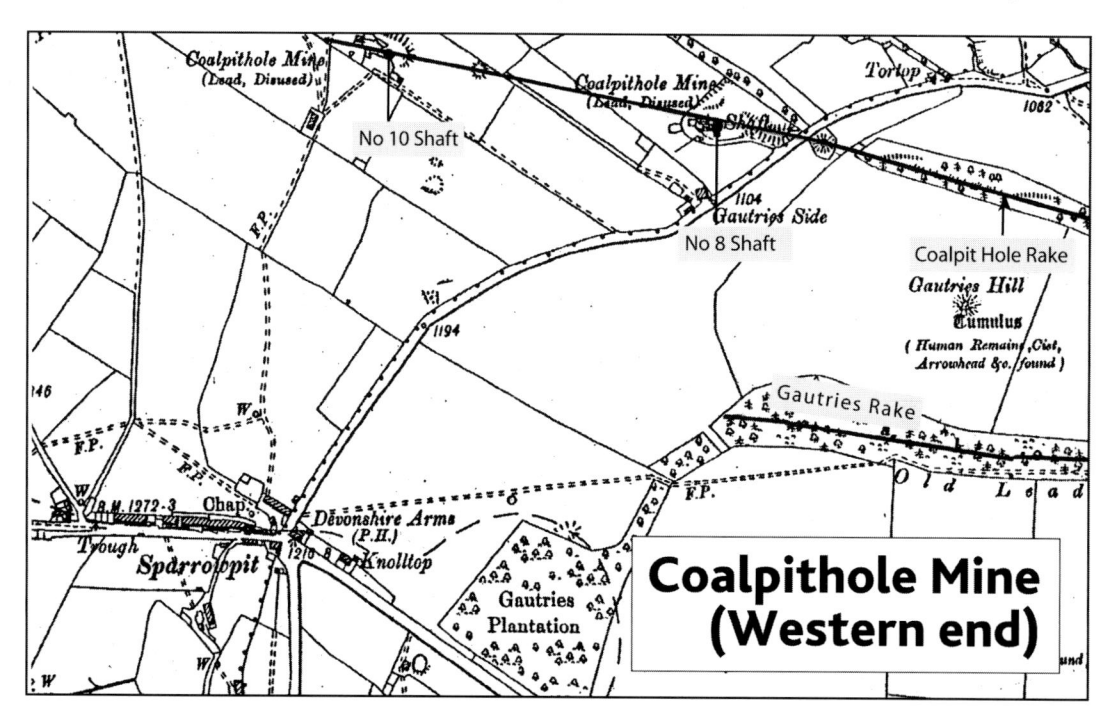

8 shaft at the point where shale dips down into the forefield. Crabtree [1966] provided details of ore production annually from 1760 until 1778. Total output, hillock ore omitted, reached 4,717 loads, of which 4,372 loads were saleable grove ore, the remaining 345 loads consisted of lot and tithe ore. These figures are at variance with Heathcote, who for the same period quotes a total output of 4,472 loads 7 dishes. A fragmentary reckoning from July, 1774 until the end of June, 1776 reveals a total loss to the mine of £632-14-6 [SCL, Bag 587/28].

Despite the moderate output of 200-250 loads/annum, the proprietors considered that payable reserves lay further down-dip towards the south west. A Newcomen Fire-engine was installed, described in the sale notice dated May-June, 1783 as:

a complete Fire Engine, boiler, beam, – a cylinder 26 inches diameter or more, 18 yards of pumps of 15½ inches diameter. The above engine hath been lately erected and but very little worked [Derby Mercury, extract communicated by Roger Flindall].

The pumping shaft, (the 19th century No 8 shaft) was situated in the 2nd meer west from the Founder and was 60 fathoms deep. The following century the 60 Fathom Bottom Gate West was described *as the lowest point reached by the earlier miners* and *the old man's sole*. The length of pumps, only 18 yards, or 9 fathoms appears therefore to be 11 fathoms short of the shaft bottom.

The engine was no doubt too small for purpose, and the mine owners turned to water power as a possible solution to the pumping problems. A rental paid by the mine to the Duke of Devonshire, at least by June, 1783 was the sum of 5/- *being one years rent due at Michaelmas last – for the use of water to the sd mine* [SCL, Bag 587/47/45].

John Rennie the well-known 18th-19th century civil engineer visited the mine in May, 1784 and left this account of the surface arrangements:

I passed Sparrow Pit where I saw an Engine for raising of water from a Lead Mine. This Engine had too large water wheels, apparently about 26 or 27 feet diameter, the one below the other so that the water that came from the one answered to drive the other, and they both had a spur wheel fixed to their edge which acted on one common Pinion which was fixed on a Crank which worked two Levers and consequently two Pumps. These spur wheels were just the same size as the water wheels and the water was conveyed away from the wheel by a subterraneous passage to a deep Valley where it ran for some distance and then went below a Mountain [Matkin, 1980].

The wheels were offered for sale in March, 1787, the sale notice adding a little more detail, some of which is contradictory to Rennie`s description. The wheels were each 24 feet diameter, the spur wheel (probably what Rennie described as `one common Pinion`) 6 feet in diameter; the two beams (`Levers`) were each 50 feet in length and there were two double cranks and four sets of pumps [Derby Mercury, extract communicated by Roger Flindall]. The dam that served the wheels still exists in the next enclosure immediately north of the No 8 shaft, and recently has been re-filled with water.

The sale notice also lists *a wind engine (with) crank etc.*, presumably a ventilation device, maybe large bellows, also activated by the water wheels. The only other example of a `wind engine` recorded from the orefield was situated at Cowclose Mine, Elton [Rieuwerts, 1998].

The depth from which the wheels lifted water was probably the same as that achieved by the Fire Engine and there can be little doubt that they too discharged water into the 40 Fathom Level. Both pieces of machinery, complex and expensive, provided little or no benefit to the working of the mine. The extent of any stoping and/or development west from No 8 shaft is not known, but most, if not all was abortive. It is not known when the Fire Engine and Water Wheels were installed, maybe a little ore was obtained in the 1770s, but from 1778 until 1796 a mere 10 loads 7 dishes were measured at the mine. From then until 1857, immediately previous to the mine being re-opened by the Peak Forest Mining Co., only 42 loads and 2 dishes were measured in sixty one years.

The Peak Forest Mining Co. was formed in 1858, and was owned mainly by a consortium of Sheffield businessmen. Their intention was to exploit the vein beneath the shale cover in Chapel Liberty [DRO, Rieuwerts L 252]. The main shafts along the vein were numbered from 1 to 10; No 1 was an old shaft at the eastern end of the title at Perry Dale; Nos 2 to 5 were

The ruined remains of the pumping and winding engine and boilers at Coalpithole Miine, No 8 shaft. It was made in 1865 by J. Mitchell and Sons, Worsborough Dale, near Barnsley. The photograph, along with several others of the mine, was taken in 1926 by the Sheffield photographer Frank Brindley.

of no significance; No 6 was Edward Fletcher`s Old Founder in Peak Forest Liberty; No 7 is known to modern explorers as `Veer Shaft`; No 8 was the late 18th century pumping shaft in Chapel Liberty, deepened by the 19th century Company from 60 fathoms to 75 fathoms and used as the main haulage shaft and a pumping shaft; Nos 9 and 10a were incompleted trials; No 10 the most westwardly shaft on the vein, was sunk to 103 fathoms by the Peak Forest Mining Co., then deepened by them to 113 fathoms in 1878.

The first work undertaken in 1858 consisted of reopening No 1 shaft. Widening and clearing the 18th century 40 Fathom Level, or Swallow Gate was begun in the following year and No 8 shaft was widened to 12 feet x 9 feet and re-ginged. The 40 Fathom Level was also driven eastwards 100 yards and connected with No 1 shaft. A small, portable winding engine made by Davy Bros., Sheffield was placed at No 8 shaft. Costing £160 it was christened `The Johns` in honour of four of the directors. The engine was later moved to a trial sinking before returning to its original site. The engine served ancillary duties and although a small pump was attached later, it was not a major feature of the mine equipment.

Refurbishment of the 40 Fathom Level had been completed to No 8 shaft by June, 1864. The 18th century title in Chapel Liberty consisted of a Founder meer and seven taker meers and it was not until October, 1866 that the title began to be extended westwards. Meanwhile, a larger engine was installed at No 8 shaft. Built by J. Mitchell and Sons, Worsborough Dale, near Barnsley, it cost £390-16-0. The engine served the dual purposes of winding and pumping. Initially steamed by one Cornish boiler, a second was added in 1869 [DRO, Rieuwerts L 252]. Ground water appears to have been an irritant rather than a major problem until the final years of operations when several strong springs were cut at depth. A section of the mine dated 1875 shows that they considered extending the 40 Fathom Level through to No 10 shaft [DRO, BSA LP 66], but the proposal does not seem to have been implemented.

Two vertical sections of the western part of the mine, one dated 1875, the other 1878 [Rieuwerts, private collection] show a series of levels and stopes. Levels at 60, 65, 70 and 75 fathoms were driven from No 8 shaft through to No 10 shaft. The 75 fathom level was known as *Gantry Level* and the 84 fathom level driven east from No 10 shaft as the *Plating Level*, but the derivation of these names is not obvious. The two deepest levels, at 84 and 93 fathoms respectively (depths were measured from the collar of No 8 shaft), extended both east and west from No 10 shaft. By 1879 the Plating Level was 30 fathoms west of the shaft, the bottom level 50 fathoms, *until the vein is cut by the dip of the shale*. The forefield of the lowest level stood at a distance of 1850 feet south west of No 8 shaft.

The 1875 section demonstrates that above the Gantry Level most of the vein had been stoped out by *Captain Sidebottom and the old man*, though as noted earlier little ore was produced in this part of the mine before 1866. A noticeable feature of the 1875 section is the considerable extent of uncut ground at depth; for example east from No 10 shaft below the Plating Level, west from No 8 shaft and also, perhaps more surprising, uncut ground east of the shaft above the horizon of the Gantry Level (the Level did not extend to the east beyond No 8 shaft). No 10 shaft was sunk between 1870 and 1874. A dual purpose winding and pumping engine was also installed at No 10 shaft. Built in 1853 by Bray and Co., Leeds, it worked first at Brightside Mine, Hassop and was purchased by the Peak Forest Mining Co. for £188 in 1870. Rated at 25HP, the cylinder was 22 inches in diameter. Steam was generated from a boiler 30 feet in length and 6 feet diameter [DRO, Rieuwerts L 252]. A newspaper report made in January, 1937 waxed lyrical about it:

The engine at No 10 shaft was a remarkable piece of work arranged alternatively for winding on a flat rope or by disengaging a dog clutch for pumping by means of a train of spears down the shaft balanced by a big bell crank. It was a beautiful piece of millwright`s work and bore the plate of James Bray of Leeds and the number 17. [Heathcote, in press].

Water was lifted from the shaft bottom, 28 fathoms up to the Gantry Level, then taken along that level in launders to the foot of No 8 shaft from where it was lifted to the 40 fathom Level *leading to the Swallow*. The 1875 section shows a 1:3 inclined *Travelling Way for Men* extending from the 65 fathom level down to the Plating Level. The feature is not mentioned in the Company Minute Book, which it presumably post-dates, but whether it was an inclined stairway, or flagged road, or merely modification through old stopes is not known. Ore production between 1858 and 1865 was negligible, but the following ten years lucrative, ore output reached 14,833 loads, the largest measures being achieved in 1869 and 1870 when 2,826 loads and 3,336 loads respectively were recorded. The mine could be described as large in terms of output and surface and underground management and development. Unfortunately output began to decline in 1875 and the mine ceased work in 1880.

PERRY PITTS SOUGH

Along the west side of Snelslow the reef limestones dip beneath the shale cover and towards the south west there is a small `embayment` of the rather flat and featureless land that forms the southern slopes of Rushop Edge. The area is known as Perry Pitts. North of Bull Pit, at the interface of the reef limestones and the shale, a short east west vein has been worked. The eastern portion of the vein formed the Lum title, west of which lay Speedwell title. The natural swallow hole known as `Jackpot` or P8 is located at the extremity of the Lum mines. Situated on the shale `flat` north of Speedwell Mine are three shaft mounds composed of shale sinking dirt.

Only one reference to Perry Pitts Sough has been found in contemporary mining documents. The jury of a Barmote Court held in June, 1768 for Peak Forest Liberty gave their opinions that Henry Kirk and partners were to pay £8-8-0 for a horse *killed by falling down a shaft belonging to the Sough in Perry Pitts*.

There appear to be two possibilities for the location of the sough. The three shale mounds north of Speedwell Mine were possibly air shafts sunk onto a shale gate sough seeking sub-shale extensions to Foreside (Faucet) Rake or other buried veins, or maybe even associated with Pilkington`s [1789] *pretended copper mine at Rushup Edge*. Alternatively, the sough may have been driven from the lower reaches of the P8 cave into the Lum and Speedwell titles. A sough driven from the surface into the rake is highly improbable, being too shallow, providing relief of only 30 feet or thereabouts. Within P8 miners have removed a calcite curtain, allowing them access at stream level into lower sections of the cave. There is also a partly mined section, near to the entrance, at or very close to the Lum mines. Derbyshire lead miners sometimes referred to caves as a `lum`, as for example at Lumb Hole in Cressbrook Dale.

SOUGHS and LEVELS within PEAK FOREST LIBERTY having uncertain provenance or mistaken function

WINDLE AND RUSH, BIRCH HALL MINE, (LOWER) SLITHERSTONE MINE

Royse and Co., (Jeremy, Samuel and Isaac, lead merchants of Castleton) began to develop deep workings at the Windle and Rush Vein about 1825. The Rush Engine Shaft was eventually deepened to 70 fathoms and the workings carried down to 110 fathoms. The mine was marked on the 1840 OS map as *Lower Slitherstone*. The Royse`s workings reached the boundary with the Birch Hall title in 1832. They entered into an agreement with the owner Thomas Hill, whereby Hill conveyed to them one meer of ground [DRO, Br-T, L36]:

for convenience of relieving Thomas Hill`s mine of Wind and Water. Hill shall have priviledge of driving a forefield two yards high through the aforesaid meer, taking the ore and having priviledge of gates and shafts at Royse`s mine. He shall have a lower level if at any time he requires it, or even a still lower level(if) not then cut by Royse`s.

The agreement indicates that Royse and Co. were intent in developing the deeper workings, below Hill`s stopes. Heathcote [2001] has speculated that Royse and Co. knew about the P8 passages that must run close beneath Windle and Rush mines and were already draining their own water into the cave before 1832. A letter from Samuel Royse at Castleton, dated 7th December, 1849 after noting a rise in the price of lead suggests: *we ought to make the most of these times and at our enormous depth too – the expense is serious* [DRO, D 1836 Eyre, M/L7].

Richard Niness, manager of the Coalpithole Mine, writing in August, 1891 about the Slitherstone mines gave the following information:

They managed to get down 110 fathoms (which is 10 fathoms below the swallow) with a horse whim – A cross-cut might be driven from the swallow 100 fathoms deep and would drain all the veins to that depth [Lafferty Papers, courtesy D. Nash].

[NOTE; A considerable proportion of the information given above about Coalpithole Mine has been derived from the manuscript of Chris. Heathcote`s forthcoming extended article on the history of the mine [Heathcote, in press]. The author is indebted to him for his generosity in allowing information to be taken from the manuscript. Remaining references have been cited as normal].

5. THE MINES OF TIDESLOW RAKE AND HUCKLOW EDGE RAKE

Historical development of mining and technology along this major vein must be considered under several separate sub-sections, so too drainage of the mines is more conveniently discussed using the same format. Nevertheless the entire vein complex, together with its multitude of individual mines, must be dealt with as one entity, encompassed within one overall section.

Current published geological maps mark the western extremity of the vein situated adjacent to New Farm, but 18th and 19th century Barmaster entries record meers of ground being set out well beyond, extending to the vicinity of the Chesterfield to Stockport main road. Beginning from this extreme western point, and until New Farm is reached, the surface range is very ill-defined. Recognisable surface expression then begins and the vein crosses over Tideslow Top, reaching to the old Tideswell to Castleton road. On Tideslow Top there are parallel, open trenches cut into the vein, probably of great antiquity. They, along with the large hillocks hereabouts, form an impressive visual feature and the site is further enhanced by several dressing floors with associated leats, water-storage ponds and buddle dams [Barnatt and Penny, 2004]. All are now preserved, this latter stretch having been designated a Scheduled Ancient Monument. The continuation of the vein ranges past Windmill hamlet to Great Hucklow village. Beyond, the vein becomes concealed beneath the shale and sandstone cover forming Hucklow Edge and Eyam Edge, the extensive workings and stopes all finally terminate north of Eyam village.

Though as yet unproved by documentary evidence, there seems to be every likelihood that the entire vein outcrop within the limestone had been discovered well before 1600. The eastern extension beneath the shale cover was probably found at Great Hucklow in the mid 17th century. Working progressively eastwards, the vein was cut into Grindlow Liberty in 1711-1712, and was freed in Eyam Liberty more or less at the same time.

Because of the considerable variability in rock types along the tract of ground under consideration, geological detail will also be discussed within each sub-section, and therefore only an outline is provided here. Along Tideslow Rake and beyond, the western section was worked in the Monsal Dale Limestones and variously through the Litton Tuff, Upper and Lower Millers Dale lavas and into the Potluck Sill. The well-known deep sinking at Clear-the-Way Mine, or Black Hillock Mine was located within the Sill, but the vein was found to be totally devoid of lead ore. Ore was mined from the toadstone at the Tideslow mines; several late 18th and early 19th century writers noted the occurrence of native sulphur at Tideslow Rake. Near Windmill, High Rake Mine exploited ore shoots both in the upper limestone, and significantly, within the Cressbrook Dale Lava. Current geological thought is that the abnormal thickness of toadstone or channel penetrated at High Rake Mine can be attributed to a feeder to the Potluck Sill intruded into the Cressbrook Dale Lava [Walters, 1981].

The Monsal Dale and overlying Eyam Limestones incline beneath the shale cover at Great Hucklow. Along Eyam Edge and Hucklow Edge the vein was reached by shafts penetrating through the overlying and generally unproductive Namurian shales and sandstones. Beneath these newer rocks the vein complex was exploited in strata ranging from the Eyam Limestone, into the underlying Monsal Dale Limestone and downwards to the top of the Cressbrook Dale Lava.

From west to east, the rake is known within Tideswell Liberty as White Rake and Tideslow Rake, in Little Hucklow as High Rake, within Great Hucklow Liberty and Grindlow Liberty as Hucklow Edge Rake, and through Eyam Liberty as Hucklow Edge Vein, Eyam Edge Vein, or the Old Great Vein. During the early to mid 18th century the continuation beyond Middleton Engine Mine was sometimes known as Middleton Engine Old Vein and/or Hucklow Edge Vein, Ladywash Old Vein, or Old Edge Vein. The irregular rectangle of land bounded by Middleton Engine Mine, Ladywash Mine, Eyam village and Black Hole Mine is traversed by many veins, the most important being Black Hole Vein or Little Pasture Sun Vein, or

Ladywash North-East Vein; Middleton Engine New Vein.

A series of law-suits, one of major significance that passed into Court of Chancery, ensured that the alignment of veins shown on old plans was often altered to suit litigants requirements, so too their naming was not always consistent in contemporary mining documents. Thus the major break discovered in the 10th meer at Miners Engine was claimed as a new vein by that partnership, but counterclaimed to be Middleton Engine Old Vein by the Little Pasture partners.

The individual `compartments` along the vein complex, as noted above, are discussed in the following order from west to east:

A All mines worked within the limestone outcrop:

Tideswell Liberty

White Rake and Clear-the-Way or Black Hillock Mine

Tideslow Rake, including Cleatons Grove in Little Hucklow Liberty

Little Hucklow Liberty, from east of the old Castleton to Tideswell road [Castleton Lane] to Windmill hamlet

High Rake and adjacent mines

Great Hucklow Liberty

Nether Liberty Grove to Milldam Mine

Cowpasture Vein (and in Little Hucklow Liberty)

B East of Great Hucklow village, all workings were beneath the shale cover:

Mines within Great Hucklow Liberty

Smithy Coe or Greenhead Grove to Have-at-All Mine

Grindlow Liberty

Bank Grove, Speed Grove and Silence Mine

Mines within Eyam Liberty

Old Grove.

Butlers Old Engine to Middleton Engine

Miners Engine (Twelve Meers Mine) to Brookhead Mine

From Clear-the-Way Mine, or Black Hillock, eastwardly to Great Hucklow, all the mines were drained by soughs or watergates driven within the confines of the vein structure and all discharged their water into a series of underground swallow holes or shacks.

The apparent variation in the contour of the water table along the rake from Nether Liberty to Milldam Mine and then at a higher level from Greenhead Grove eastwards, during the 17th and 18th centuries, is difficult to reconcile, but is probably due to legal disputes about mining rights, rather than being a reflection of underground geology. The disputes revolved around whether the miners had any legal rights to sink and work lead mines in parts of Great Hucklow claimed as *Ancient Freeholds,* exempt from the laws of the Kingsfield. The area around Milldam Mine was supposedly one of these Freeholds, and maybe a considerable pillar of un-cut vein existed at this time, effectively holding back water at the mines east of Great Hucklow.

Dr. John Beck [pers.comm.] believes that two distinct horizons of natural drainage flow northwards from the rake and resurge at Bradwell. The lower conduit is almost at the contour of the Bradwell resurgence and hence flow rates are very slow, water taking three days from Dowse (or Duce) Hole to the resurgence in Bradwell. He confirms that the lower stream passages within Bagshawe Cavern as far south as Hill (Earl) Rake lie only about three feet above the resurgence at Bradwell. The swallows in Cowpasture Grove and Hilltop Mine (both are discussed below) are part of this system.

The upper system, 30-60 feet higher, still takes overflow in times of spate and the swallow in Nether Liberty, and another in Beech Grove at about 240 feet in depth, are associated with it. Flow rates in flood are very fast, water taking only thirteen hours for the journey from Dowse Hole to Bradwell. This upper cave system was utilised for drainage purposes by 17th century miners working along the rake west of Milldam.

East of Great Hucklow, Old Edge Grove and New Edge Grove may have been un-watered by a cross-cut sough originally constructed to drain Greenhead, or Smithy Coe Grove. Kirkham [1963] considered that both Old Edge Grove and New Edge Grove were partially drained by shale gates driven from the Dowse Hole, but 17th century documentary evidence, coupled with the geological structure render this proposition highly unlikely. Shale gate soughs were certainly important further east within Grindlow and Eyam liberties, not only for dewatering purposes, but initially in locating the line of the vein, buried deep beneath the shales of Eyam Edge.

The sough postulated by Kirkham [1954], beginning about 1000 yards north west of Greenhead Grove, would have reached the mine at about the same contour as the roof of an underground swallow there. If the higher water table east of Milldam Mine was due to uncut ground holding up ground water, then natural drainage from the Greenhead Grove swallow would have been slow and indeed it may well have been partly choked and inaccessible to the miners until much later. The necessity for a sough that would by-pass the Milldam area and discharge directly to the surface thus becomes obvious. A sough must have been driven into Greenhead Grove, probably by 1671, whilst in 1682 it was to be extended into the adjacent Old Edge Grove. Later, by the 1690s, the swallow in Greenhead Grove was probably partly cleared out and used to receive water from New Edge Grove at a slightly deeper level than the sough.

Summarising the available information it seems that a high level series of swallow holes exist in Tideslow Rake, the most important situated at Poynton Cross; another was situated in Nether Liberty Grove and one in Beech Grove. Further to the east another swallow at approximately the same horizon exists in Greenhead Grove (Smithy Coe Mine, discussed below), but that mine was originally drained, pre-1682 and possibly by 1671 by a cross cutting sough. A deeper series of water channels is represented by the swallows in Cowpasture Grove (also discussed below) and Hilltop Mine, but the implications must be that this lower series was only accessible and servicable for mine drainage in periods of dry weather.

ALL MINES WORKED WITHIN LIMESTONE OUTCROP

TIDESWELL LIBERTY

WHITE RAKE AND CLEAR-THE-WAY OR BLACK HILLOCK MINE

The workings in White Rake were developed in the limestone beneath the Upper Millers Dale Lava and, according to Green [1887], were quite shallow, having being worked only to 8 or 10 fathoms depth by the `old men`. His source for this information is not stated. Little is known historically about the mines, but White Rake was in operation between 1711 and 1716, during which time Richard Bagshawe of Castleton was a major shareholder. Ore production was very small and the mine recorded a loss for each year [Rylands, Bag 12/1/60: SCL, OD 1505]. At the western end of White Rake, just north of New Farm, a disastrous sinking through the *channel* [or toadstone] was attempted at Clear-the-Way, or Black Hillock Mine, in an effort to work the vein and others in the *under Lime*, beneath what contempory miners believed was a stratum of channel of limited thickness.

Adjacent mines, for example at Heath Bush, Calvestones and Maiden Rake, had sunk through only a few fathoms of channel, represented by either/or the Litton Tuff, and Upper and Lower Millers Dale lavas [Walters, 1981]. The deep adventure was directed by the well-known 18th century Derbyshire mining engineer and geologist George Tissington, who was convinced of the presence of rich ores at depth. He seems to have specialised in sinking deep shafts elsewhere in the orefield. The geology met in the adjacent mines prompted Tissington and his partners to seek ore at depth in White Rake. Though totally unaware of the situation, they chose to sink their shaft at the most inappropriate position possible, directly into a feeder to the Potluck Sill, of which they had no understanding of structure or depth. Whitehurst [1778] rightly argued that Black Hillock shaft had been sunk in a vent or fissure up which molten rock had formerly risen, but the failure of 18th century miners and geologists to understand these complexities before Whitehurst`s time can only now be fully appreciated.

Sinking commenced in 1757 under Tissington`s direction, but work was discontinued in 1761, the Engine Shaft being 26 fathoms in depth and the climbing gates down to 30 fathoms. Sinking was restarted in 1764 and continued until 1771. During this second phase there are three references to drainage. The first occurs in March, 1766 when they were *Sludging and repairing the Level*; the shaft was then about 50 fathoms in depth. One year later a dam was built to prevent water from returning from a Swallow into the shaft, whilst in March, 1769 they were *Sludging the Drift to ye Swallow*. A swallow hole would not be expected in dolerite, and maybe it was an open part of the vein-fault rather than a true swallow. The Level was probably of no great length, its function being to deliver water into the Swallow, raised from the shaft

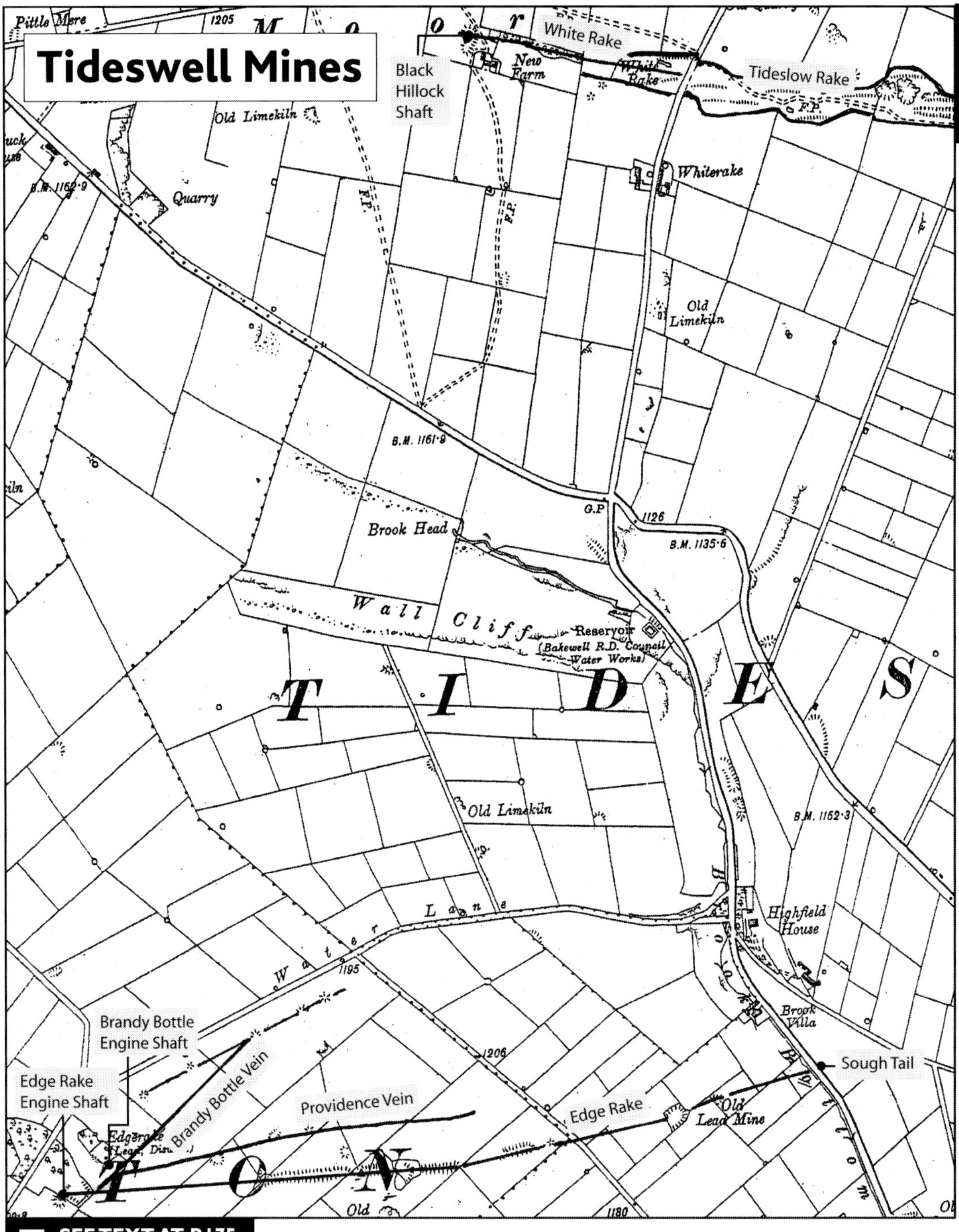
Tideswell Mines
Black Hillock Shaft
White Rake
Tideslow Rake
New Farm
Whiterake
Pittle Mere
Old Limekiln
Quarry
Brook Head
Wall Cliff
Reservoir (Bakewell R.D. Council Water Works)
Old Limekiln
Highfield House
Brook Villa
Water Lane
Brandy Bottle Engine Shaft
Edge Rake Engine Shaft
Brandy Bottle Vein
Providence Vein
Edge Rake
Old Lead Mine
Sough Tail
TIDES
TON

SEE P.89

SEE TEXT AT P.175

foot by means of horse power or even hand pumps.

The precise function of a *Tub Engine,* purchased in March, 1765, is not known, but it cannot have been a conventional Tub Engine, or water-balance used for pumping, no surface water supply was available and likely it was a horse operated gin winding large barrels. The mine was again left from 1771 until 1789, and when the `tryall` or adventure was finally abandoned in 1793, after a third phase of sinking, expenditure totalled very nearly £5,600 [SCL, Bag, 401, 402]; no ore had been found, although the vein fissure had been followed down to a depth of about 74 fathoms before being `lost`. The shaft was 100 fathoms deep in 1786 and still in channel [Whitehurst], 1786 but it is now considered that the limestone was breached at 120 fathoms in 1793 and the sudden in-rush of water noted by Farey [1811], defeated the miners.

TIDESLOW RAKE, INCLUDING CLEATONS GROVE IN LITTLE HUCKLOW LIBERTY

The earliest references to mining at the Tideslow mines date from 1195 and there was continuous production there from 1216 to 1249. During these thirty three years nearly 13,000 loads of ore were extracted. Much of this output may have been obtained from the large, distinctive `v` shaped opencast trenches visible in the rake at Tideslow Top [Rieuwerts, 1994].

Following the late 12th century and first half of the 13th century ore production records, nothing is known about the Tideslow mines until the late 16th century. About 1578 three miners were mining in *ffrost close and dogge hillocke* but little was obtained due to the hardness of the rock/vein-stuff. Sixty years later, i.e. in 1638, a dispute arose about ownership of the duties of Lot and Cope and Edward Allen the Lord of the Manor of Tideswell laid claim to them, specifically the lot and cope due from eight meers of ground in three closes called *greate dogge hillock, little dogge hillock and ffrosts close*. He claimed that during the previous two years over £400 of lead ore had been dug. A little earlier, in 1612 lead was being mined in the Great Dog Hillock Close and in 1633-34 ore had been mined in a grove in *Joanes Half Close* [SCL, Bag 549]. Barmaster entries and other information enables Jome (Joame) and Little Jome meers and also Dog Hillock to be located, all within eight meers west from the old, Tideswell to Castleton road.

Much of the vein was cavernous, or `shacky` as the old miners termed it. Lying between the old Tideswell to Castleton road and Tideslow Top there were at least three large swallow holes in the vein, the deepest, adjacent to the road, was some 270 to 280 feet beneath the surface. A series of mid to late 17th century soughing agreements prove that workings along the rake had penetrated to depths of at least 275 feet and exploitation must have been intensive [DRO, Br-T, uncatalogued]. Sough drainage along Tideslow Rake reached a zenith in the second half of the 17th century when virtually the whole length of the vein, a distance of nearly 1,000 yards was served by a series of soughs.

There are problems in interpretation of available documents, but the Burton family and the Bagshawes of Great Hucklow appear to be the common financial link in carrying forward the main sough. This present account of drainage along Tideslow Rake is slightly different from the conclusions reached in the first edition of this work [Rieuwerts, 1987]. Unfortunately no production statistics are available for this period.

The above mentioned agreements covering the period 1648 to 1685 allow some impression to be formed concerning the progress of four drainage adits driven along the vein. The principal level was probably begun in c.1654 and extended for over half a mile westwardly along the rake. In addition there was a high level sough serving mines adjacent to Tideslow Top, one sough was driven eastwards into Little Hucklow Liberty and a fourth level drained part of the rake within Tideswell Liberty, but its location is not known [DRO, Br-T, uncatalogued]. Water from mines on High Rake within Little Hucklow Liberty was drained into an underground swallow known as *the swallow at Poynton Cross* or *Tideslo Old Swallow*. An agreement dated 1654 proves that water from the first meer of ground eastwardly, within Little Hucklow drained into this swallow. From the swallow, all drainage presumably flows northwards in natural channels to resurge at Bradwell.

SOUGH [UNLOCATED, BUT DRIVEN ALONG TIDESLOW RAKE]

The first agreement to construct a drainage level at Tideslow Rake is dated November, 1648, but other than it referring to a sough or watergate extending through two meers of ground at Tideslow Rake in the parish of Tideswell, the agreement gives no indication of its precise location. Where the old Tideswell to Castleton road crosses Tideslow Rake at Poynton

SECTION ALONG TIDESLOW RAKE AND HIGH RAKE FROM BLACK HILLOCK SHAFT TO WINDMILL

―――― TIDESWELL LIBERTY ―――― HUCKLOW LIBERTY ――――

AOD
1200
800

Scale: 0 – 2000 feet

Road to Bradwell

High Rake Shaft

Flow of water taken from the 1780s high level water drift at High Rake Mine, through old workings and into *Tideslo Old Swallow*

Poynton Cross Swallow

surface of *Channel* (after Jos. Cook 1780s)

Robinsons old Grove

Nall Grove

The upper sough level (pre 1685)

UPPER MILLERS DALE LAVA
LIMESTONE

LOWER MILLERS DALE LAVA

Black Hillock Shaft

The stepped black line terminating at the foot of Robinsons old Grove is the sough level driven between 1654 and 1685. The level commences on the east side at Poynton Cross Swallow, but despite clauses in the soughing agreements *to be carried on at the same Levell which the present watergate is att* it rises gently westwards on, or near to the upper surface of the Lower Millers Dale Lava. The three black dots represent the underground swallows at Poynton Cross, Jome Meers and Swallow Groves respectively. There were probably changes in level at these points, in addition to the rise of 24 feet at the east end of Nall Grove.

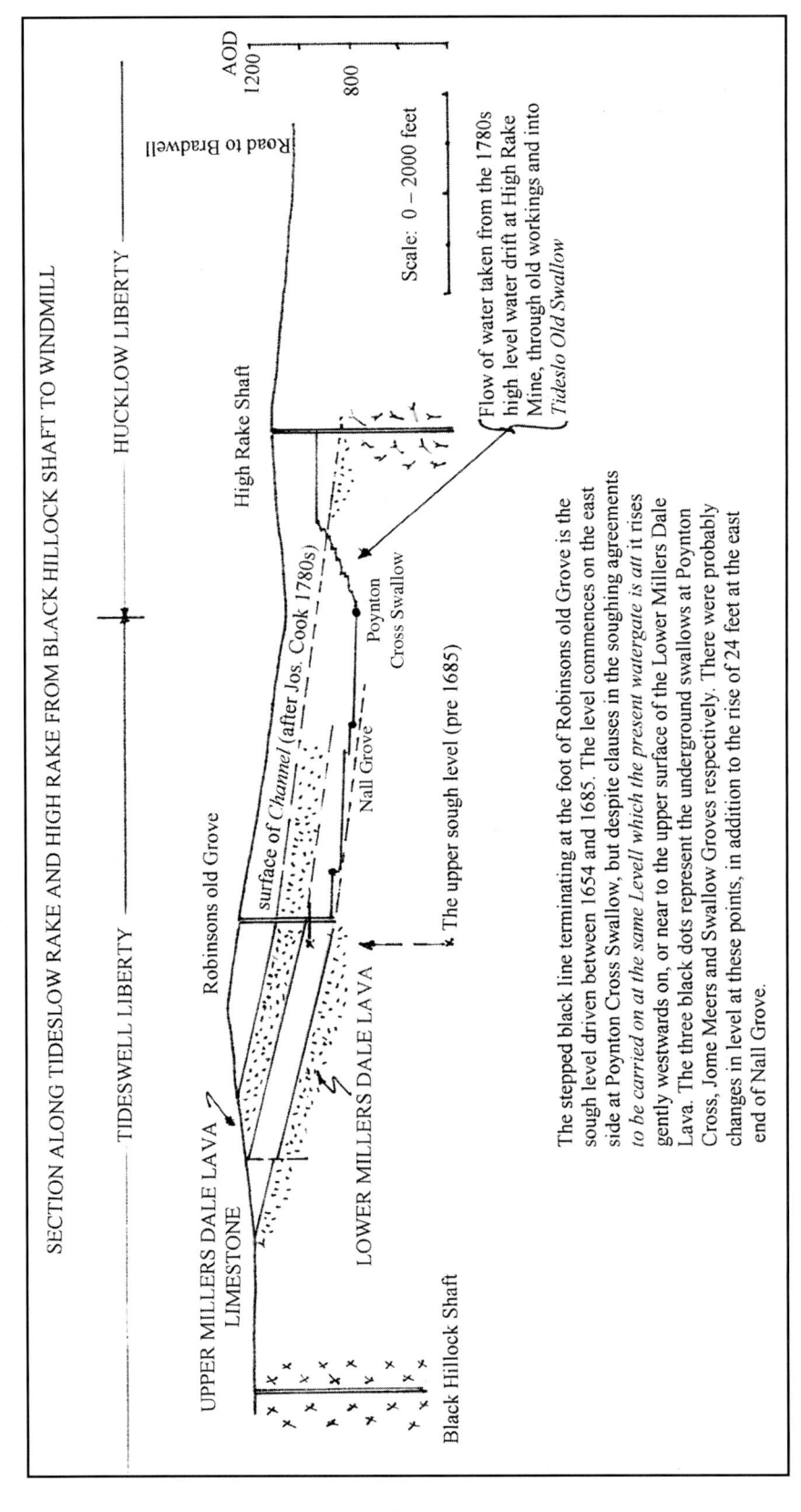

Cross marks the boundary between Hucklow Liberty and Tideswell. The sough therefore must have been situated west of Poynton Cross for it to be situated within Tideswell Parish. Attempted correlation with historical data and driveage rates and thus progress in the main sough (Tideslow Rake Sough, below) implies that the 1648 level must be separate from the principal sough along the vein. This level too, the earliest of the known soughs along Tideslow Rake, must have been driven from an underground swallow hole.

SOUGH FROM POYNTON CROSS SWALLOW INTO CLEATON`S GROVE IN LITTLE HUCKLOW LIBERTY

The only known record of this sough or water-gate occurs in Articles of Agreement signed in September, 1654 between Michael Burton, William Bagshawe and Anthonie ffoxe of Litton and Robert Cleaton and three others, all of Tideswell:

> *concerning the workeing, usinge and orderinge of two meers of ground lyinge at Poynton Crosse, the one within the Lordship of Tidswall the other within the Libertie of Little huckloe* - [DRO, Br-T, uncatalogued].

Each partnership owned a meer of ground either side of the swallow, Cleaton`s meer was situated within Little Hucklow, whilst Burton`s meer was within Tideswell. There had been previous trouble between the parties about keeping open and maintaining a swallow hole and Cleaton and partners agreed that:

> *the sinke or swallow now found betwixt the parting of the said grounds – shall at all times hereafter – keepe the same open and cleansed so farre as the ground – extend.*

Another clause referred to working both a day shift and a night shift. They also agreed that in future they would not *hinder or stopp anie watergates now runninge or hereafter to be made decendinge from the ground of the said Michael Burton and his partners into the sinke or swallow.*

Cleaton`s meer eventually became a part of the five meers within the Mock Mine title, which title extended eastwardly to the High Rake Mine possessions. During the 1780s water collecting above a toadstone clay wayboard at High Rake Mine was to be conveyed westwardly through a drift then being driven to the end of their ground, from which point it was intended to *thro the water westerly into old works to go into Tideslo old Swallow* [SCL, Bag 587 (18/1)]. The `old works` were those belonging to Mock Mine, whilst there can be little doubt that Tideslo(w) old Swallow and the swallow at Poynton Cross are identical. The water-gate owned by Burton and partners within Tideswell Liberty is fully discussed next under the heading Tideslow Rake Sough.

TIDESLOW RAKE SOUGH

The second agreement relating to soughing exclusively within Tideswell Lordship or Liberty, is dated September, 1654, it being also concerned with two meers of ground at Poynton Cross and cleaning and keeping open the swallow hole found there. This document has greater significance, the author considers that it marks the commencement of the main sough that was driven westwardly along Tideslow Rake from the Poynton Cross swallow hole for at least 28 meers, a distance a little in excess of half a mile, in the period 1654 until 1686. This would represent an average daily advance of just under three inches, appropriate for late 17th century sough driveage.

There were other underground swallow holes along the vein, for example in 1732 the 7th, 8th and 9th meers west from Poynton Cross were known as *Swallow Meers*. These same meers had been known in the previous century as *Little Jome Meer* and *Jome Meers*. The 23rd and 24th meers west were also known as Swallow Meers. A `Jome` or `Joiernel` refers to a passage through rock, and might be either natural or man-made [Rieuwerts, 1998]. The next agreement in the series, dates from July, 1661 and concerns that part of the vein adjacent to the Jome Meers. The sough masters, Francis Burton, William Bagshawe and partners:

> *will cause to be made a sufficient sough or water gate two yards high beginning - on the west side the little Jome Meere and soe from thence all along to a Swallow at ye west side of Jome meers att a leavil of 46 fadoms.*

Beyond lay the groves of Burton and Bagshawe and partners, Ellis Poynton, and Ellis Timperley and Robert Morton, the sough was to be continued through these meers. The next agreement, drawn up in 1663, though no month is quoted, relates that the sough was to be continued through the groves of William Palfreyman and John Cresswell (Nall Groves), Coffer Grove, Lawyer Grove and old Edward Outfield Grove. This agreement contains two other important statements. The first being that the continuation of the sough was to be excavated *at the levy or deepness of four fathoms above the roofe of the watergate or sugh now driven.* This pre-conceived and dramatic loss of level was carried out in order to rise and continue driving above the channel (Millers Dale Lava). The scheme avoided the lava and a long driveage through that rock. The second important item contained in the agreement states that the sough was to be continued through the meers as a *height drift.* The term has not been seen in any other Derbyshire lead mining document, but it occurs in 1573 at coal mines at Selston and Wollaton, Nottinghamshire where level driving and shaft sinking were paid by the *height* of six feet [Graham Crisp, pers. comm.].

The sough had reached the end of Outfield Grove by January, 1670 and the next stage was to drive it through Saltes Grove into Taskers Grove, 1,056 feet to the west. It was to be carried forward at the same level as previously and to be six feet in height. An interim agreement was made in November, 1685, when it was affirmed that Francis Burton and William Bagshawe

> *are now bringing up an under watergate which – will much advantage Anne Radcliffe and partners – who hath certain meers called Taskers meers.* Burton and Bagshawe were to continue their sough *through two meers called oldfield meers and soe to Taskers meers which sd sough shall be thirteen fathom under ye first sough* (see below for discussion of the higher sough).

After receipt of £40 by Burton and Bagshawe from Anne Radcliffe, the deep sough was then to be driven by her and her and partners beyond Tasker Meers to Gill Meer lying on the west side, or permit Burton and Bagshawe to continue it. [Confirming the locations of three meers on the vein each known as Outfield, Ouldfield or Oldfield Grove, proved confusing, but not quite so taxing as locating the five Swallow meers].

An un-dated plan [SCL, Bag 549], depicts the line of a sough extending from a *selfe Swallow* westwards along Tideslow Rake to a forefield on the east side of Tasker Meers at Tideslow Top. The plan is not drawn to scale, but it is clear that the sough was of considerable length and there can be little doubt that it is the 1654–1685 sough and the `selfe swallow` and the swallow at Poynton Cross are the same.

SOUGH ALONG TIDESLOW RAKE FROM OLDFIELD GROVE TO TASKERS GROVE

Toward the surface summit of Tideslow Rake, the high level sough, recorded in the agreement drawn in November, 1685, was under construction in 1663. An agreement dated December, 1663 indicates that the sough was already in existence and the proposal was to continue it from the foot of a sump in Pump Grove through to Taskers Grove or Meers. There is no indication of how far the level had already been excavated, but in November, 1685 it was said that:

> *Whereas there was heretofore a Certaine Watergate brought up by Mr. William Bagshawe, now deceased, through oldfield meers in Tidslow Rake which sd sough did according to its depth lay dry and unwatered severall meares in ye sd Rake but is now useless ye oare lying under ye watergate.*

This old sough was thirteen fathoms (78 feet) above the main sough. It may have been cut partly within the Upper Millers Dale Lava.

LITTLE HUCKLOW LIBERTY

HIGH RAKE AND ADJACENT MINES

Mock Mine title consists of five meers of ground situated at the extreme western end of High Rake, adjacent to the old Tideswell to Castleton road. Though Mock Mine is located in the Liberty of Little Hucklow, adjacent to High Rake, its 17th century drainage has been discussed coupled with Tideslow Rake.

There are no soughs draining High Rake, neither are there any specifically named `water-gates`, `water-drifts` or `swallow gates`. However, during the 1780s proposals were mooted, and at least some work carried out, in driving levels both east and west from the Engine Shaft in order to drain water from the upper workings. The deep, 19th century workings

Tideslow Rake and High Rake

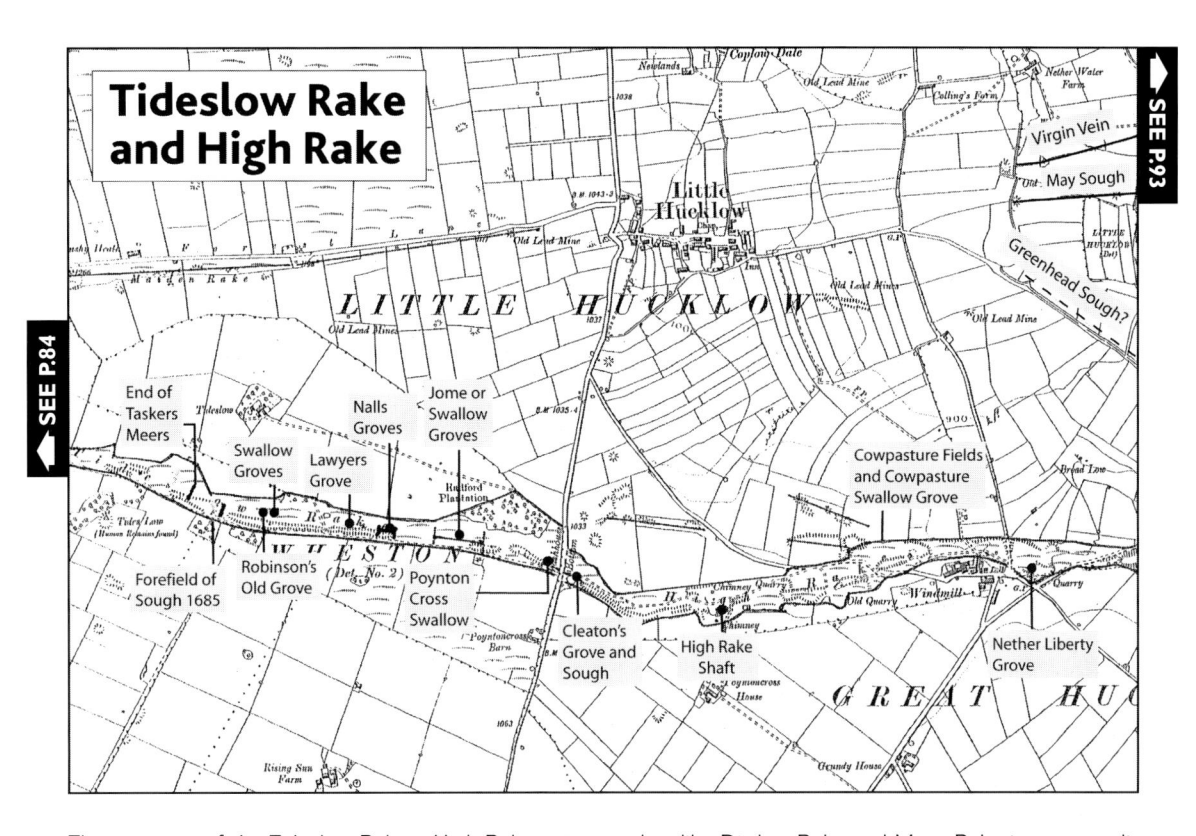

Map labels: SEE P.84; SEE P.93; End of Taskers Meers; Swallow Groves; Lawyers Grove; Nalls Groves; Jome or Swallow Groves; Forefield of Sough 1685; Robinson's Old Grove; Poynton Cross Swallow; Cleaton's Grove and Sough; High Rake Shaft; Cowpasture Fields and Cowpasture Swallow Grove; Nether Liberty Grove; Virgin Vein; May Sough; Greenhead Sough?

The structure of the Tideslow Rake – High Rake vein complex, like Dirtlow Rake and Moss Rake is too complicated to plot individually. The surface expression of the complex has been defined by highlighting the boundary walls.

were dewatered by a large Cornish Engine, but no details of a pumpway serving it, or other drainage levels are known. Lack of commercially viable ore-shoots and the great depth of the mine, rather than water problems were the reason for its closure in the mid 19th century.

No date is known for the beginnings of lead mining at High Rake, but in about 1577 Robert Dolphin, a Bradwell miner worked lead ore in Little Hucklow Waste; High Rake was situated within the Little Hucklow Waste [PRO, DL 4 62/19].

An un-dated plan, but c.1735–1736 depicts five shafts, or groves lying between the Tideswell – Castleton road and Windmill hamlet, these being from west to east; *Thos. Dudin Shaft, 2nd Shaft in Dudin Title, Houson Shaft in his Title, Adam Willson Shaft, Vallantine ffurnnis Shaft in his Title* [Chats, Dev Coll]. Fragmentary ore accounts for Hucklow Liberty record small measures of ore for *Valentine ffurness, Robert Howson, and Thos Willson* in 1726-1727 and *Thomas Duding, Tall Hill Grove* in 1734–1735, but output totalled only 16 loads 1 dish [Chats, Dev Coll].

During 1745 the Barmote Court jury heard a complaint by Isaac Morton against Thomas Dudin and partners for non-payment of £13-17-9 due to him at High Rake Mine in the Liberty of Little Hucklow [Chats, Dev Coll]. Tall Hill Grove, which included High Rake Mine, was consolidated with *Luck-in-a-Bagg* or Little Grove Engine in June, 1749 [SCL, Bag 547], only four months later Thomas Dudin was again billed in the Barmote Court by *Mr francses Mortin and Mr John Beech – for not keeping company at a mine called Luck in a bag* [Chats, Dev Coll]. The same two men were listed as owners of High Rake Engine by May, 1754.

The main 19th century shaft at High Rake Mine was situated almost halfway between Dudin's 2nd Shaft and Housons Shaft. The position of the Engine at this time is verified in a surveyor's field book, dated 1758. Coincident with the site of the large scale 19th century mine are the words *Old Grove Hills* and *Gin for Mines* -The gin-circle is plainly depicted, also a small building immediately to the west, probably a coe [SCL, Fairbank FB 13].

Somewhat earlier, in October, 1744 a complaint

The ruined, but substantial remains of the engine and boiler houses and chimneys built in the 1840s at High Rake Mine, Windmill. The original is a photographic postcard dating from the earlier part of the 20th century.

was made to the Barmote by Samuel Bunting for non-payment of 13/10d for wages by Thomas Dudwin at the quaintly named *Will-if-I can* in Little Hucklow; a mine presumably very close to Tall Hill Grove. A Bill of Complaint heard at the Barmote Court April, 1746 contains an isolated reference to Stone Shaft (or Slack) Mine at Tall Hill [Chats, Bar Coll]. Thomas Dudin lived at Smalldale, Bradwell and had shares in some of the Bradwell mines.

Black Hillock Mine had already been sunk 82 fathoms (492 feet) at a cost of £2,529 without any success by June, 1768, neither the *Under Lime or 2nd Limestone* had been breached and no ore had been found. Notwithstanding the already impending failure of that venture, ore shoots already discovered in the channel at High Rake, led the miners to speculate on the possibilities of payable ore existing at yet greater depths, not only in that stratum, but in the underlying limestone too. A decision was made therefore to undertake a similar deep trial at High Rake, which was put into operation in 1768 [SCL, Bag 587(19)]. The workings eventually reached a depth of 87 fathoms (522 feet), but only limited production of ore was obtained from the channel. The igneous rock was not bottomed and the mid 19th century sinking to 120 fathoms showed no underlying limestone.

High Rake Mine was valued at £480 in 1767 [SCL, Bag 587(12)], and the evidence seems to be that whilst before 1768 High Rake and the adjacent mines had been worked mainly in the upper limestone above the *1st toadstone or Channel*, this was not exclusively so. For example a memo dated 1786 observed *the Old Man had sunk as low as our Engin foot* [SCL, Bag 587(18/5). After 1768, the first reference to progress occurs in June 1783, at which date the Engine Shaft was then 61 fathoms deep, the following year the shaft had reached 68 fathoms (408 feet) in depth, or 20 fathoms into the Channel. A series of sumps, climbing gates and stopes took the final depth of exploitation to 87 fathoms. Production of ore from the channel amounted to 157 loads in 1785 and 121 loads in 1786, a small, but significant quantity derived from a rock often thought to be devoid of commercially viable ore.

Although the workings reached such considerable depth, drainage does not seem to have been a major problem. A section of the mine dated 1784 demonstrates that water was collecting on top of a clay bed about 120 feet beneath the surface. To facilitate drainage they were driving westwardly on top of a second clay bed 42 feet beneath the other. The drift began about one meer west from the Engine Shaft and at the end of their seventh meer west in High Rake title, they intended *to thro the water westerly into old works to go into Tideslo old Swallow* [SCL, Bag 587(18/1)].

Water on top of the main toadstone or channel was to be taken eastwards by a drift at that horizon and driven to the end of their seventh meer About 1786–1787 a scheme was mooted to carry forward a stope some 40 feet in height in the top of the channel, from the Engine Shaft, westwardly to the end of the ground, but with the added rider *which we cannot do for water at present* [SCL, Bag 587(18/5)].

Details about the history of the mine after 1786 become sparse for nearly half a century, but available evidence is that a little work was done in the higher levels and nothing at depth. High Rake Mine still retained its alternative name of Luck-in-a-Bag in the 1790s and first decade at least of the following century. Joseph Cook of Tideswell, who was involved in a sinking through the channel at Lees Rake, Burfoot, was the agent during the similar excercise at High Rake in the 1780s and perhaps before. Acting on behalf of William Longsden and partners, in May, 1791 he freed the 7th meer at *Luck-in-a-Bag in the old vein ranging west from the Engine Shaft* [SCL, Bag 452].

Despite the failure of the 18th century venture, but encouraged by highly profitable finds beneath the toadstone at Crich, a second grandiose deep sinking scheme was agreed upon in 1834. The new venture was headed by William Wyatt of Foolow, who entered into an agreement with his partners:

that a Company be formed called the High Rake Mining Company for the purpose of sinking through the Toadstone to work the vein in the underlying second limestone. [SCL, Bag 587(19)].

It proved to be a disastrous failure. The shaft took eight years to complete [SCL, Bag 587(80)]. and after sinking 120 fathoms, involving considerable sections being walled with ashlar stone, the toadstone had not been bottomed, indeed modern geological interpretation is that the shaft was sunk in a sill feeder, intruded into the Cressbrook Dale Lava.

Expenditure was lavish, the mine was equipped with a large Cornish Engine, made by Graham and Co, Milton Ironworks, Elsecar. The engine was constructed on the Simms Compound principle, having two cylinders, 36 inches and 70 inches diameter respectively. It began work in 1843, the shaft by then being 80 fathoms in depth. Working levels were driven off the shaft at intervals, but the base of the toadstone was not found, even at 120 fathoms beneath the surface. A report to the proprietors by F. C. Gillatt, a Chesterfield Mining Engineer, submitted in October, 1850, was not optimistic. On the west side of the shaft little had been done *for fear of tapping a large quantity of water which is supposed to drain through the upper strata in that direction.*

At 118 fathoms, very near the bottom of the mine, a crosscut thirty yards in length was driven northwards to the vein. A flank level was driven east and west, but despite the vein being two to three feet wide very little ore was found; unfortunately a small spring of water was intersected, and work was abandoned. The higher levels fared little better. The largest was at 80 fathoms and by 1852, when Gillatt submitted a second report, it was 272 yards in length. His earlier report from 1850, had stated *the width of the vein here being 2 to 5 feet – and in some parts yields a fair quantity of ore.* Mid 19th century memoranda confirmed that ore was found in the toadstone and *was very nice - but it was very bad in quality on account of the toadstone.*

A vertical section through the workings, drawn to accompany Gillatt's second report shows these workings all in toadstone and some small stopes and a small patch of stoping in the limestone which had been proved by rising upwards from the 80 fathom level to 65 fathoms. The vein was 18 feet in width but contained little ore. After sustaining losses totalling in excess of £19,000, a more accurate figure of £16,417 is quoted elsewhere [SCL, Bag 587(80)], the company was wound up in 1852. The Cornish Engine had been valued at £2,705 in 1850 and was sold to the Mixon Copper Mine, Staffordshire in 1853. The shaft was also equipped with a Cornish winding engine purchased from Magpie Mine in 1847. This latter engine was also used for crushing bouse raised from the mine. It too was sold to Mixon Mine in 1853.

An un-dated, but post 1852 document commented that at High Rake *there was some very fine Pyritis got in this mine – the miners called Brazil or Cocks Comb Silver –* [SCL, Bag 587(80); Rieuwerts, 1998].

A fine photograph/postcard dating from about 1910-1920 illustrates what then survived of the still substantially complete engine houses and chimneys at High Rake Mine.

GREAT HUCKLOW LIBERTY

NETHER LIBERTY GROVE TO MILLDAM MINE

At Windmill, eastwards from the Tideswell to Bradwell road, formerly known as Bradow Lane, the vein passes into Great Hucklow Liberty. There are records extant of 15th century mining at Hucklow, but unfortunately the locations of meers set out in 1456 by the Barmaster, Robert Midleton, at *Syndringes* and *Makulsmyres* cannot be traced [SCL, Bag 3435]. Over 160 years later there was a dispute between the King and Sir Charles Cavendish about the ownership of Lot and Cope and the power to appoint a Barmaster and hold Barmote Courts within Hucklow. This document, dated 27th November, 1618 relates that John Wilson of Great Hucklow pretended to be Barmaster to Sir Charles.

Barmaster`s entries, together with 19th century mining plans and a series of 17th century Barmote Court disputes, prove the existence of a large number of shafts and small mines occupying the rake between Windmill and Great Hucklow. Many had the typical, strange or poetic names so often given to their mines by the Derbyshire lead miners. Along this part of the vein were *Stand to thyself; Peace for ever; – Buy the truth and sell it not; Kill Tom* and *Watch and Ward*. By the 19th century all of them had been consolidated into just five large titles. Commencing at the western end, at the parting of Little Hucklow and Great Hucklow liberties, and extending eastwards to the village of Great Hucklow, these were; Nether Liberty, Watch and Ward, Hilltop and Beech Grove, Gateside and Milldam mines. Cowpasture Grove was situated on Hucklow North Vein, north of Windmill hamlet, in Little Hucklow Liberty. One reference relates to *the Swallow in Cowpasture Rake*.

All the aforementioned mines were worked in the limestones above the Cressbrook Dale Lava, but during the mid 19th century, Hilltop Mine, Gateside Mine and Milldam Mine penetrated into that stratum. William Chapman of Great Hucklow claimed that when it was found at Milldam Mine *it completely upset the mine* [pencil notes in the author`s copy of Whitehurst, 1786]. Explosive slickensides occurred at Milldam Mine [Strahan, 1887]. The mine manager,

Leonard Maltby told Strahan that the explosions took place where the vein was very hard and appeared to be under great pressure and he considered these factors to be the cause. When Sidney Addy was collecting words for the addendum to his *Glossary* [1933], he obtained several mining terms from Mr. Chapman of Hucklow. Amongst them was *Tollmans Dots* which he defined as *specks of lead scattered among the spar.* The term has not been seen elsewhere in the orefield [Rieuwerts, 1998].

This portion of Hucklow Edge Rake, in similar fashion to Tideslow Rake, was also `shackey` and at least three major underground swallows were utilised by the miners for drainage purposes. A fourth swallow, this situated in Cowpasture Grove in Little Hucklow Liberty, is more conveniently discussed within this section because a major drainage level was intended to be driven from it as far east as Smithy Coe Mine, east of Great Hucklow village.

Benjamin Bagshawe [1863-1864] said that the vein had been cut down to the water in 1650. Unfortunately he gave no other details, or the source of his information, but he added that coins dating from the reign of Charles I (1625-1649), plus many mining tools and equipment were found at depths ranging from 50 to 70 fathoms. All other evidence contradicts this claim and it is highly likely that *t`owd man`* reached 50 fathoms only on rare occasions.

A Barmote Court dispute between the partners at Yate Grove, dating from 1671 implies that working below 35 fathoms required special arrangements, probably intensive hand pumping, necessitating legal articles of agreement:

> *William Tatton Esq., and Edward Creswell complayn themselves to this Court against Edward Pointon for unjustly entering into and for wrongfully detayning from ye Complaynants one halfe of ye yate grove under ye levill of five and thirty fathoms according to an agreement of severall articles under hand and seale wch said grove is lying and being on hucklow rake – to ye Complainants damage of Two hundred pounds.*

This hypothesis receives support from a case tried at the Barmote Court in September, 1669, when the jurors heard that Humphrey Wardle had not paid his part of the wages *expended about drawing of water*

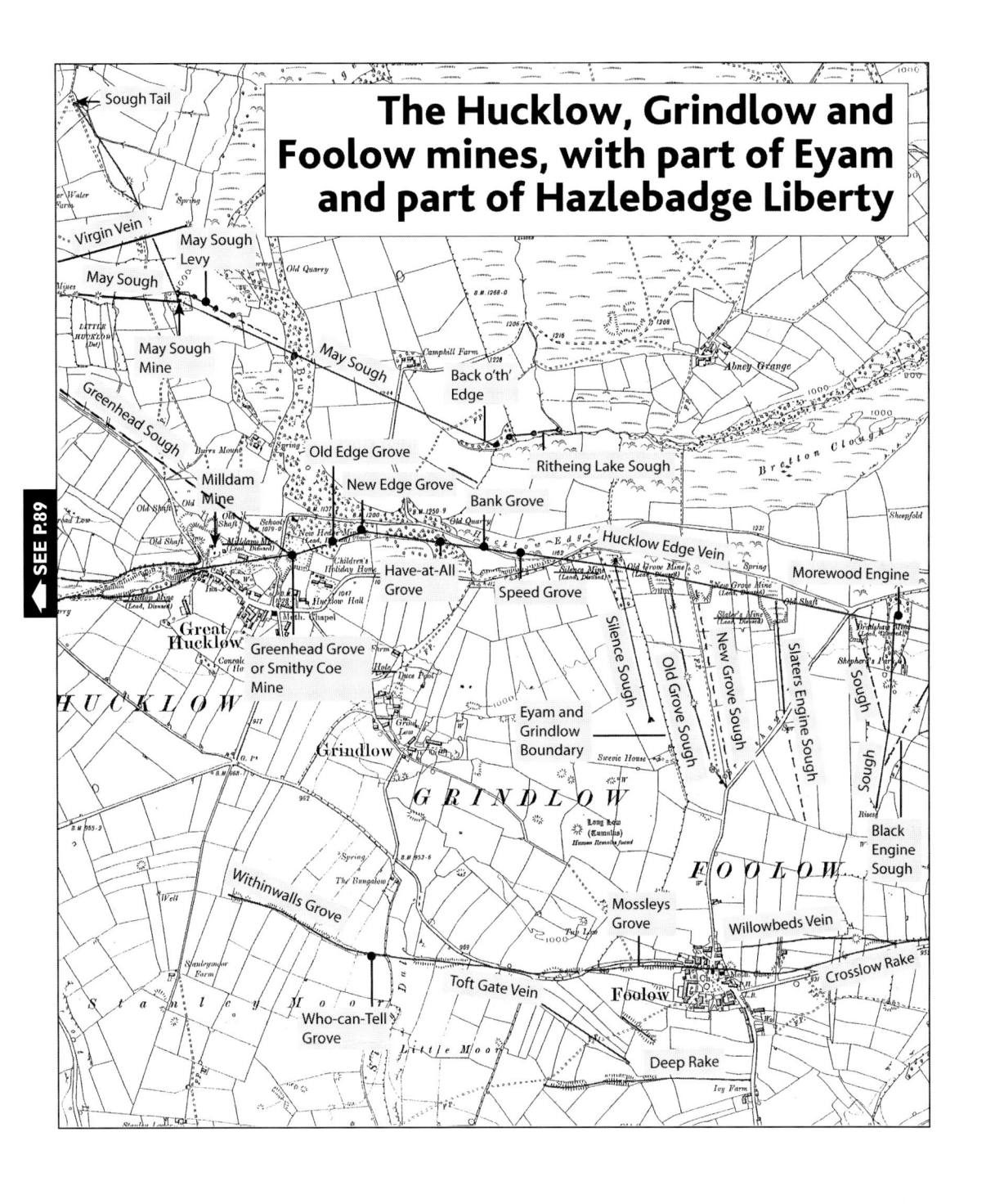

5. The Mines of Tideslow Rake and Hucklow Edge Rake

The Hucklow, Grindlow and Foolow mines, with part of Eyam and part of Hazlebadge Liberty

for drayning and unwatering two groves called Swans Grove and Claytons Grove on hucklow rake according to agreement. This agreement was again referred to in August, 1671, when the Barmote Court heard evidence about Garden End Grove and adjacent mines. The mine was also known as Nalls Grove and Hilltop Mine [SCL, Bag 671; Chats, Bar Coll]. Some time previously, unfortunately no date is specified, an agreement had been reached about sharing the costs of mutual drainage, the groves being:

> *much troubled with water* – (and) – *That ye water could be drawne forth to ye soales at an equal charge and all the said parties did fully agree to draw ye water without ceasing.*

The mines concerned in this agreement were; Garden End Grove, Bramwall Grove, Andrew Grove, Cleaton Grove, Swanne Grove, Ashtons Grove and a half meer called Primgapp Grove [SCL, Bag 702]. Claytons (Cleatons) Grove must have been a rich mine because in November, 1669 the partners there complained that other miners had committed a trespass into their meer and had illegally mined 500 loads of ore valued at £600 [SCL, Bag 702].

NETHER LIBERTY WATERGATE AND COWPASTURE SWALLOW GATE

Windmill Nether Grove *on hucklow rake* was working in 1669 when the owners alleged trespass had been committed into their meer by neighbouring miners and 10 loads of ore worth £15 had been removed illegally [SCL, Bag 702]. This mine might have been the 17th century title for what was known later as Nether Liberty Grove. Work was in progress at the *Swallow in Nether Liberty* in 1714-1715. Richard Bagshawe owned a 1/6th part of the mine, but expenditure ending 31st December, presumably for the preceding year, was only £2-7-0 for his part, or £14-2-0 for the total charge. The only other record, this ending 31st December, 1715 amounted to only 10d for 1/6th, or 5/- total charge, so work must have ceased very quickly in 1715 [Rylands, Bag 12/1/60].

A mid 18th century agreement to drive a water-gate from Cowpasture Grove refers to *the level called Nether Liberty Swallow or Water-Gate* and confirms that the swallow was 234 feet beneath the surface, i.e. at a contour of about 775 feet above OD [SCL, LD 171-172]. The agreement was signed in 1766, whereby partners at Cowpasture Mine, sometimes called Cowpasture Swallow Grove, were to sink down to a swallow in their own mine, this at a deeper horizon than the one in Nether Liberty Mine. They were to sink to the lowest convenient level and from there were to drive a drainage adit eastwardly. Experienced miners believed such an adit or sough might unwater mines as far away as Smithy Coe. Certainly the proposed level from Cowpasture Swallow to Smithy Coe was never completed and the little available evidence is that it did not even reach Hilltop Mine, and very little was driven.

BEECH GROVE SWALLOW GATE, MILLDAM MINE – WATER-GATES AND DRIFTS

The first documentary evidence so far located that refers to Milldam Grove dates from 1679 when the owner, William Bagshawe refused to pay Lot and Cope [Chats, Dev Coll], claiming that the mine lay within what were called `ancient freeholds` or `free land`, originally granted by King John and free from Crown duties. Milldam Grove was also known as Little Grove, and was at work in 1737, whilst in the same year Little Grove was stated as being *in Hucklow Rake on the Hill-top near Great Hucklow*. Bowman`s Hill Top and also Gateside Grove measured ore in 1734-1736; disputes were heard in the Barmote Court in 1736, 1745 and 1748-1749 concerning Gateside Grove. [Chats, Dev Coll]. Nalls Grove, sometimes called Garden End Grove, was also involved in litigation in the Barmote Court at various dates between 1744 and 1752.

Unfortunately, after 1737 nothing is known about Milldam Mine for over a century. The 19th century history of Milldam Mine, Gateside Mine and Hilltop Mine and Beech Grove was reviewed by Kirkham [1963]. Consolidation of Hilltop Mine and Beech Grove into one title owned by the Great Hucklow Mining Company took place in the mid 19th century. Within their title there were two swallows, one on the north side of the vein at about 240 feet beneath the surface and a lower one about 60 feet deeper. The Milldam Mining Co. was formed about 1855 [Kirkham, 1963], but it seems to have been the autumn of 1857 before serious working got under way. Between the Great Hucklow Co`s. ground and Milldam lay Gateside Mine, the latter obtained by the Milldam Co. in 1858, but only that part below the water level. .At the same time the Milldam Co. acquired Smithy Coe Mine below 50 fathoms, for which privilege they were to pay a royalty of 4/- for each load of ore obtained below that horizon.

A protracted lawsuit soon ensued, pursued by The Great Hucklow Mining Co. against the Milldam Co. The trouble began when water was taken along a *Level or old Drift road* from Milldam Mine, through Gateside Mine, and turned into the lower swallow in Hilltop Mine. The water was originally lifted to this Level by `gin-pumps` [Kirkham, 1963], but she gave no evidence for this statement. If correct it must have been before 1859, because in that year the Milldam Co. installed a combined pumping, winding and crushing engine, rated at 12 horse power, made by Davy Bros. of Sheffield, and which cost £300.

The Great Hucklow Co. at Hilltop Mine and Beech Grove then dammed up their lower swallow, probably in 1861, consequently the lower workings at Milldam Mine were flooded. An un-dated, but mid 19th century section of the disputed mines shows the Great Hucklow Co`s main shaft 596 feet in depth [SCL, Bag 603(3)]. The shaft is not named but it must be the Hilltop Mine Engine Shaft. The water at Hilltop/Beech Grove was lifted by a 14 horse-power steam engine, installed in 1855, then turned into an old shaft, through sumps down to 40 fathoms, were it ran off along the Swallow Gate into the higher swallow. The water was taken from the workings by the Swallow Gate and a plan dated 1861 shows it connecting with an irregular passage, presumably a natural stream passage. A little further east in Gateside Mine, a lime door in Sidingate Vein (a small break on the north side of the main vein), is depicted connecting with a similar irregular passage; both (natural ?) passages then join and run northwards off the plan [Plan, in private possession].

The Milldam miners were forced to consider driving eastwards at a higher level and to drain their water into a swallow in the Smithy Coe title, though unfortunately they did not know its exact position. The Milldam Co. installed a Cornish engine in 1862-1863; for which no details seem to have survived, but it pumped from 75-80 fathoms depth, initially lifting water to the higher water-gate, until agreement

A view of Milldam Mine, Great Hucklow, demolished c. 1874. The pumping shaft was 75 fathoms in depth, but little is known about the engine. This fine drawing was copied from a photograph. (Malcolm Newton)

between the parties was reached in July, 1864 which allowed the swallow in Hilltop Mine to be used again. Milldam Mine had produced some £14,500 of ore, but all that revenue had been swallowed up, plus considerable capital collected from shareholders.

The adjacent Smithy Coe title below 50 fathoms, acquired by the Milldam Co. in 1858, produced over 1,000 loads of ore per annum from 1868 to 1878 and perhaps this `mini-bonanza` persuaded the owners to consider the installation of another Cornish engine in 1870. According to pencil notes made by William Chapman in the mid 20th century quoting depths for various mines in the Hucklow district, Smithy Coe was worked to a total depth of 82 fathoms (492 feet). This depth is coincident with the depth unwatered by the pumps at Milldam Mine [Chats, Bar Coll].

Before the Milldam Co. installed their Cornish Engine all work along this portion of the Hucklow Rake seems to have been carried out above the toadstone. A detailed description and cross-section of the vein, made in the late 1860s at the time the mines were at work, was provided by Green [1869]. The vein is a large fault, the strata downthrown to the north by nearly eighty feet. Toadstone was not met on the north side of the vein until 73-75 fathoms (438-450 feet) from surface, the vein having contracted to only 10 yards in width at that depth. On the upthrow side of the fault, few workings were affected, most of them being at a higher contour than 62 fathoms.

The deep shaft at the Hilltop Mine, sunk to almost 600 feet by the Great Hucklow Mining Co. presumably sometime between 1872 and early 1873, does not seem to be described elsewhere, but the implications are that it was sunk about 150 feet deeper than the Milldam pumping shaft. A pencilled note in the author`s copy of Whitehurst [1786] states:

The Great Hucklow Mining Co. found it [ie. toadstone] *at 73 fathoms in 1864 and it completely upset the mine, no attempt is at present made to sink it through. Wm Chapman, Agent.* [A note above in the same hand gives the date 12th January, 1872].

The Great Hucklow Mining Company raised the pump trees and rods from their shaft in June, 1873 [SCL, Bag 671] and shortly afterwards the Engine House and Boiler House were demolished [Rieuwerts, private collection].

The Milldam Company was soon in great financial difficulties and the Secretary, Horatio Bradwell wrote to the Barmaster in January, 1879 that *the mine cannot pay because of the poorness of the veins and the extent of the `old man`s` workings* – [Chats, Bar Coll] and the mine finally closed in October, 1884. The head gear was taken down in 1895-1896 and in the latter year the shaft collapsed.

WORKINGS BENEATH THE SHALE COVER

EAST OF GREAT HUCKLOW VILLAGE TO GRINDLOW LIBERTY

The preceding sections have demonstrated that west of Great Hucklow village, the vein system, where it outcrops in the limestone, has been exploited from early times. East of the village it passes beneath the cover of shale; various dates have been given for the first exploitation in that direction, perhaps about 1650 might be approximately correct. Certainly by 1676 the miners had progressed at least 250 yards beyond the shale outcrop, through the Milldam and Greenhead (Smithy Coe) titles. The vein was gradually pursued through Grindlow Liberty and was freed in Eyam Liberty in 1711-1712. Nellie Kirkham believed that Milldam Mine and both Old Edge and New Edge groves drained into Dowse Hole, the latter by means of shale gates. This hypothesis, accepted in the first edition of this work [1987] for Old Edge and New Edge groves does not now appear to be correct. More likely, drainage was provided by water-gates discharging into swallow holes in the vein and possibly by a cross-cut sough driven from the side of the trackway leading from Great Hucklow to Little Hucklow. Shale gates may have existed, but if so they were more likely to have been used largely for purposes of locating traces of the vein-head some 120-150 feet beneath the contour of any mine level driven from Dowse Hole.

SOUGH TO GREENHEAD GROVE

The late Nellie Kirkham, in a general article discussing the drainage of Derbyshire lead mines [1954] noted:

An old trackway runs from Great Hucklow to Little Hucklow and in a field by this there is a

Above: A tracery of very fine pickwork in the Breakholes – Old Grove mines beneath Masson Hill, Matlock Bath. The work dates from the 15th or early 16th century (Paul Deakin).

Left: Hillocks derived from very shallow shafts excavated on a boxwork of small scrins. Whitelow Mines, Bonsall Moor (J.H.Rieuwerts).

A short and very small section, hand-picked level in the Breakholes – Old Grove mines, Masson Hill, Matlock Bath. The level probably dates from the 16th century (Paul Deakin).

Above: A classic example of fire setting within a pipe or flat-type deposit in the Northerndale Pipe or Lords and Ladies Mine, Snitterton (Paul Deakin).

Opencast scrins, Pindale, Castleton. The lead workings date from the 17th century (J.H.R.ieuwerts).

The Dun Rake branch level from Longe Sough or Cromford Sough. Driven through shale into the underlying limestones, it probably dates from about 1661-1663 (Paul Deakin).

Oxclose Old Sough or Crowholt Level, Snitterton. A mid 17th century hand-picked drainage level. They are often known to modern explorers as *coffin levels* (Paul Deakin).

Hadings in Harrybecca Mine, Hassop Common (J.H.Rieuwerts).

Steeply inclining *Hadings* in Harrybecca Mine (Paul Deakin).

The well-known Cartgate in Oden Mine, Castleton. The gate dates from the second half of the 18th century. Much of the floor and the vein beneath was stoped away in later times (Paul Deakin).

Another view of the Cartgate in Oden Mine, this portion in original condition (Paul Deakin).

A view looking up 'Leviathan' from just above the 'Boulder Piles' in the Speedwell Mine stream caverns. Note the long stemples; both they and the dressing floor were referred to by James Plumtree during his exploration of the mine in 1793 (Paul Deakin).

Underground dressing floor situated part way down the enormous 'Leviathan' cavern in New Rake, Castleton. This portion of the rake was worked in the 1750s by James Hall and partners, but was later worked as part of the Speedwell Mine title (Paul Deakin).

The stream passage in Speedwell Mine. Part of the streamway was covered by a planked haulage way used to convey ore and deads to the boats (Paul Deakin).

Sunken boat in the far canal in Speedwell Mine (Paul Deakin).

Moorwood Sough, here driven along the sole of Ashton's Pipe between Middleton Dale and Cliffe Stile Mine. This part of the sough was driven in the period 1795-1802 (Paul Deakin).

A late 20th century drivage along the top of the Cressbrook Dale Lava near Ladywash Mine. The mine was then being worked for fluorspar (Paul Deakin).

A steeply hading vein in the Samuel Mine – Slack Rake system beneath Middleton Moor, Middleton-byWirksworth (Paul Deakin).

water trough and marshy land in direct line with a shaft mound close by and just above are other mounds in a direct line up the rising ground towards Milldam and Greenhead Mines and which could have drained them over 100 feet.

Later, in a detailed article on the Hucklow mines, she made no reference to it [Kirkham, 1963] so that it is not possible to be sure if further field work and consideration had led her to reject the idea. Current field work is not very rewarding. The marshy hollow and trough are still in existence, but there do not appear to be any shaft mounds close by and none can be seen *in a direct line up the rising ground*. The hillocks at Shale Grove (or Gorse Bush Mine) still exist, but they are some 1,800 feet from the supposed sough tail. Nevertheless, there was a sough at Greenhead Grove and which was in existence by 1682, for in that year it was proposed to extend it to Old Edge Grove, situated immediately to the east of Greenhead title. Presumably water from it must have discharged into an underground swallow above the level of Greenhead Sough. A large swallow is depicted in the eastern end of Smithy Coe (Greenhead) Mine on a mid 19th century section of the Great Hucklow mines [SCL, Bag 603].

SOUGH TO OLD EDGE GROVE

The Old Edge Groves, consisting of four meers of ground, were purchased by John Bagshawe and partners in August, 1676. The meers were described as lying at the forefield of Hucklow Edge Old Vein [SCL, Bag 549]. He owned a 1/4th share in the venture, Ralph James, a miner from Grindlow also owned a 1/4th share, but he became in debt and in due course his share passed to Bagshawe. There is a hint, though nowhere explicitly stated, that the four meers were originally set on work by James.

The partners at Old Edge Grove made an agreement in September, 1682 *with Mr. Radcliffe and his partners at a mine called Greenhead Groves and who had a Sough for un-watering the same - for the liberty and benefit of a watergate for the unwatering of the Hucklow Edge Grove*. Mr. Radcliffe was give a 1/4th part of the four meers at Old Edge Grove for the use and extension of the sough from Greenhead [PRO, DL 1/461]. Miners were recruited to sink the shaft, at very great expense, the venture being *looked upon to be a very bold and hazardous undertaking*

the expense being so great and the hazard so much. [PRO, DL 1/461].

The shaft cost about £150-£160 to complete. Little ore was found, so a drift was driven through the shale towards the north and this located the parallel Hucklow Edge North Vein. Later, the workings in the North Vein merged back into those of the old South Vein and the Barmote jury gave several verdicts that the two were part of the Hucklow Edge Vein and merely separated by a rider. A great deal of litigation ensued, principally involved with disputed ownership of several taker meers set in the random of the two supposed veins [PRO, DL 1/462]. The next fifteen years (1683 to 1698) saw 7,400 loads of lead ore mined within the title *with hand labour only, no engines*. The charges incurred during the same period amounted to £4,063. The absence of a horse-gin is remarkable given the depth worked.

SOUGH TO NEW EDGE GROVE

About 1697, deeper drainage for the Old Edge Grove and drainage for the next meers lying to the east, known as New Edge Grove was in contemplation. Mr. Ashton and his partners took four meers of ground in October, 1697, continuing eastwardly from the meers belonging to Old Edge Grove [SCL, Bag 549]. Bagshawe and partners made an agreement with the partners at New Edge Grove, or Ashton`s Groves:

whereas the mines of Ashton and partners are overburdened with water and in need of a shaft, Bagshawe and partners will drive a watergate from a place called Greenhead Gound at the east end of Burnditch – until they come to the west end of Ashtons groves [DRO, 394Z/B1].

The level to Ashton Groves, also begun at the Greenhead boundary, must refer to the deeper level. New Edge Grove mined 3,100 loads of ore between October, 1697 and September, 1701. Both Old Edge and New Edge groves continued to produce moderate quantities of ore annually until 1711. This first phase of working in the upper limestone beneath the shale cover then declined rapidly and by 1714 their combined total was only 145 loads [SCL, OD 1505].

Kirkham [1963] believed that both Old Edge and New Edge groves were drained by shale gate soughs driven from Dowse Hole. She noted slight mounds in two enclosures between the mines and Dowse Hole, which she thought were the sites of shafts sunk on the line of the two soughs. The evidence presented in this current account must now throw serious doubt on this proposition. There is a possibility that a shale gate was driven towards Old Edge Grove, not for drainage purposes, but to locate the vein-head buried deep beneath the shale cover. If correct, then it must date from c1676 and thus pre-dates the shale gates driven to prove the eastwardly range of the Hucklow Edge, or Eyam Edge Vein by at least thirty five years and it would be the earliest example known in the Derbyshire orefield.

HAVE-AT-ALL SOUGH

Ashton and partners followed the continuation of the great vein system eastwards toward Grindlow Lordship. Lying next east from New Edge or Ashtons Groves was the Gorse Bush title containing four meers of ground, Mr. John Rotherham, George Bennett and John Lee were the principal shareholders. The last mine in Hucklow Liberty was Have-at-All, the shaft being about 870 feet to the east of New Grove shaft. Immediately beyond, the vein passed into Grindlow (sometimes referred to as Greenlow) Liberty. Have-at-All Mine was in production by 1711, concurrent with the demise of New Edge Grove, and ore output peaked at 3,598 loads of grove ore, exclusive of Lot, in 1712. Production declined significantly in 1713 and 1714 [SCL, OD 1505].

Little is known about drainage arrangements. A continuation of the Old Grove-New Grove sough system appears unlikely at this early date, there being no documentary evidence, yet only very limited drainage could have been provided by a shale gate sough driven from Dowse Hole. A legal agreement, catalogued by Sheffield Archives as being permission to drive a sough through the lands of Mr. Wright of Eyam, to drain Have-at-All Mine, dated 1711, is incorrect [SCL, Bag 712]. The document is dated March, 1711 (i.e. 1712). Have-at-All Mine is referred to solely in the context of its being the most eastwardly mine in Hucklow Liberty and that the miners believed that the vein worked at the mine and also mines within Greenlow (Grindlow) Lordship would range through into Eyam Lordship. The anticipated continuation of the vein into Eyam encouraged fourteen partners, who *are minded to adventure – which be suggested not to bee feisible without a Sough or Drain to unwater and lay drye the same* – [but] – *agree* – (to drive it) *thorow the ground of John Wright of Eyam – called*

ffoolow pasture – The agreement continues:

> *the said Sough upon the finding or discovering of the said Grove or Lead Mine called Have-at-All or any other Grove or Groves, vein or veins, Lead Mine or Lead Mines in driving or carrying on the said Sough shall have been entitled to and enjoy such parts therein as they pay and beare in the said Sough to bee driven.*

Quite clearly this is not an agreement for draining Have-at-All Mine, but one describing construction of a sough through Foolow Pasture and the distribution of shares, as and when the Have-at-All vein (i.e. Hucklow Edge Vein) and its continuation through Grindlow should be found within Eyam Lordship. This document relates to the Old Grove Sough (see Eyam Edge section of this work).

HAVE-AT-ALL LEVEL

Not a sough, but a level driven in shale through Hucklow Edge to the head of Bretton Clough where it tapped a spring of water. During 1869 a legal dispute arose concerning the original use and purpose of the level. The miners maintained that the level had been driven by the original owners of the mine as a water supply for ore washing purposes. The landowners counterclaimed that they believed it had been made at the expense of their forbears as a water supply for Great Hucklow and had been repaired by the ratepayers for at least the previous eighty years [SCL, Bag 3439]. The entrance has collapsed, but access is possible for a short distance.

THE MINES WITHIN GRINDLOW LIBERTY OR LORDSHIP

Three major mines worked the Hucklow Edge Vein within this liberty. From west to east these were Bank Grove, Speed Grove and Silence Grove. Bank Grove being the nearest to Hucklow Liberty was the first to be exploited and production began in 1712. Output in 1713 reached a peak of over 4,550 loads of grove ore, plus 2,300 loads of hillock ore, all exclusive of Lot. Total production of saleable ore from 1712 to 1714 was 8,000 loads of grove ore and 3,180 loads of hillock ore [SCL OD 1505].

Ore production at Speed Grove commenced in

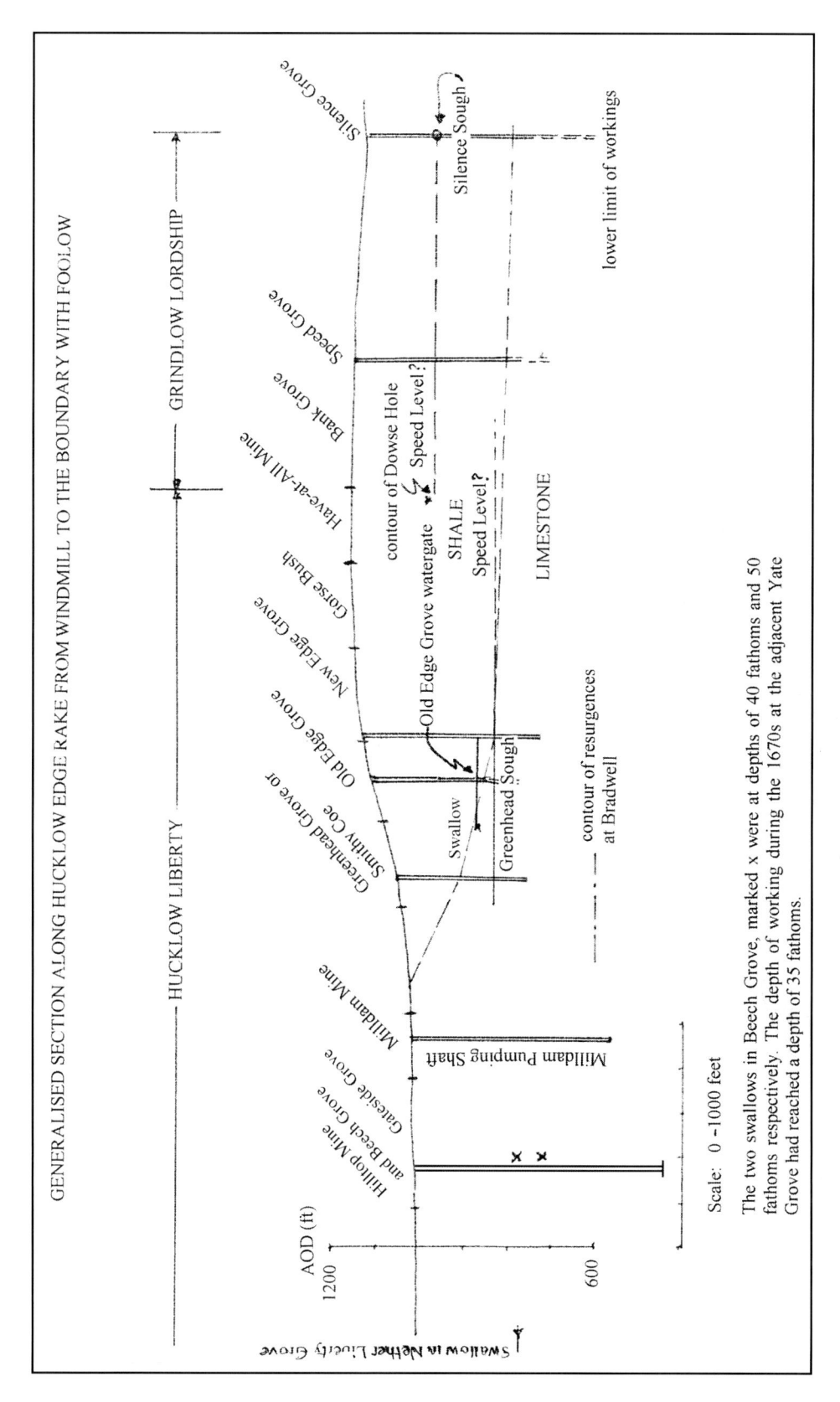

5. The Mines of Tideslow Rake and Hucklow Edge Rake

GENERALISED SECTION ALONG HUCKLOW EDGE RAKE FROM WINDMILL TO THE BOUNDARY WITH FOOLOW

HUCKLOW LIBERTY — GRINDLOW LORDSHIP

Features labelled (left to right): Swallow in Nether Liberty Grove; Hilltop Mine and Beech Grove; Gateside Grove; Milldam Mine; Milldam Pumping Shaft; Greenhead Grove or Smithy Coe; Old Edge Grove; Swallow; Greenhead Sough; New Edge Grove; Gorse Bush; Have-at-All Mine; Bank Grove; Old Edge Grove watergate; contour of Dowse Hole; Speed Level?; Speed Grove; Speed Level?; SHALE; LIMESTONE; Silence Grove; Silence Sough; lower limit of workings; contour of resurgences at Bradwell.

AOD (ft): 1200, 600

Scale: 0 – 1000 feet

The two swallows in Beech Grove, marked x were at depths of 40 fathoms and 50 fathoms respectively. The depth of working during the 1670s at the adjacent Yate Grove had reached a depth of 35 fathoms.

99

1713 and at Silence Grove in 1714; at the former output was just respectable, but at Silence 2,235 loads of grove ore were measured, plus 580 loads of hillock ore. Through to 1722 the Grindlow mines were still producing considerable quantities of ore, but after 1723 there was a steady decline at all three and they became only medium sized mines, certainly until December, 1733 when the output accounts cease.

No references to the drainage of Bank Grove or Speed Grove in the first two decades of the 18th century have been seen, but if they and Have-at-All Mine drained into Dowse Hole, then their shale gates could have acted only as pumpways for water lifted by horse gins, assisted by hand pumping at deeper levels. Silence Grove enjoyed its own shale-gate sough.

The Grindlow mines were the scene of considerable litigation during the 1730s and serious riots occurred between the miners and representatives of the Lords of the Field. The disputes have been dealt with in some detail by Kirkham [1964]. The very voluminous evidence relating to these disputes contains some comments about drainage difficulties. By 1734, or thereabouts, the lower workings were greatly troubled with water, but about 1738 the mines were looking forward to the:

> *prospect of being very soon relieved of ye water - by means of a Sough or Levell that is now bringing up (and) would in a short time unwater and lay dry the deepest soles.*

This cannot refer to any potential relief from Stoke Sough at such an early date. Deep drainage provided by Stoke Sough was only partially achieved even in the mid-18th century. Similarly, Magclough Sough, its forefield still several thousand feet to the east, could not have provided any immediate benefit. Perhaps a continuation of the Greenhead Sough beyond Old Edge Grove and New Edge Grove was in contemplation, but likely nothing was done for half a century when Speed Level holed into Have-at-All Mine in 1763 [SCL, Bag 587/44].

(* see also under Middleton Engine Sough)

SPEED LEVEL

The only documentary references to the Level occur in reckonings relating to Stoke Sough. None of the work appears relevent to events at Stoke Sough and quite why this shale sough was important to them is a mystery.

During October, 1760 driving began at Speed Level, the cost being 5/- per fathom, so obviously excavation must have been through shale. In January, 1762 there is an unexplained item: *Michael Simpson garding the Water from Dowse Hole* [SCL, Bag 391]. After a driveage of 1176 feet they were: *Making a Water Mark at Have-at-All* and an entry in July, 1763 reads: *Given the Workmen for getting a hole through to Have-at-All, 5/-*

The position of the Level is not known, only two solutions seem feasible; either a shale gate sough driven west from Silence Sough, or a continuation of Greenhead Sough eastwards beyond the New Edge Grove title. The latter hypothesis is the more attractive, but there is no supporting documentary evidence. If begun from a forefield at the eastern extremity of the New Edge meers, then 1176 feet would terminate close to Speed Engine Shaft, but well beyond Have-at-All Mine.

Until 1763 when references cease, Speed Level had been driven 1440 feet, always at 5/- per fathom.

SILENCE SOUGH

A shale-gate sough and pumpway for which no documentary evidence seems to have survived. The level was probably driven sometime during the years 1710–1712. Kirkham [1964] recorded seeing the tail section re-opened by the farmer; it had a flat roof of shale, propped at intervals of a few feet by larch poles, but it ran-in again soon afterwards. The sough intersected the mine at a depth of 27 fathoms (162 feet) after a driveage of a little over 1,200 feet. Silence Mine was worked to a depth of 526 feet, 328 feet being in shale and 198 feet -within the limestone. The mine was greatly troubled by water by 1734, but in about 1738 there appeared the curious statement that there was *a prospect of being very soon relieved of ye water – by means of a Sough or Levell that is now bringing up*. This cannot refer to any sough driven at high level in the shale, or an optimistic forecast about the westward progress of either Stoke Sough or Magclough Sough. The only feasible explanation appears to be a proposed extension of the deeper sough from New Edge Grove referred to under Speed Level.

MINES WITHIN EYAM LIBERTY

Previous historical accounts of lead mining and soughing beneath Eyam Edge, by Hopkinson, Kirkham and the present author, have contained inaccuracies of varying magnitude. The dates quoted for the first exploitation of the Hucklow Edge Vein within Eyam Liberty are incorrect, but the major omission has been the failure by all three authors to realise the presence of a major vein breaking southeastwards from the Hucklow Edge Vein at Middleton Engine Mine. Kirkham [1965] stated that before the main vein was discovered in Eyam Liberty, some mines, such as Miners Engine and Little Pasture were already working on veins to the south; this is not correct.

The first mine sunk into the the Hucklow Edge Vein within Eyam Liberty was Old Grove, or *Have-at-a-Venture;* proceeding eastwardly the succeeding mines were New Grove, or Butlers Old Engine, Slaters Engine, or Butlers New Grove, Bradshaws Grove, Morewood Engine, Milns Engine (or Black Engine) and the Middleton Engine Grove or Mine. Butlers mines and Bradshaws were consolidated into one title at an early period, being usually referred to as `Old, New and Bradshaw`s. They were sometimes also known as the `Foolow Mines` [Guildhall, Marples Papers].

The many mines worked along the vein and its branches proved to be exceedingly rich, for example when first found at Old Grove in Eyam Liberty it was described as being twenty feet in width *well filled with oar.* The reckoning account for Old Grove Sough records that when *symptoms* of the vein were first found in the forefield, the possession stows already set were checked and consisted of 69 meers in the south vein and 70 meers in the north vein. These meers in Middleton Engine Old Vein (= Hucklow Edge Vein) terminated at the eastern end of Middleton Engine possessions; the last 12 meers within the 69/70 meers on the vein were subsequently allocated to Miners Engine title. Richard Bagshawe and partners were said to have owned the Miners Engine title before 1720 and Little Pasture had the next 9 meers [Wolley 6677 ff.61-62; ff. 203-212].

Research has established that beyond Middleton Engine Grove, all the Barmaster`s title entries and freeings made between 1715 and 1720–1721 relate to *Middleton Engine New Vein,* a branch from the Old Vein ranging south eastwards. This passed through lower Miners Engine (Old Twelve Meers), Little Pasture Mine, Haycliffe Mine in Gregory`s Plantation, Old Ladywash Shaft and Brookhead Founder Shaft.

The presumed extension of Middleton Engine Old Vein (Hucklow Edge Vein), beyond (upper) Miners Engine, was found c.1721 by *the second cross-cut driven by Francis Drable an Agent --- at Little Pasture about Eighty Yards, above twenty years ago, in order to discover Middleton Engine Old Vein* -[PRO, C12 1131/2]. A little later similar cross cuts proved this vein from within Haycliffe and Ladywash titles. When in 1736 a break vein was discovered at Miners Engine, numerous complicated arguments arose in deciding which was the new break and which was the Middleton Engine Old Vein. The Barmote Jury changed their minds on more than one occasion, this with all the financial and ownership implications depending on their decision. Kirkham [1965–1966] discussed the ensuing complicated legal debates in some detail, but unfortunately, she missed several important facts resulting in mis-interpretations. Many of her conclusions were copied by this author, thus compounding the errors.

Returning now to earlier matters, the New Vein at Middleton Engine Grove was freed for `old` or `new` on the 10th March, 1715 and 26 meers were taken ranging eastwards and 44 meers westwards to the Grindlow boundary. In the following month 16 meers were set for Little Pasture or *Mr. Ashton`s Haycliffe* as takers at Middleton Engine`s stows. Haycliffe Grove, or *Helen Mower`s Haycliffe* title lay to the east followed by the possessions belonging to Ladywash Grove. A fine plan of the Eyam and Foolow mines, drawn by Samuel Hutchinson about 1715 shows the line of the vein, but at that date nothing is shown beyond Middleton Engine ground, so presumably it pre-dates April, 1715 [SCL, Bag 181]. The most eastern title on the vein belonged to Brookhead Grove who set 40 possessions extending from Ladywash title as far as the *Stoke Wall.*

Examination of the remaining hillocks at Haycliffe Mine reveals a large quantity of vein-stone, intimately mixed with dark grey shale, strongly suggesting that the vein was worked up into the shale. The miners faced problems in working New Vein so that in December, 1716 an agreement was drawn reciting that:

in consideration of the great charges and trials at the Little Pasture called Mr. Ashton`s Haycliffe and Hellins Moor haycliffe being upon the east side – and the Ladywash being on the east, takers at Hellens Moor Haycliffe -- it is agreed between Mr. Ashton – at the Little Pasture and Mr. Robert Clay – at Hellens Moor haycliffe and

Mr. Robert Middleton at the Ladywash –it is agreed that Mr. Ashtons Haycliffe shall be worked with all speed – and that Hellins Moor Haycliffe and Ladywash shall pay two third parts of the wages at Mr. Ashton`s Haycliffe - until such time as the ore shall be found there - [DRO, D 3304, Robinson].

The vein system running beneath Eyam Edge was worked in the Eyam Limestone and Monsal Dale Limestone above the Cressbrook Dale Lava. Recent underground work carried out principally by Laporte Chemicals has established that lead ore was not worked beneath the lava. The cover of shale lying over the limestone increases eastwards so that the shafts at the extreme eastern end of the Edge were amongst the deepest in Derbyshire, 900 feet to over 1,000 feet at Ladywash Mine and New Engine Mine. The miners` method of tracing the course of the vein beneath the shale has been discussed by several writers, eg. Hopkinson, Kirkham, Willies and Rieuwerts. Shale gate soughs were driven from the lower ground at the southern foot of the Edge, at a right-angle to the presumed alignment of the vein. Usually, the presence of the vein beneath was revealed by sparry leaders in the shale, these termed by the miners *symptoms* or *mudds,* the latter term apparently unique to the Eyam Edge mines.

Virtually all of the many plans of the Eyam Edge mines drawn between 1735 and 1780 show the shale-gate soughs beginning only from the engine shafts on the lower slopes of the hill, omitting the first sections from the tail to those shafts. It is not clear from either the plans, or other documentation whether they were continuous at the same contour, or whether the northward extensions were driven from a deeper horizon within the mines. One plan calls all of them, from Old Grove to Old Ladywash, *A Drift made at (mine) in search for the Hucklow Edge or Haveadventure Vein* [DRO, BSA LM/D/69]. The plans depict virtually all of the horse-gins protected within a single storied building, most roofed with thatch, the doors protected by stout locks.

Deep drainage of the Eyam Edge mines by Stoke Sough and partially by Magclough Sough, also the drainage offered by natural caverns and water-courses will be discussed later under the headings of those two sough levels. The setting of *Water-marks* by the Eyam Barmote jurors for composition payments at all the mines along the Edge in 1733 will also be discussed.

OLD GROVE SOUGH, FOOLOW EDGE SOUGH, THE MINERS SOUGH

Richeard Bagshawe and partners began work at Old Grove, or Haveadventur in the spring of 1712. An agreement dated March, 1712 begins *severall Veins, Groves or Lead Mines may – range – out of the Lordship of Greenlow and in time be workt into the Lordship of Eyam* [SCL, Bag 712]. Plainly before that date no work had commenced in Eyam. Bagshawe then:

sunk a shaft and gates and discovered a vein and proved it to be all one and the same vein that was brought through Hucklow and Grindlow liberties and worked it eastward in their title. A group of wealthy `adventures` formed a partnership and were *minded to adventure – in the Groves or Lead Mines wch be suppos'd`not to bee feisible without a Sough or Drain to Unwater and lay drye the same – wch (they) agreed to doe thorow the ground of John Wright of Eyam, Gent. lying in ffolow called ffolow pasture* [SCL, Bag 712].

The document continues that after the vein had been found the partners were to enjoy the benefits in proportion to the costs they had borne in the construction of the sough. This level can be identified with Old Grove Sough, it being also known as Foolow Edge Sough and on one plan as `The Miner`s Sough` [SCL, Bag 181]. The sough had been begun slightly before the agreement was signed, the reckoning book recording *February 9th, 1711 (*ie. 1712*) - Fowlow Edge - They began the sough.*

The next entry was *for trenching* clearly a reference to cutting a trench to form the bolt section of the sough tail. Six miners were employed, some were employed in shaft sinking. Beyond the bolt section, the first 100 fathoms were driven at a cost of only 2/6d per fathom, reflecting the ease of driving through the soft shales. Thereafter, bargains rose steadily from 4/- per fathom, then 9/- per fathom. As the sough was pushed northwards beneath an increasing depth of shale, under levels were driven and sweep pumps and churn pumps were used to lift water into the sough. Rather more difficult to explain are references to two *Upper Levells,* one called the *Upper most level* and also a *Middle levell* and *Under Levell,* or *Nether levell* all driven through shale.

The reckoning book notes on July 18th, 1713:

This reckoning we found the oare in the shiver and on July 22nd I viewed all the stoces on the north runs and – for this south vein just discovered 69 pairs of possessions and for the north leading 70 pairs. – Agreed with the partners at Fowloe Edge that Richard Bagshawe, Benjamin Ashton and Charles Potts shall be at one half of the charge at sinking the shafts from the founder and sumps and gates down to the vein – the miners to bring up the Levell to the Shaft at their own charge.

Shiver was the miners` term for shale [Rieuwerts, 1998]. By the early August reckoning they had found the top of the vein and were to work three shifts. The cost of the sough from the beginning to September, 1713 amounted to £459-3-0, but the total cost of the undertaking was very nearly £634. The length of the level was 1,900 feet, the Old Grove shaft being 50 fathoms in depth, or to the base of the shale.

BUTLERS OLD ENGINE SOUGH, NEW GROVE SOUGH

A shale-gate sough about which nothing is known historically except that it must have been driven soon after Old Grove Sough, no doubt for the purpose of locating the vein-head further to the east. The sough is marked on George Langstaffe`s very rough sketch of the Eyam Edge soughs and allocation of meers, dated July, 1736 [SCL, Bag 587/63].

BUTLERS NEW ENGINE SOUGH, SLATERS ENGINE SOUGH

Rather more is known about this sough than the preceding one. Shown on Langstaffe`s plan, a portion of the course of the sough is also shown on two mine plans dated 1790 and 1861 respectively [SCL, Bag 202; 377]. The sough ranged almost due north from the Foolow–Bretton road (Bradshaw Lane) to the mine and an ochery spring at the road side is stated to have been the tail. This cannot be correct because the shale gate was at the base of a shaft, 8 fathoms in depth at this point. The sough therefore must have been driven from very close to Waterfall Swallow, some 770 yards to the south east of Bradshaw Lane. The 8 fathom shaft was known in the 19th century as Nether Slaters. The plan dated 1861 marks a Firehouse on the north side of the hillock, used no doubt to facilitate ventilation in the shale gates and upper workings.

BRADSHAWS ENGINE SOUGH

Again, no historical details are available save for Langstaffe`s crude plan, but it must have been driven as a shale gate sometime during the years 1712-1714. The water must have discharged into the drain taking water from the other soughs to the west, toward Waterfall Swallow.

MOREWOOD ENGINE SOUGH

Another shale-gate sough, this driven into Morewood Engine Mine. Known only from George Langstaffe`s 1736 plan. Four Barmote jurymen were sent into the shale gate in October, 1721, but could find no sign of mineralisation in the shale. The workings at the mine had reached a depth of 483 feet by the 1740s, but the engine shaft was only 173 feet in depth [SCL, Bag 539].

MILLNS ENGINE SOUGH; BLACK ENGINE SOUGH

Kirkham [1953] was of the opinion that the bolts from Bradshaws Engine, Morewood Engine and Millns Engine shale gate soughs all joined, before continuing as a communal drain into Waterfall Swallow. On the same day as the jurymens` examination in Morewood Engine Sough, the same men examined the shale sough at Milnes Engine and some 200 yards south from the Engine Shaft *said there was a firm vene with mud and cavil and oare about a handful thick.* [DRO, D3304, Robinson]. (Cavil = a general name for vein-stuff or gangue [Rieuwerts, 1998]). During 1725 the mine produced 1520 loads of ore. The profits at Black Engine from 1748–1759 amounted to £3814 [SCL, Bag 587/80].

MIDDLETON ENGINE SOUGH

Middleton Engine Grove was freed in March, 1715 [SCL, Bag 517], so the shale-gate sough was probably begun in early 1714, though no historical details appear to have survived. The sough is marked on George Langstaffe`s plan dated July, 1736. The sough tail is situated at a trough situated some 250 feet north of Waterfall Swallow, from where it runs north eastwards to the mine, intersecting it at a depth of about 150 feet below the surface. The level must have been driven entirely in shale for a distance of approximately 1970 feet. A curious statement dated June, 1738 recites that: *It is believed the Level carried forward from Middleton Engine will settle the Water at Grindlow mines several fathoms which I have ordered to be tried to-morrow* -[SCL, Spencer Stanhope, 60506/67]. Middleton Engine Sough, if continued westwards in the shale, but along the line of the vein, and assuming little loss in contour, could have provided only 30 feet to 60 feet additional drainage beneath Silence Sough, and then only from the shale formation. The very limited benefit from such a scheme, in relationship to the great volume of work involved, is difficult to understand.

In 1738 it was stated that at Middleton Engine the horses drew forty barrels of bouse each working day [SCL, OD 1505]. The earliest reference to the use of edged boards so far located at a Derbyshire lead mine occurs at Milnes and Middleton Engine in December, 1748. These were wooden planks with a raised edge, thus forming an `L` shape and were used as plateways in early cartgates. The *wharle*, a primitive aerial ropeway described by Hooson in 1747 [Rieuwerts, 1998] is also first recorded at the mine, this in June, 1753 [SCL, Bag 379]. There was a Firehouse at Middleton Engine, referred to only in April, 1750, but with no accompanying detail.

MINERS ENGINE SOUGH

Driven in shale from the shallow gully north east of Little Waterfall, for a distance of 410 yards to the lower Miners Engine Shaft (Old Twelve Meers Mine). The sough is shown on Langstaffe`s rough plan; the only other reference dates from March, 1745 when the Level was repaired – *from the Sough taile to ye Engine shaft – 410 yards* [SCL, Bag 660]. The lower Miners Engine shaft was found to be in poor condition, when examined in the mid 20th century. Sometime after 1720 the shale gate was extended northwards to the Hucklow Edge Vein (Middleton Engine Old Vein). At upper Miners Engine (Twelve Meers Mine), one Engine Shaft bottomed in shale at 300 feet, it was noted as being 49 fathoms in depth in September, 1742. The total depth of the workings reached 616 feet. The adjacent shaft was investigated to a depth of 500 feet, but trouble was then experienced with instability of the shale walls [Dunham, 1952].

The mine was very rich, for example in 1725, some 2,976 loads were obtained, whilst from 1733 to 1736 10,760 loads of ore were sold; in one week in September, 1743 over 1,000 loads were raised. During 1743 forty one men were mining ore in cope gangs [Rieuwerts, 1981].

LITTLE PASTURE SOUGH, LITTLE (`OLD`) PASTURE SOUGH

The rough sketch plan of the soughs serving the Eyam Edge mines [SCL, Bag 587/63] shows only one sough to Little Pasture Mine, this equates to Kirkham`s `Old Pasture Sough`. Unfortunately, as with many of the Eyam Edge shale-gate soughs, little, or no contemporary documentation is available. Little Pasture Grove was known originally as *Mr. Ashton`s Haycliffe* and was freed in April, 1715, so again, the sough was begun at, or a little before this date. The tail is situated at sunken troughs in Well-field. Kirkham [1953] noted a line of sinking dirt mounds marking the line of `Old` Pasture Sough from the troughs to the Engine Shaft. The distance is 1,158 feet, all in shale. She also stated that the sough from Little Pasture Mine drained into the troughs.

About 1720-1721, Francis Drabble, the agent at Little Pasture and described as *a very Skillful Miner*, drove a shale gate northwards from the mine and discovered the continuation of the Miners Engine Break Vein, (during the great lawsuits of the 1740s–1750s, it was sometimes considered to be Hucklow Edge Vein). This exploratory shale gate may have been an extension to the original sough. During 1720 no less 2,181 loads of ore were raised, whilst from 1721 to 1724 profits amounted to a staggering £6,976.

The mine became well known nationally during the Lisbon earthquake of November, 1755, when the shocks were felt in some of the Eyam mines and the reckoning house at Little Pasture was slightly damaged [Phil. Trans, 1755]. The two-storey building still standing at the mine is almost certainly the original reckoning house.

HAYCLIFFE SOUGH

More is known about this sough, Old Grove Sough, Ladywash Sough and Brookhead Sough than any of the other shale gates driven to the Eyam Edge mines, due to survival of reckonings for all four.

The precise position of the sough tail is not known. Between Haycliffe (Gregory`s) Plantation and Town

Head troughs, there is much wet and marshy ground, some of it badly disturbed. However, a comparison of the water marks made at Haycliffe Mine in 1733 with surface contours suggests that the tail lies at about 850 feet above OD, very close to the troughs. The sough ranged almost due north for a distance of 1,150 feet to a climbing shaft, of which all that remains is a small upstanding mound, topped by a run-in shaft hollow. The sough continued for another 250 feet to the Haycliffe Engine-Shaft, also run-in. There is no trace of the gin-circle, it having been removed by fluorspar hillocking that has virtually destroyed the entire site. A shale-gate crosscut was driven from the engine shaft for a distance of 850 feet to a point near the Ladywash North-East Vein rither point. Whether this crosscut was at the same contour as the old sough, or at a somewhat deeper horizon, is not known. This latter level, or perhaps a yet deeper shale gate, was then continued northwards towards Broadlow Mine.

The available reckonings for Haycliffe Sough cover the short period between early July and early December, 1714 [SCL, OD 1149]. Richard Bagshawe owned a 1/12th share in the sough and mine. The first driveage record relates to 50 yards being excavated at only 2/6d per yard, the very low price probably reflecting construction of the bolt and/or the initial underground section of the sough. There follows three more payments for *sinking and driving* a total of 141 yards. The total cost of the sough during these few months amounted to £65-8-6.

Haycliffe Mine was famous for its explosive slickensides, known to the miners as *cracking-hole,* or *looking-glass*. First recorded at the mine by Short [1734], a significant explosion took place there in 1738, at which time one natural blast detached approximately 40 tons of material from the vein walls; several other explosions were noted in later years.

An un-dated section of that part of the mine worked in Hucklow Edge Vein (actually Old Edge Vein) shows a cartgate entering the mine from Little Pasture to the west, driven along the vein throughout the 11 meers of the title, extending into the Ladywash ground on the east. The cartgate declines from west to east. Sumps descend beneath the cartgate to, and in places, below the standing water level. Beneath the soles the vein was very *shackey*. The sloping shale-limestone interface is also clearly marked [SCL, Bag 587/63].

The mine reckoning book makes reference to several interesting items including *Paid Little Pasture Mine for 9 mettle Knockstones at 16/- each* in April, 1772, in 1773 to the *Long Cartgate* and the *Nether Cartgate*. Other entries include a reference in December, 1781 to *The New Shale Tryal* and in June, 1782 to *Sinking and Driving in the First Mudd* and the *Second Mudd,* these are late usage of the word [SCL, Bag 387]. The mine had a Fire-House in 1768, presumably this must have been either over the climbing shaft in Gregory`s Plantation, or a shallow shaft at the side of the Engine Shaft, the latter with suitable ventilation trap-doors above the thurl. Haycliffe Mine, like the others on Eyam Edge, was very rich, though details are incomplete. However, from June, 1736 until December, 1756 the profits amounted to £6,755-12-0; from March, 1756 to June, 1759, profit was £1,537-10-0. The year 1796 saw £1,049-0-0 realised [SCL, Bag 587/70].

OLD LADYWASH SOUGH

Old Ladywash Sough or shale gate was begun on the 15th January, 1714 [SCL, Bag 587/15]. Nellie Kirkham [1966] believed that the tail was situated on the 850 feet OD contour, on the east side of Jumber Brook, about 500 feet north of the Royal Oak Inn at Eyam Townhead. This position had been pointed out to her by Edwin Maltby, an old Eyam lead miner, whose family had long been associated with the industry. Distances driven in the sough in the year 1714, suggest that the tail must have been further south and at a lower contour. A flow of water feeds into stone troughs at the lower end of Edgeside (Hawkhill) Road and this would be a far more likely position for the sough tail. From the tail the sough ranged northwards, all in shale, for some 1,050 feet to Old Ladywash Shaft, or the Old Ladywash Coe on the Common. A distance of at least 1,032 feet were driven in 1714, so the level had reached the shaft by the end of the first year. An intermediate shaft was sunk near the sharp bend in the road, nearly 500 feet from the sough entrance, and would have been about 50 feet in depth. There is no obvious surface trace of the shaft. Kirkham [1966] states that there were two shafts on Old Ladywash Mine, one a gin shaft, the other stepped, *or as the miner expresses it, they hopped-it*. This term has not been seen in any other mining book or document. The depth to the sough at Old Ladywash is about 130 feet.

Total expenses, including driving, shaft sinking and materials, until the end of December, 1714 were £107-15-4 [SCL, Bag 587/15; OD 1149]. The potential success of the adventure can be gleaned from the purchase by Charles Turner of Swanwick of a 1/48th share in October, 1715 for £61, the value placed on the sough and mine amounting therefore to £2928 [SCL, OD 1502].

Old Ladywash Mine was sunk on the random of the Middleton Engine New Vein, but no ore was found. There are many plans of the Eyam Edge mines and veins, yet none show the original sough from the tail to Old Ladywash Shaft. The shale gate sough was continued northwards eventually reaching the Old Edge Vein, the Founder there being freed on 28th March, 1717. For reasons not presently understood, ore was not raised from the beginning, this confirmed by a note on a sheet of mine accounts stating: *Oct`r 14th 1721 to this time Rec`d no Oar at Ladywash* [SCL, Bag 587/15].

The shale gate intersected the vein about 410 feet beneath the surface, but the standing water level was 150 feet beneath it, lying just above the shale-limestone interface. Mining then became intensive. Ore began to be mined in December, 1721 and from then until the end of September, 1739 a total of 19,482 loads of ore were raised, exclusive of duty ore. Total charges reached £11,517-10-6 realising an overall profit of £8,448-3-6 to the fortunate shareholders [SCL, Bag 587/56].

Plans show a shale gate continuing beyond the Old Edge Vein, intersecting the Ladywash North-East Vein a little on the west side of Ladywash Engines (details of the deep mining at Ladywash and the sinking of the two shafts are discussed in the section dealing with Stoke Sough). The shale gate is shown as either a dotted line, or a full line on plans dating from c.1736 onwards and no doubt it had reached the North-East Vein by about 1740; the level had definitely been completed by 1749 [DRO, BSA, LM 14]. The plans do not make clear whether the shale gate was a direct continuation of the old sough, or a shale gate driven at a lower contour as the thickness of shale increased northwards.

BROOKHEAD SOUGH

Brookhead Sough, begun in the summer of 1714, is the furthest east in the lengthy series of shale gate soughs within Hucklow, Grindlow and Eyam liberties, primarily driven seeking the concealed continuation of the Hucklow Edge and Eyam Edge veins.

The tail is sited at the Townend troughs, north of the Miners Arms Inn, in Eyam village. From the troughs the sough ranges slightly east of north to the Old Brookhead Shaft, now concealed beneath the Edgeside Road. Formerly there was a horse-gin at the shaft, but all traces have been obliterated by road construction. The random of Middleton Engine New Vein was considered to run from Old Ladywash Shaft to here and the sough proprietors set taker meers along it. Beyond, Brookhead Sough continues along the same east of north alignment to the crossing with Old Edge Vein, here deeply buried in the underlying limestone. The sough was then driven yet further north, at least as far as Shaw Engine Mine [SCL, Bag 191]. The last portion was completed after 1735-1736, earlier plans merely show it as a dotted line.

The sough was begun in, or slightly before July, 1714, a document of that date lists the partners in the venture. Richard Bagshawe of The Oaks, Norton, Sheffield owned a 1/3rd share [SCL, Bag 3509]. A reckoning covering the period August to December, 1714 reveals that 60 yards had been driven, but there was an additional 56 yards *sinking and driving* part of which may have been in the sough. The first 44 yards were driven at a cost of only 1/6d per fathom, very easy excavation in the shale; the price had risen to 4/- per fathom by October [SCL, OD 1149]. A detailed section from Middleton Engine to Brookhead and Shaw Engine reveals that the Old Brookhead Shaft was sunk to a depth of 20 fathoms, followed by a series of six internal sumps to a final depth of 84 fathoms (504 feet). An un-named level at the bottom of the second shaft at 30 fathoms depth is the northward continuation of Brookhead Sough connecting through into the range of Old Edge Vein [SCL, Bag 191]. Brookhead Shaft was situated about 1020 feet from the sough tail, the sough met the random or symptoms of Old Edge Vein at 1600 feet and Shaw Engine shafts at 1,900 feet.

The Brookhead partners took title to 40 meers of ground *on Eyam Moor* in March, 1715, these were takers at the Ladywash possessions on Middleton Engine New Vein. A little later, in July, 1715 they took 10 meers west:

Francis Drable and Isaac Wilde went into that Grove that the Sough at Edward Mortens House in Eyam Edge is driving up at that time was their forefield shaft and gave their opinions – that there was a Symptom of a Vein and brought some of the Cavil up with them and showed it me [SCL, OD 1502].

These 10 meers fit exactly with the distance from `Old` Brookhead Shaft to the division with the Ladywash ground in Middleton Engine New Vein. They verified their title to the 40 meers on three subsequent occasions, in April and October, 1717 and in August 1718. Brookhead Sough met `symptoms` of another vein in September, 1718, and 16 meers were taken ranging eastwards. This must refer to their title in Old Edge Vein, plans indicate that only 13 meers were worked to the extreme eastern forefield, approximately 870 feet north of Riley House. The partners next took 38 meers as takers at the Ladywash North-East Vein, these meers terminated in Magclough Hollow, near the brookside.

Ore production began in 1736, due no doubt to the deep level drainage afforded by Magclough Sough and Stoke Sough, but output was not spectacular being 88 loads in three months [SCL, Bag 539]. Details of the post-1736 history of Brookhead mines are discussed in the sections about Stoke Sough and Magclough Sough.

BULL PIT SOUGH
MR. WINCHESTER`S SHALE GATE SOUGH

Bull Hole Pipe is shown on a map of mines and veins dated 1819. The area covered by the map extends from the north side of Middleton Dale, as far west as Cucklet Delph, northwards to Eyam village and the lower slopes of Eyam Edge and east to Riley. The pipe ranged north west from Mill Lane, passing through Brookhead Mine, then to its intersection with Rush Bed Vein [SCL, Bag 199]. On the south side of Mill Lane a shaft is marked, served by an Engine; it was sunk by *Arons Well partners or Little Meadow*. An un-dated, but slightly earlier plan, essentially of the Greenlee mines, marks *Aarons Engine* in the tongue of land lying between the Eyam – Grindleford road and the track to Riley Farm [SCL, Bag 587/63]. The shaft was still open in the 1950s, but was almost hidden in undergrowth and dangerous to approach.

Contained in the Palmer Morewood Papers [DRO, D1763/9/15k] is an agreement dated 12th May, 1715 made between Mary Morewood, landowner and a group of mine owners, including Robert Greenwood of Dronfield and Robert Clay of Sheffield, lead merchants. The latter were partners in:

The Lead Mines, Sough or Shafts commonly called the Bull Pit lying and being in Stoney Middleton in the parish of Eyam – to work and carry on the said Works of the said Mine, Shaft and Sough – to discover all the – Rakes, Pipes and Veins under the Lands and Tenements of the said Mary Morewood.

The miners were to pay Mary Morewood every 12th dish of ore as composition. This agreement constitutes the earliest known reference to mining beneath the shale cover between Eyam and Stoney Middleton. The sough also dates from much the same period as the shale gate soughs seeking the Hucklow Edge Vein. The implication must be that Bull Hole Vein had been discovered and worked already within the limestones forming The Cliffe, south of Mill Lane. Nothing more is known about the venture.

The story moves forward nearly three quarters of a century. In February, 1785, Mr. Wright of Eyam Hall wrote to Humphrey Winchester and partners at:

The Sough or Shale gates now driving up in the Land of George Morewood Esq; Gentlemen – having reason to believe that your workmen are driving the above mentioned Sough or Shale Gates in such a direction as will lead you into a Freehold piece of land of mine, called Greenlee, without any consent first obtained from me – if you enter any part of the Greenlee with the said Sough – I shall – take such measures – and defence of my Freehold Right – [DRO, Wright Papers].

Bull Hole Pipe certainly passed beneath a part Greenlee, being shown on the mine map dated 1819, referred to above [SCL, Bag 199]. Whether Mr. Winchester`s Sough was diverted, or an agreement reached with Mr. Wright is not known. The sough formed part of a mining title called Broomheads Venture. A division of ground between Moorwood Sough and Broomheads Venture, agreed in November, 1786 stipulated that the soughers were to take the ground south of Steeple Torr Vein and the miners all the ground north of that vein in *Moorwoods Ground* [SCL, WH 10]. The Morewood family owned the ground known as The Cliffe, the large enclosure bounded by Middleton Dale, Cliffe Stile Vein and Mill Lane. They also owned land north of Mill Lane, lying east of Mr. Wright`s Greenlee enclosures, and also ground at Riley. The inference from this agreement must be that Broomheads Venture and Mr. Winchester`s Shale Gate Sough lay in and adjacent to Bull Hole Pipe, north of Mill Lane and largely east of Mr.Wright`s Greenlee.

A Barmaster title entry dated December, 1843 confirms that Broomheads Venture Shaft was identical with Aarons Engine, from where 18 meers ranged southeastwards on Bull Hole Pipe to the barn at the bottom of Cliff Pasture (i.e. Mill Lane) [Chats, Bar Coll]. Beyond Broomheads Venture Shaft, the pipe lay within Brookhead title.

The mining venture was commenced in late 1786, announced by the agreement noted above and by a small measure of ore in the first quarter of 1787 at the *New Title*. [Chats, Dev Coll]. Mr. Winchester owned 13/24ths. What seems to be a complete financial account is contained in two documents [SCL, WH 10; 14]. Reckonings begin in 1787 and continue to November, 1796, the operations having cost £1,090 with a return of a meagre £10-14-8 for the sale of ore. The years 1792-1796 saw a mere £35 expended. No ore was measured after 1787. There are references to both the *Upper Engine on the Common* and the *Forefield Engine on the Common*, one of these no doubt being Aarons Engine.

If the intention was to drive Mr. Winchester`s shale gate along the random of Bull Hole Pipe, up to Little Brookhead Engine, (where Mr. Winchester held a 1/16th share by 1783) there is no evidence to suggest that the objective was reached. The Little Brookhead shaft was 56 fathoms (336 feet) to water in 1819, so the shale gate sough could have drained only the upper strata to around a depth of 300 feet. The last reference to Broomheads Venture, in Farey`s list of mines, it is noted as *at Riley, in Eyam, in Shale and 1st Lime, Lead* [Farey, 1811].

GREENLEE SOUGH

The Greenlee Sough exploited Old Oak Vein, probably Rowland Scrin, Stub Scrin and perhaps mines in the Shoulder of Mutton Close.

The entrance to the sough is situated within an enclosure known as Greenlee, on the north side of the conspicuous bend in Mill Lane. When it was examined in about 1959, the sough was found to have run-in within about 30 feet from the tail. The first 15 – 20 feet had a slabbed roof and the level then turned sharply towards the west, through about 80 degrees, passing into unlined shale, before a fall halted further progress.

An old Eyam miner, Edwin Maltby believed that this sough was Brookhead Sough, but research by Nellie Kirkham [1966], proved this supposition to be incorrect and that the latter lies north of the Miners Arms and issues into Townend troughs.

The date of commencement is not known, but a reckoning book for Townend Mine, later called Townend Cross and Green Lee Sough covers the period from December 1783 until July 1788 [DRO, Wright Papers]. During 1786 expenses amounted to £105-17-4.

Two undated and very diagrammatic plans of the sough and associated veins are both very difficult to reconcile, not only with each other, but with existing field boundaries [SCL, Bag 587(63) and DRO Wright Papers].

The curious sharp turning just inside the entrance is shown on both maps; the former plan has 'Coe at Suf tail' and beyond the turning it shows the Greenlee Sough shale gate following a reasonably straight line to a forefield at the crossing of Stub Scrin, lying within an enclosure known as Bocking Close. The other plan is contained within the above mentioned reckoning book for the Greenlee mines, but it is very sketchy and impossible to equate to field boundaries. This plan shows the shale gate sough following an inexplicable and remarkably sinuous course, quite unlike the Bagshawe plan.

The first vein crossed by the line of the sough was Old Oak Vein, worked by means of sumps sunk into the underlying limestone and by means of a drift driven south westwards as far as Philip Sheldons Shaft on Ashtons Pipe. The shaft was 150 feet in depth. Ore was obtained in the whole length of this drift [SCL, Bag 199].

No details are known of any workings developed on Rowland Scrin. The Green Lee partners sank a shaft on Stub Scrin; the scrin was worked to the end of Shoulder of Mutton Close where they were drowned out, 4 fathoms deep in the limestone. The plans suggest that Stub Scrin passed through Bocking Croft, somewhat too far south to pass into Shoulder of Mutton Close north of the road, so this remains a mystery.

There is no direct evidence that the sough was

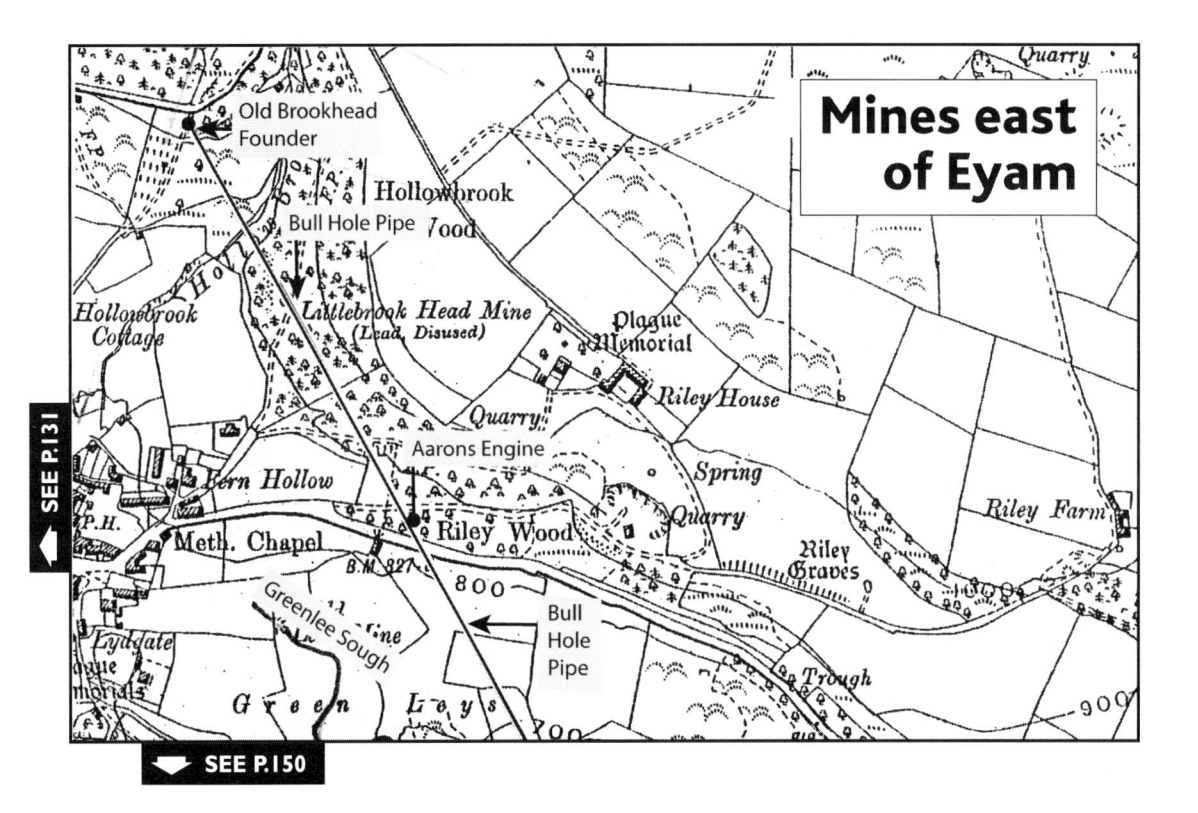

driven to the north side of the Eyam – Grindleford road into the Shoulder of Mutton Close. The Green Lee partners obtained liberty from the Reverend Carver in October, 1786 to work all veins beneath this close, but they could not sink shafts in it. He was to receive 1/24th of the ore as royalty. They were not given permission to work Sheldons Vein already owned by Philip Sheldon and partners [SCL, Bag 587(44)].

All mining seems to have ceased by August, 1788 and from that date until March, 1801 the entries are very spasmodic and refer only to security and filling old shafts and holes.

6. THE DEVELOPMENT OF THE EASTERN END OF THE EYAM EDGE MINES, AND THE CONSTRUCTION OF STOKE SOUGH AND MAGCLOUGH SOUGH

From Grindlow Liberty boundary the continuation of the Eyam Edge, or Hucklow Edge Vein, sometimes known as the *Great Old Vein,* and its important north east and south east break veins, was proved partly by driving a number of north trending shale gate soughs from the lower ground at the foot of Eyam Edge until the position of the great vein, buried deep below could be established. These shale gates, by their very position and contour could not offer deep drainage to the large mines established on the Edge, neither could they offer any hope of exploration or de-watering of extensions to mining eastwards beyond Brookhead Mine. This latter situation was exacerbated by a sudden and pronounced steepening of the shale-limestone contact beyond Brookhead Mine.

The first major branch from the Hucklow Edge Vein was a break discovered in 1715 just east of Middleton Engine Mine; it was named Middleton Engine New Vein. At the time of its discovery the precise picture underground was far from clear, but subsequent development proved that the vein was indeed a break and not a continuation of Hucklow Edge Vein (or Middleton Engine Old Vein), at that date proved only as far east as Middleton Engine [SCL, Bag 181]. The New Vein passed through lower Miners Engine (Old Twelve Meers) and before 1721 had been proved at Old Ladywash and probably at Brookhead Shaft.

Meanwhile, about 1720–21 the Hucklow Edge Vein had been re-located beyond Miners Engine by means of a crosscut driven north from Little Pasture Mine under the supervision of Francis Drabble, and it was to the eastern random of this perceived main vein that Stoke Sough was aimed, also based on Drabble`s recommendation.

STOKE SOUGH

Mine owners realised that their problems could be solved only by driving a long, deep level sough from the Derwent. The work would involve `state of the art` mining technology and require large financial resources. Proposals were mooted and an un-dated plan, c.1734–1735 has the following note:

> *ffrancis Drabble – Incouraged Some Gentlemen to begin a Sough Levil which the(y) accordingly did – he always concluded that Hucklow old vein would range verry near that Stone at top of the Coast* [Chats, Dev Coll].

Drabble was a well esteemed, practical miner, involved at Hucklow, Grindlow and Eyam Edge and eventually was overseer at Stoke Sough. The Coast Stone is a very large, isolated gritstone boulder beyond the south eastern end of the prominent gritstone outcrop known as Rock Hall, and some 1,350 feet north west of the shafts at Stoke Old Engine.

The first section of Stoke Sough was driven within a sequence of interbedded shales and sandstones for a distance of about 1,000 feet before it encountered the Shale Grit or Eyam Edge Sandstone. The sough was continued through this unit for some 1,200 feet before it entered the underlying Edale Shale. Consequent to much confusion, which included finding symptoms of veins in the shale, thought by some to be the long anticipated Hucklow Edge Vein, limestone was eventually met in the sough forefield some 170 feet south of east of the Coast Stone, more or less as forecast by Drabble.

The sandstones in the first part of the sough are of sufficient strength to require blasting, the shot holes are short, but very regular; the passageway hereabouts is low, only about four and a half feet in height. Excavation through the Shale Grit has produced an interesting profile. Shot holes some 1 foot 6 inches in length are common, the rock being very strong and thickly bedded. The rock has a general dip toward the east of 10 degrees to 15 degrees and the miners were obliged to develop the roof of the sough along the underside of a convenient bedding plane. The gradual rising of the plane to perhaps 8 or 10 feet above floor level dictated that a `forefield` was formed, driveage then continuing along the next convenient lower bedding plane. The roof therefore presents the appearance of the underside of a slightly sloping staircase with very long steps, but short risers. Initials carved into the walls include *IB* possibly John Botham the overseer, but there are no dates.

Later driveages in the sough included several branch passages passing variously through shale and limestone and along veins. Their more detailed geology will be discussed in the second part of this account dealing with events post 1747. According to one document Stoke Sough was begun in 1724 [SCL, Spencer Stanhope 60050], but this cannot be correct because in October, 1723 a charge was made on shareholders *For ye Carrying on ye Sough in Eyam Edge* [DRO, Wright Papers]. The major shareholders were Henry Thornhill of Stanton, Francis Sitwell, James Mower, James and William Milnes. By 1726 a 1/32nd share was owned by Richard Marples, Auditor to the Dean and Chapter of St. Paul`s Cathedral, London. Much of the available information relating to the period 1725-1737 is contained in a series of detailed letters from Henry Thornhill, William Soresby and John Botham written to Marples in London [Guildhall, Marples papers]. Extensive extracts from this source are quoted below.

A financial account dated 1726 referred to the level as *the Sough in ye Peak*. The potential was enormous, reflected in a valuation of £100 for a 1/48th share in 1729. Little is known about progress of the forefield until the latter part of 1732. From then until January, 1735 the letters written from Derbyshire to Richard Marples enable a detailed picture to be formed.

Before 1733, when the deep shafts at Stoke Old Engine were completed, by holing through into the sough over 3,450 feet from the tail, ventilation must have been a great problem. Two air shafts were sunk within a short distance of the entrance, *the shaft in Youle Close* and *the shaft on Stoke Moor* [DRO, BSA LP32]. Recent exploration of the sough has revealed that a few yards before the second air shaft is reached, a neat doorway has been carefully cut in the shale, though nothing remains of the door itself. Although positive evidence is lacking, the top of the Stoke Moor shaft was probably covered by a fire-house. The shaft would have contained a brattice, fresh air descending down one side, carried along the level to the working face by means of a fang, foul air extracted from the contemporary forefield by the up-draught created by the fire house. The door would have been placed to prevent a short circuit of air to the sough tail.

In October, 1732 Thornhill wrote to Marples: *The shafts will be through as ye overseers compute by Candlemass, when in my opinion the greatest hazard of the tryal will be over.* The shafts at Stoke Sough Old Engine were completed in early January, 1733. The main shaft was sunk vertically for about 350 feet beneath the surface and then continued downwards by a series of slightly off-set sumps to a depth of 693 feet, there connecting with Stoke Sough [DRO, BSA LM/D/44C].

Henry Thornhill informed Marples:

we shall be able to make an effective tryall – which carries of all others in ye minerall county the richest prospect – our bitterest enemies only objected the impossibility of getting these shafts through and consequently of carrying forward ye Leavill.

Thornhill, for ever optimistic, wrote to Marples soon afterwards:

They cannot from ye Symptoms they have in the Forefield of ye Levill be a great way from ye Limestone and as soon as it is discovered they cannot miss finding the vein a short time after.

In March, 1733 Thornhill wrote yet another account of their progress:

They have lately met with in ye Leavill stronger symptoms of a vein than ever, for before we had only loose lumps of what they call Keavills and mudd but now we have a pritty strong continued leading of sparr.

The initial optimism of the soughers turned out to be disappointing. The contour of the shale/limestone interface at Black Engine, Middleton`s Engine and Ladywash mines, when projected towards Stoke Sough, would have led to the belief that limestone could be expected in the sough forefield a little beyond Stoke Sough Old Engine. Francis Drabble, the miner who had first proposed the idea of a sough from the Derwent, believed that the Hucklow Edge Vein would be found somewhat further west, near the Coast Stone. Drabble`s forecast proved the more accurate, limestone was eventually found in the forefield, some 1180 feet west of Stoke Sough Old Engine, very close to where Drabble had predicted. There had been several false starts, thin beds of limestone, interbedded in the shale having been found on more than one occasion.

Thornhill wrote to Marples in March, 1734: *John Botham tells me that he believes We are now in ye*

Strong bouther that caps the lime Stone. The *bouther* or *Boulder Stones* occur in a bed at, or near the base of the shale. On being broken some were found to contain inflammable bitumen and this was used for illumination. Rock-oil was also found floating on the water and these circumstances gave rise to a rumour hat a burning spring had been found. The bitumen was also collected by the miners and used for greasing boots, but they soon discovered that it shrivelled the leather and the idea was rapidly abandoned !

Eventually, in late July, 1734 the sough masters were able to report: *the(y) are struck to A greate Spring of Watter at Stoke Sough that hath taken all ye watter from Ladywash and Haycliff so they may work their sole*. Ladywash in this context refers to Old Ladywash Grove, and subsequent development along Old Edge Vein, not the later mine near the top of Sir William Hill. The vast inrush of water caused a great deal of damage as John Botham explained: *When we lett of the watter – Its violence – pulled down A Great deal of Shale – from the roof and Sides of the Sough*. There was a tragic human event associated with the damage. Lack of an appropriate air circulation resulted in four men being killed by bad air in September, 1734.

Our men went Bouldly on – But there was unfortunately Lodged the damp – it is death to any that Comes Near it, which was the fate of four of Our Workemen on Tuesday Last [John Botham to Richard Marples].

The dead miners were; Joseph Marsden and Richard Holmes, both of Grindleford Bridge and John Taylor. The name of the fourth man is not recorded. The site of the water inrush at the forefield could not be reached, so that by October the sough masters were under the obligation of driving an over drift for ventilation purposes, the drift connecting the Engine Shaft to the beginning of the damaged and run-in section *We – can't get Wind up to ye Breach till this over drift from ye Engine Shaft is perfected* There was considerable delay in clearing falls and repairing damaged sections of the sough, but in January, 1735 all had been accomplished.

Water levels in the Edgeside mines had begun to fall immediately after the first breach in July, 1734, one reference claiming the benefit was felt as far west as Middleton Engine. Immediately the question arose of composition payment to the sough masters. No legal agreements had been drawn between the mine owners and sough masters, so a series of disputes began which led eventually to the sough being dammed-up in June, 1738. The *Four and Twenty* jurymen of the Eyam Barmote Court had decided in October, 1733 that when any mine was unwatered by a sough, the sough masters were to have $1/4^{th}$ part of all ore laid dry by virtue of the sough. A footnote added a note of caution asking whether a jury had the power to make a law for soughs near finished, when no complaint had been made to them [Steer, 1734]. Water marks were set at the Edgeside mines during 1733, the standing level being referred to as the *Levell Watter*.

The soughers discovered several veins of their own, but most were thin and poor and were not pursued for any distance, although extensive runs of taker meers along them were entered into the Barmaster's Book. Some of them were described merely as a *mudd*, or a symptom of a vein running through the shale rather than within the limestone [Rieuwerts, 1998]. Middleton Engine New Vein reached as far as Brookhead Grove, but somewhat to the south of the position of Hucklow Edge Vein as postulated by Drabble. Historical indications are that beyond Haycliffe Grove or possibly Old Ladywash Grove, the vein deteriorated eastwardly into worthless stringers. Of far greater importance, the predicted range of Drabble's Hucklow Edge Vein (later known as Old Edge Vein) proved to be remarkably accurate, though the vein was not freed by the soughers until January, 1749. Before then the most important was known Fair Dealing Vein, later called Stoke Sough Vein. The Founder was freed in January, 1736, followed by a Lord's Meer and six takers, the 6th taker was freed in June, 1738.

The dispute with the mine owners escalated, culminating in June, 1738 when driveage in the sough forefield was abandoned on the north-west cross cut between Fair Dealing (Stoke Sough) Vein and the later discovered Simon Vein. A wall or dam was built in the sough a little downstream from Fair Dealing Vein, thus effectively preventing any water flow from the Edgeside mines outwards towards the tail. The sough masters claimed that by then the sough had cost them £12,000, but had received only £3,000 to £4,000 in composition ore and ore mined in their own vein [SCL, Spencer Stanhope 60506/66].

STOKE SOUGH AFTER 1747

After remaining walled-up from July 1738, the sough was re-opened in April 1747. A letter written in May, 1747 observed that:

6. The Development of the Eastern end of the Eyam Edge Mines, and the Construction of Stoke Sough and Magclough Sough

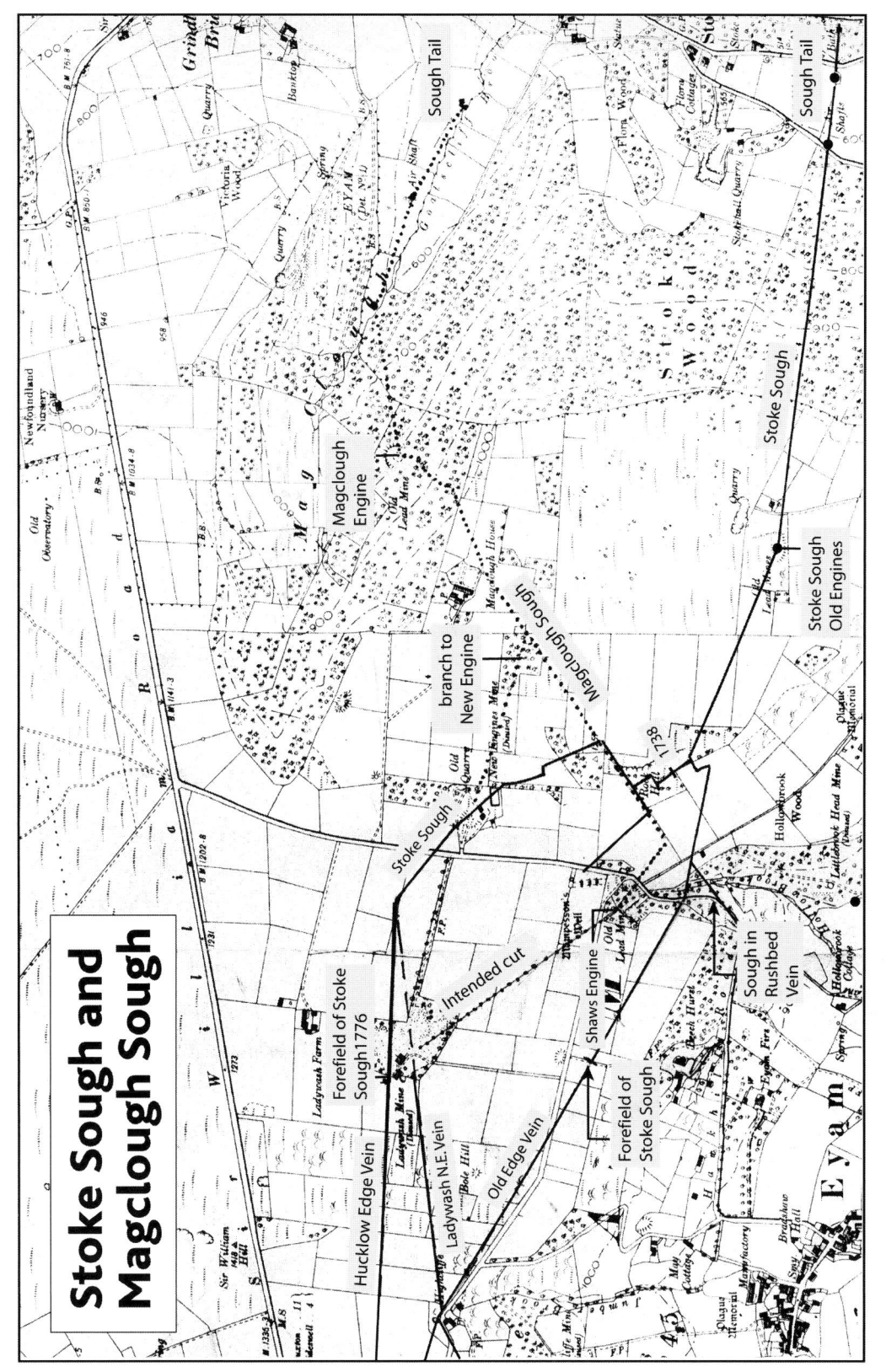

a great deal of time and money will be spent before the sough be perfectly cleaned, the Shaw Engine sunk down to the limestone – and a shale drift cut cross to Stoak Sough Vein [SCL, Spencer Stanhope 60506/270].

These comments are reflected in expenses at Stoke Sough in the immediate aftermath of its re-opening. Very considerable charges accrued, just over £1,196 being paid in six months in 1747, followed by £929-10-0 during 1748 [SCL, Bag 547].

The construction of the sough became complicated, various levels were driven in different directions, but often discontinued in favour of an alternative target. The events are chronicled by a long narrative written on a plan of the mines drawn about 1761 by Francis Mason, an overseer [DRO, BSA/LM/D/20]. The level was cleared and operations commenced by continuing the north west driveage beyond the point where the sough had been abandoned in 1738. Simons Vein was crossed, but having reached Magclough Vein, driving this forefield was suspended and work concentrated on continuing a drive south westwards down Stoke Vein towards the intersection with Old Edge Vein or Brookhead Vein in Brookhead title (also known as Ladywash Old Vein within their own title). The confusion generated by these alternative names can be partly alleviated by understanding that when Francis Drabble persuaded the adventurers to begin Stoke Sough to find Hucklow Edge Old Vein near the Coast Stone, he was referring to what later became known as Old Edge Vein.

The forefield encountered very hard ground and to avoid it a short cross-cut was driven south east to meet Brookhead Vein (i.e.Old Edge Vein), described as *driving in the cross vein to carry the sough to Ladywash*.

Nellie Kirkham was confused by this entry believing it to refer to the site of the later, deep Ladywash Mine on the moor [Kirkham, 1966]. The soughers soon met mineralised ground and in January, 1749 they:

Gave a dish to free a taker meer in Brookhead Vein (if it proves so) – and one dish to free a new vein discovered by driving in the Low Levill of Stoke Sough (if it proves).

The sough masters obviously took the precaution of double freeing, they could not be sure whether they had found the eastern part of Brookhead Vein (Ladywash Old Vein; Old Edge Vein) in Brookhead title, or a completely new vein. Soon after, composition ore began to be paid to the sough masters, but details are very sketchy.

Financial accounts for 1749 are incomplete, nevertheless operational costs remained high, from 1750 to 1758 inclusive no less than £7,843 was spent, in 1753, 1754 and 1755 annual costs exceeded £1,000. Details vary slightly in different documents, but the charges are a fair reflection from each source [SCL, Bag 389 and OD 1498]. There was a dramatic fall in 1759 only £201 was spent and in 1760 only £132.

The driveage, referred to in the reckoning book as *the low levill*, continued in a north west direction along Old Edge Vein in Brookhead title towards Ladywash title. The division point was reached in December, 1755, the event recorded thus: *Given to workemen holeing sough and Ladywash together* [SCL, Bag 389]. The sough was continued within the Ladywash title for about 210 yards.

Having accomplished their objective in relieving Ladywash title in Old Edge Vein, the sough masters once more returned to the suspended forefield at Magclough Vein. The sough was then continued south west down Magclough Vein in 1757, but as they approached Shaw Engine a north west trending vein was discovered and the level was turned in that direction. The reckoning for December, 1760 records that Joseph Hadfield was *driving in ye Chun Levelle up towards Ladywash* [SCL, Bag 389]. The intention was to drive along this alignment to the newly sunk deep shafts at Ladywash Mine on Ladywash North East Vein. The position of the Ladywash deep shafts was set out by George Tissington in March 1746 and work began in August, 1747. The main engine shaft, known as the *South Shaft* or *Great Shaft* was sunk 104 fathoms (624 feet), arguably the deepest vertical shaft in Britain at that date The adjacent North Shaft was sunk 60 fathoms (360 feet) followed by a series of sumps for a further 36 fathoms (216 feet) [SCL, OD 1152]. The work was finished by December, 1748 the total cost being £1,959-0-2 [SCL, OD 1497]. Ventilation was effected by *thorls* driven between the shafts and a Firehouse built over one of them. One reckoning records that there were 15 *men – whole partnership sinking in the Engine Shaft 10 fathoms at £1-5-0 per fathom*. The principal miners or gang leaders were Henry Hodkinson and Edward Sellers.

The Chun Levell discovered Masland, or Marsden Vein and a little later reached another cross vein called the New Vein, but had to be abandoned soon afterwards,

6. The Development of the Eastern end of the Eyam Edge Mines, and the Construction of Stoke Sough and Magclough Sough

the soughers having struck a great feeder of water; in addition the ground was very hard and would have cost £10 per fathom. This driveage was abandoned in favour of the Magclough Vein north east drive.

An aside to this concentrated, major mining work, in April 1758, Thomas Martin was paid 11/- for binding and securing the old Stoke Engine Shaft; a little over two years later they sold *Stoke Sough Engine and firehouse timber - to Jos Newbould, £27-19-0*. [SCL, Bag 389]. Later, in May, 1767 the Stoke Old Engine Shaft was re-opened and a coe was built over it.

From the north eastern forefield of Magclough Vein the sough was continued north westwards towards the eventual site of the New Engine shafts. The section was begun about 1760. Magclough Vein had been discovered in 1735 whilst driving Magclough Sough (see under that heading for discussion). The Stoke Sough was to be driven in shale, but with limestone forming the sole of the level. The proposal was clearly defined on a plan drawn about 1759-1760 [DRO, BSA LM/D/102; SCL, Bag 194]:

> *A line signifying where a level might be Carried in the Shale with its point as near as can be supposed so as to make the Limestone the sole of the sough all along and which may also show where the Huckloe Edge Vein and Ladywash Vein (northeastwardly) will dip under the level of the Sough.*

The soughers realised by driving along this interface, effectively the strike of the shale-limestone contact at sough contour, they would be able to discover and drain all veins ranging east and north east from the vicinity of Shaw Engine and between there and Ladywash Mine. On one plan, un-dated, but c.1760, it is described as *The Shale Sough which is now driving to meet Bagshawes Break* [SCL, Bag 195a].

Robert Middleton`s plan dated May, 1776 shows the line of *Hucklow Edge old Vein or what at Ladywash is calld Bagshawes Breck* [DRO, BSA, LM/D/10]. Geological predications proved correct up to and beyond New Engine shafts and in 1761-1762 it was reported that *they have at this Sough been skirting the limestone in order to relieve the veins watered and to make new discoveries near 300 yards of which has cost 15/- yard* [SCL, OD 1161].

Nellie Kirkham [1966] misinterpreted several plans and stratum contours hereabouts, claiming that Stoke Sough could not have been driven in shale through this section, and it must refer to a branch of Magclough Sough. She was mistaken, Stoke Sough was driven along the shale–limestone interface. A geological section from Magclough Sough tail to New Engines proves that the sough was at this horizon [D. Nash archives], the fact also verified by notes made by White Watson [Cambridge University] and mid 19th century annual reports of the Eyam Mining Company.

Several new veins were discovered; in October, 1763 a rib of ore 17 inches in thickness was found in the forefield [SCl, OD 1504]. A peculiar, unexplained item dating from November, 1763 was for *Wm Bradshawe Bill for making a bote £1-2-8*.

New Engine Mine was originally known as Stoke Sough New Engine or the Deep Sough Shaft. The first reckoning at New Engine dates from November, 1765, so work must have begun a little earlier [SCL, Bag 391]. They were completed in April, 1769 *Spent at getting the Shafts thro`*. There were two gin shafts, one at least 135 fathoms (786 feet) in depth, or 4 fathoms below the contour of Stoke Sough. According to White Watson the shafts encountered *Millstone Sandstone, Shale Grit and Shale – deepest in Derbyshire 270 yards.*

Ventilation was obtained by means of a Fire-house built over the second shaft, this 67½ fathoms deep (405 feet) connected to the deep shaft by a thurl. The reckoning for August, 1767 saw the purchase of 28,000 bricks, plus an additional 20,000 three months later. The bricks would have been used in the construction of the fire-house and its chimney at New Engine shafts. A rather inaccurate sketch section of the arrangement was drawn by White Watson in August, 1810, whilst he was at Mr. Longsden`s at Eyam. Longsden had bought all the materials from the New Engine site in June, 1805, including: *the Old Fire House, Smithy – walls, stone, coes, gin races – for £21* [SCL, Bag 391 and 587/64].

Near New Engine the sough encountered a warm spring and in June, 1776 Joseph Mosley spent six weeks at 7/6d per week timbering between *Warme Spring* and New Engine. The shale gate sough, still skirting the limestone, continued beyond New Engine Mine, but along a more north west alignment. It was called *The Great gate wherein we take our Levy*. An un-located part of the sough was known as *Guinea an Inch*.

The forefield reached the intersection of Hucklow Edge Vein with Ladywash North East Vein about 1770 or shortly thereafter, and two plans dating from that year [DRO, BSA, LM/D/35; DRO, 3266 R 310d]

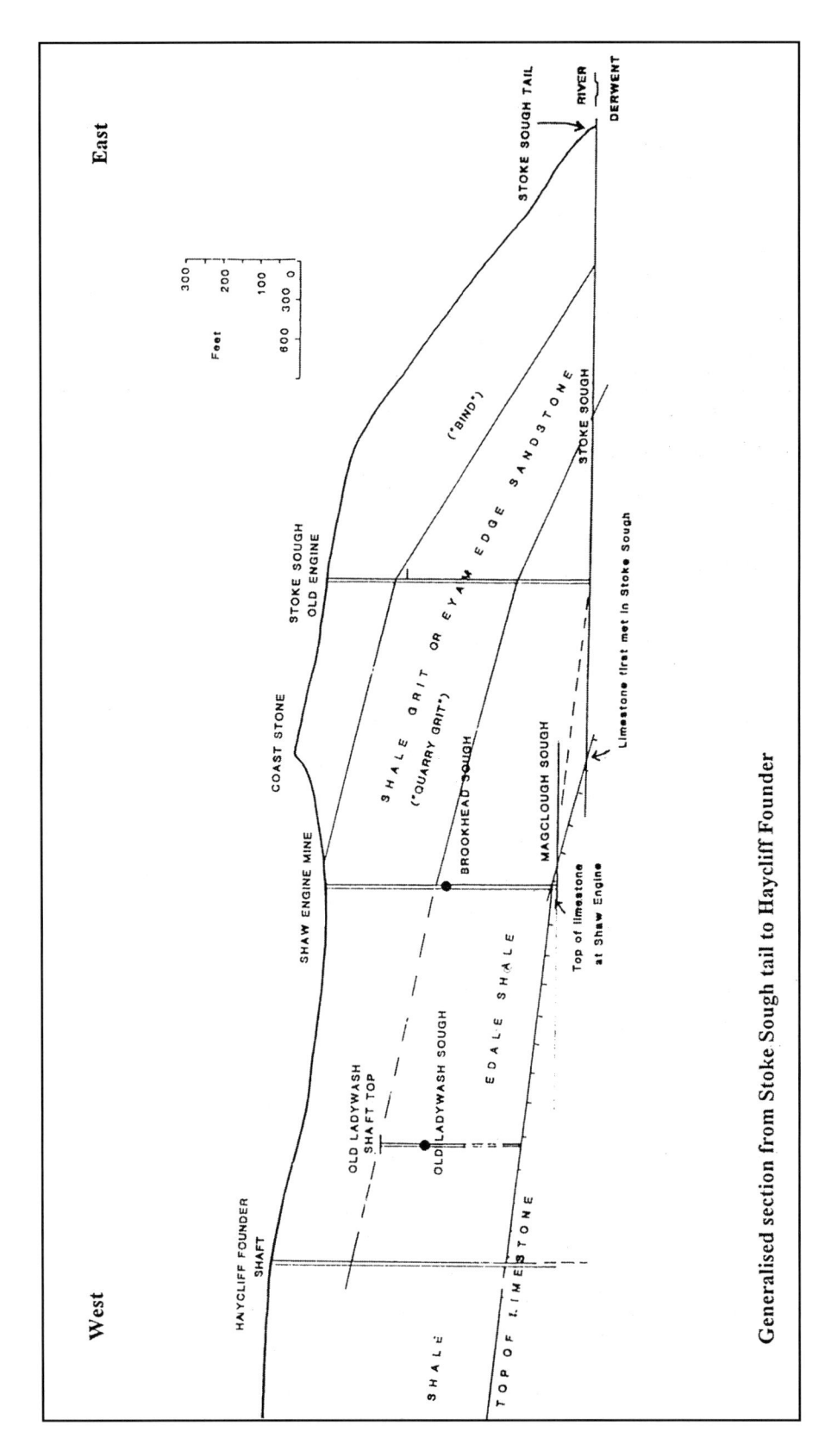

Generalised section from Stoke Sough tail to Haycliff Founder

name Hucklow Edge Vein as Broadlow Vein. During the summer of 1779 Thomas Bagshawe and Co. were paid a bargain of £4-4-0 *For reesing the Roofe of the Levill in the Bouder for the Newcastle wagin to roon in* [SCL, Bag 391]. This entry has two points of interest, the first being continued use of the term *bouder (boulder, boother)*, the second reference being to the Newcastle waggon. Laporte`s, when working in this area of the mine in the late 20th century, discovered large cross section wooden rails, obviously part of the Newcastle Road. This is one of only three known examples in the orefield, the others being in White Coe Mine, Hassop and Pindale Mine, Castleton.

The sough forefield in Hucklow Edge Old Vein by May 1776 had reached some 285 yards beyond the rither point with Ladywash North East Vein. The forefield in a branch level along the North East Vein stood nearly 60 yards from the rither point and was some 30 yards distant from the forefield of a shale drift driven above the vein-head being worked towards it from the opposite direction [SCL, OD 1233b]. Reckonings are available from 1790 until 1802, but without any detail of expenditure. Charges amounted to £2275-9-1, partly offset by sale of 583 loads of ore which produced revenue of £1221-0-9 [SCL, Bag 482].

According to White Watson, Stoke Sough was driven to near the top of Sir William Hill and the forefield abandoned in the channel [Derby Local Studies Library]. Kirkham [1966] recounted how an old Eyam miner named Edwin Maltby told her that the end of the sough on Hucklow Edge Vein was *towards Broadlow*.

By 1804 work was at a standstill and a meeting of the proprietors resolved that no more money was to be expended and that a valuation was to be made by Francis Mason and William Wyatt of all the materials [SCL, Bag 391]. During June, 1805 Mr. Longsden bought *The Old Fire House, Smithy and all the Stone about the Engines at Stoke Engine for £21-0-0*.

Another document of the same date [SCL, Bag 587/64] also records the sale thus: *Inventory of what Mr. Longsden bought of the Proprietors of Stoke Sough and situated at New Engines – walls, stone, remains of buildings, coes, gin races*. Farey [1811] recorded that the sough had cost £35,000. After 1804 Stoke Sough lay abandoned until the Eyam Mining Company began to take an interest in the Edgeside mines in the 1860s.

The Company deepened New Engine shaft to 156 fathoms (936 feet), and installed a dual purpose steam engine for pumping and winding. The horizontal engine and boilers, made by Davy Brothers of Sheffield, was ready for work by late 1863, but the shaft deepening did not begin until summer, 1865 [DRO, Wright Papers]. Stoke Sough must have been in poor condition because the intention was to lift the water into a branch of Magclough Sough. (The detail of this work is discussed under the heading of Magclough Sough). A drift driven from the foot of the newly deepened New Engine shaft towards Hucklow Edge Vein struck a very large feeder of water which drowned them out and flooded the shaft to the contour of Magclough Sough. The Eyam Mining Company had by then expended £25,000 on the work.

A direct result of this misfortune was the clearing out of Stoke Sough; the work began in 1868 and was finished up to Hucklow Edge Vein by 1876. Ore was produced from New Engine only in 1877 when 237 loads 5 dishes were measured [Chats, Dev Coll]. All working ceased in 1884 and the plant was offered for sale in April that year.

The final chapter in the history of Stoke Sough is perhaps not yet complete. During underground fluorspar working beneath Eyam Edge in the 20th century, the sough drained water from the extreme eastern parts of the mine. Should underground production of fluorspar re-start, the old sough will again provide some drainage relief.

MAGCLOUGH SOUGH, (GOATSCLIFFE SOUGH, or GOATLEE SOUGH),
MAGCLOUGH (NEW, DEEP OR VENTURE) SOUGH (a proposed sough, but not driven)

Magclough Sough was begun in either December, 1723 or January, 1724. The tail is situated on the north side of Goatscliffe Brook, south west of Grindleford, and not as might be expected on the bank of the River Derwent, which would have provided gravity drainage for an additional 18 fathoms (108 feet). During the period of the dispute with the Stoke Sough masters in the mid 1730s and early 1740s when the latter was dammed-up, the Magclough soughers actually considered bringing up a new level from this lower contour, the `Magclough Venture Sough`.

The sough tail is a low, slabbed bolt which issues a trickle of ochreous water. The bolt runs north west beside the brook for 350 feet to a very shallow, but run-in air shaft. The actual underground level begins at this shaft and is driven through the Eyam Edge Sandstone, or Shale Grit for 1,100 feet to an overgrown hillock that marks the site of a drawing shaft, named on one plan as Brookside Shaft. Here the level turns to the south west and then runs for 1,000 feet to Magclough Engine Shaft, 157 feet in depth, below which are three sumps reaching sough level 293 feet beneath the surface [SCL, Bag 517]. The level continues along a rather irregular course in Shale Grit for 180 feet before passing into the underlying shales and ranging for a further 3,000 feet until limestone was met in the forefield near Shaw Engine Mine.

The principal proprietor of the venture was Richard Bagshawe who owned $1/4^{th}$ and $1/96^{th}$ parts in it; Bagshawe was also a major partner at Brookhead Mine and Sough. There is evidence to suggest that Magclough Sough was planned to discover and drain Brookhead`s title in the Ladywash North East Vein. An un-dated plan, but c.June – December, 1735, depicts the Ladywash North East Vein beginning at Haycliffe Founder, passing through the Ladywash title into Brookhead title, its random or presumed range terminating at the Brookside Shaft [DRO, BSA, LM/D/7]. The will of a shareholder, John Nodder, directed that after his death certain sums were to be paid to beneficiaries when the sough reached the east end of Twelve Meers Grove. This substantiates the author`s belief that the sough was originally intended to be driven along the Ladywash North East Vein into the Hucklow Edge Vein (Old Edge Vein) at Haycliffe Mine and so to Twelve Meers. Failure to locate any mineralisation at the Brookside Shaft (in any event, the vein deeply buried beneath sough contour, would pass well to the north of the shaft) led to the deviation to Magclough Engine Shaft and the subsequent driveage towards Bagshawe`s Brookhead Mine. A slightly earlier plan [DRO, BSA, LM/D/33] again un-dated, but pre June, 1735 shows the forefield of Magclough Sough about 300 feet short of the Brookhead workings, but Magclough Vein had not then been discovered.

Early in June the Barmote Court jury observed that: *Magclough Sough yet wants 100 yards driving to come to the vein freed by Brookhead* [DRO, Grant Papers].

The sough had cost £4859 by December, 1734 and by March, 1735 had risen to £6,447 [SCL, OD 1505]. The sum of £1,000 was expended on landowners for the liberty of driving the sough through un-mineralised ground. The soughers were soon comforted by the discovery of *a leading which gives hope of a new vein*. On the 17th June, 1735 the Barmote jury were requested *by Richard Bagshawe and partners at Maggcluff Sough to go Down there and to View whether there be a Vein or Veins*. The jury inspected and reported that:

> *wee have been down the Little Sump below the Levell of the Sough and have gone on the Little Drift at the Sump foot Northwardly and then wee go to the forefield and there wee find a Vein and Oar and a Cross Leading but wee say that there is but One Vein till further workmanship be made.*

Magclough Vein was freed, the sough masters taking 58 meers south west and 35 meers north east, the latter terminating at Goatscliffe Brook. Ore began to be raised in January, 1736 and within 6 months 466 loads and 6 dishes had been measured [SCL, Bag 539]. The soughers eventually worked the vein to a depth of 14 fathoms beneath their sough level. These events activated the Stoke soughers into claiming composition ore and also checking the validity of the title to this new vein.

Sometime in 1736 the sough masters entered into an agreement with the owners of Brookhead Grove. The sough was to be driven southwestwards down Magclough Vein into Brookhead Vein (known subsequently as Old Edge Vein) and then westwards along that vein. From the intersection to the west end of Brookhead title adjoining Ladywash title, the ground was to be divided equally between Magclough Sough and Brookhead Grove. When the sough reached Brookhead title that company was to have liberty to carry the sough westwards at their own cost and charges. However, in the event of non-compliance, the Magclough partners were to have liberty to cut the level to the partition with Ladywash and have the ore within that length. Whether the sough was ever driven into Old Edge Vein and for what distance is not known. The agreement concludes with a clause stipulating that an Engine Shaft was to be sunk at joint charge and an Engine erected on it, again at joint charge [SCL, Bag 587/58]. The intended shaft must be one of the two engine shafts at Shaw Engine.

A letter dated 6th April, 1736 records, *ye new engine at Magclough is near finished* [SCL, Spencer Stanhope 60506/44]. A cross cut was driven from the sough to Shaw Engine Mine about 1735. What must be the second engine shaft at Shaw Engine is referred to in a letter dated 11th June, 1738: *they have got into ye shale with the new shaft – I had it measured this morning it is sunk above 40 fathom and but about 10 to sink*. The depth to the sough at Shaw Engine was 100 fathoms 4 feet, but: *Will not lay Brookhead dry by 3 fathoms 4 feet and 5 inches* [SCL, Bag 191].

A little to the east of Shaw Engine a cross cut was

driven north west, certainly as far as the New Vein. However, the original intention (no date, but definitely by 1735) was to connect this cross cut with the Ladywash North East Vein, a plan depicting the line as: *what Magclough partners drove with intent to carrie Magclough Level to Ladywash North Vein – before any Consolidation was proposed by Stoke Sough and Magclough partnerships* [DRO, BSA, LM/D/14].

After the sinking of the Ladywash deep shafts the scheme was again resurrected, but probably never carried out. A diagrammatic section drawn between Old Brookhead, Shaw Engine and Middleton Engine mines marks details of the shafts and depth of workings. The deepest soles at Middleton Engine were 85 fathoms or 510 feet beneath the surface, it being considered that Magclough Sough would drain the mine 12 fathoms beneath the soles [SCL, Bag 191]. The soughers speculated that their sough would reach onto the toadstone at or close to Middleton Engine Mine. All historical evidence is that no extensions to the sough were driven westwards even for short distances along either Brookhead Vein (Old Edge Vein) or Ladywash North East Vein.

The dispute with the proprietors of Stoke Sough was bitter and prolonged and was not resolved until 1747 when Stoke Sough was re-opened. The Magclough Sough partnership had very little to give them any optimism for future development. Their own vein had deteriorated very badly, one document declaring:

The Maggclough Vein is perrished dead or Seems to be Seerd up with hardness and of no Value – the Magclough Vein is Dead Westwardly almost cut out Eastwardly [SCL, Bag 587/106].

The proprietors considered the possibility of driving a deeper level, virtually at the same contour as Stoke Sough, the so-called Magclough Venture Sough. The ground was measured in July, 1742 from the sough tail, down the fields to the Derwent, a distance of 712 yards [SCL, Bag 587/58]. The proposal was doomed to failure, due to the long drivage through barren ground, though one writer was rather more optimistic:

The Magclough partners have an Opportunity of bringing up another Levell 16 fathoms or more under their present Levell, by means of which several rich Veins might be discovered and would very well pay the proprietors the expence of such an undertaking [SCL, Spencer Stanhope 60050].

After Stoke Sough was re-opened it seems that all work at Magclough ceased and the deeper contour Stoke Sough was continued.

Nearly a century later the Moorwood Sough Co. began to consider re-opening the old sough. A letter dated 21st April, 1843 from James Sorby to Thomas Fentem reported:

Capt`n Skimming – says respecting the Mag Clough it would appear that mine, Ladywash and New Engine and perhaps Shaw Engine would be more readily and cheaply brought into profitable work by means of Goatley Sough than by the Morewood one [DRO, D2160, PDMHS Coll].

During the mid 19th century the level was also referred to as Goatscliffe Sough [eg. Mining Journal, October, 1857]. Nothing was done at that period, but shortly after the formation of the Eyam Mining Co. in 1859 that company decided to drive a branch level from a point south west of Magclough House to New Engine Mine. The branch, a little over 1,200 feet in length, was driven through shale. Rock-oil was encountered in 1860 [Stokes, 1878-1879] and the level had definitely been completed before 1865. The New Engine shaft was enlarged and deepened to 156 fathoms (936 feet) some time previous to September, 1863. The Magclough Sough branch entered the shaft at a depth of 672 feet and was used as a pumpway for the winding and pumping engine made by Davy Bros. of Sheffield and installed in the latter part of 1863.

The condition of the level caused the Eyam Mining Co. considerable trouble:

the timbers supporting it decay so fast – yet – they do not think they would do right to incur the great cost of arching it with stone [DRO, Wright Papers, Eyam Mining Co. Annual Report, 1865].

A large spring met with in the lower levels at New Engine necessitated the clearing of Stoke Sough, and Magclough was again abandoned in favour of the lower level. There are no records that any part of Magclough Sough has been entered for a period of around a century and a quarter.

7. WATER GROVE MINE AND THE SOUGHS IN UPPER MIDDLETON DALE

Several spellings of the mine, vein and pipe occur and include Water Groove, Watter Groove, Water Grove and Watergrove; after about 1750 it was usually known as Water Grove (Mine). Variants in the spelling can be found in the same document.

The first reference to *Water Groove* occurs in 1715, but the mine was `old` by that time, though no date for its original discovery seems to be known. The Founder Shaft for Water Groove Vein was situated at the side of Fielding Yate (Tideswell Lane), immediately beyond the western end of 13 meers of ground owned by two miners named Edward Drabble and David *ffeepound*. Their meers were described in April, 1724 as extending from *Dale Head (and) west towards the ffielding Yate*. The meers had been given to them by the Barmaster in April, 1715. Eastwards they terminated at the head of Middleton Dale, very close to the range of Brushfield Rake. David ffeepound also owned three meers more northward than *Old Water Grove*.

Close Head Shaft is either a later name for the Water Groove Founder Shaft, or they are very close together. The earlier of the two Newcomen `Fire-Engines` was situated in the original Founder meer adjacent to Fielding Yate and in the second half of the 18th century meers were set out *from fire Engine by Sweet Bottoms up towards Burnt Heath 42 Pair* [SCL, Bag 587/2].

Entries in Barmaster`s books, together with an early 18th century map, indicate that originally the Water Groove title was confined to eight or nine meers on Water Groove Vein west from the Founder Shaft, extending from there to the Foolow to Housely road, about 440 yards east of Brosterfield Farm. At the end of January, 1726 William Millns bought from David ffeepound his 13 meers set for Water Groove Vein for £10, but the latter was to retain a 1/24th share in the mine. When the main sough articles were signed in January, 1740, the old Founder was still regarded as the division point where the Water Grove possessions began, but this seems to ignore the purchase by Millns of ffeepound`s 13 meers in Water Groove Vein. During October, 1723 the partners took 37 meers west from Water Grove *for their vein or pipe*, but it seems highly improbable that this was the main pipe.

The position of Water Grove Mine marked on modern OS maps was a later development of the main pipe and dates only from the 1770s and later.

Brushfield Rake extends along the north side of Middleton Dale, very close to the top of the dale side and parallel with it. However, when the Water Grove possessions were checked in January, 1764, they had no title in Brushfield Rake, only 15 meers in Streaks Vein, ranging east to Streaks End. A later entry dated July, 1786 verified the situation: *From the East end of Brushfield Ground on the Great Rake to Stocken side 15 meers*. At Streaks End the vein complex crosses the Dale at the sharp bend opposite Upper Cupola Quarry. Yet further east it was known as Oakenedge Vein, terminating opposite to *Charles Work* (Carlswark Cavern). In 1730 when possessions were set out ranging west from Charles Work to the Fielding Yate, the whole vein was called Oakenedge Vein, neither Brushfield Rake nor Streaks Vein were mentioned. Resolution of soughing agreements in the 1730s and 1740s proved troublesome, the complex interplay within the rake system leading to claims and counter-claims by both the Water Grove partners and also the partners at Oakenedge Sough.

The Founder situated at the side of the Housely to Foolow road was set for the main Water Grove Pipe and was not freed until July, 1771. It was not the original Water Groove Vein Founder as proposed by Kirkham [1967], this was situated adjacent to Fielding Yate as discussed above. Beyond the Water Grove Pipe Founder Shaft the main pipe was worked along an extremely sinuous course in a general south westwardly alignment to a point a little beyond the 19th century Forefield Shaft and adjacent Fairbairn Engine Shaft.

The very name of the mine testifies to its nature and susceptibility to problems with ground water inflows. Contemporary mining documents refer to the presence of large, open fissures in the limestone and the fragmented nature of the rock. These observations have been confirmed by explorations carried

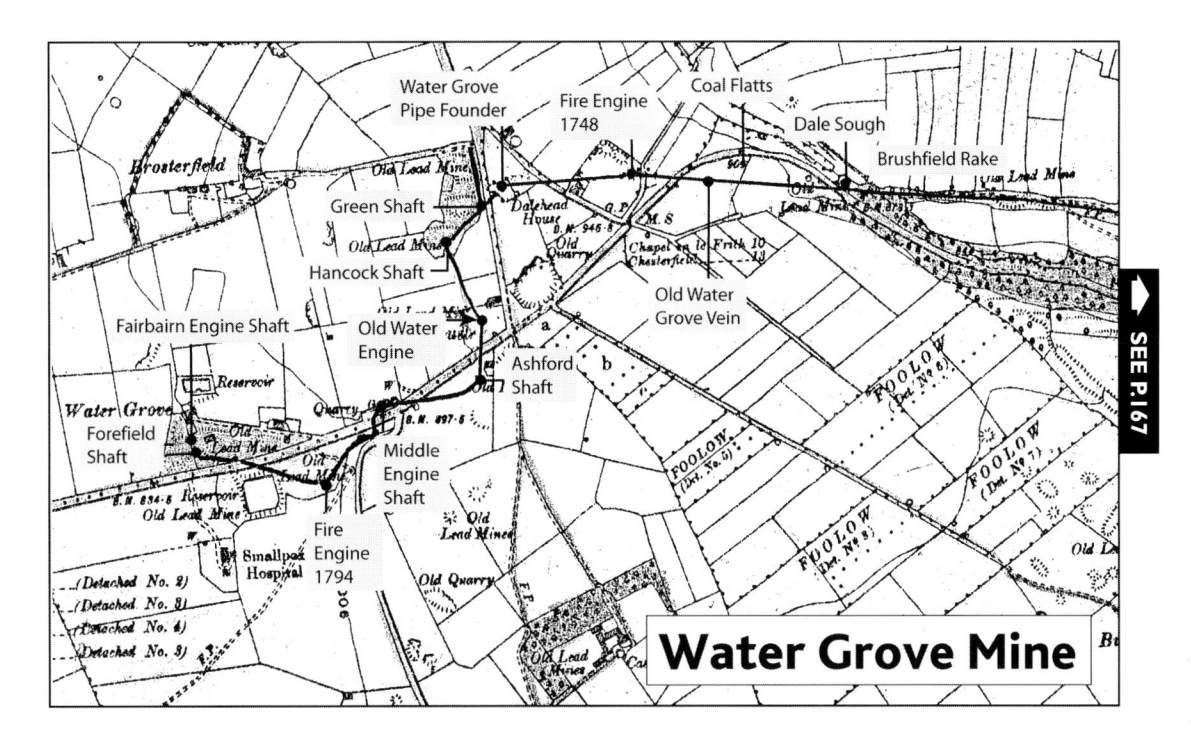

7. Water Grove Mine and the Soughs in Upper Middleton Dale

A tiny walled and slabbed level of uncertain function associated with a natural cavern. First explored and modified by lead miners, who were possibly seeking lower levels in Brushfield Rake. The Level is in 'Lay-by-Pot', Middleton Dale (Paul Deakin).

out in the late 20th century. The explorations revealed major instabilities in several parts of the mine, enormous slabs of limestone having slid away from the vein walls, causing huge blockages in the workings [D. Nash, pers. comm].

During the eighteenth century two soughs reached the mine, whilst at least two more were intended to do so, but abandoned before reaching their objective. Two Newcomen engines operated at the mine, at least one `water-engine` and two *Machines* of unknown design. A large, side lever Cornish engine was installed in the mid 19th century. These combined efforts to drain the workings occupied a period of one hundred and thirty years.

There is a peculiar problem concerning identification of the numerous soughs in Middleton Dale. The situation is very acute with reference to the Water Grove Mine because two different drainage levels were, at various times, each known as Eyam Dale Sough, the problem being compounded by the existence of at least two Dale Soughs, plus Oakenedge (Dale) Sough and Nether Dale Sough and Upper Dale Sough, both of which are un-located.

Few 17th century references to these mines have been found. Earnslow Shaft was situated on Brushfield Rake and in September, 1663 Earnslowe Rake and Earnslowe Close were sold [SCL, Bag 2866]. Maybe Earnslowe Rake was the earlier name given to Brushfield Rake. Sweetbottom Grove, near Dale Head was at work at least by 1671 [SCL, Bag 702]; by the mid 18th century it was owned by the Water Grove partnership. Streaks Vein is aligned along the eastern continuation of Brushfield Rake. Richard Torre and Thomas Ashe were in partnership there in 1685 at *ye taker meer in ye Streaks* [SCL, Bag 3505].

Nothing is known about any other activity in the area before 1715, but by then James and William Millns were partners. They must have been in possession of meers along Oakenedge Vein/Streaks Vein before 1723 because in that year two miners were working at a mine *in the Stockins – within the compass of Mr. William Millns and Partners possessions that belong to Watergroove* [SCL, OD 1502]. The Stockins is almost opposite the end of Farnley Lane. The above mentioned possessions were probably held by them even before 1715 because there are no freeings recorded there after that date.

SOUGH AT COAL FLATTS HEAD, DALE SOUGH, UPPER DALE SOUGH

The earliest sough driven to the Water Groove seems to have been begun from the upper reaches of Middleton Dale. No trace of the sough has been found, but very probably the tail was situated on the south side of the dale close to the point where Brushfield Rake crosses at what was known in the 18th century as *Dale Head*. The sough was then driven almost due west along Water Groove Vein, but how far is not known. The maximum depth of gravity drainage would have been only about 90–100 feet. The first edition of this work [Rieuwerts, 1987] postulated that Coal Flatts Sough was situated near the Mill in Stoney Middleton village, this based on the position of a location known as Coal Flatts given by local information. Slightly later another local source stated that the Coal Flatts fields were on the south side of Middleton Dale, `near to White Rake`. Both are now known to be incorrect.

The Coal Flatts are the two fields immediately south of the long, sweeping bend in the main road before the Foolow road junction is reached [DRO, Eyam Enclosure Map]. Here, in March 1731-32, three miners were given three meers *for an old vein on north side of the Sough at Coal Flatts head* [DRO, Br-T, L56]. In May, 1733 another miner *took five taker meers east in a vein at Coal Flatts Head* these being takers at the other three meers. Perhaps significantly, when some few years later the Barmaster gave five meers at the Dale Head, lying north of Brushfield Rake, written alongside the entry is *1757 Dale Sough*. What was to become the main, deep drainage level to Water Grove Mine had not reached the Dale Head by 1757, so the foregoing information all appears to suggest the existence of a high level sough begun from the Dale Head, maybe soon after January, 1726 when Millns purchased Drabble and ffeepound`s 13 meers. The mine was then just beginning to become a major producer [Guildhall, Marples Papers].

The sough was no doubt used as a pumpway for the first of the Newcomen engines installed in 1748. Sometime before June, 1748 William Soresby, a Chesterfield lead merchant was able to report:

The greate beame is upp and I hope the house will be covered before we get thither – Mr Curr (Mr Carr ?) thinks ye pumps will be going down and are making the place ready for the boyler [SCL, Tibbetts 530/21].

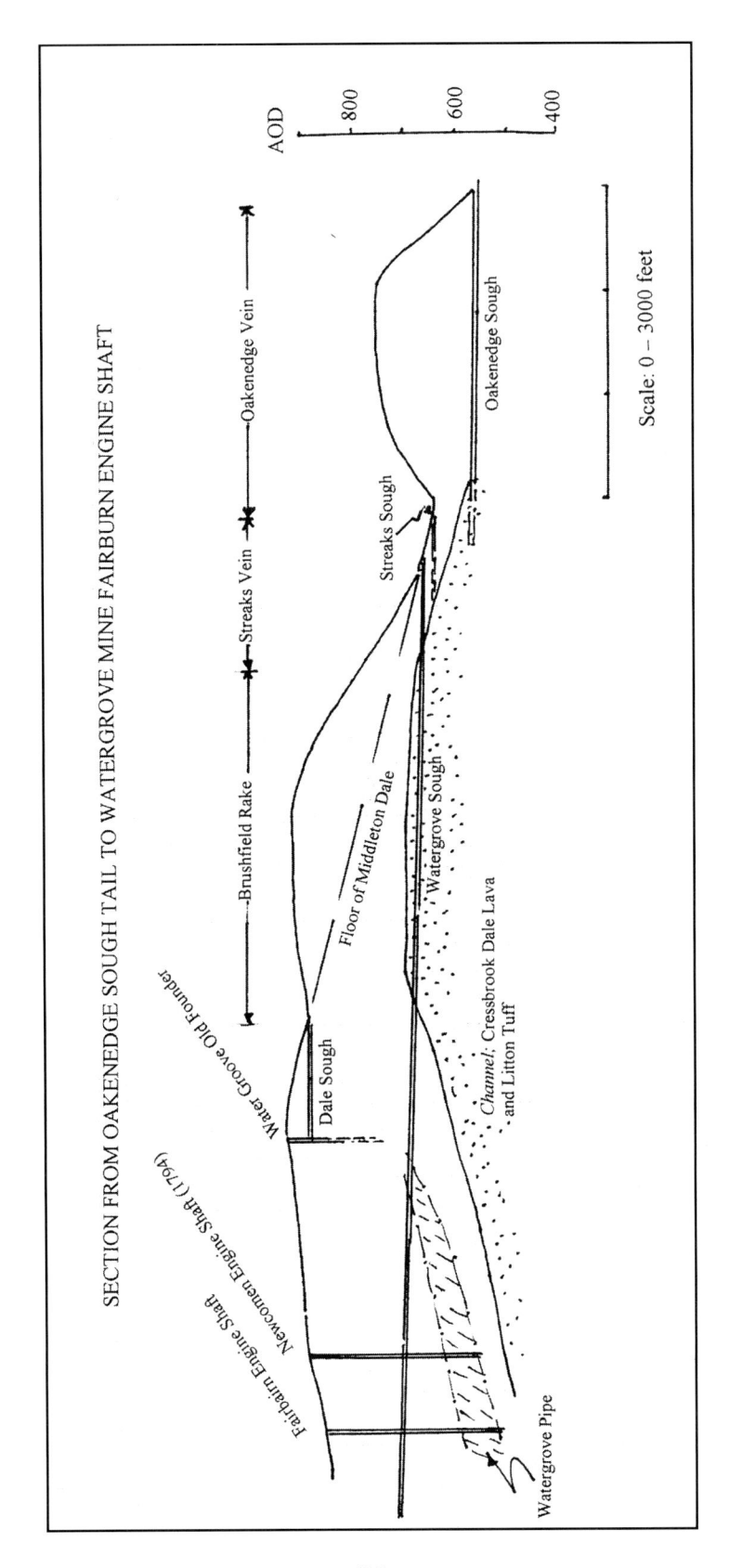

7. Water Grove Mine and the Soughs in Upper Middleton Dale

SECTION FROM OAKENEDGE SOUGH TAIL TO WATERGROVE MINE FAIRBURN ENGINE SHAFT

Mr. Carr has not been identified, but a possible reference to `Mr Curr` is intriguing. John Curr, the Sheffield-based mining engineer was not born until 1756, but his father, also John Curr, was a coal viewer in the North Eastern Coalfield, though no connections with Derbyshire are known. The Fire-engine had a 34 inches diameter cylinder, but it was a failure and was already advertised for sale by March, 1751. The engine was sold to Cowclose Mine, Elton in 1753 for £403-18-2 [SCL, Bag 486]. Two years later the pumps were sold to Portaway Mine, Winster for £80.

Upper Dale Sough is a mystery. Kirkham [1967] acknowledged that its location could not be deduced from the slim evidence available and since that time nothing further has emerged. Information is restricted to two entries in the Eyam Barmaster`s Book, both dating from 1747. They refer to an arrest of 22 meers at the sough, subsequently delivered to the Rector of Eyam for non-payment of £5-8-6 tithe. There is a possibility that it may be identical with Dale Sough, the 22 meers corresponding with Drabble and ffeepound`s 13 meers ranging west from Dale Head, plus the original 9 meers in Water Groove Vein west from the Founder at Fielding Yate.

MILLNS SOUGH, STREAKS SOUGH

Water Groove began to be exploited on a large scale in 1721–1722, probably coincident with the onset of work at Millns Sough, though the two never had any physical connection. Expenditure at the mine in 1722 was £288, rising to £923-13-6 in 1724-1725. By September, 1725 the total charges amounted to £1,638-8-8, whilst 570 loads 6 dishes of ore had been raised, of which 448 loads were mined in 1725. The loss *from the beginning* to that date was £1,132-16-6 [Guildhall, Marples Papers]. Reckonings for the mine continue until July, 1734 but despite at least 3284 loads of ore being sold, the mine lost a few shillings short of £5,000 (ore accounts for September, 1726–August, 1727 and June, 1733-July, 1734 are missing).

No starting date is available for the sough at Coal Flatts Head, but it is probably pre-dated by that James and William Millns were driving in Middleton Dale from at least October, 1723, when two miners were allowed to work a grove:

In ye Stockins – within the compass of Mr William Millns and partners possessions that belong to Watergroove – until Mr Millns doth bring up a Sough to them from the west end of Oakenedge [SCL, OD 1502].

In the above context the words *from the west end of Oakenedge* are taken to mean that the sough began from a point west of Oakenedge, ie. at or near the Oakenedge Vein founder in the Streaks. There is no remaining surface evidence of the sough tail, the surface having been disturbed by road widening, waste tipping from quarries and fluorspar extraction.

Nothing is then heard about the sough until April, 1730 when an agreement was made between the Oakenedge Sough masters and the Water Groove proprietors. Oakenedge Sough was to be extended to the mine and the document concludes:

If the Soogh Levill that Mr James Millns and Mr William Millns – have now in Eyam dale, will not get 15 yards of Levill under the deepest Soles at the Water-groove – then Mr John Wright and Mr Thomas Middleton – is to pay to Mr James and Mr William Millns – at the Water-groove – thirty pounds.

The peculiar wording of this complicated arrangement presumably means that Millns Sough was to be abandoned in favour of Oakenedge Sough, already well under construction and driven from a lower contour. Furthermore, another agreement made on the same day indicated that Oakenedge Sough was to be driven to the west of Oakenedge and then they were to *join Partners with James Millns and William Millns – at Watergrove and to have one half of all Veins or pypes – in Driving up their Soogh to the fielding yate.* There is every likelihood that by 1730 Millns Sough had met channel (Cressbrook Dale Lava) within 1,100 feet from the tail at the Streaks.

The only references to Streaks Sough (rather than Millns Sough) seen by the author date from January, 1737 when the partners there freed an old vein and April, 1744 when a founder was freed *in Streaks Soogh Old Vein lying nere to Brushfield Yate in Eyam Dale.* This last entry must relate to the vein being encountered and freed as the main Watergrove Sough was pushed westwards towards Brushfield Rake.

OAKENEDGE SOUGH, EYAM DALE SOUGH

The date when Oakenedge Sough was begun is not known, but it was about 1715. The original purpose of the level was to unwater Oakenedge Vein and the numerous veins and scrins crossing Middleton Dale; it was not intended to be driven to Water Groove. The latter idea seems to have taken place early in 1730, after Millns (Streaks) Sough was on the point of becoming redundant. John Wright and Thomas Middleton, soughmasters, were *To bring up their Soogh that they are Driving – at their own Cost and Charges.*

After the sough had reached the bottom of the Dale at Streaks End, they were to enter into joint partnership, the partners at Water Groove were to bear half the charges in driving the sough to the vein at Fielding Yate and Wright and Middleton were to have 1/4th of the ore when Water Groove had been drained. Wright and Middleton *is to have all the Veins or pypes – to themselves from Charles-Work to the place in Eyam Dale where their possessions join.* On three days in late December, 1731, the Barmaster set out 63 meers of ground on Oakenedge Old Vein, ranging west from the Founder in Streaks End to beyond the Fielding Yate; 6 additional meers were added in January, 1732. Eastwardly from the Founder in the Streaks End, 31 meers were set *Down to the End of the Sough.*

This entry places the sough tail on the south side of Middleton Dale, nearly opposite to Carlswark Cavern. Until the 1950s–1960s there was a stone trough by the brook side, but Nellie Kirkham thought that it was not associated with Oakenedge Sough, but was fed from a short, un-named sough driven from the north side of the road, north west beneath the old quarry at the foot of Shining Cliff, then northwards to the veins crossing beneath Eyam Dale. Charges for Oakenedge Sough from July, 1733 to December, 1735 reached £272-4-0 [DRO, Grant Papers microfilm], and from August, 1740 to December, 1741 an additional £347-12-0 was incurred [SCL, Bag 544]. Duplicate references for September and December, 1741 refer to the level as Eyam Dale Sough [SCL, Bag 587/47]. A vein was freed by the soughers in December, 1742.

There are several versions of the agreement to construct the main Watergrove Sough, these dated from 1738 to 1740–41. This suggests that work on the main sough was delayed, or that work on both soughs was concurrent for a short period until Oakenedge Sough was abandoned about 1741–1742. The Watergrove Sough agreements confirm that both parties claimed title to meers of ground along Brushfield Rake or Oakenedge Vein and Streaks Vein, and only after resolution of that problem did abandonment of Oakenedge Sough become realistic; another and equally important reason was that channel was met in the forefield of that old sough.

WATERGROVE SOUGH, EYAM DALE SOUGH, FIELDING YATE SOUGH

After the failure of both Millns Sough and Oakenedge Sough, the partners at Water Grove decided to start a completely new level from a point in Middleton Dale opposite to the bottom of Farn(s)ley Lane. The new sough is at a higher contour than either of the older soughs and immediate reaction is of surprise that Oakenedge Sough was not persevered. The reasoning seems to be that the soughers considered by rising to a slightly higher contour they would be able to drive above the horizon of the channel (toadstone). This anticipated bonus did not succeed.

There are at least three copies of the articles of agreement for constructing the sough, two dated 8th June, 1739, one dated 1738 (no month) with schedules signed and dated January, 1740. The different dates may be associated with a delay in the decision to abandon Oakenedge Sough. The new level was to begin at Streaks End in Eyam Dale (the older name for upper Middleton Dale) and driven westwards to the Fielding Yate where the Watergrove possessions began. East from Fielding Yate the mines were variously claimed by both Eyam Dale Sough (ie. Oakenedge Sough) and the Water Grove partners. They were to be amalgamated and shared equally between the two parties. This clause seems to be an affirmation of the 1730 Oakenedge Sough –Water Groove agreement. West from Fielding Yate, that is along the early 18th century *Water Groove Vein*, 1/4th part of the ore obtained below the level of the sough was to be taken as composition.

There are a number of isolated reckonings from the late 1730s, and during the 1740s and 1750s to `Dale Sough` and `Eyam Dale Sough`, but there is insufficient detail to identify them. The earliest definite correlation dates from January, 1759 when a reckoning was made for *Water Grove or Eyam Dale Sough* [SCL, Bag 485]. Subsequent freeings at certain points along the route of the sough, together with confirmation of the possessions belonging to the Water Grove company, are compatible with a driveage rate of about 7 inches per day. During April, 1758 a meer was freed in Earnslow Vein, nearly 3,500 feet from the tail; the Water Grove Pipe Founder was freed in July, 1771, a distance of a little under 6,000 feet from the sough mouth. Despite the siting of the sough horizon, much of the section along Brushfield Rake, about 3,300 feet, was in channel (toadstone).

Reckonings appear for Eyam Dale Sough in 1763 and continue through to 1772, but after the latter date they are referred to as 'Watergrove'. By 1763 ore began to be mined so presumably the sough had passed into limestone again. These reckonings confirm that beyond Fielding Yate the ground belonged entirely to the Water Grove proprietors and was not under joint ownership. Between 1763 and 1772 the sale of ore amounted to £7,580, unfortunately charges exceeding £8,600 resulted in a net loss of £1,063 [SCL, Bag 431a].

Beyond the Water Grove Pipe Founder Shaft, the pipe assumes a sinuous, but overall south westwardly alignment towards Wardlow Mires, within a short distance it also begins to dip below sough contour. The pipe was gradually exploited ever deeper beneath the sough, but the immense volumes of water in the workings was a constant problem. One document describes *a great pipe* ranging from Hancock Shaft to Water Grove Mine. Much of the ore was found in lumps embedded in clay and sand, in what Farey [1811] called *softs or soft-veins*.

Despite the problems, Water Grove Mine was now on the brink of a period of great prosperity. Profits from 1771 to 1786 reached £16,000 [SCL, Bag 432], whilst in the seven years beginning in 1771 no less than 18,674 loads of ore were obtained with an additional 5,900 loads from 1783 to 1786. The workforce was large, in 1784 150 men were employed.

Mr. Joseph Clay of Sheffield was one of the major shareholders and the remarkable circumstances of his appointment of Benjamin Barber of Bradwell as agent were recounted by Seth Evans [1907]. Barber was one of the founders of Methodism in his native village and was so steadfast in his faith that having applied for the post, when Mr. Clay told him he would have to renounce the Methodist cause and attend the Church of England, Barber replied that though a poor man he could not do so and thus expected to lose the position. Clay however was so impressed by his answer that Barber was appointed, served for many years and on the death of Mr. Clay he left his silver watch to *my trusty servant Benjamin*. Barber received a salary of 14/- per week and remained at Water Grove until March, 1805. He was succeeded by his son, Josiah.

The 1780s and 1790s saw the installation of three or four large pieces of pumping equipment, though no descriptions of their design or application seem to have survived. Often merely referred to as a *Machine*, an Engine, or a *Water Engine*, installation took particular skill, requiring specialist engineers. Machinery at the mine also included a Horse Engine, possibly associated with drainage, but of unknown design [SCL, Bag 422; 423; 655/1].

At several dates during 1783, men were paid 1/2d per day for attending the *Water Engine* and for frequent repairs to the *Water Engine race*. Payment was also made to men for *Guarding the Water Engine*. The July–October, 1783 reckoning includes: *Given men at different times when getting the Horses out* whilst in 1784–1785 a reference occurs to *driving the under Level from the Horse Lodge*. Much later, in the second half of 1794, men were paid for *Getting out beam at Old Horse Engine*.

The foregoing information suggests that the Water Engine was a conventional horse-gin winding water barrels, though `getting the Horses out`, `the Horse Lodge` and `Getting out beam` all hint at an underground installation at sough level. Lifting water to surface from considerable depth, or from a higher horizon than sough level would seem unlikely, though it cannot be eliminated. The Old Water Engine Shaft, a few yards south west of Housley may have been the site.

During the later part of 1783 and the first few months of 1784 preparations were in hand for installation of the first of the large `machines`. Miners were: *Shooting room for the Great Pump* and *Shooting room for the Upper part of the New Engine Frame*,

Rowland Hill and Co. Shooting room for the new Engine Frame, 121 yards at 13/-

John Thompson and Co. Expenses when going into the Mine £1-1-9.

This underground work may have been at Green Shaft because in 1783-1784 meers were set out from the shaft *from the New Machine*. Nothing is then heard until the period August, 1787 to October, 1788, when a series of events were recorded in the reckoning book. These include:

Joseph Middleton and Co assisting the Engineers, 10 weeks 4 days at 8/- per week

William Furniss ditto 13 weeks 1 day at 8/- per week – also assisting *in the Pipe*

Expenses to Jno Thompsons men £7-15-0
to men assisting to set the Engine up £3-0-0
Going to Winster to see the pumps 7/8d
John Thompson Bill £167-1-4

This engine was installed at Middle Engine Shaft. Sometime between June and November, 1803, £5-5-0 was paid for *James Drabble and Co. getting out the Machine at Middle Engine* [SCL, Bag 423]. Unless long delays were involved with installation of the previous engine (1787–1788), for which there is no supporting documentary evidence, then apparently yet another *Machine* was erected at the mine during 1789-1790. The new engine was set up close to the Stoney Middleton – Peak Forest road, the site identified by a Barmaster`s entry to the *New Machine Shaft or Water Engine Shaft* [Chats, Bar Coll].

The reckoning book covering the period from November, 1789 and August, 1790 contains the following:

Shooting room for Cistern and Barrels to work £17-10-0

Rowland Hill and Co. Assisting Engineers in putting up the Machine, 252 shifts at 1/4d, £16-16-0

Expenses by Miners when assisting the Engineers to put in the Machine, allowing them dinner and a quart of Ale each for staying double shift £4-3-11

John Thompsons Bill (unspecified) *£87-18-3*

and in March, 1790; *at Water Groove with Thompson fixing of a new engine to draw Water at top of Mire began drawing ye water* [SCL, Bag 655/1].

In April, 1790 *got ye new shaft thro` at top of Mires into ye Pipe* whilst in June, 1790 the reckonings record that *at Water Grove – the new Water Engine by Warm Dale was gated and took off about 50 pumpers.*

A second Newcomen engine was installed at an Engine Shaft south of the main road, almost opposite to the houses at Watergrove. Very ruinous foundations and walling remain at the site which may be connected with the old Newcomen engine house.

Building work began in the second half of 1794 with Robert Eley and Co., masons *walling the Engine House* and smithy. The engine was made by Booth and Co. of Brightside Iron Foundry, Sheffield. The cylinder was 38 inches diameter, the engine rated at 16HP. The pumps, each 32 yards in length, were 16 inches and 15 inches in diameter. During 1795 (month unspecified) the mine proprietors *paid Messrs Booths £673-8-4* [SCL, Bag 422].

During the same period 7/6d was paid: *for repairing a house damaged by the Boiler at Stoney Middleton.* There are no references to building a boiler house, or boiler installation, only to building *Chimney Pipes and Arches*. The Engine House and other ancillaries were offered for sale in 1836 and 1853, but on neither occasion was a boiler house, or boiler installation included. The situation leads to speculation that the boiler may have been located at the bottom of a long-necked bottle-shaped chimney structure, the boiler itself an integral part of the chimney. A similar arrangement, though with two boilers and two `bottle` chimneys, was made by John Curr for the Attercliffe Common Colliery, Sheffield in 1790.

The reason why Curr placed the boiler outside the engine house is explained by Rolt and Allen [1997]:

The dimensions of the engine house were governed by the diameter of the boiler and its surrounding furnace – this necessitated the use of beams of considerable span. Inevitably cylinders tended to `work` on their supporting beams, causing the failure of steam joints, breakage of pipes and generally increased wear and tear. Curr placed the two boilers of his Attercliffe engine – adjoining the engine house – This arrangement enabled him to contract the walls of the engine house and support the cylinder firmly by two sets of beams, each of very short span.

John Curr`s Park Ironworks were close to Booth`s Foundry, and he had close connections with the principal Water Grove proprietors who were also concerned at Hills Rake Mine, Hazlebadge, where Curr installed a Newcomen engine in 1795 [SCL, OD 1500]. The boiler and chimney arrangement at Water Grove may have used Curr`s solution and may have been the first, and only such example in the orefield, though John Milnes claimed an almost identical arrangement at Westedge Mine, Ashover and later at Magpie Mine, Sheldon. It must be stressed that little is known about surface planning at most of the Newcomen engine sites, but at Water Grove archaeological excavation might provide some answers.

Men were paid 14/- per week for working the engine, but it was troublesome and there are frequent accounts for its repair. Nearly a decade after

19th century graffiti in Water Grove Mine (Paul Deakin).

installation the reckoning for June – November, 1803 included payment to Messrs Booth and Co. for £249-7-11, plus £24-8-8 to Messrs Barrett and Co., engineers [SCL, Bag 423]. Despite setbacks with the engine, prospects at the mine were so optimistic that in October, 1797, Mr. Greaves, one of the major shareholders proposed installing another Fire Engine [SCL, Bag 656/3].

The Newcomen Fire-engine worked until 1820, expenditure on coal was usually £17 to £21 per week [SCL, Bag 423]. After a brief trial of the mine, when it was again put to work, albeit briefly, it was offered for sale in August, 1836 [Sheffield Mercury], but was not sold. The engine was still on site when the mine closed in 1853, when it was again offered for sale. The Engine House had a leaded roof and said to be 40 feet in height. It was demolished in mid 1847 it being *ordered that the Old Engine House be pulled down, the slate, stone timber being made available for the new building for the Whim Engine* [SCL, Bag 518].

Ore valued at £14, 075 was raised in the decade beginning 1790 [Hopkinson, 1958]. A profit of £508-2-2 was made in just seven weeks in July-August, 1802 [SCL, Bag 655/2]. The fortunes of the mine suffered dramatic fluctuations in the years 1800 to 1835. For example the years 1803–1806 saw 2540 loads sold realising £5,398 profit. The year 1806 was very intense. A profit of £2,725 was made on the sale of 1274 loads of ore at prices typically 90/- per load [SCL, Bag 587/85]. Ore getting was performed by one hundred and twelve copers. One of the gangs consisted of twenty four men.

By 1808 only fourteen men and five women were employed, but the second half of 1811 was rather better with an influx of miners from Eyam, Bradwell and Castleton. During 1817 only four men worked at the mine, rising to forty one in 1818. The workforce fell to a mere three men in 1820. The mine made an overall loss of £8,900 during the period from 1812–1835 [Willies, 1983].

Very heavy expenditure was recorded in 1819, somewhat at variance with the foregoing information. Mason work, stone and bricks and clay amounted to £24-19-1, whilst castings (£107), millwright work (£110-15-3), and boiler maker (£86-16-4) resulted in an additional £320-7-1. Not included above was board and lodging for fifteen men. Whether all this signifies radical work at the Newcomen engine, or otherwise un-recorded engineering work is not known.

From the date of its first freeing in 1771, the main Water Grove Pipe had been pursued in the general direction of Wardlow Mires. Progress can be judged by the working dates at Green Shaft, old Water Engine Shaft, Middle Engine Shaft and the (Newcomen) Engine Shaft, a short branch level serving as a pumpway [P. Deakin, pers. comm.]. Local information asserted that Watergrove Sough was completed in 1805. Considering the foregoing historical information, the statement is probably correct, but branches from it were driving until at least 1814. *North End Level* was probably a branch, so too *Dam Level*, though their locations are not known. The sinuous windings of the pipe directed that the sough forefield could be extended only as the position and direction of the underlying pipe was revealed. Reckoning books also refer to Watergrove Sough as the Main Level and the *Mean Level*.

The last phase of working at Water Grove Mine began in 1834–35. George and William Greaves, Benjamin and William Wyatt and James Barker formed the nucleus of the new venture, William Wyatt became agent in 1836. They invited Absolam Francis and I. T. Leather to submit reports advising their opinions on how the mine might be de-watered and brought back into production. Francis believed that a 70 inch Cornish engine, lifting 200 gallons/minute to surface from a depth of 480 feet would be sufficient. He did not envisage Watergrove Sough being used as a pumpway, having been informed that it was in poor repair, small in size and was *a very imperfect thing*. A large pumping engine, complete with pumps, plus engine house and ancillaries, including enlarging the existing shaft, would incur expense of approximately £6,400.

Leather considered that a 45HP Boulton and Watt engine, pumping to the sough would be the preferred option, using the 15 inch and 16 inch pumps from the now defunct 1794–1795 Newcomen engine. He recognised the great amount of work needed to repair and clean the sough for use as a suitable pumpway. The alternative was to pump to surface, but as Francis had advised, this solution would need a 70 inch engine.

Eventually, the partners embarked on a hybrid solution. They decided to install a 70 inch Cornish-type engine, using the sough as a pumpway. An unusual, and probably unique for mining purposes, Cornish-type engine using Side Levers as opposed to the more conventional single beam mounted on the bob wall, was ordered from William Fairbairn and Co., Manchester. It was rated at 200HP. The Side Lever engine had been developed for use in ships where its low centre of gravity was a benefit; two similar engines had also been erected in textile mills in Stockport and Stalybridge. A new engine shaft was sunk, 350 feet in depth, connected to the Forefield Shaft by a short cross-cut. The engine at Water Grove Mine was installed by 1839 and the mine cleared of water by 1840.

Willies [1983] noted that no profits were recorded at the mine from 1812 to 1841 and that by 1840 expenditure from the onset of the new venture in 1835 had reached £18,800. A healthy output of ore ensured that by 1846 the very large deficit had been erased and turned into a profit of £2,760 [SCL, Bag 693].

Despite the capacity of the huge Fairbairn engine, the deep pipe workings were frequently flooded, larger pumps were installed and eventually six boilers served the engine. To facilitate stoping in the ever deepening pipe, a Deep Level was driven from the foot of the 1794 Newcomen engine shaft. The length of this gate not known, but before it reached the Forefield Shaft it was already above the pipe horizon. Water was lifted from the deep workings by means of a *Trail Pump* attached to the main lift of pumps, but to facilitate isolation of the heavily watered deep pipe from the remainder of the mine during periods of large rainfall, water-tight metal doors were installed 70 feet above the bottom of the Fairburn Engine Shaft, these recessed into dressed gritstone portals and fitted with tensioning rods. The doors more or less coincide with the base of the down-dip pipe workings.

Watergrove Sough was continued westwards towards Wardlow Mires. Driving the extension, known as the Day Level, occupied 1843–1844, the forefield eventually abandoned in barren limestone 600 feet beyond the Forefield Shaft. The total length of the sough from its tail at the bottom of Farnley Lane to the western forefield was 3,342 yards, construction of which had occupied a period of just over a century.

The mine again began to lose money and by 1849–1850 operations were virtually at a standstill. The half century from 1800 to 1852 saw Water Grove Mine lose £23,000 [Willies, 1983]. The plant and ancillaries were offered for sale in 1853, the Fairbairn engine being sold to Cawdor Mine, Matlock.

8. THE VEINS AND MINES LYING BETWEEN FOOLOW AND EYAM VILLAGE

Mine drainage within this relatively small portion of the Eyam mining field is but poorly understood. With the exception of Black Hole Level, the various soughs were all intimately connected with the series of natural swallow holes that occur along the shale-limestone boundary between Foolow and Eyam, but evidence concerning their dates of construction and alignments is somewhat contradictory.

Crosslow Rake runs east-west from Foolow, passing just south of the Waterfall Swallow and Crosslow House, from where it begins to curve towards the south east, terminating north of Hungerhill Farm. Several 17th century documents refer to a *North Syde and South Syde Vein*. Between Waterfall Swallow and Foolow the vein splits, a mining plan drawn about 1715 by Samuel Hutchinson names the northern branch as Willowbeds Rake and which extends nearly to Foolow village. The southern branch, *Crosloe Rake*, also ends to the east of the village [SCL, Bag 181a]. From the Waterfall eastwardly, Hutchinson marks the rake running almost to the position that eventually became the site of Dusty Pit Mine. A number of shafts are shown, but none are named.

Crosslow Engine must have been located very near to the highest point of the rake adjacent to Crosslow House. The shaft was 237 feet to the water level, the collar some 58 feet higher than *Dusty Old Shaft* [SCL, Bag 587/70]. Nearby, a working west of Black Hole Lane was described by Robey [1964]. Here a shallow shaft gave access into a cavern, largely filled by miners deads and washed gangue mineral. The cavern is considered to be that described by Farey [1811]. The site has been obliterated by `hillocking` operations.

Modern geological maps show the southern branch vein on the west side of Waterfall Swallow, continuing through Foolow village reaching into Grindlow Lordship. They name the whole of it as Crosslow Rake, but the Hutchinson plan names the vein west of Foolow as Moseleys Grove. East of the Waterfall the vein lies at the boundary of the shale and limestone, or just beneath the shale cover, but at surface the remainder is wholly within the Eyam Limestones. Farey [1811] records the vein entirely *in 1st Lime*. A vein breaking north eastwardly near the Waterfall is known initially as Black Hole Vein, but beyond Black Hole Mine it becomes known as the Little Pasture Sun Vein. At Black Hole Mine, a pipe vein trending south eastwards towards Dusty Pit Mine, was known as Redfearns (Founder) Pipe.

Crosslow Rake and Willowbeds Rake feature in several 17th century legal disputes. However, the first available record dates from 1612 when the inventory of Francis Burton of Foolow included mining tools at a grove on Crosslow Rake and *a knocking bucker*, the first notice of the word in the Derbyshire orefield, though by then the term must have been several hundred years old [Kiernan, 1989].

A case was heard in the Duchy Court in September, 1638 disputing ownership of shares in a grove sunk about 1635 in a close in Eyam called Willowbeds. Five miners were original partners at the venture, but a new partner, Shorland Adams of Eyam found *great store of lead* [PRO, DL 1/356]. Two months later Adams had a 1/4th share in *a grove or meer of ground upon a place called Crosloe Rake – commonly called the Northsyde*. Three other Eyam miners, his partners in the mine, joined with John Morrill of Eyam to defraud Adams of his share. Adams claimed that in the previous two years 200 loads of ore, worth £250 had been obtained, but they had given him neither account or allowance [PRO, C3 395/5]. Disputes were heard in the Eyam Barmote Court in 1670 about a mine on Crosslow Rake on Waterfall Flatt [SCL, Bag 702].

SOUGH TO WILLOWBEDS VEIN AND CROSSLOW RAKE

Before 1676 it would appear that mining activity along these veins was not hindered by water problems, but in that year the first record of artificial drainage occurs. Previously, the Waterfall cave system must have taken all water from the upper workings in these mines, recent cave exploration has shown that the water-table in the immediate area must lie below 755 feet OD.

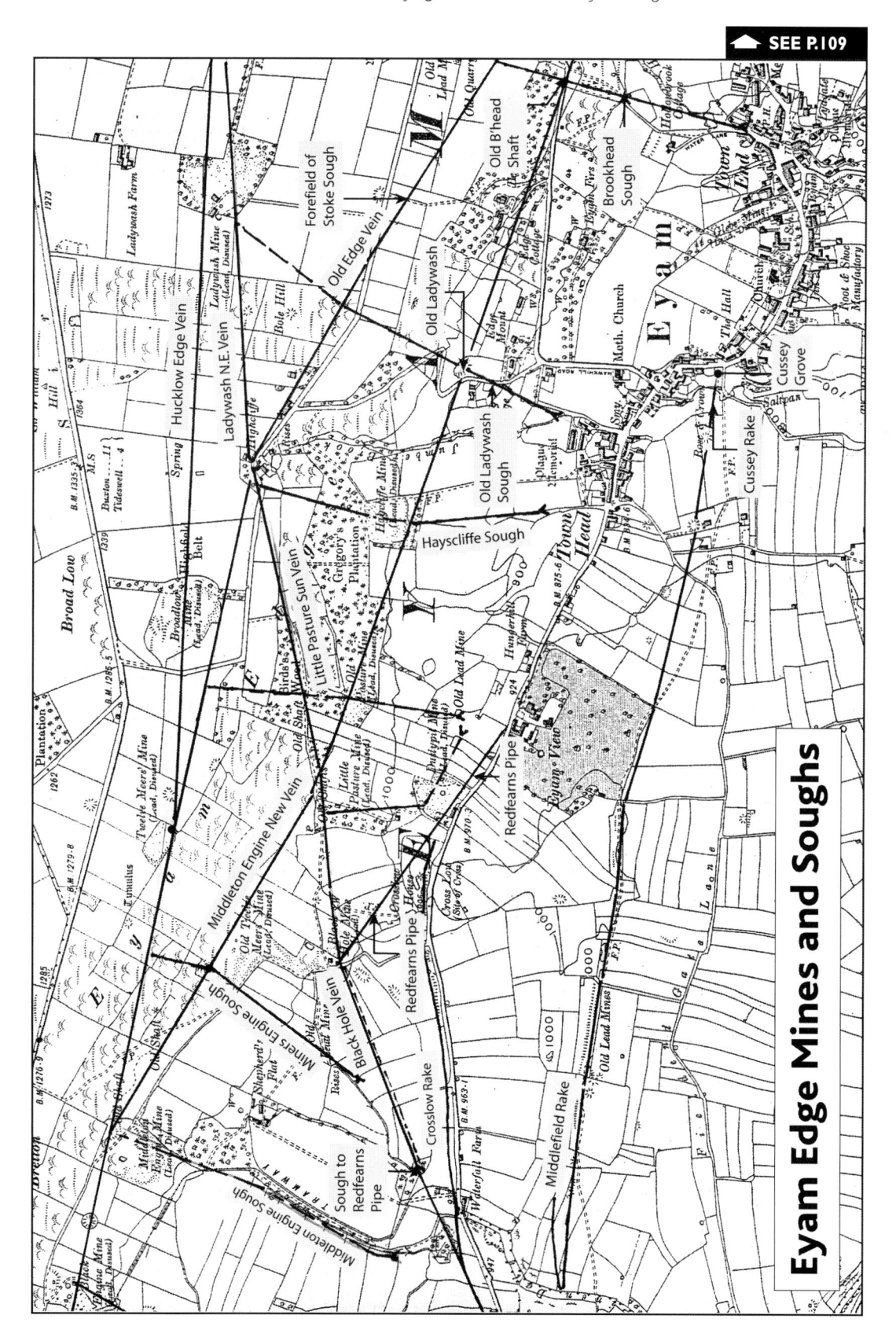

8. The Veins and Mines lying between Foolow and Eyam Village

Eyam Edge Mines and Soughs

A soughing agreement, made between Robert Eyre, Robert Broomhead and partners and a group of miners, dated 30th March, 1676 recites that:

Whereas in a certaine Grove or Meare of Ground in or upon Croslow Rake now in possession of Robert fox and his partners a self open is already found which leadeth southwardly from the said Rake about the space of sixty yards there is discovered it to open itself into a shacke or Wide opens such as Miners commonly call a Swallow at the depth or levell of four or five and thirty fathoms and (- ?) to be of sufficient wideness to receive and carry of – the water – that anoyeth and overflows – the meares and Workes [Chats, Dev Coll].

The miners must have explored the self open and passage southwards into a larger cavern from which Eyre, Broomhead and partners agreed to *bring up* (the sough) *from the said Swallow northwardly – to Croslow Rake, Waterfall flatt and Willowbeds*. Unfortunately, the agreement does not provide the location of the swallow, though an 18th century Barmaster entry notes the existence of a swallow in Frith Pingle, an un-located enclosure, thought to be the very small field west of the head of Linen Dale. The field was known in the mid 19th century as Waterfall Pingle. The surface contour of Waterfall Pingle is 952 feet above OD, therefore the sough was driven at about 742 feet above OD, very close to the present limit of exploration in Waterfall Swallow.

There are no further definite references to the drainage level, but Crosslow Rake Sough mentioned in the Eyam Barmaster`s Book in January, 1721 may be identical (see below).

CROSSLOW RAKE SOUGH

The following entry in the Barmaster`s Book of Entries constitutes all that is known:

January 20th, 1721. Then Roger Shore bid me bring 2 of the 24 – and me and Isaac Wilde and Hugh Bagshaw went into ffrith pingle – where Croslow rake Soogh and the Swallow was – I arrested a pair of Stoses – and Roger Shore took up 2 meers of Ground from thence westwardly and then I arrested a pair of Stoses under a Thorn tree – and then Roger Shore Crosed from thence westwardly to the old Myners Shaft.
[DRO, D3304, Robinson].

This places the `old Myners Shaft` at least 128 yards west of Frith Pingle (Waterfall Pingle?), therefore probably just on the north side of the Foolow-Eyam road and in the range of the Crosslow Rake – Willowbeds Rake vein system. If this hypothesis is correct, then Crosslow Rake Sough in Frith Pingle is unlikely to equate with Waterfall Sough (below), and more probably it is the same as the old, 1676 sough.

WATERFALL SOUGH

Waterfall Sough is yet more obscure. The sough is listed in a 19th century index of mines and soughs [SCL, Bag 432] and in a list of shares held by the Barker partnership in 1776, in the latter merely as: *Eyam Liberty – Waterfall Sough* [SCL, Bag 587/111]. There appear to be three possibilities for the location of this level; the sough driven north from the underground swallow in 1676; a sough driven north eastwards from the Little Waterfall, along Black Hole Vein, through the Deep Sitch enclosures to Redfearn Pipe, or a sough driven eastwards along Crosslow Rake from Waterfall Swallow. The author suggests that the first possibility is very unlikely and can be discounted. A sough driven north eastwards from the Little Waterfall swallow towards Black Hole and Redfearn Pipe sits uneasily with other information (see below under SOUGH TO REDFEARN PIPE).

A sough eastwards along Crosslow Rake is a more attractive proposition though cannot be proven. The standing water level in the shaft at Crosslow Engine was at a depth of 237 feet (753 feet above OD), this contour equates very closely with the drainage offered by the 1676 sough, which in turn suggests communication with the lower natural passages in Waterfall Swallow. A reckoning book concerning Crosslow

---

See map overleaf: The shale gates that extend northwards beyond the Middleton Engine New Vein, may not be direct continuations of the original sough levels, though most plans do suggest continuity. One plan [SCL, OD 1232c] dated August, 1761, definitively names the shale gates extending from Miners Engine, Little Pasture and Haycliffe as soughs. The precise locations of the following drainage levels are not known; Crosslow Rake Sough; Waterfall Sough; Dussey Pitts Sough; Cussie Rake; Sough in Buxtons Close.

Rake Grove covering the period June, 1747 to March, 1750 contains one entry for March, 1749 *for the Levill repairing 5/-,* but there is no additional information [SCL, OD 1154]. Whether the `Levill` refers to a sough along the rake is not known.

SOUGH TO REDFEARN PIPE

An agreement was drawn in March, 1766 between John Wright of Eyam and John Burton, gent. and a group including nine miners, who were partners in Redfearns Founder *a grove or leadmine in Eyam which they cannot work effectively because of water.* For the consideration of £10-10-0 Wright gave permission for them to *bring up a sough from the bottom of a close called Deep Syche – to the mine to unwater it* [DRO, Wright Papers].

Redfearns Founder Pipe ranges north westwardly from opposite Eyam View, rapidly passing beneath the shale cover. It ranges close to Dusty Pit Mine, then continues to Black Hole Mine. No additional information has come light concerning this venture. The surface contour of the enclosure now known as Deep Sitch is far too high for there to be any possibility of a sough tail issuing into daylight there and it is suggested that other closes bearing that name formerly extended as far west as Little, or Lesser Waterfall swallow and the sough was driven north eastwardly from there to the lower, down dip end of Redfearns Pipe. No supporting documentary evidence has been found to suggest this sough may be identical with Waterfall Sough, though the possibility cannot be entirely discounted.

DUSTY (DUSSEY) PITS SOUGH

A mid 19th century memorandum gives the depth of Dusty Pit shaft as 38 fathoms (228 feet) to the Cart Drift and water level [SCL, Bag 587/70]. The water therefore was then standing at about 747ft above OD, very close to the level recorded at Crosslow Engine shaft and also the contour of the 1676 sough level driven into Crosslow Rake. Only one reference to the Dusty Pit Sough has been seen, when in January, 1775 it was noted: *Dussey Pitts Sough will be drove to relieve Cote Close sixty yards* [SCL, Bag 587/47].

There is no further information and it is therefore impossible to speculate on the meaning of the note. Nellie Kirkham believed that Cote Close was at the top of Linen Dale, but gave no other details. She also believed that a mid 19th century, high level pumpway from Dusty Pit Mine drained into the Well Field troughs north west of Hungerhill Farm.

BLACK HOLE LEVEL

This level is even more enigmatic. Logic dictates that Black Hole Level could well be the section of the above mentioned postulated sough from Little Waterfall to Redfearn Pipe at Black Hole Mine. However, the only reference so far located states that the level discovered Bradshaws North Vein [DRO, Wright Papers]. If this vein is to be identified with Bradshaws Engine Mine, just east of Slaters Engine, then it is very difficult to understand where either the sough or the North Vein might have been located.

9. MINES AT EYAM AND THE NORTHERN SIDE OF MIDDLETON DALE

Previous to the arrival of Moorwood Sough beneath Eyam village in the mid 19th century, the mines at Eyam Townend were subject to a localised, very high water table. A detailed plan of veins and mines, dated 1819 [SCL, Bag 199] provides considerable evidence that even at that late date mines around Townend were `drowned out` at depths ranging from only 50 feet to 70 feet beneath the surface. The plan notes that *Veins in Eyam Town End never seen below 12 Fathoms and left very rich much ore got in ye water*. Away from the village, towards the south and south east, the situation was not so acute. For example, Mosley Vein near the top end of Eyam Dale, was worked to 15 fathoms before being drowned and further away to the south east, shafts in Rakey Pingle towards Cliffe Stile were worked 20 fathoms to 25 fathoms in depth before drainage problems occurred.

The extensive natural drainage system, extending from beyond Waterfall Swallow, near Foolow, on the west, to the well known caves in Middleton Dale, has been greatly modified by lead mining activities. The system was partly explored and described by Short [1734]. Persistent local stories are told of old miners introducing chaff into Waterfall Swallow and which was traced passing through Dusty Pit Mine and Hungerhill Swallow, to re-appear in Charleswork (Carlswark) Cavern [Kirkham, 1951]. Moorwood Sough intersected this underground stream system in the mid 19th century, diverting the flow into the sough and all later testing of water flowing into Waterfall Swallow has been traced into the sough. The local stories about the chaff must therefore pre-date the mid 19th century.

Before any intensive lead mining took place, water

Moorwood Sough near Cliffe Stile Mine (Paul Deakin).

sinking underground at the Waterfall Swallow and also at other swallow holes along the shale-limestone boundary between there and Eyam, resurged either from Charleswork (Carlswark) Cavern, or by bottom springs rising in the floor of Middleton Dale [Dr. J. Beck, pers comm.]. Short [1734] was able to explore Charleswork as far as the sump at the bottom of `The Rift`, proving that even then the cavern was probably functional as a resurgence only in times of spate. Construction of a sough driven in the 1680s and 1690s, from the dam of Middleton Mill, along Ashtons Pipe towards Cliffe Stile Mine, almost certainly diverted some of this water away from the Charleswork Cave system and Middleton Dale. Cliffe Stile Sough, (1738–1740) must also have tapped some of this water, further lowering the water table, but details are lacking. One reference notes that shortly after Cliffe Stile Sough was completed the workings were soon dipping below water level and pumping would be necessary.

Water presently sinking at Waterfall Swallow follows a largely unexplored underground course, but it now emerges from Moorwood Sough. It is considered that in flood conditions the Merlin Cavern streamway–Charleswork (Carlswark) cave system takes some water from the Wardlow Basin, the result of capture in the 1760s during the driving of Watergrove Sough. [Dr. J. Beck, pers. comm.]. Auton Croft Sough (which may be identical with the Nellie Kirkham`s `Sough in Eyam Dale`) may have been driven in response to the substantial increase in water flow induced by Watergrove Sough into the Merlin streamway and thus into the veins worked at depth in Merlin Mine and adjacent groves.

Moorwood Sough terminated beneath the lower slopes of Eyam Edge, its forefield in the Cressbrook Dale Lava. Victory Level, a major branch driven a short distance beneath Middleton Pasture towards the Moisty Knowl mines and the Burnt Heath mines, perished in the toadstone on the south side of Middleton Dale. Beyond Cucklet Delph, the same stratum of toadstone, (Cressbrook Dale Lava), was also intersected by the various soughs driven towards Watergrove Mine, but this mine and its soughs are dealt with elsewhere in this book.

The above terminal events excepted, all mining took place within the Eyam Limestones and the Monsal Dale Limestones, but operations were carried out in limestone beneath the shale cover at the Green Lee mines, Bull Hole Pipe and Brookhead Mine. Although these sub-shale mines and their shale gate soughs impinge onto the history of Moorwood Sough, they are more satisfactorily discussed under the collective heading of the Eyam Edge mines and soughs. The limestones dip to the north and north-east, disappearing beneath the shale cover along a line approximately coincidental with Mill Lane, an old trackway that connects Stoney Middleton with Eyam.

The lead ore was obtained from rakes, scrins and pipes. Old plans mark innumerable south west-north east aligned veins and scrins ranging across Cucklet Delph, Eyam Dale and over `The Cliffe`. Many of them are well exposed in the precipitous sides of Middleton Dale and in Eyam Dale and the Delph. The pipes range south east-north west, the most important being Ashtons Pipe, Paul Pipe, Philips Pipe, Bull Hole Pipe and Merlin Pipe. Ashtons Pipe and Merlin Pipe, and no doubt others, do not take the form of a traditional Derbyshire `pipe-vein`, but appear to consist of detached pieces of galena enclosed within a glacial/alluvial infill, occupying near vertical, water enlarged joints; similar examples can be seen in `*Nicker Groove*` in Cucklet Delph.

Records of pre-18th century mining are sparse. Kirkham [1952], discussing the mines around Cliffe Stile, referred to *le Cluff plumbi* and quoted a date of 1396, but she cited no reference. Her interpretation is incorrect, in fact the document is in the Bowles Deeds [SCL], but it refers to *le Stuff plumbi*, i.e. lead ore.

The earliest positive available date is contained in the will of a farmer-miner named John Mosley from Eyam, who in 1587 owned *one grove of the Clyfe In Eyam paryshe* [Kiernan, 1989]. Stoole Grove, at work during the first decades of the 17th century, may have been associated with the Cliffe Stile mines, but positive evidence is presently lacking. No documentation has been located that relates to the period from 1620 to 1670. During the last quarter of the 17th century Sidcop Grove, *Bockinge Old Grove* on Cliffe Rake, Auton Croft Grove, *Pingle Veyn*, New Close Grove, Stub Scrin and Cussey Grove were all at work. So too were several workings situated on The Cliffe and also adjacent to Cliffe Stile, these being associated with a sough driven from Middleton Dale.

A sough was also in existence somewhere near the top of Eyam Dale serving mines in Buxton Close and Needhams Acre. A miner named Edward Torre was killed at a mine near the Parsons Fold, Eyam, in 1699, his death being recorded as due to *plug and wing* [Wood, 1859]. It is difficult to believe that ordinary plug and feathers were responsible, and Torre may have been killed by a premature explosion of gunpowder firing the iron plug out of the shothole. Iron plugs were used for holding the gunpowder charge in the shothole before clay/stone powder became widely utilised for stemming purposes [Rieuwerts, 1983, 1998].

SOUGH FROM BUXTONS CLOSE.

Within the mining liberties of Eyam and Stoney Middleton this sough, in existence before April, 1677, is pre-dated only by the sough to Crosslow Rake and Willowbeds Vein, the agreement to construct the latter being signed in the previous year. John Wright, gentleman, the freehold owner of Buxton Close, along with Francis Wild, Robert Wild and Godfrey Brightmore, of Eyam, miners, were all partners at a lead vein in Buxtons Close. John Wilson, yeoman, along with Robert Thorpe and Robert Berry, two Eyam miners were owners of a shaft in an adjacent piece of land called Needhams Acre, the freehold of Wilson. (A miner named Robert Berry was killed in an Eyam mine in 1690 [Wood, 1859]). The parties agreed that Wilson and partners:

> *may enter into the said Buxton Close into the shaft and Meare of ground next adjoininge to the said Needhams Acre and to drive a drift out of the said Meare into the said Needhams Acre for the unwateringe of the Mine or Mines within the said Needhams Acre, at the levell of the Mouth of a sough now found in the said Buxton Close beinge about ten or eleaven fathom in depth untill it run under the sole of the shafte now sunk or to be sunke in the said Needhams Acre* [DRO, Wright Papers].

The agreement continues with various additional covenants. Wilson and partners were to bear all the charges for sinking the shaft in Needham Acre down to the level of the drift, Wright and partners were to pay one third of the charges for driving the drift, but they were to have all the ore obtained in doing so. After the work had been completed they were to become joint owners, but then Wilson and partners were to pay two thirds of the charges and receive two thirds of the profits.

Needhams Acre was situated on the east side of Eyam rectory and as Buxton Close adjoined to it, then there seems to be a reasonable probability that the grove worked by Wright, the Wilds and Brightmore in Buxton Close was the original Wilds Old Grove, later known as Townend Mine, or Glebe Mine, and the un-named vein referred to in the agreement being White Rake. The mouth of the sough, only ten or eleven fathoms in depth, presents something of a problem, it being unlikely to have had a surface outlet. Probably it emptied into an underground swallow at that depth, in which case it might be identical with the Pippin, or Piping Hole swallow, because in 1751 Wilds Old Grove founder was called `piping hole` [Kirkham, 1966]. When Glebe Shaft was explored in the late 1930s, small levels were seen at about 50 feet in depth.

SOUGH FROM SWALLOW IN CUSSIE RAKE

Cussey Grove was situated at the top end of the Saltpan, the name given to the small limestone gorge at the upper end of Cucklet Delph [SCL, Bag 206/1]. The mine was at the eastern termination of New Close Vein, but the site was obliterated by tipping many years ago.

Cussey Coe Shaft and Cussey Hillock and also New Close Grove were producing very small quantities of ore during 1687 [SCL, Bag 3508]. An un-dated agreement, probably drawn up about 1699–1700, was made between John Bradshawe Esq., and four Eyam miners. They were partners in two taker meers in *Cussie Racke* and were then given shares in the founder meer and Lord`s Half Meer in the rake for which they agreed that Bradshawe *shall have libertie to convey watter to ye Swallowe through ye sd two meers.* The document is not detailed enough to allow the position of the swallow to be located, but it was probably near the Saltpan [SCL, Bowles Deeds 175]. The mine was very close to the shale-limestone boundary and possibly the swallow was located at depth within the workings and formed the underground continuation from a surface sink-hole at the aforesaid boundary.

In September, 1725 John Blackwall of Foolow, acting on behalf of the owners:

> *Shewed me* (i.e. the Barmaster) *9 possessions belonging to William Milns of Grindlow and his partners at Cussey Groove in Eyam Liberty 6 of them for Cussey Old Vene and 3 of them for what they can finde.*

The award of the latter three meers precipitated action in the Barmote Court because in the following month the jury decided that Croft Grove *in Eyam Town Street* and Cussey Old Vein was all one vein; four months earlier two jurymen had descended into Cussey Grove *and said they saw the old man`s dirt that had work`t there before* [SCL, OD 1501]. The year 1725 saw 132 loads of ore mined at Cussey [DRO, Grant Papers].

`EYAM DALE SOUGH`, AUTON CROFT SOUGH

The fields lying above the cliff tops between Eyam Dale and Cucklet Delph and rising slightly towards Eyam village, are known as Auton, or Awton Crofts. Merlin Mine and Pipe, together with several scrins lie beneath these fields and there is at least one capped shaft on Stub Scrin, accessible from Merlin Mine.

The precise location of Auton Croft Grove is not known, but it was at work in 1685 and a reckoning has survived for the period between March and October. Three people were employed, William Bamford, who was paid 9d a shift, plus a drawer and a lad. Expenditure totalled £10-17-10 [SCL, Bag 3508].

Nellie Kirkham [1951] wrote briefly about a probable sough, which she believed drained mines in Eyam Dale and possibly extended northwards to Glebe Mine. She mentioned a local tradition relating to the existence of the level, but did not elaborate on the nature or source of this tradition. No authentic name could be found and therefore she called it *Eyam Dale Sough*. This was a rather unfortunate choice because several 18th century mining documents refer to other drainage levels by the same, or similar names. Kirkham [1968] again briefly discussed the old sough, but gave a slightly different account.

Virtually all traces of the `Eyam Dale` sough tail have disappeared, but until the 1960s a small, walled recess could be seen in the bank on the north side of the Middleton Dale road, about 600 feet east of the junction with Eyam Dale. Water tricked through the base of the walling and then ran in pipes under the main road and fed two stone troughs by the brook side. In her account Kirkham also described a shaft on the floor of the old quarry, behind the former Ball Inn, at the base of Shining Cliff. The shaft was situated at the intersection of Shining Cliff Scrin and Merlin Pipe and had been descended into a sough with flowing water. She thought that from this point the level turned more or less northwards beneath the electricity sub-station and ranged towards Glebe Mine in Eyam village. The present author disagrees with this hypothesis and believes that this level and Auton Croft Sough (see below) may be identical.

The tail of the sough is almost on the projected line of Merlin Pipe. The author considers that the first part of the level would have been constructed as a slabbed bolt, parallel with the road, then continued as a driven level until it intersected the actual line of Merlin Pipe at what must have been a very shallow shaft in the old quarry a little to the north west of the former Ball Inn, as described by Miss Kirkham. Beyond the `quarry shaft` the sough would have passed beneath Eyam Dale to a run-in shaft situated in the wood below the entrance to Merlin Cavern, the former shaft eye being a little above road level. From the run-in shaft the level would have been continued north westwards along the sole of Merlin Pipe.

Only two reckonings exist for Auton Croft Sough, they date from November-December, 1764. Within this short period 16 fathoms were driven at costs varying from 10/6d to 21/- per fathom. The level was used as a cartgate and payments for sludging it prove that flowing water was present. In 1771 the title was given to Joseph Burrs. A reference in an index to `Clayton Croft Sough` is obviously a mis-reading and transcription from an earlier document. Kirkham [1968] considered that Auton Croft Sough might have been driven from a point at the south eastern corner of Cucklet Delph, along Stub Scrin. A level beginning at this position can be explored for about 200 feet along a narrow worked-out scrin, exploration being terminated by a large fall of deads. It is possible that this level may be Auton Crofts Sough, but as discussed above, it is considered that the `Eyam Dale Sough`, driven along Merlin Pipe, and at a contour almost 50 feet lower than the narrow level along Stub Scrin, is more likely to be Auton Crofts Sough.

SOUGH FROM MIDDLETON MILL DAM TO MINES ON THE CLIFFE

This late 17th century drainage level seems to have been long forgotten. No record of it has been found in 18th century documents, or in any printed works; no memory of it has survived in the locality. Yet for a period of some fifteen years considerable sums of money were expended and letters from Robert Ashton to Lord Halifax, owner of the mineral duties in

Stoney Middleton and Eyam, stress the importance of its anticipated success to the local economy.

The agreement for making the sough is dated 7th June, 1683 [Chats, Dev Coll]. The level was intended to drain *Mr. Joseph Ashton Rake, ye Cliffe Rake and ye Dale Groves*. The sough was to begin:

> *at ye Taile of Middleton Mill dam and from there by a ditch or water course – driven into Mr. Bowler`s Meare in – Mr. Ashton rake, Thence through yt Rake to ye Cliffe Stile, Thence up ye Cliffe Rake to ye upper most Meare in Eyam dale and Middleton dale and soe forward as farr as ye same can be Carryed on.*

Before considering historical events, it is necessary to discuss the likely position of the sough and the mines it was intended to unwater. Considerable difficulty has been experienced in arriving at a tentative solution to this problem [Rieuwerts, 1987]. The author's original assumption was that the Middleton Mill Dam referred to in the sough agreement could not equate to the mill in Stoney Middleton village, it being too far distant and at a too low contour for a late 17th century drainage adit. A site in Middleton Dale at or near to the (later) Lord`s Cupola was also rejected. The author concluded that the sough was begun from Mill Lane at a point a little below where Cliffe Stile Vein runs across the lane and close to a postulated and now long forgotten mill, *Middleton Mill*, although there is no supporting documentary evidence. It was suggested the sough discharged its water here. *Mr. Ashton rake* was considered likely to be the north eastern continuation of Cliffe Rake, or Cliffe Stile Vein and was so-named before continuity between the two was proved. The hypothesis was unsatisfactory, but an alternative was elusive.

The situation has now been reviewed and revised in the light of documentation held in the Lichfield Record Office. Papers concerned with the will and probate affairs of the principal shareholder in the adventure, Godfrey Haslehurst, now lead to the view that the mill mentioned in the sough agreement was after all at or very close to the present mill in Stoney Middleton village, and `Mr. Ashton rake` became known later as Ashtons Pipe, the title it bears to-day. The sough emptied into the mill dam, from where it ran along the floor of the Dale as an open ditch until it met with Ashtons Pipe a little west of the village.

The level was then driven along the pipe into Cliffe (Stile) Rake, where it turned southwestwards along that rake to the Dale Grove in Middleton Dale. The positions of two, or perhaps three horse-operated rag and chain pumps are not known with any certainty. Probably one at least was situated on the north eastern end of Cliffe Rake adjacent to Mill Lane.

The sough agreement contains a clause that *where the Levell of ye Sough cannot be carryed deep enough – Pumping, Laundering and other helps* were to be provided by the owner of the sough, Godfrey Haslehurst of Carter Lane and Teversall. He was described in 1687 as, *A great dealer in Coles, thought to be worth £10,000.* Haslehurst was to have a half share in all the mines lying above the level of the sough, and was to bear one half of the costs.

Despite the date and wording of the agreement the sough had by then already been begun, a letter from Robert Ashton of Stoney Middleton, dated 4th March, 1683 speaks of: *ye suff which is now in doinge – ye suffmaster – hath already spent above Two hundred pounds and is dayly spendinge very considerabely* [Chats, Halifax Papers]. Proposals to drive a sough had been mooted by April, 1682, Robert Ashton writing,

> *I have consulted with several Eminent Gentlemen about Soughing of the Dale Grove which seeme thorrow my p`swasions and me takeing pte with them to be very willing.*

A little earlier, about 1680 Thomas Wright, George Moore, Joshua White and Penelope Wright owned *several meers of ground at Middleton Clyffe and a taker meer eastward in a south veine next to the White Coe upon Middleton Clyffe*. Their workings were then stopped by water, but Thomas Held and John Daniel obtained permission from Wright and partners to work the veins above the water level on condition that Wright could redeem them. Held and Daniel refused to do so [PRO, E 112]. However, by April, 1684 Robert Ashton wrote to the Marquis of Halifax:

> *ye mines now are very Bad and almost worked out – so that if it was not for ye expectation of ye Sugh I cold give your Lordshipp Litle or noe Incaragement – but as for ye Sugh if once effected I do not question but will doe very well   And hitherto the Sugh masters Thorrow*

my Incouragement goes on verye well [Chats, Halifax Papers].

A complication arose in the summer of 1684 when a group of miners and speculators took 20 meers of ground, *every meare containes 24 yards* (surely an error ?) *in ye heart of ye worke Mr. Hasleburst hath undertaken to free them from water*. Another setback occurred in October when Ashton reported suspension of the work *by Reason of the Largeness of ye springs is drowned foarth untill the springe, but hitherto hath gone on very prosperously*. Matters were still not encouraging in September, 1685 when Adam Dunkersley, agent to the Marquis wrote to His Lordship, in less than glowing words, *I dout Hasellhurst will not run to his purpose for I feare his levell will not reach it*.

Disputes relating to the sough and mines began to arise in 1687. In February freeing dishes were given to the Barmaster for Steeple Tor Vein, Thomas Frith Vein and at the same time there is the first record of *The Over Ingain Pitt Meer*. Steeple Torr Vein takes its name from the very distinctive, isolated pillar of limestone standing above the cliffs on the north side of Middleton Dale. The vein ranges north east-south west on the south east side of Cliffe Stile Vein; it was known later as Siddalls, or Limekiln Vein. From Ashton Pipe in Middleton Dale to its crossing with Steeple Tor Vein is about 980 feet, representing a driveage rate at the sough forefield of 8 inches/day for the four year period (c.March, 1683 to February, 1687). This rate of advance is somewhat high, but as Dr. John Beck has pointed out [pers. comm.] Ashton Pipe is partly cavernous and contained alluvial fill, both facilitating easier excavation.

The soughers also found signs of near surface mineralisation, the curious entry below appears to relate to a deposit of flott ore found on top of the limestone bedrock [Rieuwerts, 1998]; *Mr. Hazleburst in ye Ingian Pitt – no veyn but a flotter on ye top of ye quarrell – he would not free it* [SCL, Bag 3508]. The site of the Over Ingain (Engine) Pitt has not been positively identified, but from the tenor of Barmaster`s freeings recorded in March, 1687 it was probably on the random of Cliffe Stile Rake, or the South Vein in Little Meadow. A position adjacent to Mill Lane at the point where crossed by the random of the veins is possible. This position is consistent with dewatering the north eastern random of the vein as it approaches and then disappears beneath the shale cover.

The Over `Ingain` can probably be identified with the *Great Gin pit: 2 Gins, 4 chains that contained 142 yards* (and) *52 yards of pumps* [Lichfield R.O.]. Thus at each gin two sets of rag and chain pumps each lifted water from two pump barrels, each approximately 40 feet in length, placed one above the other, providing drainage to a depth of 80 feet or thereabouts beneath the surface.

The sough masters freed two meers in the South Vein *on ye Cliffe next Torr Topp* in March, 1687, a few days later the Barmaster noted *Mr. Benj Ashton making a chaleng concerning ye meer of ground in difference in Little Meadow* [SCL, Bag 3508]. Little Meadow is the small enclosure on the south side of Mill lane where it is crossed by Cliffe Stile Vein, the challenge no doubt relating to Haslehurst not freeing at the `flotter`.

Other information concerning these affairs can be gleaned from a letter dated 21st May, 1687:

Mr Haslehurst in the driving of his Sough meets with a Veyne or Rake got several measures of Oare, paid the Lot for the same, but not a Meere dish – Mr Haslehurst at the first three times of the taking up of the Oare refuses to pay a Meere dish – but would do it if the Barrmaster would set him out a meer of ground and pretended the Proprietors or Posessors of the Myne ought to doe it and that he had no reason to free for them [Chats, Halifax Papers].

This probably relates to Cliffe Stile Rake. The affair takes another twist when one of the owners of the vein and Haslehurst argued about the cost of sinking the *Gyn pit* and its position. An interim agreement was reached and work was to proceed. The letter continues: *Soe we concluded the worke should goe on – The Pit to be sunke must still be 18 yards deeper, 4 yeards long and one yeard wide which is in hard rock*. Eventually, during March, 1688:

Mr. Turner agreed with Mr. Haslehurst for ye Ingain Pitt meer which was forfeit for want of freeing. Mr Haslehurst works the ground at his own proper cost and charges giving a just account of ye charges.

Ore accounts for Eyam and Stoney Middleton liberties are not available for another century, but a rare glimpse is given in a letter dated May, 1690 which rejoiced that 172 loads had been obtained from Dale Grove in two weeks. The higher levels of the mines were poor and by August, 1692 Mr Hazlehurst was dead, but as ever optimism remained:

As to Dale Grove Mr Hazzlehurst`s Executors continue yett working there and are at great charge in endeavouring to bring up the Sough which they hope according to their computation of going all to effect in 24 weeks; in which if they succeed there will without doubt be gotten very great quantities of good Oar [Chats, Halifax Papers]

The papers associated with Godfrey Haslehurst held at Lichfield Record Office tell some of the story between 1690 and 1698. Charges at the *Middleton Dale and Cliffe Lead Mines* from 29th December, 1691 and 2nd July, 1698 amounted to £1,865-14-7 Charges were high in 1694, £693-4-11, but these were somewhat offset by income of £508-2-4. They reflect payments to miners for ore mined and receipts for ore sold. Receipts are not available until 11th, September, 1692, from then until 2nd July, 1698 they totalled £1,048-1-4.

Interspersed with the main accounts are several isolated papers of significance. An inventory of tools and equipment taken on the 4th January, 1692 makes reference to *the nether Ginn, 60 yards of Chains upon 2 Rag wheeles* (and) *28 yards of pumps*. The position of the gin is not known, but like the Great Gin, each pump barrel must have been about 40 feet in length. There was 130 yards of spare chain, *2 Sesternes,* and *20 pare of possessions*. There was also *a Horse gin not set up*. Tools listed include, picks, hacks, a maul, *3 stone nogars, 2 pluggs, 2 wings, 2 small stone wedges*.

Four pages of detailed reckonings have survived covering the period from the end of December, 1691 until 15th May, 1692. Five miners were employed, earning 8d per day on wage, but they were paid by bargain for sinking and driving. The miners included *francis Drable,* perhaps the same miner who was instrumental in setting out the line of Stoke Sough beneath Eyam Moor.

But the most intriguing entries occur in April-May, 1692 when 23/- was paid for *Covring 22 yards over Charlswark* and *Covreing 23 yards at Charlswarke mouth*. The meaning of these entries is not understood. Old workings are visible in several places in the near reaches of Carlswark Cavern and old man`s workings lying beneath the cavern entrance are shown on a late 19th century plan of Victory Level.

CLIFFE STILE SOUGH

When Thomas Short visited the area in 1733–1734 he was able to enter the lower entrance into Charleswork (Carlswark) Cavern and to proceed for 50 yards or more to where the passage was flooded; this point is identical to the sump which to-day prevents further progress without diving gear. The resurgence point for the water flowing through the cave system in the 18th century is not known. Cliffe Stile Sough entered the mine 240 feet below the Engine Shaft eye and some 50 feet beneath the standing water in Carlswark sump.

The sough was begun in the early months of 1737 and by midsummer 1739 the sum of £466 had been expended on it [SCL, Bag 430]. Unfortunately, ore accounts are incomplete, but 68 loads 6 dishes were raised in three and a half months in 1737, which seems to indicate that the level was being driven along a vein. In June, 1738 it was remarked that *Cliffe Stile Sough goes on prosperously*.

An agreement was reached in April, 1739 between the partners at the sough and several owners of sundry adjacent veins. The owners of Stanley Meer Grove sold all their title under forty fathoms deep to the soughers for 1/-; similarly two meers in the South Vein were sold for 1/-; several meers in a vein or scrin north west of Cliffe Stile Grove for 1/- and three meers in Middleton Vein in Cliff Close for which: *the sough partners to give them what they please*. Cliffe Close Vein is shown on a mining plan dated 1716 [SCL, Bag 182] ranging north westwards from Cliffe Stile Rake; Cliffe Close Vein and Middleton Rake may therefore be identical and became known in the 19th century as Paul Pipe. All the aforementioned transactions referred only to the mine titles below forty fathoms deep, the original owners retaining the upper parts [SCL, Bag 542].

The sough probably reached the mine in 1740 because at Cliffe Stile by 11th May *ye Engine is fixed and hope to get oar next week but shall want Mr. Philips Pump part of the oar dipping below the level of our Sough* [SCL, Spencer Stanhope 60506]. Richard Bagshawe Esq., and William Spencer Esq., were freeing veins around Cliffe Stile in the autumn and winter of 1741 [DRO, Br-T L56]. Between September, 1741 and May, 1742 the sum of £396 was spent, during which time 245 loads and 3 dishes of ore were obtained. The adventure terminated about 1744 when the engine and ropes were sold.

The Barmaster's Book of Entries for Stoney Middleton and Eyam records gifts in 1795 to the proprietors of Moorwood Sough of many veins lying on the north side of Middleton Dale. Amongst these gifts one concerned a vein: *wherein a Sough Level is driven up to the Cliff Stile Vein, from the Lord's Cupola, 3 pairs of Stowces – takers at the Stone Pit Pipe Mine* [Chats, Dev Coll]. A sough driven from this position, at a contour of about 500 feet above OD would enter Cliffe Stile Mine at 40 fathoms depth and it is therefore proposed that this otherwise unrecorded sough equates to Cliffe Stile Sough.

MOORWOOD SOUGH OR WILLIAM FROST'S SOUGH, OR EYAM SOUGH

BRANCH LEVEL, VICTORY LEVEL OR WATERGROVE NEW SOUGH

The sough was probably begun soon after 1780, for a letter dated 6th March, 1820 states: *this Sough was begun of 40 years since and driven near half a mile without proper agreements being made* [SCL, Bag 654/132]. The sough was projected by the Morewood family, a document dated 1825, affirmed that the late Mrs. Morewood of Alfreton Hall had an interest in it, reserved to her at the sale of her property in 1799 [Goodchild]. The information is also quoted by Bagshaw [1846] who commented that the family were the original proprietors, but then added incorrectly, that they drove it about a mile. The intended destination of Moorwood Sough is a little obscure, but Wood [1859] asserted that it was intended to drain the Edge-side mines.

The tail of the sough, which has been extensively modified, lies within the grounds of Stoney Middleton Hall, the water discharging into Stoke Brook. Various 19th century plans [eg. SCL, Bag 199 and 206/5] show the line of the sough trending north westwards, approximately in alignment with Mill Lane. Had the level been continued in that direction it would have passed through the enclosures known as Green Lee, towards Brookhead Mine [SCL, Bag 199]. The hypothesis receives some support from events at Broomheads Venture and in the terms of an agreement made by that partnership with the owners of Moorwood Sough. Mr. Humphrey Winchester owned 13/24ths of Broomheads Venture and his Shale Gate Sough was being driven in 1785 towards Brookhead Mine, almost certainly along the line of Bull Hole Pipe, beneath land owned by George Moorwood Esq. Mr Moorwood's ground therefore lay to the east of Green Lee. A division of ground between Moorwood Sough and Broomhead's Venture, was agreed in November, 1786 [SCL, WH 10], whereby the soughers were to take the ground south of Steeple Torr Vein and the miners all ground north of that vein *in Moorwoods Ground*. The implication must be that the original intention of the Moorwood Sough masters was to drive along a line very close to Mill Lane.

For reasons not presently understood, the sough did not continue forwards along the line originally intended, parallel to Mill Lane, but having reached True Pen Vein (probably originally known as Wilds Vein [SCL, Bag 182]), it was turned to the south west and carried along the sole of that vein to a shaft situated in what is now the garden of Rock Cottage in Middleton Dale. Moorwood Sough reached the shaft in the summer of 1795 and numerous veins, mostly un-named, were freed. The principal shareholder in the sough was William Frost and the Barmaster's Book refers to the level as `Mr. William Frost and partners at Moorwoods Sough` [Chats, Dev Coll]. Contemporary levellings taken at Dale Grove and Cliffe Stile Mine refer to *Frost's Sough* [SCL, Bag 518]. By 1790 at least the Barker and Wilkinson partnership owned 10/24th shares in the sough [Willies, 1983].

Beyond the shaft at the foot of Middleton Dale cliffs, the sough was driven north westwards along the sole of Ashtons Pipe. The forefield reached Cliffe Stile Mine about 1805. The sough was some 3400 feet in length to this point; the overall drivage rate being about five inches per day, which is consistent with True Pen Vein being reached about 1790, the shaft in Middleton Dale in 1795 and Cliffe Stile Mine about 1805. The sough was 33 feet under the water mark at Cliffe Stile, the engine shaft being 285 feet in depth to the level.

Unfortunately, no costs are available before 1790, but from that year until 1802 the soughers expended £3,108. The sale of 408 loads of ore reduced the loss to £3,084 [SCL, Bag 482]. From 1803 to 1805 a further £329 was spent, but no ore was found. A note in a diary of the pioneer Derbyshire geologist White Watson, stated that in 1803 Cliffe Stile Mine was very rich, but gave no other information [SCL, Bag 317].

The sough was then abandoned until the 1840s, though proposals were mooted in the period 1819 to 1823 to extend it to the mines beneath Eyam village. A plan, sketched in December, 1819, probably by Thomas Birds, shows all the veins and pipes within an area bounded by Middleton Dale to the south, Cucklet Delph on the west and Eyam village on the north side. The plan, which is endorsed *Plan of veins below Eyam to show the line of the sough necessary to drain them,* includes notes and comments on the depth to water and depth of the workings at many of the veins and mines [SCL, Bag 199]. The comments confirm that most of the mines beneath and adjacent to the village were usually drowned out at no great depth. The veins in Eyam Town End had not been worked below 12 fathoms. They had been left very rich, though much ore had been got in the water. Therefore, whatever natural drainage was afforded by the Waterfall Swallow–Merlin–Charlesworth cave system, it did not extend far enough northwards to benefit the Eyam mines.

A further proposition was put forward in October, 1823, various points being itemised on a document headed *Eyam Sough* [SCL, Bag 518]. A new partnership was to be formed to carry on the sough, the distance from Cliffe Stile Mine to White Rake in Pippin Close in Eyam village being 770 yards. Again, nothing materialised and another twenty years were to elapse before work finally re-started. The well known mining engineer, Stephen Eddy made a report in July, 1841 in which he recommended that Mr. James Sorby should be granted permission to continue the sough to the glebe land in Eyam, driving it 7 feet in height and 4 feet in width, and utilising at least six men [SCL, Bag 587(105)] adding: *The Moorwood Sough at its commencement must be intended as a general drain for mines not at present in the possession of Mr. Sorby.*

The Moorwood Sough Company was formed in 1843, James Sorby of Sheffield being the major shareholder and driving force; his partners included Thomas Fentem, William Cantrell, John Harrison, William Hattersley and the Duke of Devonshire. John Alsop, another partner was the Agent for the sough. The level was continued along the sole of Ashtons Pipe and several plans dating from the 1840s to 1870s show the line of it beyond Cliffe Stile Mine. A much earlier plan, dated 1716 names the pipe, ranging from Middleton Dale to White Rake in Eyam village, as Pingles Rake. Small quantities of ore were measured at *Pingle veyn* and *ye Cliffe* in 1687 [SCL, Bag 3508].

The new sough masters were in hopes of reaching Nut Scrin, 112 yards beyond Cliffe Stile Shaft by January, 1844, but in a letter to Sorby it is apparent they had not yet found it: *the Forefield is carrying but little ore, I do not suppose we have yet arrived at Nut Scrin* [DRO, D2160 PDMHS Coll]. By May 1844, Sorby wrote to Thomas Fentem that he hoped they would soon be able to get ore at Baulk`em Shaft, at the crossing of Shining Cliff Scrin with Ashtons Pipe. Baulk`em Shaft is situated 180 yards beyond Nut Scrin, so certainly ore getting at the shaft cannot have been due to any direct communication with the sough forefield. There were more encouraging signs by September, for ore had been found in the roof of the sough. The miners driving the forefield were receiving 14/- per week. An un-dated plan [SCL, Bag 206/6] shows the forefield 72 yards past Baulk`em Shaft, from where a cross cut had been made in Shining Cliff Scrin, south westwards to intersect Paul Pipe and some ore had been mined. Bagshaw`s *Directory of Derbyshire* [1846] made the unlikely claim that the Sough Company had already driven 250 fathoms *towards the great veins in Eyam Edge,* but of course this cannot be correct, although a total driveage in both the sough and associated veins may have been included in the figure.

Unfortunately, Sorby went bankrupt in 1847; the Moorwood Sough Company was purchased and the Eyam Mining Company formed. They invested £3,200 in the venture and became one of the more successful of the many mid 19th century Derbyshire lead mining companies. After 1855 they sold ore and pig lead worth £41,617 and paid £17,400 to the fortunate shareholders [Hopkinson, 1958]. By July, 1847 driveage of the forefield was costing between £2-5-0 and £2-15-0 per fathom [DRO, Wright Papers]. The following month the sough had reached Eyam glebe land. The rector objected to it being continued beneath this ground, but changed his mind when the Eyam Mining Company paid him £125 for the privilege of so doing.

The sough was continued past Glebe Shaft and the forefield was standing 700 yards beyond the shaft in May, 1858. This would place it north of the sharp bend in the Edge Road and a little short of the Old Ladywash Shaft (not to be confused with the later Ladywash Mine). The toadstone was soon intersected and the forefield, which had employed six men in driving it, was suspended at least by May, 1860. There is no evidence that the level was ever continued beyond this point, though it was within 1,200 – 1,250 feet of Haycliffe Mine. A note dating from June, 1878 comments that from the formation of the Eyam Mining Company until abandonment in the toadstone, Moorwood Sough had cost some £6,000 to £7,000 [Chats, Dev Coll].

Several small branch levels were driven out of the main sough, most along scrins or veins and of no great length. One, of unknown length was driven north eastwards towards Little Brookhead Mine, but nothing is known about its history. The most extensive and potentially important was Victory Level, discussed below and another, rather more enigmatic branch, driven south west from Glebe Mine along White Rake. This was identified by the Eyam Mining Company as the 40 fathom level. During April, 1857 the forefield of this branch level intersected a large spring of water, believed by the miners to issue from Charleswork Pipe. Presumably it was this event that diverted the water running from Waterfall and the Eyam Edge swallows through the Carlswark Cavern system, into Moorwood Sough.

BRANCH, VICTORY LEVEL OR WATERGROVE NEW SOUGH

The important branch level driven from Cliffe Stile Mine, beneath Middleton Dale and toward Victory Mine, may have been commenced previous to the formation of the Moorwood Sough Company. Indeed, one report hints that it may even have extended as far as Middleton Dale by 1843–1844. The level, like several others in Middleton Dale, eventually perished in the toadstone, well short of its target.

Shortly after the formation of the Moorwood Sough Company in 1843, the proprietors of the Hazard title lying on the Middleton Pasture vein complex, immediately south west from the Middleton Dale road, began negotiations with the Sough Company for a branch level to be driven along the vein from Cliffe Stile Mine. A report by Stephen Eddy to the proprietors of the Victory Mine, submitted in March, 1844 commented:

> *An agreement is about to be made between the Moorwood Sough proprietors and a company holding ground on the Middleton Rake Vein for the purpose of driving a branch level westward on this vein.*

He continued by advising the Victory Mine partners to obtain as much ground as they could on the vein, north east from their own possessions, towards those held by the other company (i.e. the Hazard Mine proprietors). Eddy advised that the branch level might be extended to the Victory Mine and *it might not be necessary to erect a steam engine.* Early in the following month a miner named William Brickhill, who had worked in Victory Mine:

> *made particular enquiry into the state of their Counter Level which is drove into the great Vein, part of which we now have in our possession; in the part that belongs to the Moorwood Sough Company there is no ore at present* [SCL, Bag 587/25].

Counter, or Caunter Level means a branch level, an unusual term in the Derbyshire ore-field [Rieuwerts, 1998], although references of a similar age survive from the adjacent North Staffordshire orefield.

Some time previous to the Eddy report, Brickhill had examined the mines owned by the Victory partners. He had recommended to them deepening the Victory Shaft from forty fathoms to sixty fathoms and erecting a 60HP steam engine on the shaft. He believed that all the bearing horizons in the veins and pipes then in their possession would be drained by this arrangement. A crude, diagrammatic and undated plan of the veins around Victory Mine is probably contemporary with Brickhill`s report. It marks *Grate Vein, Jackson Vein, Victory Shaft, Crow and Bone, Dirty Rake, Burnt Heath Shaft and West Side Pipe* [SCL, Bag 587/25].

Subsequent to Eddy`s report, Brickhill was informed that within two or three meers south west from Middleton Dale the branch level would enter the toadstone *and in going West the Channel rises to within 25 meers of the Victory Engine Shaft.* He calculated that even if the Victory Shaft was deepened to 60 fathoms, because of the synclinal structure in which that shaft was situated, no more than 16 or 18 meers of ground on the Middleton Pasture vein(s) would be relieved northeastwards.

At much the same time James Skimming issued a similar report, this on behalf of the Hazard Mine proprietors, but directed at the Victory and Burnt Heath partnership, suggesting the benefits of a consolidation of the two titles. They should together drive forward the branch level through to Victory Mine, thus unwatering the whole of this mining field. The drainage afforded at Victory Mine would be at considerable depth under their present workings. The need to purchase Hallam title lying between Hazard and Victory was recognised [SCL, Bag 587/25].

Despite these detailed reports reviewing the options for deeper drainage of the area, nothing seems to have been done by the parties concerned and all was left until the Watergrove Company began operations in earnest in January, 1847. Before discussing the known development of Victory Level, particularly significant information is given in part of the last paragraph of Skimming`s report which states:

> *That arrangements be settled as soon as possible with the Moorwood Sough Company for the right of clearing out and carrying forward the level and that immediately after such arrangements be completed, the same to be continued with all possible speed.*

This implies that at least a part of the branch level was already in existence by the spring of 1844, but at what date it was made, or its length in 1844 are not known. This statement is also supported by an earlier comment in his report: *This branch level is said to be drove to the Dale road on one of the Hazard Veins.* Meanwhile, James Sorby of the Moorwood Sough Company was troubled on hearing that the Victory Mine partners were contemplating approaching the Sough Company with a view to turning their water, via the branch level, into Moorwood Sough. He was worried that the constricted nature of the lower end of their sough would be overwhelmed by the additional water flows.

The Watergrove Mine partners purchased the Victory and Burnt Heath titles in May, 1844, for £200, appointing William Wyatt as agent. By December, 1844 they were already reviewing the proposed branch. Further interim development took place when Wyatt `nicked` the Hazard possessions in late February, 1846. Work on Victory Level, or as it was termed in the reckoning book, Watergrove New Sough or Branch Level, began in earnest in January, 1847. Unfortunately, the distances driven in the forefield are not recorded, the miners being paid on wage-work rather than by bargain. A typical entry gives: *Sundry persons on wages driving the Branch Level forward along the vein in a south west direction from Cliffe Style Engine Shaft* [SCL, Bag 426b].

Peter Harrison, the gang leader was paid from 2/6d to 3/- per shift. Sometimes seven men were involved, at other times as many as eleven, earning from 2/2d to 2/6d per shift. During 1850–1851, 8 men spent up to 175 days *stoping the sole of the Old Moorwood Sough in order to regain some lost Level.*

Expenditure during the eight years to January, 1854 totalled £1585-8-10. Reckonings continue until the end of September, 1857, a further £743-12-8 being spent during this time, resulting in a total charge of £2,329-1-6. During this latter period the sale of lead ore amounting to just over £73 barely offset the considerable losses; no ore sales were recorded during 1847-1854 [SCL, Bag 587/25]

The well-known `Shaft-under-the-Rocks`, or New Victory Level Shaft, at the foot of the cliffs on the north side of Middleton Dale was being sunk during 1854–1855. The forefield of the Level had reached a point beneath the Dale road by 1856 and was 180 yards beyond the New Shaft by January, 1857. The forefield of the Level ran into toadstone 215 yards south west of the road. A plan of *Watergrove and Victory Level* drawn by George Maltby in February, 1872, notes that the forefield had reached the toadstone by February, 1865, about 95 yards beyond the old Hazard Founder shaft. There is no evidence that any attempt was made to extend the Level through the toadstone and Kirkham`s [1952] assertion that the forefield was in Dirty Rake, 2,300 feet south west of the Middleton Dale road cannot be verified by documentary evidence.

10. MINES ON THE SOUTH SIDE OF MIDDLETON DALE

The most important veins on the south side of Middleton Dale are those associated with Middleton Pasture Main Rake, Thunder Pitts Groves and Dirty Rake and further west, White Rake. The development of the Middleton Pasture and Main Rake veins is fully discussed below. The Burnt Heath mines form a complex of veins, scrins, pipes and flats lying north west of Victory Mine on Middleton Moor. The mines were rich, attracting lead merchant, landowner and entrepreneur alike. Consequently they feature in many legal disputes heard in the Barmote Court and some heard in the Duchy of Lancaster Court during the last quarter of the 17th century. They were not troubled by water problems in their higher levels, the earliest references relating to drainage occur only in the mid 19th century when proposals were mooted to drive the Victory Level branch from Moorwood Sough at Cliffe Stile Mine into the Victory Mine.

At the same period thoughts turned towards steam pumping power. Victory Level was abandoned in the toadstone, hundreds of yards away from the mine and nothing materialised in the form of mechanical pumping. White Rake was worked north eastwardly from the Burnt Heath mines, across Middleton Dale, into Cucklet Delph and in Glebe Mine and Brookhead Mine. North of the Dale drainage of White Rake was effected by the Merlin streamway and associated natural caves, nearer to Eyam village by Moorwood Sough and at its extreme north eastern end by Stoke Sough.

The veins associated with Frith Sough lie on the west side of the bottom end of Coombs Dale and range towards Middleton Lane at the upper end of Stoney Middleton. They were worked beneath a thin cover of shale, but appear to have enjoyed little success.

MAIN RAKE SOUGH AND PASTURE SOUGH

Main Rake or Middleton Pasture Main Rake ranges south westwardly from the south side of Middleton Dale for a distance of 80 meers (2,560 yards) to the boundary of Stoney Middleton and Ashford Northside liberties. The rake is accompanied by many break veins and scrins and also adjacent parallel veins which contemporary documents often recorded as separate titles, yet confirm they merged into Main Rake, Willow pitts Rake being a typical example. The broad belt of workings, extending from the Dale side to Victory Mine, is referred to by Stokes [1880–1881] and later edition OS maps, collectively as Dirty Rake. This is incorrect, Dirty Rake was only 16 meers in length and ranged from Farnsley Pipe, past the north side of Victory Mine, before crossing Thunderpits Lane. The 1 inch to 1 mile OS map (1840 edition) more or less confirms the correct position. A diagrammatic mine plan dating from 1844 shows Victory Shaft and the *Grate Vein,* (obviously Main Rake) on the south east side of the shaft, with *Crow and Bone Vein* and Dirty Rake on the north west side [SCL, Bag 587/25]. Neither Dirty Rake nor Thunder pitts Groves are mentioned in the list of veins in the sough title.

Virtually the whole length of Main Rake has been destroyed by quarrying, hillocking and activities associated with the Cavendish Mill processing plant. No trace of the sough tail remains, but Kirkham [1968] stated that many years before she wrote that article, a friend could remember stonework with water flowing from beneath it into the Dale brook. He considered this to be the tail of a sough and Miss Kirkham believed it was probably the site of Main Rake Sough.

The earliest reference to these mines located so far, dates from 1669 and refers to a dispute heard in the Barmote Court concerning trespass and illegal removal of twenty loads of ore from *a p`cell of freed ground upon – ye Maine rake at Middleton pasture head upon ye moore* [SCL, Bag 702]. One of the defendants was Jonas Crosgill, a miner from Great Longstone who had been implicated some years previously in litigation concerning the so-called Mines Royal in Nether Haddon. The original Middleton Pasture fence was about 1,600 feet north east of Victory Mine, so that the site of this 17th century working has disappeared into the Darlton Quarry extension.

Barmaster entries confirm much activity at Benninsons Grove in the 1720s, characterised by transactions in shares in 1729. The title in 1732 was 15 meers in Middleton Pasture. Ruth Hole branched from the rake at the east end of Rakey Pasture, formerly a part of Middleton Pasture. Main Rake Sough was begun in the autumn of 1740 and was intended to reach the complex of mines on Moisty Knowl. The level would have been some 450 feet beneath the surface at this point, but available evidence from geological data indicates that assuming a dip of 2 to 4 degrees, the forefield would have encountered toadstone (Cressbook Dale Lava) between 1,600 – 3,500 feet from the tail and it was probably abandoned well short of its destination. John Blackwall, the agent at Main Rake Sough requested the Barmaster in 1752: *To send down 2 of his 24 men into Mistey Know Engen – and – found willow pitt rake which was poor at the levell* which might indicate that the rake was in the toadstone at the contour of the sough.

The first reckoning at Main Rake Sough is dated October, 1740 and three months later they freed a founder in Halfroods Old Vein at *the New Sough in the Dale*, whilst in February, 1741 a first taker was freed in the same vein *in Main Rake Sough*. During May, 1742 their possessions were viewed in nine veins totalling 197 meers, or over 6,300 yards. In addition to 80 meers in Main Rake they had 26 meers in the attendant Willow Pitts Rake and 17 meers in Halfroods Vein [DRO, Br-T L57]. A note of optimism had been sounded only a few days previous to the viewing: *They have found some ore at Middleton Main Rake Sough which is likely to be very good* [SCL, Spencer Stanhope 60506/172]. A note written in the following century refers to Willow Pitts or Mean Rake, whilst in July 1844 it was referred to as lying on top of Moisty Knowl and the south side of Victory Mine.

A vertical survey along the line of the sough was carried out in June, 1742:

An Account of what Levell the Main Rake Sough driving up Middleton Pasture will gain to the following places;
From the Sough Tail to Paul Shaft 42 fathom 3 feet. From thence to the Engine Shaft 6 fathom 4 feet.
From thence to the top of Misty Knowl upon Middleton Moor 30 fathom
Which makes 79 fathom 1 foot
According to Jno Botham and Jos Drabble`s Levelling [SCL, Bag 546].

The Engine Shaft is marked by a run-in hollow on the south side of Darlton Quarry, approximately 1,800 feet along the vein from Middleton Dale. The run-in had occurred before 1898 [OS maps].

Miners driving the sough were paid 25/- to 28/- per fathom in 1743–1744, occasionally dropping to only 20/- per fathom [SCL, Bag 546]. The last available reckoning dates from May, 1746, total expenditure by then having reached nearly £760. A trifle under 60 loads of ore were raised in the same period, realising £102. Though no reckonings are available there seems every likelihood that the sough was in work until 1747–1748, for in August, 1748 a quantity of edged boards were supplied [SCL, Bag 547]. This is an early date for edged boards, they are recorded first at Ladywash Mine in 1747 [Rieuwerts, 1998]. The last record of the level dates from 1783–88 when Joseph Timperley obtained some ore from *Pasture Sough* [Chats, Dev Coll]. Timperley`s Grove contained 8 meers in Main Rake and was situated immediately downhill from Benninsons Grove. Little underground mining was carried out on Main Rake during the 19th century, being confined to a few relatively small scale operations. Benninsons Grove had been split into 10 meers in Siddalls Grove and 5 meers in Mortons Grove [SCL, Bag 518].

FROGHOLE SOUGH

Immediately south west of Stoney Middleton village a vein runs north west from the side of Middleton Lane towards the Dale. Southeastwards, surface traces are soon lost, but the vein appears to lie on the continuation of Peakstone Rake, worked at Wren Park in Coombs Dale and in the mid 18th century at Frith Sough title. Towards Middleton Dale the vein diverges into two branches, the more eastwardly one terminates north of the Dale at the side of the very steep footpath up The Grip. The other vein probably extended as far as Cliffe Stile Vein at the top of the limestone tors on the north side. (Cliffe Stile Sough was probably partly driven along this latter vein, identified in the Barmaster`s Book as *takers at Stone Pit Pipe Mine*).

Virtually all surface traces of both veins have disappeared, due principally to extensive quarrying operations and other developments. During the 1950s, the Sheffield Caving Club and other individuals visited an old working on the south side of the Dale, opposite to The Grip. The mine was pointed out by locals as

`Froghole Mine`. A short level gave access to a substantial stope slanting upwards, then descending, but lack of equipment, dictated that a thorough inspection was impossible.

The only historical records located date from 1772-1773. The first is dated July, 1772, when ten meers were set out on Froghole Vein for William Frost and partners at Stone Pit Rake Mine, the meers ranging south west from the Dale side. Four months later a new vein was freed at *Luck-at Last* lying at Middleton Town Head. The founder was situated on the north side of Middleton Lane. Finally in April, 1773 eight meers were given to Edward Timperley at Codders Venture:

> *on a vein on the south side of Middleton Dale called Luck-at-Last. The north west end of this range stands at the Sough End which is called Frogghole Sough and rangeth southeast.*

The sough was probably driven south west along the sole of Froghole Vein, but reference to the *Sough End* at Luck-at-Last may just mean that it drained that vein instead; although this proposition seems unlikely.

The above scanty references excepted, nothing is known about the history of this sough, but it seems reasonable to conclude that it was of limited importance and extended no further than beneath Middleton Lane. No trace remains of the sough tail, but this is not surprising considering quarrying and building developments, not least the re-alignment of the brook course and construction of bankside retaining walls.

FRITH SOUGH

Peakstone Rake, worked in Calver Liberty from at least the 17th century, crosses the lower end of Coombs Dale at what became known in the mid 19th century as Wren Park Mine. On the west side of the Dale the vein passes into Stoney Middleton Liberty. The Frith Sough title, or Wilds Venture, set out in March, 1758, was situated wholly within Stoney Middleton; it included 23 meers in Peakstone Rake, ranging west from the Calver Liberty boundary through Frith Pasture, up into Jane Close, 20 meers in Bull Hole Vein and sundry meers in two veins *in the Frith*.

The course of the sough is not known, but it was probably begun at Stoke Brook and constructed as a bolt beneath the flat valley floor, following the boundary between the two mining liberties. A search for surface features revealed nothing. After crossing beneath the Calver–Stoney Middleton road the sough probably continued south westwards into the lower end of Coombs Dale, where it intersected Peakstone Rake. The sough would have intersected the rake at a depth of only about 60-65 feet, with an additional 100 feet or so to the highest point towards Middleton Lane. When Wren Park Shaft was examined in the 1850s a worked-out pipe vein was found at a depth of about 70 feet. (The deep drainage of Wren Park Mine is considered under the history of Calver (Mill) Sough).

Frith Sough is first recorded in June, 1757. Charges from then until December amounted to £196-6-6, with an additional £61-5-7 accruing by March, 1758 [SCL, Bag 486]. The account book continues until April, 1759 but there are no further reckonings. Four loads of ore were measured in 1761, the last reference to the venture being in March, 1764 when a share was sold.

SOUGHS and LEVELS within EYAM and STONEY MIDDLETON LIBERTIES having uncertain provenance or intended function

NETHER DALE SOUGH
UPPER DALE SOUGH

There were a number of soughs in Middleton Dale referred to during the 18th century merely as `Dale Sough`, or `Eyam Dale Sough`. Details of the two levels listed above are very sparce. There appears to be a reasonable possibility that Upper Dale Sough may have been identical with Coal Flatts Sough, situated near the head of Middleton Dale and made to serve the older, upper workings at Water Groove (for detail see under that section). A 1/22nd share in the level was sold on 11th April, 1747 and on the same day the Barmaster:

> *dispossesed twenty two pairs of stows belonging to the Uper dale Sough partners being once dispossesed and set up again and not arrested according to Custom and burned all in the Mineral time of the Day* [DRO, Br-T, L56].

A few months later the sough title was given to the Rector of Eyam for non-payment of £5-8-6 due to him for Tithe, but he was not satisfied and took the shares of Mr. Longsden and Mr. Mower in Stoke Sough, Brookhead and Shaw Engine. Nether Dale Sough is more enigmatic. The title was given away for want of workmanship and except for the note below, nothing further is known about the sough: *Then delivered to Joseph Mossley the Nether Dale Sough Mine and the taker meers thereto belonging* [DRO, Br-T, L56].

LEVEL IN UPPER MIDDLETON DALE

A mine shaft 40 – 50 feet in depth, communicates at its base with an `old man`s level driven into a natural cave system known to cavers as `Lay-by Pot`. The slabbed level follows a sinuous course and extends for some 200 feet to a collapse beneath the Middleton Dale road, the original entrance presumably destroyed by road construction. The level is of very small cross section and cannot have served as an access point [pers comm. Dr. J. Beck]. A possible explanation is that miners, having found the cave system, believed it might lead them into the lower levels of Brushfield Rake. Fearing a water inrush, the level was constructed as an intended sough in anticipation of such an event. Considering the dates of construction for the soughs into Water Grove, this level may be of considerable antiquity.

SHEFFIELD SOUGH

This sough was situated in Eyam Dale (the name often given to Middleton Dale west of Oakenedge, Hawken Edge on OS maps). The only reference to it occurs in a document dated March, 1752, but which harks back to about 1730, detailing fines on mine owners when the Barmote jury were denied access to a mine, as apparently was the case at Sheffield Sough [SCL, Bag 587/44].

SOUGH ALONG CHARLESWORK PIPE

The line of Charleswork Pipe is shown on several mining plans [SCL, Bag Coll] and ranges northwestwards from the entrance to Charleswork (Carlswark) Cavern, passing beneath Eyam Dale and probably beneath Cucklet Delph. The pipe would have intersected Merlin Pipe where the latter is crossed by Cowlishaw Scrin. Contrary to popular belief it is not aligned along the line of the Carlswark Cave, although old mine workings are met at many points within that system. The pipe must lie at depth, at or beneath the water table, but no evidence has been seen during the course of recent (post-1940s) cave or mine exploration. Pipe leaders were seen in Victory Level in the 1860s. Kirkham [1968] was given local information about the existence of a supposed sough driven to drain the workings, but dismissed the idea. The author agrees with this and does not consider that a sough of this name existed. Maybe short passages driven within the cave system, for example beyond the Lower Entrance sump, may have given rise to the notion of a sough.

HOLMES SOUGH

Shares in the sough were offered for sale in August, 1782, along with mines on Eyam Edge. No other details are available and it is impossible even to speculate where this level might have been situated.

MOLL`S DRAIN

Depicted as a straight line on Moll`s map of Derbyshire, with the words `A Drain` alongside. The position of the tail on the west side of the Derwent in the general area of Calver–Grindleford is completely inaccurate and the north of west line cannot be satisfactorily matched with any known sough, but most likely it was supposed to represent the intended alignment of Stoke Sough.

11. THE MINES AND SOUGHS OF CALVER, HASSOP AND ROWLAND

The limestones forming the western side of Calver Peak and the eastern flank of Hassop Common belong to the Monsal Dale beds, the overlying Eyam Limestones occur in Northcliffe Wood and around the eastern side of Calver Peak. Along their fringes the limestones dip to the north east and east at angles ranging from 20 to 35 degrees, before disappearing beneath the shale cover.

Igneous horizons were not important, except at Backdale Mine where a mid 19th century branch level from Brightside Sough met toadstone in Deep Rake which resulted in its abandonment about 1844–1845 [Willies and Fletcher, 1975], yet there is evidence contained in a mining report dated 1853, that it was continued in that stratum in the 1850s until final abandonment [Rieuwerts, 2005]. There is no other evidence that toadstone was met elsewhere in either mine workings, or the deep soughs driven to drain them.

Within Calver Liberty the most important veins were Brunda Croft Vein, Peakstone Rake, running across the northern flank of Calver Peak into Coombs Dale, Red Rake rises from beneath the shale cover a little east of the Calver–Hassop road, from where it then ranges more or less south west, passing the Muse Mine shaft, eventually joining into Deep Rake. Situated on Peak Pasture were Catsall, or Cat Rake at the top of Northcliffe Wood and Dog Rake, both veins running almost due south into Hassop Liberty adjacent to Backdale Mine. A little higher up the hillside was the site of Gospel Mine, largely destroyed by hillocking.

Within Hassop Liberty, the eastern end of the great Deep Rake complex splits into many smaller veins in the vicinity of Backdale Mine. A mine plan dated 1728 names Deep Rake as the *Engine Vein*. The Breech Veins break out of the Engine Vein in the vicinity of Busks Mine and an *Engine* close-by, though not named, is probably Busks Grove [Wolley 6676, ff198-199]. Backdale Mine was formerly known as Busks Grove, *Hassop Busks Grove* or *Backtill Engine*. Between Deep Rake and Water Hole Mine, the latter mine situated on top of the hill above Hassop Common, there is a great complex of mineralised ground. Many veins and scrins occur, but much of the ore bearing ground was worked from within the steeply dipping bedding planes and in vertical joints, the former being known as *hadings*, the latter as *plumbs* [Rieuwerts, 1998]. A plan of the workings adjacent to White Coe Mine, just east of Water Hole, names no fewer than thirteen of these hadings, worked both there and in Brightside Mine [SCL, Bag 200]. Much of the very rich ore mined in Breachside Sough, Brightside, Harrybecca and White Coe mines was obtained from these deposits. Ranging north east-south west along the brow of Hassop Common and more or less coincident with the Hassop-Ashford Northside boundary is the *White Coe Great Vein*.

Mining in the area is very ancient, but the most important development was the involvement of William Humphrey and Christopher Schutz and the Society of Mineral and Battery Works. Humphrey took a lease of all the lead mines in Calver Lordship about 1570, whilst around 1571 William Furneys (Furniss), a miner from Calver, was working at *the old Rake in Calver*, the location of which is not known [Donald, 1961]. Humphrey and Schutz introduced the water vat and wire-meshed sieve into the Derbyshire ore-

Hadings in Harrybecca Mine, Hassop Common (Jon Humble).

Stoney Middleton, Calver and Hassop Common

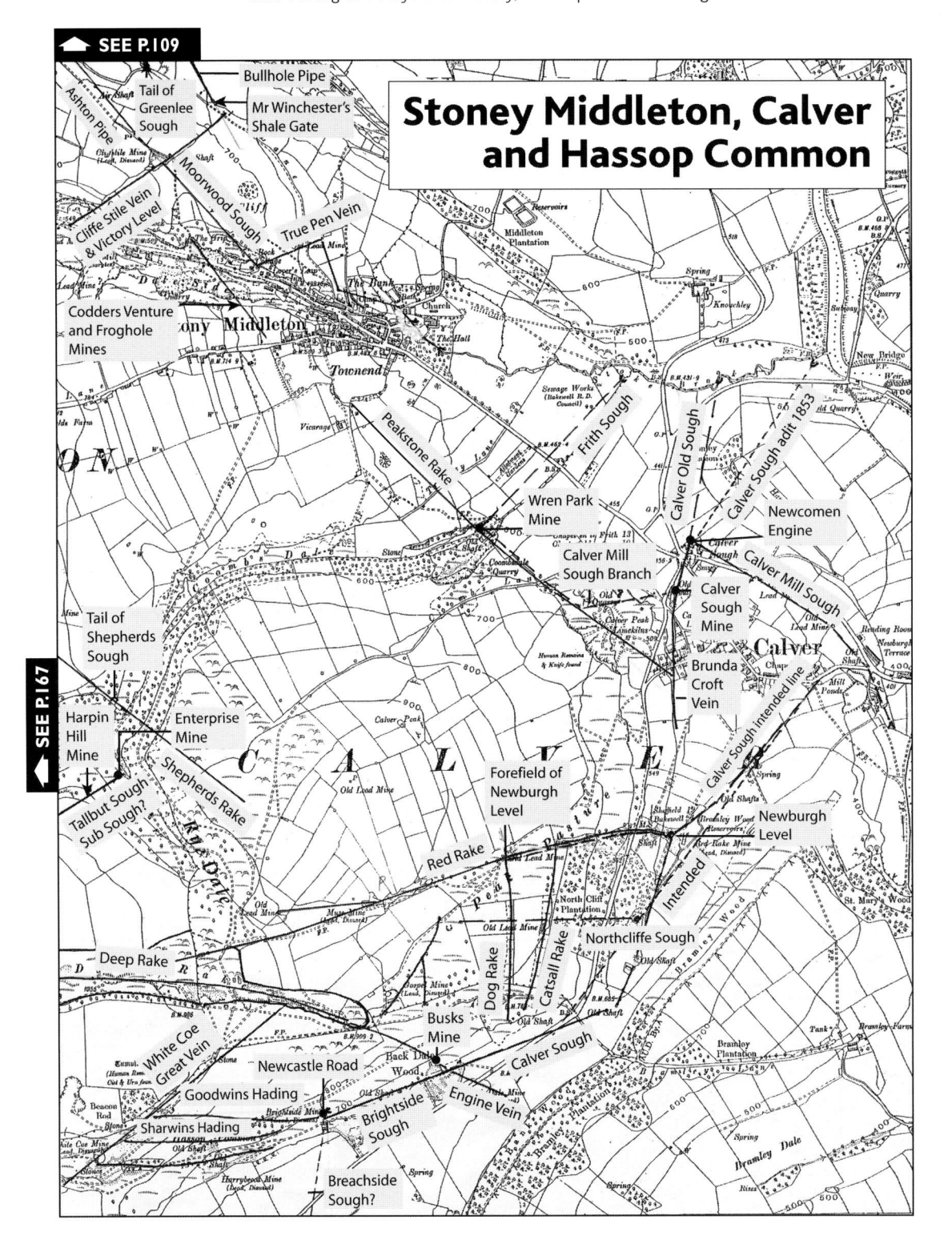

field about 1570-1572 [Kiernan, 1989]. At the same period, Humphrey established his ore hearth lead smelting mill at Beauchief, near Sheffield. This mill was the earliest water powered ore hearth serving the Derbyshire mines, the ore supply being maintained largely from the old hillocks at mines on Calver Peak. The monopolies claimed by Humphrey resulted in a protracted series of law suits, fully discussed by Kiernan.

During 1581 a Special Commission acting on behalf of the Society reported:

> *there is noe order kept in getting* (ore) *thereof and in keeping open of the same rakes but that sifted earth is cast upon the rakes – whereof there is much spoiled* [PRO, E 134/24].

For example it was reported that at *Calver Northcliffe*, bouse containing much good ore was being discarded in 1582. During October, 1586 a survey carried out by Edward Stanhope, surveyor of the Duchy of Lancaster, spoke of much small sized ore that could be obtained by use of the sieve and vat from the huge heaps of waste formerly taken out of the *forsaken workes known as the old Rakes* [PRO, DL 44/390].

The importance of lead mining is reflected in the holding of a Barmote Court at Calver in 1577 under the direction of Anne Shakerley, Lord of the Manor. Two of the nine mineral articles written at this Court relate to washing ore [SCL, Bag 343].

The next available record of mining dates from over half a century later. There was a dispute in 1653 about ownership of four meers of ground at Red Rake on Calver Peak A part share had been purchased in 1646 by Humphrey Ellis *a poore labouring myner in the lead mynes within Calver* [PRO, C3 442/43].

Complaints were made in the Barmote Court in 1660 concerning a half share in three meers in *Catsall Rake* (Cat Rake) [DRO, D 598, M/M5]. Somewhat later, during the period 1669 to 1673, the Barmote Court for Calver Liberty heard complaints arising at Peakstone Rake, Northcliffe Rake, *Dogg Rake*, and the presently unlocated *Sourduck flatt upon Calver peake* [SCL, Bag 702].

The Duchess of Devonshire brought a case into the Exchequer against five miners, claiming non-payment of tithe ore. The evidence included information that *Bushes Grove in a Rake in Hassop* (obviously Busks Grove) was working in 1679 and that no tithe had been paid. George Ruddiard owned 1/4th of the mine [PRO, E 112, 383/95].

Excellent examples of sooting and fireing in narrow veins can be seen in the swarm of veins in the plantation at the south western end of the Harrybecca title, adjacent to White Coe Mine [Barnatt and Worthington, 2006]. Radio-carbon dating has established a date for this work to have been carried out within the period 1650–1700 [J. Barnatt, pers. comm.].

Mine drainage did not become a problem until the latter part of the 17th century. From that date until the final abandonment of lead mining in the late 19th century, at least six drainage soughs were driven and steam powered pumping engines were installed at Calver Mill Sough, Brightside Mine, Wren Park and Calver Sough Mine.

CALVER CROFTS SOUGH AND CALVER OLD SOUGH

Two soughs were driven into the veins and mines adjacent to the north and west side of Calver village and the northern slope of Calver Peak, the above named level and Calver Mill Sough. There is evidence to suggest that Calver Crofts Sough, begun in 1694 and Calver Old Sough are identical though the link cannot be proved at present. An agreement dated 6th September, 1694 allowed Daniel Mosley, Cornelius Dale, Cornelius White and their partners:

> *to dig, Myne, sough and worke – any Mynes, Veynes or Rakes – and – bring up a sough into ye old Rake or Veyn called Calver crofts Rake* [Chats, Dev Coll].

The location of Calver Crofts Rake is not known, but it may be the same as Brunda (Brunder, Branda) Croft Vein; no other references to Calver Crofts Sough are known. A map of the possessions of the North Derbyshire Mining Co. dated 1853 shows the line of the Brunder Vein ranging nearly due south from Stoke Brook. It passes through the site of the mid 18th century Newcomen engine at Calver Mill Sough Mine (behind the old Eyre Arms public house), skirting the western end of Calver village, before terminating near Red Rake [DRO, Br-T LP 4]. The map also shows *Calver Sough Adit* emptying into Stoke Brook at its confluence with the Derwent, then driven beneath Hare Knoll for some 2,000 feet, terminating at Calver cross roads. No trace of the sough tail remains at the position shown on the mine plan and no air shafts have been located, but the plan is almost certainly inaccurate and a more feasible interpretation is that the sough ran into Stoke Brook, but some distance further upstream, maybe on the *random* of Brunda Croft Vein. It would then follow beneath the flatter ground around the flank of Hare Knoll rather than directly beneath it. The section would have been driven almost entirely through shale.

The sough could have offered only very shallow drainage to Brunda Croft Vein, for example, about 35 feet at the shaft behind the Eyre Arms. There is no evidence that the level was continued southwards along the sole of the vein, or to its intersection with Peakstone Rake, a distance of some 800 feet. If it did so it would have drained that vein to a depth of about 80 feet at the intersection and the deepest section of Peakstone Rake, on the northern brow of Calver Peak, could have been unwatered to about 250 feet.

There was a lack of success, this reflected in a lawsuit heard in the Duchy Court in 1719. William Sharshaw, a Chesterfield merchant involved in the Hucklow Edge mines, had bought a 1/24th share in Calver Sough Mine for £150 in November, 1718. The mine was said to have great potential, but it turned out to be very poor and Sharshaw claimed he had been cheated by William Bradley, a Matlock miner from whom he had bought the share [PRO, DL 1/477]. There is a possibility that the Calver Sough referred to might be that at the Ball Eye mines in Bonsall Liberty, opposite to what later became the Via Gellia Mills. These mines were very rich and profitable and Sharshaw`s description of a very poor mine hardly fits.

A pain was laid in the Calver Court Rolls in April, 1722 that no one *shall go or make a footway after the Groves or Shafts belonging to Calver Sough Except those persons that hath buisness or is concerned with the said Sough or Ground* [SCL, Bag 344]. Reckonings for Calver Old Sough are available for the period 1724 to 1731. The Duke of Devonshire owned a quarter share in the venture and during the seven years a charge of £580 was only slightly offset by the sale of 67 loads of ore for £114, resulting in a loss to the proprietors of £466. Limited expenditure of £15-14-2 in 1738, was followed by only £4-8-6 in 1740; no ore was measured [Chats, Dev Coll]. Detailed ore accounts for Calver Liberty become available from September, 1740, but Peakstone Rake was not in production and Brunda Croft Vein measured only very limited quantities of ore. Clearly these veins had been worked out to the level of Stoke Brook and possibly a little deeper by means of hand pumping and the sough must have been abandoned.

CALVER MILL SOUGH

Calver Mill Sough, or Milln Sough was begun from the dam of Calver Mill, near to the Derwent. The sough tail, though much modified, still issues water. It is situated in the garden of a house near to the bottom of Riverside Close. The sough was driven close to the shale-limestone interface and until the 1960s the course of it could be traced by a line of sinking dirt mounds from three air shafts situated between the tail and the Newcomen engine pumping shaft on Brunda Croft Vein, behind the old Eyre Arms. However, building and other modifications within the last forty years has obliterated all trace of the shafts.

The sough was begun in the last quarter of 1756 and by spring, 1758 it had cost £624. A Newcomen Fire Engine was installed at the shaft behind the Eyre Arms, but no engineering details are known. The next reckoning, dated May, 1758 amounted to £806-8-0 and it may be safely assumed that the extra large charge included payment for the Fire Engine [SCL, Bag 486]. Some £2,025 had been expended before profits of £958 accrued on 2,732 loads of ore mined in 1765–1766 [Hopkinson, 1958]. Until the abandonment of the mine in 1776 at least 6,900 loads were measured, but no accounts are available for the year 1763, therefore a total yield of 7,500 loads might be expected. Production was spasmodic; 2,250 loads were raised in 1766, followed by 1,150 loads in 1767, but a dramatic fall to only 80 loads in 1768. Production declined after 1769 and between 1770 and 1774 only 6 loads were mined. The mine title was valued at £1,000 in 1768.

The Fire Engine was offered for sale in April, 1772 [Derby Mercury], but it was not sold until 1774 for the sum of £486-10-5 [SCl, Bag 431a]. An abortive attempt was made to recover the pumps, but a second attempt was more fruitful and they were sold to a colliery owned by Mr. Barnes. A memorandum written after the closure of the mine comments:

This mine raised a large quantity of ore and many people were of the opinion that it would have answered had it been carried on by a competant Overseer and the miners paid as

The Cornish Engine House at Calver Sough Mine.

they ought to have been, but it seems now that it would never be of any use to the Proprietors unless a new sough could be carried up which would completely drain it [SCL, Bag 431a].

The mine then stood idle for more than three quarters of a century, until 1857 when work began at Calver Sough Mine. The extent of Calver Mill Sough is not known, but by the mid 19th century the original title was changed to Calver Sough, the name shown on Ordnance Survey maps for the locality of the cross roads and immediate adjacent area.

Kirkham [1951] considered that Calver (Mill) Sough was finished in 1840, but she gave no references, neither did she comment on whether this included the extension to Wren Park Mine. The sough was cleared out as far as Wren Park Mine at the bottom end of Coombs Dale in 1857, according to Willies [1982] at *fairly considerable expense*. The old level was again cleared in 1860. Calver Sough Mine was aquired by Thomas Broomhead and Thomas Burgoyne and Co. in 1851. They took title to meers on Peakstone Rake as far as Wren Park Mine in Coombs Dale at the Calver-Stoney Middleton liberty boundary, as well as meers on other veins, but little is known of their activities. Maybe they drove the extension to Wren Park Mine. Nellie Kirkham also considered that a branch was driven south westwards along the line of three small shafts situated on the north eastern side of Calver Peak, but she produced no documentary evidence.

Work of a more substantial nature began at Calver Sough Mine in 1857 subsequent to the formation of the North Derbyshire Mining Co. A 70 inch Cornish engine, rated at 150-200 horse-power, steamed by three Cornish boilers, was installed in 1858. The engine was made at the Bowling Iron Works, Bradford and cost £2,280. The pumps were supplied by Messrs. Walker and Co., Sheffield. The engine house and boiler house were built by Mason and Booth and cost £1,038. Work on sinking the Engine Shaft was started in January, 1858; it was 14 feet by 10 feet, divided into three compartments, pumping, winding and man access. The shaft was sunk 12 fathoms beneath the `old man`s workings, but was drowned out at 25 fathoms [Green, 1887]. Calver (Mill) Sough was used as a pumpway for the engine.

The venture was a failure, expenditure reached about £20,000 and the mine was abandoned in 1863 along with Wren Park Mine. The Cornish engine was sold in 1869 to the Magpie Mine, Sheldon where it worked until 1883, after which it was removed to Manners Colliery, Ilkeston. The chimney and buildings which dominated the skyline at Calver Sough were demolished in 1921.

NEWBURGH LEVEL OR RED RAKE SOUGH

Red Rake was worked in the 1640s and 1650s, a case being heard in Chancery relating to a dispute about four meers of ground at *Giles Groves* on Calver Peak

The fine portal of Red Rake or Newburgh Level, Calver. The level was begun in October, 1851 (H.M.Parker).

[PRO, C3 442/43]. Various mines on the rake were producing ore for brief periods during the 18th century, but output was recorded for only sixteen years in the forty nine year time span from 1740 to 1789 [Chats, Dev Coll]. An isolated reckoning took place at *Red Rake or Calver Sough* in 1765, pointing to the existence of a branch level from Calver New Sough having reached the vein, but as no further ore measurements were recorded the level was no doubt very short and work soon abandoned.

Nothing is then known about Red Rake until the mid 19th century. Various items were supplied to `Red Rake Company, Broomhead and Co.` in 1851-1852 by a Calver timber merchant, of which the most interesting are *Two New Dressing Tables, £1-3-0* and *New Hopper to grinder, 7/6d* [Thornhill, 1965]. An illustration of a hand powered grinder, complete with hopper and two rollers can be found in Stokes [1880–1881]. The Newburgh Level (sometimes called Red Rake Level, or Red Rake Sough) was begun in October, 1851, the date confirmed by a datestone at the level portal. By January, 1852 it had already reached a point beneath the Calver-Hassop road and was expected to reach the `old man's` workings within a short distance. The first 180 feet from the entrance, lying on the east side of the road, were driven through shale. Shortly afterwards, in October, 1852 the proprietors of Red Rake and the Calver Peak Mines (Gospel Mine and Muse Mine) agreed to unite and consolidate their interests under one title [Chats, Dev Coll]. The consolidation became known as the Peak United Mines or Mining Company. A report by the well-known 19th century geologist Professor D. T. Anstead, dated April, 1853 states that the Level forefield had reached a point 260 fathoms (1,560 feet) from the entrance. This position corresponds with the intersection of Red Rake with Dog Rake. Dunham [1952] contributed an unfortunate double error by claiming that Red Rake Level reached Dog Rake and was then continued to Catlow Rake. Cat Rake, originally *Catsall Rake*, is the nearer to the adit entrance; the name Catlow does not occur in any contemporary lead mining papers. There is no evidence that Newburgh Level ever extended beyond the forefield as it stood in April, 1853, i.e. at the intersection with Dog Rake, whilst Dunham also quoted the same length for the level.

Mathew Newbould, a mining agent from Pateley Bridge, North Yorkshire reported in March, 1853 that: *This Level is constructed sufficiently large to admit of Wagons being drawn by Horse Power* [DRO, Br-T L266]. Slightly contradictory is an un-dated report noting that *15-20 tons of earth and mineral are brought to the floors by each waggoner per day.* The Company purchased a *Grove Waggon* for 10/- in 1859 [Thornhill, 1965]. The usual optimism displayed by the Mining Journal is in evidence in September, 1855 when it reported that *The Day Level will shortly reach Gospel and Muse mines,* though as noted above there is no evidence that the level was ever extended beyond the point it had reached by April, 1853.

Conflicting evidence also arises in the mid 19th century. Acting on the advice of Mathew Newbould that a sub-level 87 feet beneath the adit should be driven to connect with Brightside Sough, shortly afterwards Anstead was able to report that work was underway, but the vein had not been cut. A note in the Mining Journal [Sept. 1855] claimed that this level had been driven under the guidance of John Taylor. The precise relationships between the 1765 branch sough, any work done by Taylor and the Newbould/Anstead reports are unclear.

The last ore measured at Red Rake supposedly took place in April, 1873, yet in May, 1879 the Barmaster gave 43½ meers to Isaac Bradwell, the meers extending from the mouth of Newburgh Level, south west almost to the upper end of Ryedale [Chats, Dev Coll].

G. C. Blackwell Ltd. took both Red Rake and Northcliffe mines in the early 20th century, coincident with a long newspaper article giving the mid 19th century history of both mines. Blackwell's obtained title 1907, they were followed by the Grove Syndicate who worked the mines until 1919. Both companies mined fluorspar and lead ore from Red Rake, Catsall Rake, Dog Rake and from flats associated with Dog Rake. One flat was described as being 22 feet wide and 2 feet 6 inches in height [Dunham, 1952]. The lower level discussed earlier was also driven (continued) by these two companies to Dog Rake.

NORTHCLIFFE SOUGH

Northcliffe Sough was developed at three distinct periods of time. The initial development took place in the mid 18th century, about 1762-1773; the second phase was begun in 1853; the final work was carried out in the first two decades of the 20th century. This last episode was largely devoted to working fluorspar.

The extent of the 18th century Northcliffe Sough title is not known. A plan of Calver New Sough dated

1728 shows Lambing Holes Vein and Silver Well Vein both within Northcliffe Wood [Wolley, 6677 ff198-199], but they are not recorded in the mine reckonings. No doubt Northcliffe Rake was exploited along with Cat (Catsall) Rake, Dog Rake and possibly Camm Rake. The geologist, A. Strahan`s field map, dated 1886, shows the level taking a peculiar, almost semi-circular route beneath Northcliffe Wood between the Hassop road and Catsall Rake [BGS, Keyworth]. The author considers this may have been the alignment of the original sough. An alternative theory, that the sough was driven at depth as a branch level from Calver New Sough, has no supporting documentary evidence. The attraction of deeper drainage must have been considered; a similar branch toward Red Rake was in existence by the 1760s, but perhaps potential problems with composition payments to the soughmasters presented an obstacle to the idea at Northcliffe Sough.

The earliest record of the sough dates from May, 1762. Until the end of July, 1763 some £332-16-2 had been expended, but only 45 loads of ore were sold, plus 17 loads of hillock ore [SCL, Bag 487; 546]. Small quantities of ore continued to be raised until 1768, thereafter working carried on until 1773 when the mine was abandoned *Deserted being thought of no value. Expended upwards of £900* [SCL, Bag 431b].

Kirkham [1953] recorded that the entrance to Northcliffe Sough was still open, but very shattered. A keystone bearing date 1853 was reputed to lie face down at the partially collapsed entrance. Despite being termed a sough, like Newburgh Level it may have been intended to serve primarily as a haulage gate rather than a drainage adit; it certainly had an outlet to surface a few hundred feet south from the contemporary dressing floors at Newburgh Level or Red Rake Sough. The 19th century level may have been a rehabilitation of the 18th century sough, but the meagre available evidence does not support this hypothesis. In contrast to Strahan`s field map, Barmaster`s plans dating from 1863 and also from the early years of the 20th century depict Northcliffe Sough driven in a straight line for 1,610 feet, almost due west beneath Northcliffe Wood. It continued into the veins on the eastern side of Calver Peak, before terminating at a cross vein named on a barmaster`s plan dated 1863 as the *Gospel and Red Rake Vein* [Chats, Dev Coll].

Exploration of the sough in the 1980s or 1990s encountered what was described as a high, spectacular hading stope [Terry Worthington, pers. comm.].

Virtually nothing is known about either the 19th or 20th century operations. The mine, along with Red Rake was re-opened in 1907 by G. C. Blackwell Ltd, work being continued by the Grove Syndicate, but water problems forced closure of the mines in 1917 [Dunham, 1952]. Both companies exploited thin ore shoots in Cat Rake and Dog Rake.

A well-known photograph dating from 1908 shows a large group of men near the mine entrance, in the foreground the Barmaster prepares to measure about twelve tons of lead ore.

CALVER NEW SOUGH (known as BRIGHTSIDE SOUGH after 1775)

Note; during the 19th century the whole length of the sough became known as Brightside Sough, or even occasionally as Backdale Sough [eg. Kirkham, 1951].

The tail in Calver village to Busks Grove; c.1728 – c.1751

A very diagrammatic, extremely elaborately embellished map, drawn by Thomas Atkinson, dated 1728, marks the intended line of Calver New Sough [Wolley, 6677 ff198-199]. The plan denotes that the sough was intended to be driven in a straight line for a distance of almost 1,550 yards to the *Engine Vein* (i.e. Deep Rake, here depicted as 60 yards in width) and to the *Breach Veins*. The three Breach Veins break south westwards from Engine Vein. The `Society` or owners of the sough held title to 27 meers of ground in Red Rake, 29 meers in the Engine Vein or Deep Rake and meers in *Dogge Rake, Catsall Rake, Silver Well Vein, Black Sticking Vein and Middle Vein*. Had the sough been driven along the intended line much of the driveage would have been within limestone, Deep Rake would have been intersected east of the Hassop road, just beneath the shale outcrop. Mine maps dating from the 19th century prove that the original line was changed, thus allowing easier driveage through shale, probably for some 3,600 feet, as far south west as the head of the valley beyond Northcliffe Mine. The level then turned south west into limestone and continued through to Busks Grove.

The 1728 plan establishes that the sough was planned to terminate at Deep Rake in the vicinity of Busks Mine (Backdale Mine), although this mine is not marked on the plan. A letter from Eyre of Hassop Hall to his agent also confirms the arrangement:

the suff from Calver to the Busks you told me they intended to begin at the Milldam and carry it up the hill – I fear if they bring it up the bottom it will take away all the water from those pasters if they can secure me from that I shall be very willing to agree [SCL, Bag 363].

The sough tail, now almost completely silted to the roof, issues water into a sunken stone trough in Calver village, the flow formerly running in an open leat to the site of the original mill dam. The leat has since been culverted and its course altered by modern housing and garden developments. It is now usual to refer to it as Brightside Sough tail for reasons explained below.

No agreement to construct the sough survives, and no definite date for the commencement of driveage is known, but 1728 is consistent with later evidence. A 1/12th share in *Calver New Sough and all rakes, veins, meers and possessions in the Liberty of Hassop and Calver which belongs to it – also a 1/12th of Busks Grove in the Liberty of Hassop* were purchased in July, 1736 by Thomas Middleton from Benjamin Bagshawe for £80 [SCL, Bag 3352]. A reference dating from the 1730s records *Hassop Busks Engine or Backtill Engine,* confirming that Busks Grove was identical with the later Backdale Mine. Somewhat earlier, in 1717-1718 there were isolated reckonings at *Corver Grove or ffroggatt busks* [DRO, Wright Papers]. There exists a fragmentary reckoning for Calver New Sough and Busks Grove dating from March and August, 1739, but it is of little historical value [SCL, Bag 542]. Thomas Middleton, paid Matthew Frost in January, 1740 *for 1/24th of 8 meers of ground in the Liberty of Calver which said ground was posses`d by James Wild as Takers at ye Busks partners in a vein called Deep Rake* [SCL, Bag 542]. The eight meers, together with the twenty nine meers already possessed by the sough owners, comprise the whole length of Deep Rake up to the Calver-Ashford Northside liberty boundary.

Complete reckonings for Calver New Sough are available covering the years 1744–1752, during which time £800 was expended, but a loss of nearly £473 resulted from the sale of a mere 183 loads of ore [SCL, Bag 547]. Two accounts for April, 1745 note that Robert Platts and partners were paid £1-9-0 per fathom, followed by payment of £2 per fathom, the latter *for driving three and a half yards more in the Limestone* [SCL, Bag 598]. These two reckonings indicate that the sough level was passing rapidly from shale into limestone, consistent with modern geological interpretation that the level was excavated at, or very near to the limestone/shale interface. Busks Grove, meanwhile, mined little ore; from midsummer 1724 until the end of 1749 only 557 loads, plus some hillock ore, realised a sale value of £825. A mere 252 loads were obtained in twenty two years. The mining involved the owners in a loss of £431.

The sough probably reached Busks Grove in 1751–1752. An un-dated document, but presumably post-1752 states that: *About £1,400 spent above the oar found in bringing up the sough* [Chats, Dev Coll]. The benefits of deep drainage were quickly felt at Busks Grove where ore output between 1751 and 1754 increased, totalling 1,015 loads, exclusive of Lot [Chats, Dev Coll]. The initial optimism must have dwindled rapidly as production declined, for example from 1757 until 1762 only 334 loads were sold. Output had virtually ceased by 1771, a mere 20 loads were measured in 1774 and 1776. The loss at Busks Grove from 1750 to 1754 was £189. A loss of £1,400 at Calver New Sough and £620 at Busks was scant reward for twenty three years of barren driveage. The reason for the rapid decline in ore production from a zone of rich mineralisation is not understood. A report and valuation of Barker and Wilkinson`s shares in mines submitted in 1782 revealed the situation at Busks Grove:

ye Sough has formerly been carried almost to ye Deep Rake but ye shafts and gates are all run in: if a shaft was opened and ye Level carried on it may be of some value [SCL, Bag 634].

The level referred to above almost certainly must have been an incompleted branch from Calver New Sough, driven to tap Deep Rake, perhaps beneath the toadstone. A later, mid 19th century branch from the sough was driven for the same purpose, but was abandoned on reaching that stratum. Both Calver New Sough and Busks Grove were regarded as being of no value at a later valuation carried out in 1795.

CALVER NEW SOUGH or BRIGHTSIDE SOUGH, BREACHSIDE SOUGH.

Busks Grove to Brightside Mine; 1775 –1782

The forefield of Calver New Sough stood within the Busks title for almost a quarter of a century. A new agreement was drawn up and signed in April, 1775 whereby it was decided that the sough should be extended through Froggatt Grove to Brightside Mine, but at the expense of the Brightside proprietors [SCL, Bag 744]. The sough reached its objective in 1782, draining the mine to a depth of 41 fathoms (246 feet) at the Engine Shaft.

Before proceeding further, it is important to establish the various 18th century mining title boundaries along the foot of Hassop Common. Much confusion has arisen in the minds of mining historians in distinguishing between Old Brightside Mine, Brightside Mine and Breachside Sough. The latter included a shale gate sough and mine sharing an identical name. The confusion is not diminished by the Breachside workings being referred to in quite random fashion as Brightside Mine.

Nothing is known of the early history of Brightside Mine. The mine was worked by William Twigg from at least 1763 to 1769, but a mere 77 loads of ore were sold, reflected in an operating loss of £438-8-3. Twigg owned 21/24ths and 1/48th of the mine [SCL, WH 6]. This contrasts sharply with the high levels of output sustained at Breachside Sough in the same period, it being obvious that two separate mines were at work. The mine worked by Twigg was referred to in the 1780s as `Old Brightside` it occupied the ground between White Coe Mine to the south west and Breachside Sough (later Brightside Mine) to the north east. It was still a separate title until 1788 at least. Later, in the mid 19th century `Old Brightside` became known as Harrybecca Mine, or Middle Grove.

Breachside Sough title, established in 1759, extended from `Old Brightside` north eastwards but did not include Froggatt Grove, where between 1758 and 1765, 1,077 loads of grove ore were measured. The Breachside complex proved to be extremely rich and profitable, working the many veins, scrins, plumbs and hadings beneath the south eastern flank of Hassop Common. The net effect of this major development was to delay any extension to Calver New Sough until the mid 1770s.

The position of Breachside Sough has caused much speculation, for example by Willies and Fletcher [1975] and Rieuwerts [1987]. The author now considers that the sough tail issued into the significantly named Sough Brook, at a point about 2,130 feet almost due south of the Brightside Engine Shaft, the contour datum at this position being most appropriate to satisfy details of composition ore payable to the Calver (New) Sough due below 25 fathoms in depth at Brightside (Breachside) mine.

Breachside Sough must have been commenced about 1756–1757. No doubt it followed close beneath the valley floor as a shallow shale gate before turning north westwards, reaching the mine 25 fathoms (150 feet) beneath the surface. The main shaft here was sunk in the latter part of the 18th century as the `New Engine Shaft`. A Barmaster`s entry for the Brightside Mining Company title dated March, 1855, set out meers on each side of a *founder drift*. An accompanying sketch map shows this drift running north west-south east, crossing all the veins virtually at a right angle. The author considers this `founder drift` to be part of Breachside Sough level, running into the steeply dipping limestones beneath the flank of Hassop Common. The drift would have intersected the engine shaft about 25 fathoms (150 feet) beneath the surface.

The names `Breachside` and `Brightside` had become interchangeable by 1759, the sale of 1/24th share in April, 1759 refers to it as Brightside Sough [SCL, Bag 486]. The name was also applied in 1767, but the usual title retained until the onset of the 19th century was Breachside Sough. The profits at Breachside Sough were considerable, reflected in overall profits of £18,879-13-1 obtained between 1759 and 1790 [SCL, Bag 431a]. Hopkinson [1958], from an analysis of partnership account books, demonstrated that from 1763 to 1769, 14,140 loads of ore were measured, followed by 15,201 loads between 1772 and 1780.

The continuing ore bonanza dictated that deeper drainage below the old shale gate sough was needed and in 1774 negotiations took place with the proprietors of Calver New Sough to extend their level from its forefield at Busks Grove in Backdale Pasture, through Froggatt Grove to Brightside Mine at the New Engine Shaft. Work was to be undertaken at the expense of Brightside. Agreement was reached in 1775 [SCL, Bag 744] and the sough reached Brightside Mine New Engine in 1782 at a depth of 40 fathoms. There is no evidence that Calver (New) Sough extended beyond Brightside New Engine Mine.

At some time between 1782 and 1789 the title to White Coe Mine was acquired. Two detailed plans drawn in this period reveal that thirty eight men were employed at `Old Brightside` Mine and twenty four at White Coe [Chats, Dev Coll; SCL, Bag 200]. By September, 1791 the numbers had increased to fifty six men at Brightside, but still twenty four at White Coe. Both plans mark and name seventeen `hadings` and a few `plum` veins. From White Coe Engine Shaft a `Newcastle Road` was driven in the 1780s or 1790s along the White Coe Great Vein for about 90 yards, where it turned north west for an additional 35 yards [SCL, Bag 201]. Handwritten notes on the plan and an accompanying text prove that the intention was to extend it further eastwards along the Great Vein and also into and along the *Great Hading*. The Newcastle Road at White Coe Mine is one of only three examples of this type of haulage gate known in the Derbyshire orefield, the others being at Stoke Sough and Pindale Mine. The plan delineates the courses of thirteen named hadings. The Overseer valued a 1/24th share at £100. Profits were handsome between 1783 and 1790, the lucky proprietors reaped £3168-9-1 from the rich hadings and veins.

The final phase of this cycle of operations, probably by then named `New Brightside` title, took place after 1790. The much enlarged `New Brightside` title included Froggatt Grove, Breachside Sough, `Old Brightside` and White Coe Mine, and extended to the boundary with Waterhole Mine. Ore sales reached £17,531, showing a profit to the mines of £1,387 [SCL, Bag 482]. Output began to decline after 1798 and it became only a medium sized mine until 1809, after which it declined further into virtual obscurity [Rieuwerts, 2005].

John Taylor`s `Longstone Edge Mines` included the mines along Hassop Common. He cleared out Brightside Sough as far as Backdale Mine, from where a branch was driven towards Deep Rake in order to work that vein 54 fathoms (324 feet) beneath Sallet Hole Sough. The branch level breached the toadstone in 1844–1845, about 300 fathoms from Backdale Shaft and it was abandoned [Anstead, 1853; Willies and Fletcher, 1975]. Brightside Mine was not worked by Taylor, but in 1852 the mine was taken by another company and in 1853 it was acquired by the North Derbyshire United Mining Co. They installed a 25HP horizontal pumping and winding engine made by Bray and Co., of Leeds. The engine lifted water from beneath Brightside Sough which was used as a deep pumpway. The venture achieved some success, for example from 1855 to 1860 some 3,027 loads of ore, exclusive of Lot were mined; output almost reached 1,000 loads in 1856. The optimism did not last; the steam engine was sold to Coalpithole Mine, Peak Forest in 1863 and the so-called `El Dorado of Derbyshire` was abandoned in 1869.

SOUGHS and LEVELS within the LIBERTIES of CALVER and HASSOP having uncertain provenance or intended function.

POSSIBLE SHALE GATE SOUGH TO BUSKS, OR BACKDALE MINE

Willies and Fletcher [1975] postulated that a shallow shale gate sough had been driven from the stone lined drain or spring at the head of Sough Brook into Backdale Mine. Nothing is known about the history or nature of this feature, but considering the drainage difficulties experienced at Busks Grove by the early 18th century, then such a drainage adit would have been a logical early development.

POSSIBLE LEVEL TO OLD BRIGHTSIDE

A similar situation to that above may have existed at Old Brightside Mine. Some fifty years ago what appeared to be hillock waste and disturbed ground could be seen running downhill through the pasture towards the Hassop road, although a search in the brook below revealed nothing convincing.

LEVEL AT BRIGHTSIDE MINE [`NEWCASTLE ROAD`]

The stone arched and walled level adjacent to Brightside (New) Engine Shaft (the so-called `Newcastle Road`) may have provided access to stopes and workings in `Old Brightside` and maybe even White Coe Mine. The level may have been driven along either Sharwins or Goodwins Hading. Sometimes mistaken for a drainage sough, it did not serve that purpose, but was used as a haulage gate. Nothing is known of its history and rather having an 18th century origin it may well have been associated with mid 19th century developments at Brightside Mine.

12. THE LONGSTONE EDGE MINES AND ADJACENT WORKINGS

THE SUMMIT AND SOUTH SIDE OF LONGSTONE EDGE

The crest of Longstone Edge is dominated by the massive Deep Rake – High Rake – Longstone Edge Rake complex and its important north side branch Watersaw Rake. These very large rake veins are associated with scores of adjacent veins, scrins, flat-works and hadings. They were worked in limestones belonging to the Monsal Dale Beds, and in places through the Longstone Edge (Upper) Tuff into the underlying limestones.

A little south of the main summit complex lay Silver Hillocks Vein and at the foot of the steeper slope was the 16th century *Great Vein*, a part of the Hard Shaft Vein – Hard Nell Vein system, which continues eastwards to the Waterhole Mine in Hassop Liberty. Ranging through the flatter ground south of the Edge is the Ash Nursery Vein and its eastward continuation Oxpasture Vein and Hard Rake. Important mines operating in the 18th and 19th centuries included Ash Nursery Mine, Oxpasture Mine, 30 fathoms deep, Blue Bell Mine, and Hard Nell Mine, 40 fathoms deep. Just outwith the area were the Old Hen Mine and Waterhole Mine. It seems likely, though not everywhere proven, that they were worked down to the toadstone, but that stratum was breached at least by Hard Nell Sough and at Hard Shaft 50 fathoms in depth.

The huge surface expression of the main veins would have been apparent in very early times and it is not surprising that Roman activity has been claimed for an unknown mine location on Longstone Edge. Boles Vein probably indicates the position of former Bole smelting furnaces, whilst lower down the steep southern slope was an ancient trackway, recorded in 1575 as the *Bolegate* [Chats, Hardwick papers]. The *Great Rake*, at the foot of the slope was recorded in 1575 as being very near the southern boundary of Blakelow. The late 16th century saw the great law suits between William Humphrey and Christopher Schutz against the miners about the claimed infringements of Humphrey's patent for the water tub and iron wire sieve, used for recovering lead ore cast away as waste by previous generations of miners. Tradition says that the tub and sieve was first used in Derbyshire *at the Old rake in Longstone Lordship* [White Watson, 1811]. This must refer to re-working poor quality ore from backfilled opencast workings.

Little is known about activities in the 17th century, but a dispute heard in the Barmote Court at Ashford

A rare surface survival of a knockstone in a ruined coe at an un-named mine near Silver Hillocks on Longstone Edge (J.H.Rieuwerts).

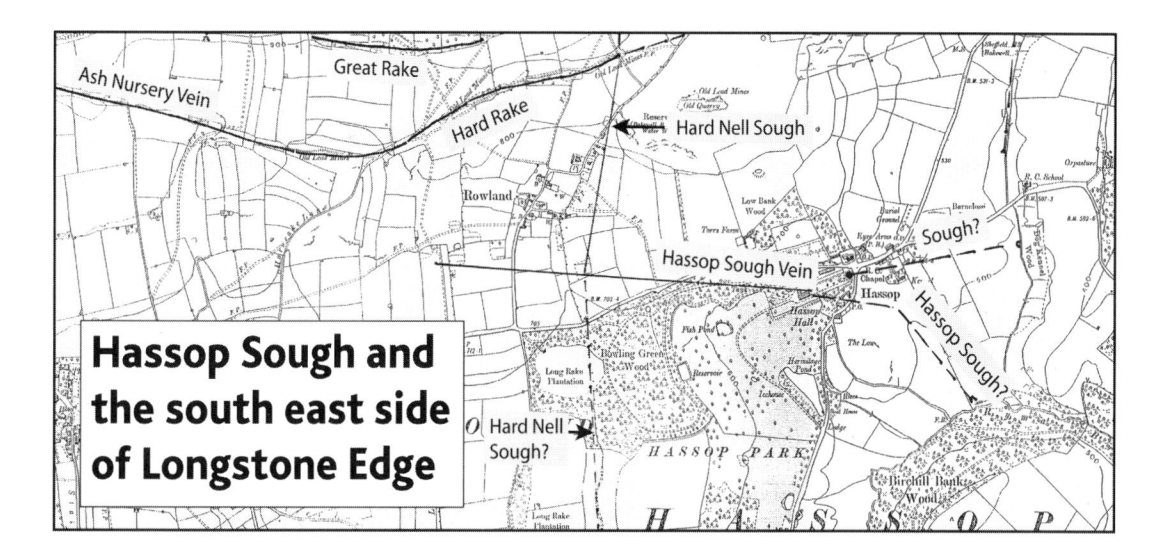

Hassop Sough and the south east side of Longstone Edge

in 1669 described trespass and illegal removal of 100 loads of lead ore, valued at £100 at *Longson edge Rake – ye ancient edge Veyne* [SCL, Bag 702]. There were disputes at *Hard Rake in Longson fields*. The Ashford Barmote Court, held at Great Longstone in October, 1673, adjudicated a case concerning the illegal sale of 40 loads of lead ore, valued at £40, taken from *Hard Rake in Oxpasture* [SCL, Bag 702]. Two large fields bearing the name lie north and south of the rake, north west of Rowland village [Wright, 1906].

OLD SOUGH AT THE CAUMS HEAD

An old spelling for Coombs Dale was Caums Dale and therefore the logical location of this sough would be somewhere towards the upper end of Coombs (Caums) Dale. The Barmaster`s setting out of meers along Boles Vein, coupled with other peripheral documentary evidence and not least the ground surface contours, all preclude Coombs Dale being the location of the sough at `Caums Head`. Cameron [1959] makes no reference to the name, neither is it shown on the Longstone Enclosure map dated 1770 and reproduced in Wright [1906]. Only one significant reference to this old sough has been found:

May 6th, 1788 Then gave to William Wager for Whant of Workmanship the following Meers of Ground on Longstone Edge ranging east and west From an Old Sough Tail at the Caums Head [SCL, Bag 448].

The Barmaster then set out meers for Wager on Boles Vein and nine other parallel, but un-named veins. This and other entries concerning the position of Boles Vein are not very clear, but it was closely associated with Deep Rake–Longstone Edge Vein, adjacent to where it was crossed by the Edgeside road. This location does not merit the description `Caums Head`, but seems the only possible position for the tail of this sough, from where it was driven north eastwards on Mr. Wager`s possessions.

A second, but much later Barmaster entry, dated April, 1841 was mis-read by Nellie Kirkham as *an old sough tail on the Mootlow Vein,* leading her to speculate on the presence of a sough draining into Hay Dale [Kirkham, 1966]. However close perusal of the original entry shows a full stop after the word `tail` and `on the Mootlow Vein` is followed by the meers set out on that vein eastwardly, not from Hay Dale, but from Mr. Wager`s Bell Holes title. No other information has been found, so the date for making the level is not known, neither anything of its length, or whether it encountered or penetrated a thin toadstone.

LONGSTONE EDGE SOUGH OR MR WAGER`S LEVEL

This was an important level, recorded in Farey`s list of mines, it does not appear in any other pre-20th century literature. Farey [1811] described it thus: *Longstone-edge-venture, in Great Longsdon, in 1st and 2nd Lime, much Lead, fibrous Spar, hades N: this Rake parts and meets again.* White Watson [Derby Local Studies Library] produced an un-dated pencil sketch section showing Mr. Wager`s Level initially driven through steeply dipping limestone and toadstone, then for a short distance in the *2nd Lime*, before terminating at *Longstone Edge Dyke Vein*. Watson used the term *Dyke Vein* to describe a faulted structure, the wall rock on one side of a vein higher than the other side, i.e. a normal fault.

The venture was an attempt by Thomas Wager and partners to explore Watersaw Rake, Longstone Edge Rake and probably the Boles veins below the `old man`s` workings. The first record dates from 1786 when 35 meers were set out in Watersaw Rake, 20 meers belonging to Cackle Mackle, 8 meers for Edge Sough and 7 meers for Mr. Wager [SCL, WHC 12]. The sough was started in 1786 and driven almost due north towards the Longstone Edge Rake (or High Rake) – Watersaw Rake intersection. Little production was recorded before 1791 and that situation is consistent with the ore content in the upper limestones having been exhausted many years previous to the construction of the sough.

Longstone Edge Sough was used as a drawing level as well as for drainage. The sough would have unwatered the Longstone Edge veins in the limestones beneath the Longstone Edge Upper Tuff, to a maximum, but beneficial depth of about 220-250 feet beneath the surface. The entrance to the level has run-in, but it has been entered in recent years and explored for over 600 feet.

The recorded bargains begin in October, 1788 when William Wager: *Set John Wain to Drife north in the forfield of the Edge sough 2 fathm at 31/6d per fa*. John Wain and partners were driving the level in the late 1780s and 1790s, the bargains rising from 31/6d per fathom to £3-10-0 per fathom. The Upper Tuff was intersected 576 feet from the level mouth in January 1791, the event recorded in the reckoning book as, when the sough *Reach`d the Chanial or Todestone* [SCL, WHC 14]. The sough was 600 feet in length by April, 1791, the vein being met at 720 feet. Two waggon gates were driven from it, one towards the west, the other towards the east. Stoping was carried out from both of these waggon gates. Two single measures of ore were recorded in 1789 and 1794, the main production began in 1797 but remained low until 1804. According to Willies [1976] output in 1806, 1808 and 1809 exceeded 500 loads per annum, inclusive of duties. His figures are underestimated, at least for 1806, because in that year alone the value of ore sold reached £2,355 on which a profit of £919 accrued [SCL, WHC 14].

The sough reckoning book provides a list of the copers` names at work in September, 1805. Ten men were raising ore in the east end, four men *in the Rouff Over Cartgate,* 3 men at the West Sump foot, and 4 men in the West forefield. Nineteen men were named as copers in 1808. The reckoning book records payments made during 1808 for *Boy Copes and Boy Spritching*. These exact terms have not been seen in any other Derbyshire lead mining document, but there is a reference to a *Boy Charge* at Haredale Mine, Bakewell Moor in 1776 and one to gangs of old miners called *spritchers* at Millclose Mine in 1917 where they were employed cleaning up in the ore-caverns after the main gangs had removed the bulk of the ore [Rieuwerts, 1998]. All the various terms therefore probably mean cleaning stopes or workings of small grains of ore and other small sized particles of waste.

A Firehouse is noted in the accounts in 1791 and Nellie Kirkham spent some time speculating about a possible Newcomen-type pumping engine, but it is very unlikely and more probably the Firehouse was a ventilation furnace housed in a small building similar to those serving the Eyam Edge mines. She noted an illustration of Longstone Church with what appeared to be a tall chimney on the Edge skyline at the appropriate location.

Serious work at Longstone Edge Sough ceased in 1816, but some small scale activity persisted for a few years afterwards. During the mid to late 19th century ore was brought from the level to a water supply in Great Longstone village for dressing and at that period it was referred to as *the levvy*, one of the very few references to the word found in Derbyshire lead mining documents [Kirkham, 1966].

HARD NELL SOUGH

Hard Nell Vein contained 25 meers of ground east from the Founder to the Rowland-Hassop boundary and 3 meers west to the Rowland-Ashford boundary. Miss Kirkham mis-interpreted the Barmaster`s entry, thereby transferring the title west of the Ashford boundary, terminating at Grisedale Hollow. She also suggested a position for the tail of Hard Nell Sough, a little to the south of Rowland hamlet. This seems unlikely because the Blue Bell Shaft, 240 feet in depth, indicates free drainage to about 620 feet above OD. A sough tail at a deeper contour, discharging into the stream towards the west side of Hassop Park would be a more suitable location. (The Hall Park did not extend so far west to this valley in the mid 18th century when Hard Nell Sough was in existence. [J. Barnatt, pers. comm]).

Hard Nell Mine was at work during the 18th century, but work was re-started in 1764 and became more ambitious in scale in 1766. The earliest available record of Hard Nell Sough dates from the mid 1760s when it was receiving attention and repairs:

June, 1766 Repairing the Old Levey
December, 1768 Joseph Dakin and Co. for repairing the Ould Suph Level, £4. [SCL, WHC 3].

The work in the sough coincides with the increase in activity at the mine and moderate ore output of about 200 to 300 loads/year during the same years. The ore shoots diminished quickly and by 1768 the mini-boom was over. The Barmaster and two jurymen laid out a road to the mine and in the same year a Lord`s Meer was purchased for £21. During the first year expenditure was £104, sale of ore ensured a small profit of £30. The next reckoning saw a profit of £105 on the sale of 130 loads and 6 dishes of ore. [Thornhill, 1967]. The situation then becomes complicated because subsequent accounts must cover workings on the vein in both Ashford Northside and Rowland Liberties or Lordships. From 1766 until 1784, 792 loads 6 dishes of ore were measured, exclusive of Lot, of which 640 loads 5 dishes (81%) was obtained in 1766-1768. The whole period recorded a loss of £1,211-2-0 [SCL, Bag 431a].

The mine was deemed to have no value in 1782. Losses continued until at least 1796. The decline can be gauged by charges of only £23 between 1791 and 1805. The mine continued in work from 1806 to 1811 during which period the rather larger sum of £362 was expended, without any ore being obtained [SCL, Bag 393]. Further work in the sough was underway in 1812 and 1813. On 5th October, 1812 the agent:

This day set Rodger Sellers and Anthony Henstock a bargain in the forefield of Hard Nell Levile in the Chanele at £3 per fathom.

A mark was made in the sough wall from where this bargain began. One month later they were driving *in the Stone* at £5-10-0 per fathom, suggesting that the channel had been breached, but the underlying rock was proving very hard. By March, 1813 the men had driven 8 yards beyond the mark. The miners used a staggering 20 lbs of powder for 1 fathom and 24.5 lbs for another fathom [SCL, WHC 3]. No later references about the sough have emerged.

HASSOP SOUGH

Nellie Kirkham [1966] believed that the tail was at the `well` on the north side of the Hassop-Great Longstone road, 250 feet west of Hassop Church. The author always considered that the site seemed to be at an impossibly high contour, but was not aware of a feasible alternative. However, the answer is to be found in the Calver, Hassop and Rowland Manor Court Rolls [SCL, Bag 344]:

27th August, 1724 – no persons shall make a footway up or down William Bowers ground called Ellers betwixt Birchill and Hassop Sough.

Ellers is situated east of Hassop Hall and south of School Lane [Mr. H. Stephenson, pers comm.], so the sough tail must have emptied into Sough Brook, maybe approximately 1,800 feet south of the Lane. The western range of Hassop Sough Vein is known from Barmaster entries, where it is recorded as passing in an east-west direction through enclosures known as Bamfurlong. The position of these fields is shown on the Longstone Enclosure plan dated 1770 [Wright, 1906]. An un-named vein or scrin is shown running from Hard Rake Lane, south of east, across the top of two of the three Bamfurlong fields [BGS, Keyworth]. The line of the vein towards the sough tail passes beneath Hassop Hall, confirming old stories of a lead mine beneath the Hall.

The Manor Court Rolls also mention the sough and associated workings in 1733:

We lay a pain of ye Partnership belonging to Hassop Sough that they sufficiently Repair their Shafts and Run holes, their Engin shaft and Engin betwixt now and ye 10th May next or Forfeit to ye Lord of ye Manor for every Hole and Every shaft and Engin not so secured and Neglected 13/4d.

Perhaps this marks the end of the first phase of working at the sough, because there is no record available for fifty six years, until John and Samuel Ashton were given: *One Meer and Eighteen Yards of Ground*

Lying at the Head of Middle Bamfurlong Betwext John Hardy`s possessions Uppon Hassop Sough Vein July 1st, 1789. The same two miners had a road laid out to their mine in December, 1789 *from the Turnpike Road between Longstone and Hassop – up a field called Bawmfurlong to (their) mine on Hassop Sough Vein* [SCL, Bag 448]. Nothing further is heard about Hassop Sough or the Sough Vein.

THE NORTH SIDE OF LONGSTONE EDGE

The major veins breaking from the north side of Deep Rake and ranging north west down into Coombs Dale are Ashtons Vein, Silcocks Vein, Brandy Bottle Vein and Strawberry Rake. Unwin Vein crosses all of them, beginning in Ryedale, from there ranging south west until it meets Deep Rake in an area of intense mineralisation associated with Bow Rake and the break out of Strawberry Rake. Numerous other veins and scrins cross this tract of ground. Associated with Unwin Vein is *Coumdale Vein or Pipe* (*Scotch Bank Vein or Pipe* or *Hairpin Hill Mine*).

TALLBUT SOUGH or TORBOT SOUGH or TURBUT SOUGH

The valley of Ryedale separates the liberties of Longstone, a part of Ashford Northside Liberty and Calver. The lower end of this small valley joins into Coombs Dale and near the confluence a swarm of parallel veins and scrins range up the hillside south westwards, eventually passing into the line of Unwin Vein high on the southern hillside of Coombs Dale on Scotch Bank. The main vein of the swarm is Hairpin Hill Mine, known also as Coumdale Mine or Scotch Bank.

Ore production is recorded at Scotch Bank in 1738, Hairpin Hill Grove in 1743 and Unwin Grove by 1745. Saleable ore from these mines totalled 923 loads from 1738 to 1753. Subsequent output was intermittent throughout and overall quantities were small.

This sough is the oldest in the area. Though first recorded in 1773 it is probably much older, associated with work carried out in the 1730s, 1740s and 1750s. Richard Talbott was involved in a title dispute at Hairpin Hill Mine in 1745 and it seems likely that the sough was named after him. There are no known records about the actual driving of the level, or anything of its extent. Financial compensation was claimed, when in 1773 two cows were suffocated at a *Leadmine Sough or mineral title Scotch Bank, otherwise Talbot Sough* [DRO, Br-T, L24].

Nothing is then heard about it until the mid 19th century. Torbut Sough title in Scotch Bank was sold for 3/- in January, 1846, with the rather baffling rider, *it likewise crosses Sallad-hole Sough,* but this must refer to Unwin Vein and not the sough level. A new company was formed in the latter months of 1853 with the intention of re-working these same mines. Named Enterprise Mine, a level was begun in the bottom of Ryedale, but all indications are that it was soon abandoned. The Barmaster and two of the Jury laid out ground *for Mining purposes* or *hillock room* at Talbot Sough on 27th February, 1854. A sketch plan in the notebook of the Barmaster, James Longsden, shows the Longstone – Calver boundary fence, a stile in the wall (it still exists), the level mouth and a channel curving away from the entrance. References in 1854 and 1858 give the name `Enterprise Mine or Torbut Sough` and `Torbut Sough on Scotch Bank`.

Mr. William Robinson, a pioneer in the working of fluorspar in Derbyshire, told Nellie Kirkham that the intention was to drive to Deep Rake, she thought to act as a horse level. A brief note in the Mining Journal [May, 1854] is curious: *Enterprise Mine – preparing ore for sale, the east, or second level has assumed the appearance of the former level and likely to be more successful.* The note contradicts an un-dated, but c.1856 document entitled *Remarks on Lead Mines and Mining Interests in the Hundred of High Peak*: *Enterprise Mine – Wrought by a Company of Adventurers for more than a year but no Ore measured* [DRO, Br-T, L 269/1].

The precise nature of the work done by the Enterprise Co. is not known. Whether William Robinson was correct and they intended to drive into Deep Rake, or whether it was an abortive attempt to refurbish and extend the old Tallbut Sough is not known. The well-arched portal of the level was destroyed by vandalism in the 1950s though a photograph of the entrance is extant.

SUB SOUGH

The 1 inch to 1 mile OS map [1840 edition] presents yet another ambiguity. At a point somewhere adjacent to Tallbut Sough and Enterprise Level are the words *Sub Sough*. The name is very curious and does not appear in any Barmaster entries or other contemporary mining documents. It pre-dates the Enterprise mining venture so it cannot relate to their level, and it must therefore for the present remain a mystery.

SALLET HOLE OLD SOUGH OR SALLET HOLE LEVEL

A map of the mining field owned by the North Derbyshire Mining Co., drawn in 1853, depicts the line of *Sallet Hole Level* running south eastwards from Coombs Dale, meeting Deep Rake close to the intersection with Red Rake [DRO, Br-T, LP 4]. No other map or documentary evidence support this peculiar alignment, yet the map is well drawn and otherwise accurate. Nellie Kirkham [1966] suggested that the old sough tail section shown on Mathew Frost`s 1811 plan of Sallet Hole Sough (see below) and approximately along the same bearing as Sallet Hole Level, may have been the first part of that level and would therefore represent a much older sough, i.e. Sallet Hole Old Sough.

SALLET HOLE SOUGH

Sallet or Sallad Hole Mine is situated on Deep Rake, the Engine Shaft and Founder being 160 yards north west of Bleaklow House. The mine in the bottom of Coombs Dale, known in the 20th century as Sallet Hole and marked on OS maps, is the entrance to Sallet Hole Sough, part of which was modified into a main haulage level by Laporte Chemicals Ltd.

The earliest available reference to Sallet Hole dates only from 1749 from which date it enjoyed modest output for a few years. Ore measurements began in 1749, from then until the end of December, 1755, some 760 loads of ore were mined inclusive of duty ore. Output continued until 1759. Thereafter, except for 1786, when only 12 loads were measured, no ore was measured up to and including 1792. After the brief spell of work in 1785–1787, nothing seems to have been done until the first decade of the 19th century. The mine title consisted of 36 meers in Deep Rake in March, 1813, together with meers on Unwin Vein, Silcocks Vein, Ashtons Vein, Strawberry Rake and Brandy Bottle Vein [SCL, Bag 448].

Sallet Hole Sough was begun about 1805–1806, the late date may signify a dual purpose, as a drainage level and as a deep trial beneath the thick toadstone sequence in Deep Rake. The earliest verification of the sough consists of a plan dated July, 1811 [DRO, D3266]. The forefield then stood just south of Unwin Vein, 450 yards from the tail. The original sough tail was situated west of the later (c. 1840) entrance and was driven south east for about 100 yards to the intersection with Unwin Vein, along the sole of which vein it was then driven south west for about 300 yards. It then turned from the vein towards Sallet Hole Engine Shaft. William Robinson informed Nellie Kirkham that the sough met toadstone about 1,200–1,300 feet from the entrance and this position roughly coincides with the point where the sough leaves Unwin Vein. However, a pencil line on the plan depicts the sough turning yet again parallel with Unwin Vein. Though no documentary proof has been seen, the sough reached Deep Rake in 1815. The vein was met in the toadstone and abortive driveages were made in both directions in that stratum. Accounts covering the years 1810-1813 and 1817 do not record any ore, only expenditure of £1,007 [SCL, Bag 393].

Little is known until 1840 when John Taylor took possession of a large number of veins and mines, which he called `The Longstone Edge Mines`. Taylor considered, with some justification, that with few exceptions the whole area had been worked by small scale methods. He proposed enlarging Sallet Hole Sough into a Horse Level to facilitate removal of low grade ore left in the `old man`s workings in Deep Rake. His scheme involved driving a new section of level from a fresh portal in Coombs Dale. This *New Cut* passed over the original tail section before re-joining the sough in Unwin Vein. The sough was cleaned out and enlarged for a distance of 660 feet along Unwin Vein. Rises and sumps were to be made in Deep Rake in the toadstone, seeking the limestones above and beneath. Driveages were planned at sough contour east and west in Deep Rake. Mechanised dressing floors were to be built at the level mouth in Coombs Dale [Willies, 1976].

Overall results were disappointing; the old miners had removed most of the ore from the vein above the toadstone, despite Taylor`s optimistic statement in his 1841 report that though the rise from the sough showed the ground had been worked in former times, yet the new company had taken out a `great deal of ore` [Willies, 1976]. The Longstone Edge Mines were abandoned in 1847 and there is no evidence that serious mining took place until 1926-1930 when the Coombsdale Mining Co. worked fluorspar from Deep Rake using Sallet Hole Sough as a haulage adit. Similarly, Laporte Chemicals developed the sough and mine in the latter part of the 20th century as a major fluorspar prospect.

13. MINES ON THE NORTH SIDE OF COOMBS DALE

The group of mines commonly referred to as the Highfield mines are situated in Stoney Middleton Liberty and lie between the upper reaches of Coombs Dale on their southern side, the gently curving boundary between Stoney Middleton and Ashford Northside Liberty on the west, their effective northern boundary being Seedlow Rake, itself of greater significance within Ashford Northside Liberty. No records about this group of Highfield mines have been found dating to before 1800.

The `older` 18th century Highfields mines were situated along Shepherds Rake and two or three parallel veins and pipes. They were not referred to as the Highfield mines after the 18th century.

Contemporary mining documents make reference to five named soughs. The first edition of this book [1987] drew attention to several unresolved problems concerning the precise nature and relationship of these sough levels. Additional research has enabled a clearer picture to be obtained and it is gratifying to verify that Brightmore Sough and Tallbut Sough are quite different and to confirm the existence of Brights Sough; remaining hypotheses contained in the 1987 edition have also been confirmed.

The early history of the mines and soughs is obscure. Shepherds Rake runs north west from the bottom of Coombs Dale, up the steep hillside known as Rough Side, into Tortops Close, then through the very prominent, but post mining plantation towards the hilltop. The vein was known in the 18th century as Highfields Old Rake, it being accompanied by the parallel Josephs Pipe and Mossley Vein. The main rake extended for 25 meers (2,400 feet) from the Calver-Stoney Middleton Liberty boundary in Coombs Dale, terminating in the field beyond the plantation, but Josephs Pipe (named after Joseph Mossley? see below) and Mossley Vein were worked only from the north west end of Tortops Close. This detail corresponds with a distinct widening of the surface expression of the veins within the plantation.

Small quantities of ore were measured at Highfields, 24 loads in 1718 and 5 loads in 1722, but the location of the mine(s) is not given [DRO, Br-T, L 62]. Joseph and William Mossley freed an old vein in 1722, presumably the vein was named after the family [DRO, Br-T, L 62/3]. The Shepherd family must have been involved before 1733, for in that year Robert Shepherd sold all his groves in Highfields and Rough Side, except Horsehole, for £3 [DRO, Br-T, L 56]. Thomas Shepherd accompanied the Barmaster when meers were laid out in March, 1766 in *the Old Rake*, *Josephs Pipe* lying on the west side and *Mossley Vein* [DRO, D2090].

Before 1776 Joseph Whitfield, the Derbyshire agent for the London Lead Co., had sold his 1/21st share in Highfield Top (location un-traced), his share of the loss being £30-10-10. The period during which this amount accrued is not stated, but a total loss of £641-7-6 represented a considerable outlay on the mine.

Seedlow Rake was at work in Stoney Middleton Liberty by 1731, and probably many years before that.

Map opposite: The problems associated with identification of the several *Eyam Dale* soughs, *Dale* soughs, *Nether Dale Sough*, and *Upper Dale Sough* have been discussed in the text. These factors should not be overlooked when examining the maps of Middleton Dale and Eyam Dale.

The exact locations and ranges of the 17th century sough from Middleton Mill Dam, the sough driven from near the Lord`s Cupola to Cliffe Stile Mine and Bull Pit Sough are not known. Neither Holmes Sough nor Sheffield Sough have been located.

Serious anomalies exist in proving the exact location for the southern range of Southside Pipe, and the positions of Blagden Vein, Cackle Mackle Vein, the Highfield Engine Shaft and consequently the upper range of Highfield Sough. Barmaster title entries do not accord with other contemporary information, but the map provides a `best fit` solution. The great Deep Rake vein system has been depicted by marking the alignment of the conspicuous main vein, but its attendant veins and scrins by highlighting the boundary walls.

13. Mines on the North Side of Coombs Dale

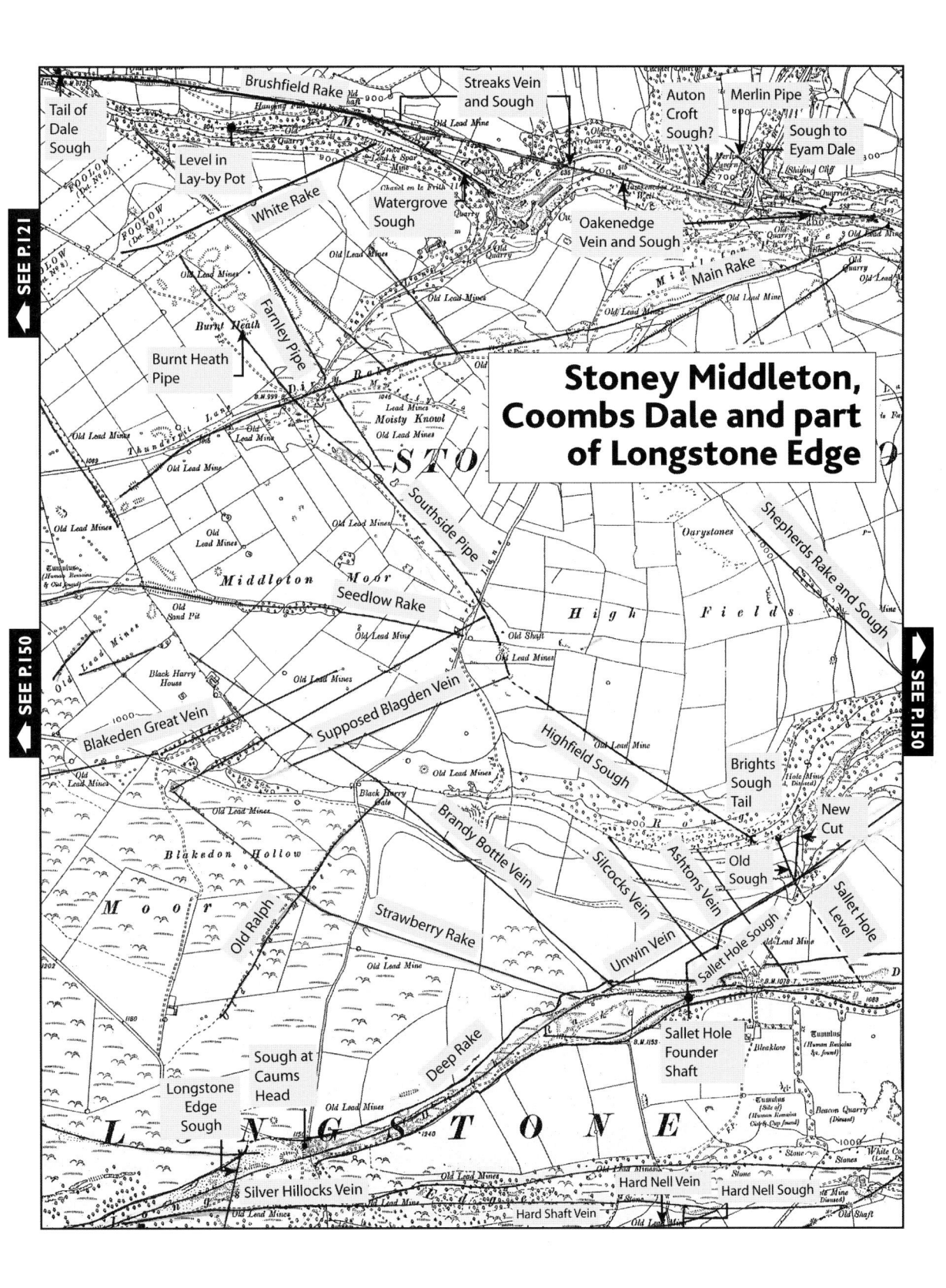

Stoney Middleton, Coombs Dale and part of Longstone Edge

The vein has been almost obliterated eastwards from Long Lane, near Wardlow, but on Middleton Moor, in the plantation west of Black Harry Lane, there has been only minor disturbance and there are several run-in shaft hollows and deep `pitt holes`. The southern boundary wall of the plantation is curiously irregular in shape, no doubt reflecting the random deposits of hillock material.

SHEPHERDS SOUGH, COOMBS (COWMS, CAUMBS) DALE SOUGH, BRIGHTMORE SOUGH

The sough level was driven along the sole of Shepherds Vein (Highfield Old Rake). Nellie Kirkham [1966] stated that Shepherds Mine was situated in the plantation 1,700 feet north west of the Calver – Stoney Middleton boundary in Coombs Dale and she added that the level was driven to the mine; in the late 19th century it was used as a drawing level. Shepherds Vein extended beyond the plantation and in 1836 Philemon Swift Marshall was given 25 meers [2,400 feet] ranging north west from the Calver Liberty boundary.

Shepherds Vein or Pipe was worked by Thomas Hallam from at least 1793 until 1804, but only 106 loads of ore were produced in the twelve year period. In October, 1804 William Hallam sold 11/12ths of Shepherds Rake or Pipe to Mr. Septimus Furniss and in December of that year Furniss took title to Josephs Pipe. By December, 1804 Furniss owned the mine and also 42 meers in other, un-located but adjacent veins including Lambhouse Vein. There is no mention of the sough in this entry [Chats, Dev Coll].

He did not offer any ore for measurement, but from 1808 to 1811 obtained 33 loads 3 dishes from *Coombs Dale.* Levellings taken in March, 1810 (see details below) prove that Cowms Dale Sough and Brightmore Sough were the same, whilst the first entry to Shepherds Sough dates from April, 1812 when a 1/24th share in *Shepherds Sough alias Caumbs Dale Sough* belonging to Richard Gregory was given to Francis Rowlands and partners for non payment of a debt amounting to £4-10-8. The two preceding references confirm that Shepherds Sough, Coombs Dale Sough and Brightmore Sough were all identical. The date when the sough was begun is not known, nor any details of the driveage or geology along the route. Whether a branch level was begun toward the Highfield mines adjacent to Black Harry Lane, as an outcome of the levellings discussed below, is not known. Furniss had one remaining measure of 6 loads 4 dishes from Shepherds Rake in 1813, but nothing further through to 1849.

HIGHFIELD SOUGH

Before the modern haulage road to Sallet Hole Mine was made by Laporte Industries along the Coombs Dale valley floor, about 400 feet west from the Sallet Hole Sough `New Cut` there was a small embankment across the old stream bed. On the north side of the wall that runs down the dale bottom, was the run-in tail of a sough. A mine plan, dated 1811 shows the tail almost opposite to the old, original entrance to Sallet Hole Sough [DRO, D3266]. No obvious sign of the tail can now be seen, but during periods of heavy rainfall, a considerable stream of water still issues at the location.

The late Nellie Kirkham was given information about Highfield Sough by William Robinson, a lead mine owner and pioneer in the working and export of fluorspar from Derbyshire. He told her that originally it was planned only as a level, not a sough, but this does not seem to be entirely correct because it was referred to as a sough by April, 1807. From the tail, the level had been driven for at least eleven meers [1,050 feet] by March, 1811 along the sole of a vein, probably East Southside. This suggests that the sough may have been started about 1805–1806, possibly at the same time as Sallet Hole Sough situated almost opposite to it, but on the south side of Coombs Dale. Whether the remaining 2,400 feet from the position of the forefield in 1811, to the intersection with Blagden Vein and Seedlow Rake at the Highfield mines was ever completed is not known. Farey [1811] noted that the sough was driven in limestone and toadstone.

The first documentary evidence available dates from April, 1807, at which time it belonged to Messrs Brightmore and Shuttleworth and Company, later Mr. Brightmore seems to have become the major shareholder: *Gave – Messrs Brightmore and Shuttleworth and Co (proprietors of the Highfield Sough) 18 meers of ground in a Vein known as – East Southside, beginning at a Shaft at the top of the Rough side.*

A memorandum of levellings gives a hint that deeper drainage to that offered by Highfield Sough was already being considered. The vertical distance between the Highfield mines and `the Cowms Dale Sough mouth` (Shepherds Sough) was checked in

March, 1810, at the time that Highfield Sough was not half finished, and there must be a strong implication that deeper drainage offered by this lower sough was already being contemplated:

> *This day leviled the ground from the old Engine Hillock down to the Cowms Dale Sough mouth viz, its 28 fathoms and 1 yard 2 feet down to Moses Taylors piece in Cowms Dale Botham, and from there to a place where Mathew Furness of Foolow made trial its 18 fathoms 2 feet and from there down to Brightmore Sough Tail its 18 fathoms. That`s 64 fathoms 1 yard* [SCL, WH 14].

Mr. Benjamin Brightmore purchased Mr. Thomas Birds share in the sough in March, 1812 [SCL, Bag 654] and he gradually acquired a compact holding. The Sough Title included the north eastern range of Blagden [or Blakeden] Vein, the eastern range of Seedlow Rake, Cackle Mackle Vein, Brandy Bottle Vein and several other veins and scrins mostly lying on the west side of Black Harry Lane. The original intention of the sough must have been to offer deep exploration and drainage to these old, well-tried veins worked so extensively in Ashford Northside Liberty. Yet amazingly, no ore was measured at any of the mines in the sough title within the fifty six years from 1793 to 1849.

During 1958 the now long defunct Sheffield Caving Club descended a large engine shaft at Highfield Mine adjacent to Black Harry Lane. The shaft bottomed at a depth of about 230 feet and a stope, roofed by shattered limestone blocks, gave access to a smaller diameter, square cut shaft, explored to standing water at about 300 feet beneath the surface. At this depth the water level must correspond closely with the contour of Highfield Sough [Rieuwerts, private coll., section by P. Tottle, c.1958].

A good deal of `hillocking` has taken place around the Highfield mines, and the shaft cannot now be identified, but to the south, down the hillside into upper Coombs Dale there are several untouched veins and scrins, but none with any associated features such as dressing floors, coes or gin-circles.

BRIGHTS SOUGH

The tail of this sough and a short level, only a few yards in length, are marked on an undated, but early – mid 19th century plan [DRO, D3266]. It was situated about 220 feet north east of Sallet Hole New Cut, behind a now demolished mine building. Kirkham [1966] noted a low crag of limestone behind the remains of this building with a jumble of stones and a definite channel leading from it into the former reservoir at the New Cut entrance. This field evidence convinced Nellie Kirkham that she had located the tail of Brights Sough. The area has been re-graded and landscaped in the intervening years and the site obliterated. No documentary evidence has been seen referring to this level, but the levellings taken in March, 1810 from the Highfields Engine Shaft *to a place where Mathew Furness of Foolow made trial* locate the `trial` 46 fathoms, 2 yards 1 foot (283 feet) below the Engine Shaft, very near to the contour of Brights Sough tail. What function Brights Sough might have achieved, is difficult to understand, but the term *trial* and very short length of level depicted on the plan enhance the belief that it was a quickly aborted attempt to discover the eastern random of Seedlow Rake.

14. VEINS AND MINES DRAINING INTO CRESSBROOK DALE

EAST SIDE OF THE DALE

Two sough levels are known to discharge from the eastern side of Cressbrook Dale, both of which drain substantial vein complexes. There may be two additional drainage levels, but the existence of one is presently unproven, whilst another may have served only as a haulage gate. The most northwardly of the known soughs, and the most important, was Wardlow Sough serving Seedlow Rake, a portion of which was known during the 19th century as Wardlow Sough Vein, or according to Green [1887] as the Sough Vein. The mine level currently known as `Neptune Mine` was designed as a drawing level, but may have acted as a sough and used for both functions. The level was associated with a group of mines known collectively

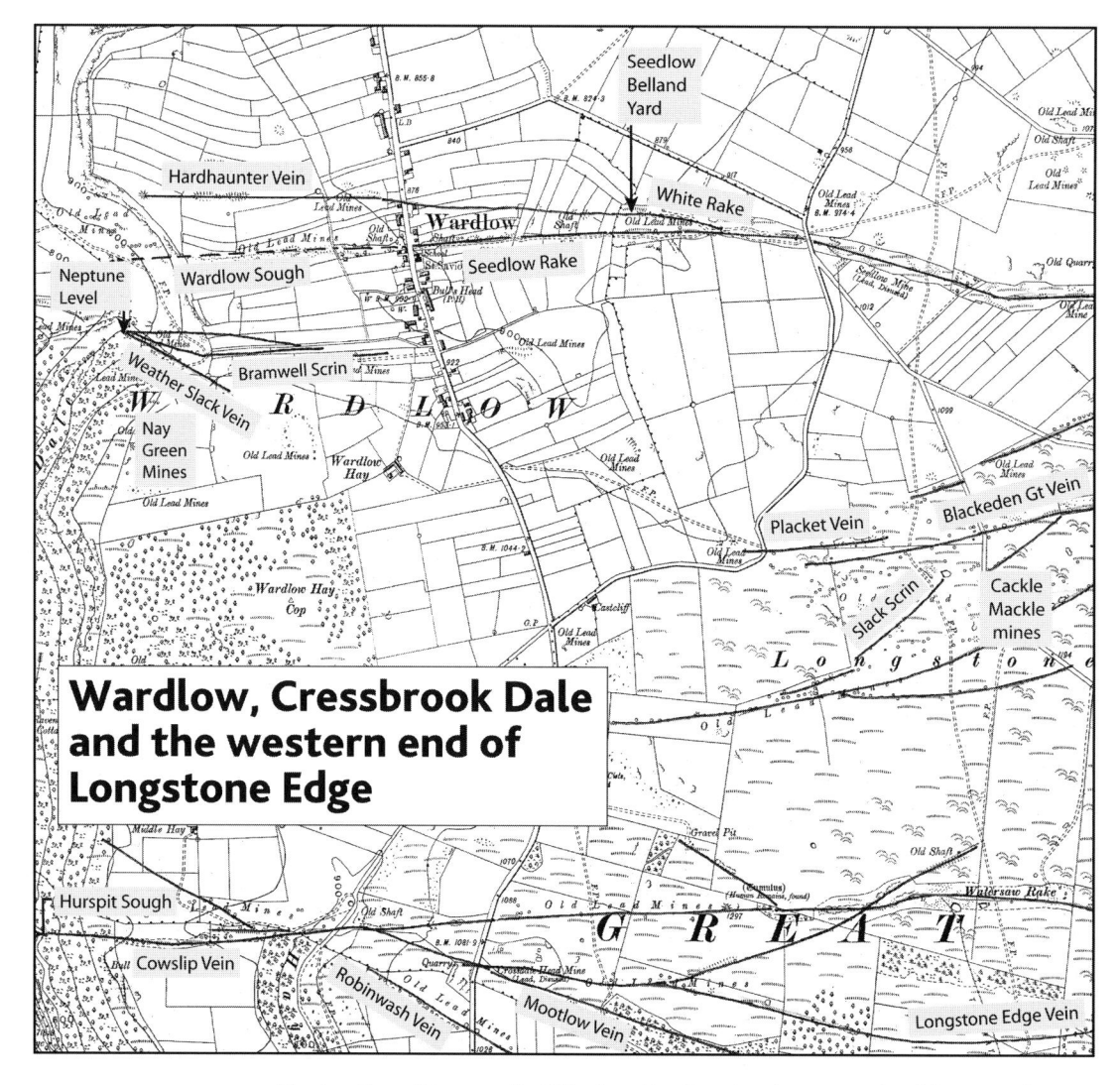

The location of the so-called Wardlow Hay Sough in Longstone Lordship is not known.

as the Nay Green mines. Hurspit Sough drained the western end of the great vein complex developed on Longstone Edge. The sough drained Cowslip Mine and may have extended to Robinwash Mine, Mootlow Mine in Hay Dale and Crossdale Head Mine. A sough for which there is only one known reference was called *Wardloe Hay or Sough* [Chats, Dev Coll]. It was situated within Longstone Lordship and may therefore be identical with Hurspit Sough. On the west side of the dale, Harbourseats Sough, or Arbour Seats Sough drained the vein of the same name. These workings are in the Private Liberty of Litton.

Very little is known about pre 18th century workings in the Wardlow–Cressbrook area.

At the time of the great dispute about the invention and introduction into Derbyshire of the wire-meshed sieve and washing vat, unsuccessful efforts were made to dress previously discarded bouse ore using these methods at the `old rake` in Wardlow in 1573 [Donald, 1961]. Despite this reference, nothing is known about the very early history of workings on Seedlow Rake, but *Robinsons Rake neare a place called Little Seedlow [and] a veyne neare Nether Seedlow* were named in a dispute about non-payment of Lot and Cope, c.1685–1688 [PRO, E112 575]. At the latter location work had been suspended, it being hindered by water. *Benchstowe or Benchstones* can probably be equated with Benstall Hollow or Benstall Bottom.

WARDLOW SOUGH

No documentary evidence has been located that provides any confirmation about the extent of Wardlow Sough, and excepting accounts of lead ore measured from the sough title, and actions in the Barmote Court, nothing is known of its history. Small amounts of ore were measured regularly for the sough throughout much of the 18th century. Wardlow Sough is first recorded in 1729; there exists a brief note of the ore mined and charges involved [SCL, Bowles Deeds 189]. Ore was mined in the Sough Title in 1734–1742 and the 1730s saw several actions brought into the Ashford Barmote Court for non-payment of shares by some of the partners. Activity at this time at least was very vigorous. Richard Marples of St. Paul`s Cathedral owned a 1/48th share in the venture and from his accounts it is disclosed that the total loss to the sough at December, 1734 was £1,495, but unfortunately the length of time covered by this reckoning is not known. By November, 1738, well after Marples` death, in *A note of Mr. Marples mines* it was stated that Wardlow Sough was *not worth anything at pr`sent* [Guildhall, Marples Papers]. The following year the title, which included Seedlow Rake, was owned by George Low, Edward Bagshawe, William Millns, Richard Soresby, William Cawton and others [Chats, Dev Coll]. Unfortunately, no reckonings have survived for the driving of Wardlow Sough; ore measurements continue through most of the 18th century and also the first half of the 19th century, but these accounts of course relate only to lead ore mined from within the sough title and give no information about progress of the sough. If, as seems likely the level was driven as far as the eastern end of White Rake title near Long Lane, then it was about 1,750 yards in length and must have taken at least 25 years for completion.

Recent explorations have demonstrated that the sough runs almost due east from the Dale, along the sole of the vein, but unfortunately an extensive collapse has occurred 950 feet from the tail. A large volume of water still issues from the now inaccessible inner reaches of the level [Beck, 1978]. The sough almost certainly must continue beneath Wardlow village and it very probably extends at least as far as the White Rake Mine, just on the west side of Long Lane. It may have reached as far as the important Seedlow Mine, east of Long Lane.

The Seedlow Rake/Wardlow Sough Vein complex is some two and a half miles in length and is accompanied by many parallel branches and break veins. Westwardly from Wardlow village it ranges through several fields before running down the steep hillside to the sough tail in Cressbrook Dale, but surviving Barmaster`s entries make no reference to this part of the workings. West of Cressbrook Dale, and within Litton Liberty, it again becomes known as Seedlow Vein and finally terminates at the head of Tansley Dale. Wardlow Sough Vein ranges east-west and in Wardlow village it crosses the main road from Wardlow Mires to Monsal Head. Barmasters` entries dating from the 1840s set out seventeen meers in Wardlow Sough Vein lying between Wardlow Town Gate and ranging eastwardly to the west wall of Seedlow Belland Yard. Immediately west of the Belland Yard was Daily Bread Mine, described in 1788 as being *three Meers of Ground set as Takers at Mr. Whites Ground at the Neather part of Seedlow Rake* [SCL, Bag 448].

The name of Daily Bread Mine seems to have been forgotten by the mid 19th century and had become absorbed into the title of Wardlow Sough Vein. The latter title too seems to have been used in preference to Seedlow Rake during the 19th century, though Benstall Bottom was described as lying on the sun (south) side of Seedlow Old Vein as late as 1810; it consisted of five meers west. This was very probably the closely parallel vein, its range of shaft hollows and hillocks still being visible. Seedlow Belland Yard was an important area and contained the founder shaft of both Mr. White`s Ground, later known as White Rake Mine, and also the founder of Old Seedlow Mine. Mr. Richard White owned 7/24ths of Seedlow Mine or `Seedlow Ingen` from at least 1764 until 1771. A horse-gin was purchased for £15 from Pic-tor-End Mine in Haslebadge Liberty. The venture was a losing concern, nearly £224 being lost in the seven years. The position of this mine is not definitely known, but there appears to be every likelihood that it too was within Seedlow Belland Yard, being *Mr White`s Ground at the Neather part of Seedlow Rake.* [Thornhill, 1962].

The Barmaster set out eighteen meers in Old Seedlow in 1846, ranging east from the founder in Seedlow Belland Yard, across Long Lane. These meers terminate 700 feet east of Long Lane in an area designated on the 25 inches to 1 mile OS map [1880 edn.] as Seedlow Mine. Immediately west of Long Lane the vein splits and it is the southern branch, which passing through the Seedlow Belland Yard, then becomes known as Wardlow Sough Vein. West from Long Lane the northern branch vein is known as White Rake as far as the western boundary wall of the Seedlow Belland Yard. Beyond lay Ashton`s Mine, Scotch Grey Grove and Hardh(a)unter Grove. The latter, in part at least, lay west of the main Wardlow to Monsal Head road. Modern ordnance maps mark a considerable stretch of the vein, even well to the east of Long Lane as White Rake, but this is incorrect. The 1840 edition of the 1 inch to 1 mile map shows that White Rake Mine was wholly within the Seedlow Belland Yard; Barmaster`s entries confirm this. Beyond the Wardlow, or Ashford Northside Liberty boundary, Seedlow Rake extends across Middleton Moor within Stoney Middleton Liberty, as far east as the Highfield mines, an area drained by Highfield Sough.

There is much surface evidence yet remaining to attract the mining historian. From the head of Tansley Dale, across Cressbrook Dale to Wardlow village are long lines of undisturbed hillocks, shaft hollows and occasional ruined coes. Seedlow Belland Yard is a very important site, the boundary walls are intact and within the enclosure are two winding shafts, several smaller shafts, a ruined coe, water channels and washing floors [Barnatt and Penny, 2004; Barnatt, 2004]. A horse operated crushing wheel was erected here in the mid 19th century but no trace now remains and it was probably removed to another mine many years ago.

East of Long Lane virtually everything has been obliterated including at Seedlow Mine, another crushing wheel and water leats, dams and washing floors. The engine shaft has also been covered (or filled?), but it was explored to a complete blockage at a depth of 240 feet in 1975. Massive stopes were considered to be too dangerous to enter [Beck, 1978]. On the highest part of Middleton Moor the remains are almost intact within two plantations; here may be seen deep `pitt holes`, opencast trenches and peculiar, irregular boundary walls which require further investigation.

HURSPIT SOUGH

Immediately north of the large resurgence known as Lumb Hole (historically *Hyrspitt Lumb*), is the run-in entrance to a sough. Beck [1978] noted that it was a `persistent rising`. The level is driven into the hillside on a mineralised fault downthrowing to the south. The fault is along the range of the important Cowslip, Mootlow, Robinwash vein complex. The tail of the sough is within the limestones above the horizon of the Ravensdale Tuff. Virtually nothing is known about the history of the level, or its extent, but potentially it may have been driven eastwardly as far as Crossdale Head Mine, a distance of some three quarters of a mile. A dispute was heard in April, 1749 at the Ashford Barmote Court, for non-payment of a debt at *Hurspit Sugh* and *Cowslip grove* [Chats, Dev Coll].

WEST SIDE OF THE DALE

The mines are all situated within Litton Liberty. During the 17th century many miners who resided at Litton worked at mines in Tideswell and Hucklow liberties and there are very few references to actual mines in Litton. A dispute at Backdale Side Rake in 1630 claimed that five Tideswell miners pretended shares in three meers in the vein and had undermined into adjacent meers belonging to William Bagshawe. The Tideswell men had illegally obtained 100 loads of ore, valued at £100 [PRO, DL 1/325]. Backdale is untraced, but it may have been an earlier name for Tansley Dale.

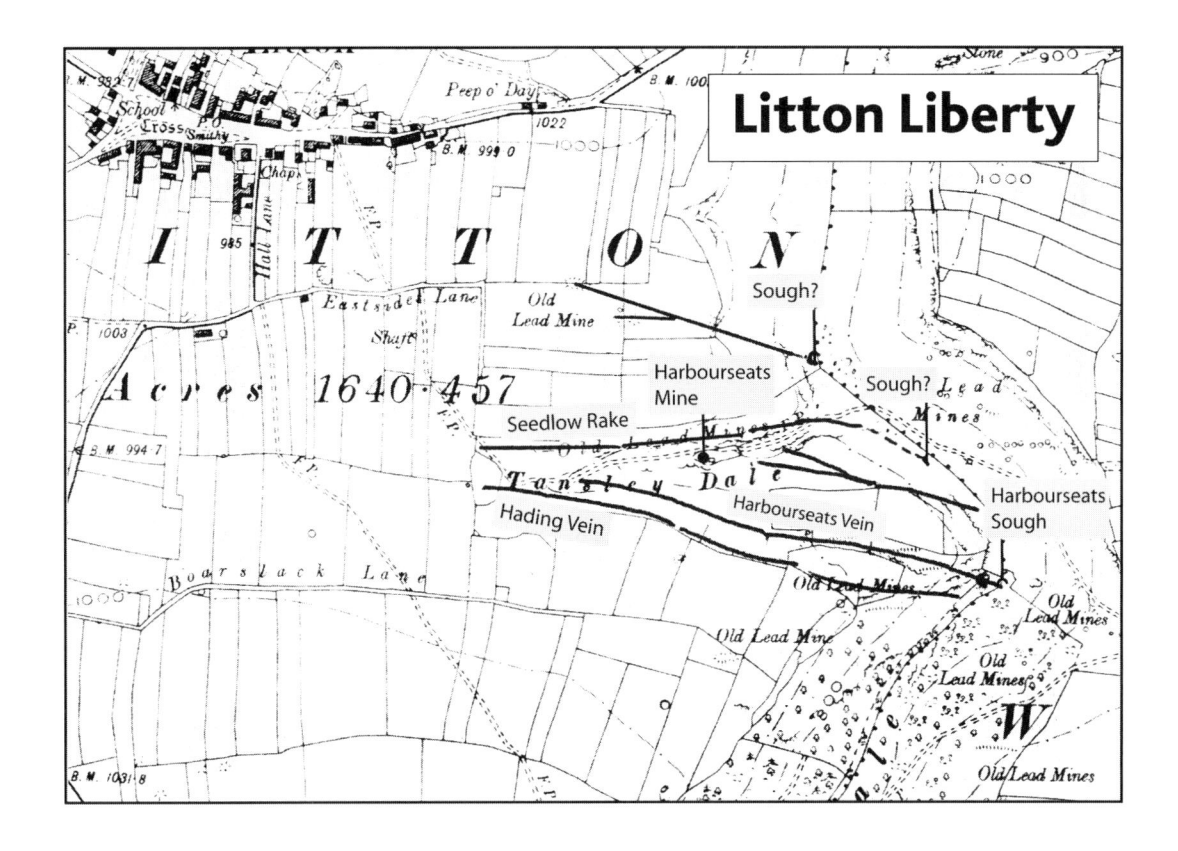

Originally, meers within Litton Liberty were 28 yards in length [eg. PRO, DL 1/325 (1630); Steer, 1734], but after the Derbyshire Mining Customs and Mineral Courts Act of 1852, the length was increased to 32 yards.

HARBOURSEATS OR ARBOUR SEATS SOUGH

In 1860 Harbourseats Vein was set out by the Barmaster for a length of 25 meers ranging west from Cressbrook Dale. These meers terminate at the upper end of Tansley Dale, close to the Engine Shaft. Hading Vein, 18 meers in length, ranges along the south side of Harbourseats Vein [Barmasters Book of Entries, Litton Liberty; in private possession]. There is little additional documentary evidence about the vein and nothing about the sough.

The late Sam Turner, an old Wardlow miner, first drew the author's attention to these workings and provided their location during conversations held with him in the 1950s and 1960s. The sough tail has run-in, but a walled channel feeds into water storage dams formerly used in ore washing operations. The flow is small, but it was persistent even in dry periods. Access into the mine and sough is by an open stope a little higher up the hill. Square section iron rails laid along the sole of the sough probably date from the 1830s–1850s. The level passes beneath several stopes, but progress is blocked after 300 feet by a collapse. A shaft about 850 feet west of the sough tail passes into `an impressive hading stope over 60 feet high` [Gill and Beck, 1991]. This stope may well be on the closely parallel Hading Vein.

The earliest written reference located so far is to be found in Hopkins [1834], who in reviewing the Derbyshire toadstones stated that Arbour Seats Mine had been worked to a depth of 40 fathoms, but no toadstone encountered. Joseph Wright of Wheston, a shareholder in Edge Rake, Tidesell and mines at Millers Dale and Stoney Middleton noted in October, 1846: *fresh bargains taken at Harbour seats Mine this last week and more men put in* [DRO, D1836 Eyre Deeds L4]. However, by June, 1853 Joseph Hall *says they are not working the Harbourseats at all and hopes they never will do again - - or not on his account* [DRO, D1836 Eyre Deeds, L 11]. A document written in 1856 by a Barmaster, James Longsden, reviewing current mining operations and those that had closed only a short time previously, observed that Arbourseats had been worked by a Company but was unremunerative [Chats, Dev Coll].

SOUGHS and LEVELS in ASHFORD NORTHSIDE and LITTON liberties having either uncertain provenance, or intended function.

`NEPTUNE MINE LEVEL`

`Neptune Mine` is not the correct title, but a name bestowed on it by cavers. The correct name of the level is not known, no direct records of it have been found in contemporary mining documents. The level forms part of the Nay Green mines, the group included Weather Slack Vein, Bramwell Scrin and two un-named veins referred to in Barmaster`s entries merely as `North Veins`. Neptune Level was driven into the first North Vein.

Nothing is known about the history of the Nay Green mines until 1732 when a dispute was heard about *Sellors Grove on Knea Green* [Chats, Dev Coll]. The year 1737 witnessed 1,115 loads of ore measured at *Nagreen* and *Upper Nagreen,* otherwise output was erratic, typically that arising from a small-medium mining venture.

Accounts of recent explorations provide little factual detail. The level is described as being either 500 feet, or 650 feet in length. Small square-section iron rails remain in-situ confirming its function as a haulage level. During normal weather conditions water does not flow in the level, though perhaps some drainage was achieved. Shafts in the floor would have required bridging launders. The mine was probably worked in the period 1840s–1850s contemporary with Harbourseats Mine and Sough. Two side branches were driven to to test Bramwell Scrin and possibly Weather Slack Vein.

WARDLOW HAY SOUGH

The position of this level is not known; it was situated within Longstone Lordship and cannot therefore have drained directly eastwardly into Cressbrook Dale from the veins on Wardlow Hay, this large enclosure lying within Wardlow. It is possible, though unlikely, that it may have been a level draining workings situated near Middle Hay Farm. An un-named vein trending north west from the Cowslip–Mootlow mines, if projected along that alignment, would issue into Cressbrook Dale adjacent to Ravensdale Cottages. A more logical explanation is that Wardlow Hay Sough may be identical with Hurspit Sough. The only historical reference is dated Michaelmas, 1734 when Lot ore was collected from `*Wardloe Hay or Sough*` within Longstone [Chats, Dev Coll].

SOUGH ISSUING FROM SEEDLOW RAKE, NORTH SIDE OF TANSLEY DALE

Seedlow Rake and an un-named scrin range east – west along the north side of Tansley Dale. At the confluence with Cressbrook Dale, a line of very denuded shaft hillocks run from the rake and scrin down into the dale bottom. They are closely spaced and have all the appearance of being air shafts on a very early sough. No other information is available.

POSSIBLE SOUGH NORTH OF SEEDLOW RAKE

A little to the north of Seedlow Rake, an un-named scrin ranges south eastwards obliquely down the side of Cressbrook Dale. Near the valley floor there is a walled channel leading to a run-in level and below are vague signs of closely spaced and very denuded shaft hollows on another early sough.

15. THE EDGE RAKE AND BRANDY BOTTLE MINES, WHESTON

This group of mines lies immediately north east of the hamlet of Wheston, some 1¼ miles north west of Tideswell. The 1:25 000 geological map (Millers Dale) depicts six veins, of which the principal, Edge Rake ranges slightly north of east to Tideswell Brook at Brook Bottom. At Brook Bottom is the tail of Edge Rake Sough, sometimes referred to as Brandy Bottle Sough.

The veins were exploited in strata from the Monsal Dale Limestone, down through the Upper Millers Dale Lava into the Millers Dale Limestone and through the Lower Lava into the underlying limestone. The strata have a shallow dip towards the north east at angles of 3 to 8 degrees. The gentle topography and geological structure have dictated that chronological development was not related to progressive exploitation in lower beds.

No dates are available for when the veins adjacent to the hamlet of Wheston were first worked in the Millers Dale Limestone lying between the Upper and Lower lavas. Historical evidence dating from the mid 19th century reveals that at least one and possibly two deep engine shafts at Edge Rake Mine and Brandy Bottle Mine penetrated the Lower Lava and entered the limestones beneath. Further towards the east, the upper workings on Edge Rake (and Providence Vein?) were developed in the Monsal Dale Beds above the Upper Lava, but again no historical details are known. Due west of the un-named lane that connects Whestonbank and Water Lane, there is a broad line of old hillocks and run-in shaft hollows developed in the Monsal Dale Limestone that give the impression of considerable age, perhaps dating from the 17th and 18th centuries.

Two large shaft mounds on Edge Rake, one east of the un-named lane and between it and the sough tail, and a second in the field next but one west of the lane, no doubt were drawing shafts, the former at least connected with haulage of spoil from the sough. At Wheston there is a complex of shafts, waste hillocks and the remains of an engine house, chimney and two gin-circles, most associated with work carried out in the mid to late 19th century. Some of the site has been disturbed and some waste tipping has taken place. Surface evidence of the smaller veins has been largely obliterated by land improvement.

The Edge Rake, Providence and Brandy Bottle mines were all interconnected, but surviving Barmasters` entries carry insufficient detail for their precise relationship to be established. Providence Mine was described in 1824 as being *situate near old Edge Rake Vein* [DRO, Br-T L 47]. The title consisted of 15 meers of ground, seven meers east and seven meers west from the Founder. These distances are in accordance with the main section of a vein lying north of, and more or less parallel with Edge Rake. The Yatestoop Mine and Golden Ball Mine were also situated very close to Wheston, but their location is not known.

The earliest notice to the mines occurs in 1709 when a solitary reference to *farr Edge Rake* is included in a list of mines with some ore measurements within Tideswell Liberty [SCL, Bag 549]. In April, 1734 a 1/6th share in Edge Rake in Tideswell Liberty, along with shares in mines in Great Hucklow, Eyam Edge and Stoke Sough, were mortgaged by John and Benjamin Hallam, miners of Stoney Middleton [DRO, Br-T L56]. There follows a gap in documentary evidence until September, 1747 when the purchase of *a Tar`d Rope* was recorded at Edge Rake in Tideswell (Liberty) [SCL, Bag 547]. *Goulden Ball* was recorded in a Barmaster entry in 1770 [SCL, Bag 587/46].

The site of the late 18th century trial known as Yatestoop Mine is not known, but very probably the shaft was begun within the outcrop of the Millers Dale Lower Lava and soon abandoned. Nellie Kirkham misinterpreted documentary evidence and presumed it to be the great mine at Winster bearing the same name. On the 18th September, 1772 two miners, Thomas Bowman senior and junior gave Robert Drabble, Barmaster a dish of ore to free, *an Old mine in the Whete yart at Wheston Now cald the yate stoop by us.* The trial was begun in December, 1772 but abandoned only two years later after expenditure of £195-14-3, no ore being mined. The miners had the mine arrested for money due to them, for which they were given permission *taking Mine, Engine and other materials for their money* [SCL, Bag 431a]. Miss Kirkham mistakenly understood this to mean that the miners were given the underground Fire Engine at Yatestoop Mine, Winster.

No documentary evidence relating to Edge Rake Sough has been found. The sough tail has run-in, recent exploration via a shallow air shaft penetrated only 250 feet before an apparent forefield was reached. The possibility that a natural cave passage continues beyond has been suggested [D. Stables, pers. comm.]. Exploration has revealed gunpowder shot holes believed to be of 18th–19th century date. Hydrological considerations lead to the conclusion that the sough did not extend far enough for it to breach the Lower Millers Dale Lava. This hypothesis is based on the completely waterlogged condition of the lowest levels at the time of the mid 19th century deep workings at Edge Rake and Brandy Bottle mines. Documentary evidence is lacking, but the sough possibly terminated at the interface with the Lower Millers Dale Lava about 3,000 feet from the tail.

Small quantities of ore were measured at Golden Ball [SCL, Bag 587/44] in 1814-1815 and similar small measures of ore recorded from 1820 to 1841 at Edge Rake, Providence and Brandy Bottle mines, but output was infrequent [DRO, Br-T L 47]. A period of active exploitation took place from about 1843 until the mid 1850s and again from 1868. The principal shareholders at the earlier venture were Thomas Meerbeck of Sheffield, Thomas Eyre, lead merchant of Castleton and John and Joseph Wright of Wheston. An isolated reckoning indicates that miners were paid at a rate of 2/6d per shift in 1846. [DRO, Eyre Deeds, L 4].

More detail emerges in June, 1851 at which time two agreements were made. Thomas Eyre agreed that John Wright was to work Edge Rake Vein *to his own profit* from June, 1851 until December, 1853 paying to Thomas Eyre 2/6d for every measure of ore, clear of all expenses of getting the same out of Brandy Bottle Engine Shaft [DRO, Eyre Deeds, L 8]. One month later Wright and Thomas Meerbeck leased to Thomas Eyre:

> To drive a waggon gate out of Edge Rake Mine, to begin at the now West End forefield – to drive as he thinks fit – the gate 6 feet high – taking to himself all the ore got in driving the gate [DRO, Eyre Deeds. L 9].

But any ore either above or below the gate was for the benefit of the Providence proprietors. Eyre was also to have benefit of *the now used Cartgate Engine*. Eyre was able to report by June, 1853 that good ore had been found including one lump weighing 3 hundredweight found by a miner named Thomas Flint.

At Brandy Bottle too there was good news. Eyre writing to Thomas Mearbeck in March, 1853 that:

> we have met with the Swallow where we were driving at the West End of the Engine shaft which I think will be all that will be required to relief us of the Water after we have cut through to it – can hear the water in it seems to be at a great depth – from the noise of it appears to be a very large open one [DRO, Eyre Deeds, L 21].

A cautionary note in the next letter dated April, 1853 explained that *getting water out of Brandy Bottle is difficult since the bottom springs are not low enough to draw the water without enormous expense.*

However, Thomas Eyre was able to report to Thomas Mearbeck that in mid May, 1853: *Got the water out of the bottoms at Wheaston ten days ago – the mine should be good if it can be managed for water* [DRO, Eyre Deeds, L 23]. The location of the swallow, well beneath the Lower Millers Dale Lava, suggests that if as postulated Edge Rake Sough did not reach the mine complex, then the water drained through its original natural course from the swallow near Brandy Bottle Shaft to resurge near the head of Monks Dale.

Ore to the value of £465-6-8 was sold in the period from October, 1852 to August 1853, heavy charges of £427-4-10 still enabled a profit of £38-1-10 to be recorded. A document entitled *Remarks on Lead Mines and Mining Interests in the Hundred of High Peak*, is un-dated but from internal evidence must have been written about 1860 states that the Brandy Bottle, Providence and Edge Rake mines *have been wrought by Company`s of Adventurers but unremunerative and are now only partially wrought* [DRO, Br-T L269/1].

A new venture calling itself `The Edge Rake Mining Company` was established in 1868. The Barmaster set out ground around the Brandy Bottle New Engine Shaft in October, 1868 and more surface land there in December, 1869 [Chats, Dev Coll]. A report in the Sheffield Morning Telegraph, dated April, 1869 reported that the shaft was 47 fathoms in depth and a gate being driven from the shaft bottom was only 4 yards distant from the vein. The documents dating from the 1850s do not mention installation of an Engine and there seems to be every likelihood that the surface remains of the engine house and chimney date from this last period of operations. Nothing more is heard of the mine and it must have been a short-lived speculation that met with little success.

16. LEAD MINING AT BURBAGE AND CHROME HILL, NEAR BUXTON

Lead ore was mined at Burbage, south west of Buxton from at least 1662 and continued, albeit intermittently, until the first half of the 19th century. At least ten rakes and pipe veins are named in contemporary mining documents, but descriptions of their location in relation to known geographical features are at best poor, or at worst non-existent. Very probably many of the meers recorded under a particular title were never worked. The names of two drainage levels occur, Chance Sough and Gate Sough, but the author considers them to be identical.

The mines were worked in the Monsal Dale Limestones on the western flank of Grin Hill (known earlier as Grin Common). The beds dip towards the west and north west at angles of 15 to 25 degrees, locally steepening, before passing beneath the shale cover. Large scale excavations carried out in conjunction with recent housing development near Anncroft Road, revealed dramatic evidence of buried karst features beneath the site in the form of large, widened joints with fluted walls and two deep swallow holes, all infilled with weathered Namurian shale, a variety of cave sediments and other Pleistocene and Recent sediments and Head deposits. Three other swallow holes, all more or less aligned along the limestone-shale interface lay outside the development boundary.

Short [1734] discussed the strata at the lead mines *next to Buxton* and noted the boundary between the limestone and shale thus:

Where a Chink happens between the Greetstone and Lime-stone it is filled up with Petrefactions. Later, he again referred to: *The Chasms of the Rocks - - wedged up with Petrefactions - - at the Lead Mines beyond Buxton*

A `Chink` is an old miners` term for a natural cavity, but `petrefactions` were usually rock fragments, tufa and stalactites and stalagmites, rather than the types of infilling recently found in the above mentioned joints and swallow holes.

Seventeenth century accounts of the Burbage and Grin mines are very sparse and confined to depositions given by miners relating to payment of tithe ore in Hartington Liberty. Anthony Clayton of Buxton deposed that in 1662 he had a 1/6th share in *Rushy Gutter* from which mine 60 loads of ore were obtained and in 1663 he had a 1/12th share in *Saw Groves*; the Barmaster was `Mr. Peters` [PRO, E 134 4William and Mary, Hilary 15].

There follows a gap of sixty seven years until October, 1730, when a complaint was heard in the Hartington Barmote Court:

Stephen Gill compaineth himself against Mr John Answorth for wages dew for him to paffrom a sertin mine called deeper ye Better Near Buxton laying in a sertin pees of ground called grin – being 16/6d [Chats, Dev Coll].

CHANCE SOUGH   GATE SOUGH

Chance Vein and Saw Rake are two closely parallel veins. Meers were set out by the Barmaster(s) along both, ranging north west - south east from near Plex Farm to Grin Low Road. The position of *Saw Grove* is shown on a map dated 1775. The grove was situated immediately on the west side of the Buxton-Leek road, adjacent to the cottage known as Grove House, opposite to where the river Wye crosses the head of Anncroft Road. (Saw Knowl was on the south west side of Grin Hill, but since removed by quarrying). Limited historical documentation suggests that the productive workings were confined to the south eastern half of the titles, that is from Dogholes Vein adjacent to the Macclesfield Old Road to Grin Low Road. Unfortunately, most has been obliterated by housing development at Ann Croft and quarrying and associated tipping on Grin.

Ore measurement accounts held at Chatsworth House encompassing the years 1730–1792 record very small quantities obtained from Saw Rake, but in 1734 and 1772 only. Measurement of ore from Chance Mine began in September, 1750 and continued until 1769. Total production reached 1,464 loads

1 dish, of which 1,015 loads 7 dishes were measured as smitham, much of it no doubt purposely beaten down by the ore dressers so as to avoid payment of Lot. A Lord`s Meer was valued there in March, 1752 proving it to be a `new vein`, not previously worked: *By the Lord`s Mear sold at Chance Myne in Hartington Liberty to Mr Hodgson and Co. £10-10-0* [Chats, Dev Coll].

Satisfactory output was achieved in 1750–1753 stimulating the proprietors into construction of a drainage level. The level was first recorded in February, 1754 when the Barmaster paid a miner named Francis Clark 3/-

For going to View and Value the Lord`s Mear in a Vein that Mr. Hodgson and Partners are driving in for a Sough to relieve Chance in Hartington Liberty [Chats, Dev Coll].

The position and range of the sough is described below under Gate Sough. Output at Chance Mine declined rapidly and was very small during the last eight years of operations, i.e.1762-1769. Mining began again at Chance Mine in 1782 and continued until 1791, but the owner, John Dawson measured only 161 loads 6 dishes, the venture was very small scale.

Gate Sough was first recorded in August, 1780. A Founder meer and first taker meer were freed immediately, the absence of a second founder meer and Lord`s Meer confirm that the sough-vein had been worked previously (i.e. Chance Sough). The venture was a failure, only 79 loads 5 dishes being raised through to 1806. A mere 22 loads 8 dishes were mined from 1784-1806 [DRO, Br-T L30].

The tail of Chance Sough or Gate Sough is now marked by a deep pool at the point where Bishop`s Lane crosses the river Wye, close to Upper Otter Holes Farm. Local information confirms the site. The position of the old Founder was noted in September, 1801 as being 10 meers from the sough tail and is the location of a shaft formerly visible just north of Gate Farm [John Leach, pers. comm]. The sough ranges slightly west of south to Dogholes adjacent to the Macclesfield Old Road. Here, Chance Vein and the closely parallel Saw Rake cross Dogholes Vein. There is little documentary information about the upper reaches of the sough. A reasonable hypothesis would be that beyond the Dogholes Vein intersection the main level was continued south eastwards along the sole of Chance Vein/Saw Rake. During abortive working in the 19th century it became known as *Sough Gate Vein*. A Barmaster entry in May, 1835 gave two miners Benjamin Bonsall and William Nall 21 meers of ground: *in an old Vein - - called Sough Gate Vein beginning at an Old Hillock - - at the north west fence of a piece of Land – called Saw Knowl – all ranging North Westwardly.*

A minor branch from the sough possibly extended for an unknown distance southwards along Dogholes Vein. The range of Dogholes Vein was described in September, 1779 as: *seventeen Meers of Ground ranging Southwardly from a Place called Gate lying to the Saw Rake* [DRO, Br-T L 30]. The vein must range parallel with Anncroft Road and extend beyond, beneath the bottom of the shallow valley at the limestone-shale boundary. Two closely spaced shafts, shown on the published 6 inches to 1 mile geological map adjacent to Anncroft Road, were most probably sunk on the vein. Between 1730 and 1792 ore was measured at Dogholes only in 1773. The absence of any additional ore measures suggests that any branch level driven along the vein was abortive.

Rushy Gutter Vein, Rushy Gutter Pipe, Bolepit Rake and Quakers Vein or Bolepit Pipe, were small veins ranging south west from Saw Rake; little is known about them but very small amounts of ore were obtained from Rushy Gutter in 1742 and 1744 [Chats, Dev Coll]. It has proved impossible to place Zachary, or Old Zachary mines; Ladmorelow foot Vein ranged west from Saw Rake, whilst the title to Ladmorelow Vein was set out for 58 meers (5,046 feet): *as far as the Thatch Marsh Wheell Engine Coalpit Shaft* [DRO, Br-T L 30]. These meers terminate exactly at the position of the Engine Pit at Thatch Marsh Colliery [Roberts and Leach, 1985].

CROOM HILL SOUGH

Chrome Hill, originally Croom Hill is a spectacular, upstanding mass of reef limestone, surrounded by Namurian shales. The shales were deposited onto a highly eroded limestone surface and several exposures demonstrate the contact of these near horizontal shales, lapping onto the steeply dipping limestone at the foot of Chrome Hill. The dip of the limestone is from 30 to 45 degrees toward the south. The geological memoirs largely ignore mineralisation on the hill, making but scant reference to a part of the Chrome Hill Fault being mineralised [Aitkenhead et.al., 1985].

Nothing is known about lead production, but presumably it was small and fairly insignificant. Calamine was obtained from both *Croom Hill* and Parkhouse Hill in 1750, the ore being taken to Mill Dale Calamine Mill, owned by the Cheadle Brass and Copper Co [Porter and Robey, 2000]. At the southernmost tip of the hill, at the point where the river Dove touches its base, a line of hillocks can be seen ranging almost due north up the precipitous hillside. Immediately at the lower end of this vein is a level, accesible until the 1970s. Only 60 yards in length, it was 6 feet in height and 3 feet in width. Locally, it is said to have been a zinc mine.

Excepting the mid 18th century zinc mining, the earliest reference occurs in July, 1808 when John Birch and partners were given:

> *an Old Founder on the south side of Croom Hill ranging East and Westwardly with Ten Meers East and Ten Meers West from the Shaft. And also gave him the Sough Levell* [DRO, Br-T, L30].

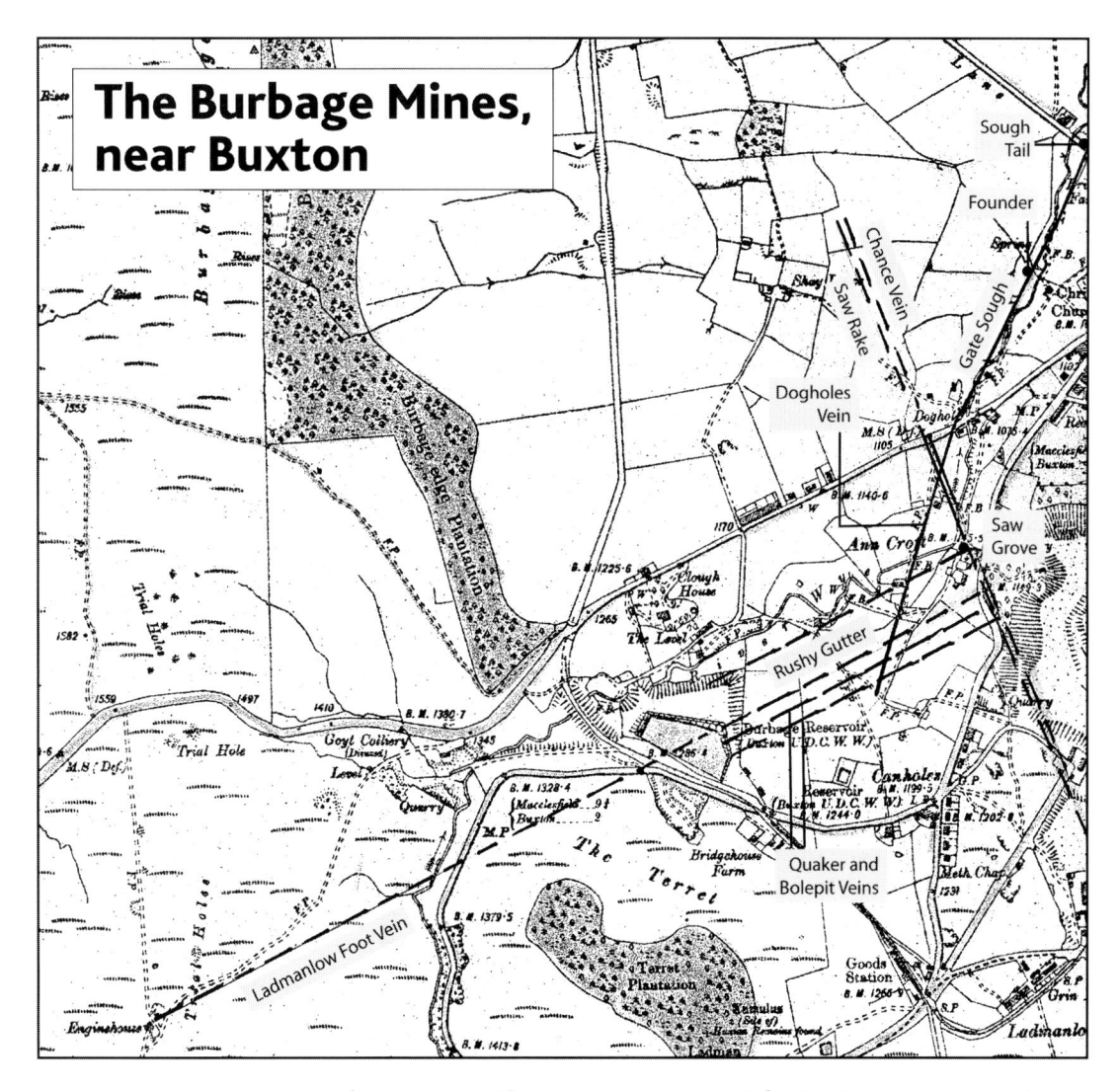

No mine plans are known to exist for this area and Barmaster entries are ill-defined and sometimes contradictory. The lines depicted on the map are a best-fit approximation. The position of Saw Grove is accurate.

(The terms `east` and `west` were an approximation, used in relation to the position of magnetic north at that date and not grid north).

The next, and only other reference occurs in 1842, when Melville Attwood, who was concerned with copper, zinc and lead mining took title:

> *put Isaac Wain (for the use of Melville Attwood Esq) into possession of twenty meers of ground in an old vein situate upon Croome Hill - beginning at the side of the River Dove near an old level and all ranging northwardly from the said river. Also three cross veins* [Chats, Dev Coll].

No other information has been seen relating to Attwood's venture at Chrome Hill, and maybe no work was undertaken.

SOUGHS and LEVELS within the LIBERTY OF HARTINGTON (UPPER QUARTER) having uncertain provenance.

On the east side of Grin Low a line of five shaft hillocks run downhill to Hillside Plantation and towards the shallow valley in Fern Wood. There is one small shaft in the plantation and surface evidence terminates well above the valley floor. They have all the appearance of a line of air shafts along a sough. The hillocks contain a few scattered pieces of gangue stuff, but they are composed mainly of rock fragments and earth. No name is known for these workings and no historical detail has emerged.

BIBLIOGRAPHY

PRINTED SOURCES;

ADAM, W. 1838 The Gem of the Peak. London. pp. 256.

ADDY, S. O 1933 Local Words and Their Meanings. Trans. Hunter Arch. Society, vol 4, pp. 113-130.

AITKENHEAD, N. 1985 Geology of the country around Buxton, Leek and et. al. Bakewell. British Geological Survey, London. pp. 168.

ANON. 1755 Account of the Earthquake as felt in the Lead Mines of Derbyshire. Philosophical Transactions, vol. x. (abridged).

BAGSHAW, S. 1846 History, Gazetteer and Directory of Derbyshire. Sheffield. 702 pp.

BAGSHAWE, B. 1863 Account of some old mining tools found in the Hilltop Mine, Great Hucklow. The Reliquary, vol. 4, pp. 43-44.

BAND, S. 1975-6 Lead Mining in Ashover. Bull. PDMHS, vol. 6, no. 2 pp. 113-115; vol. 6, no. 3 pp. 29-139.

BAND, S. 1983 The Steam Engines of Gregory Mine, Ashover. Bull PDMHS, vol. 8, no. 5, pp. 269-295.

BARNATT, J. and 2004 The Lead Legacy. Peak District National Park Authority.
PENNY, R. (issued with);
BARNATT, J. 2004 An inventory of regionally and nationally important lead mining sites in the Peak Distict.
2005 Inventory up-dated.

BARNATT, J. and 2006 Using Coal to Mine Lead: Firesetting at Peak District
WORTHINGTON, T. Mines. Bull PDMHS, vol. 16, no. 3, pp. 1-94.

BECK, J. 1978 Caves, Mines and Soughs of the Wardlow Basin and Cressbrook Dale. Bull PDMHS, vol. 7, no. 3.

BRITTON, J. and 1802 The Beauties of England and Wales: Derbyshire. London.
BRAYLEY, E. W.

CAMERON, K. 1959 The Place Names of Derbyshire. English Place Name Society. Cambridge University Press.

CRABTREE, P. 1966 The Peak Forest Mines. Cave Science, vol. VI, no. 42.

DONALD, M. B. 1961 Elizabethan Monopolies. Oliver and Boyd. Edinburgh.

DUNHAM, K. C. 1952 Fluorspar. 4th edn. Memoirs of the Geological Survey. London. 143 pp.

EVANS, S. 1907 Methodism in Bradwell. New Mills. 108 pp.

EVANS, S. 1912 Bradwell; Ancient and Modern. 135 pp. Bradwell.

FAREY, J. 1811-17 The Agriculture and Minerals of Derbyshire. 3 volumes. Board of Agriculture, London.

FEARNSIDES, W. and TEMPLEMAN, A. 1932 A boring ... at Hope Cement Works ... near Castleton. Proc. Yorks. Geol. Soc, vol. XXII. Pp. 100-121.

FERBER, J. J. 1776 Oryktographie of Derbyshire (in German). Mittau.

FORD, T. D. 1962 Long Cliffe Mine, Castleton. Bull PDMHS, vol. 1, no. 7, pp. 1-4.

FORD, T. D. and RIEUWERTS, J. H. 2000 Lead Mining in the Peak Distict. 4th edn. Matlock Bath. 207pp.

FRANCE, R. S. 1951 The Thieveley Lead Mines. Lancashire and Cheshire Record Society, volume 102.

GILL, D. W. and BECK, J. S. 1991 Caves of the Peak District. Dalesman. 257 pp.

GREEN, A. H. et. al. 1887 The Geology of the Carboniferous Limestones etc. of North Derbyshire. Mem. Geol. Survey. 2nd edn. 212 pp. 1st edition, 1869.

GREG, R. P. and LETTSOM, W. G. 1858 Mineralogy of Great Britain and Ireland. London. 483 pp.

HEATHCOTE, C. D. 2001 Mines in the Liberty of Peak Forest, 1605-1878. Bull PDMHS, vol. 14, no. 5, pp. 1-28.

HEDINGER, J. M. c.1795 A short description of Castleton in Derbyshire. Derby.

HOOSON, W. 1747 The Miners Dictionary. Wrexham.

HOPKINS, 1834 On the Stratification of the Limestone District of Derbyshire. Private publication. 47 pp.

HOPKINSON, G. 1644 The Laws and Customs of the Mines within the Wapentake of Wirksworth. Printed in 1944. Nottingham.

HOPKINSON, G. c.1958 Five generations of Derbyshire lead mining and smelting Derbys. Arch. Journal, vol. 78, pp. 9-24.

JAMESON, R.	1820	A System of Mineralogy. Edinburgh. 3 volumes.
KIERNAN, D.	1989	The Derbyshire Lead Industry in the Sixteenth Century. Derbyshire Record Society, vol. XIV, 338 pp.
KIRKHAM, N.	1950	Old drowned work in Derbyshire. Derbys. Arch. Journal, vol. 70, pp. 1-20.
KIRKHAM, N.	1951	Lead Mine Soughs of Eyam, Stoney Middleton and Calver. British Caver, vol. 22, pp. 56-67.
KIRKHAM, N.	1952	Lead Mine Soughs of Eyam, Stoney Middleton and Calver. British Caver, vol. 23, pp. 64-77.
KIRKHAM, N.	1953	The Tumultuous Course of Dovegang. Derbys. Arch. Journal, vol. 73, pp. 1-35.
KIRKHAM, N.	1953	Lead Mine Soughs of Eyam, Stoney Middleton and Calver. British Caver, vol. 24, pp. 82-100.
KIRKHAM, N.	1954	Underground Water and some Derbyshire Lead Mine Soughs. Trans. Cave Research Group of Gt. Britain, vol. 3, no. 1, pp. 5-15.
KIRKHAM, N.	1957	Glebe Mine, Eyam. Derbyshire Miscellany, Bull. Local History Section. Derbys. Arch. Soc. vol. 1 no. 7, pp. 92-97.
KIRKHAM, N.	1962	Discussion (includes Oden *Peakshill Sough*). Bull PDMHS, vol. 1, no. 7, pp. 34-35.
KIRKHAM, N.	1963	Great Hucklow Mines. Bull PDMHS, vol. 2, no. 1, pp. 31-47.
KIRKHAM, N.	1964	Grindlow mines – Derbyshire Miscellany Bull. Local History Section. Derbys. Arch. Soc.
KIRKHAM, N.	1965-66	Eyam Edge Mines and Soughs. Bull PDMHS, vol. 2, nos. 5 and 6, pp. 241-254 and 315-354; vol. 3, nos. 1 and 2, pp. 43-57 and 103-118.
KIRKHAM, N.	1966	Longstone Edge area mines and soughs. Cave Science, vols. 39 and 40, pp. 354-368 and 440-469.
KIRKHAM, N	1967	Oakenedge, Streaks and Watergrove Soughs. Bull PDMHS, vol. 3, no. 4, pp. 197-218.
KIRKHAM, N.	1968	Soughs in Middleton Dale. Bull PDMHS, vol 3, no. 6, pp. 329-338.
LANDER, and VELLACOTT	1907	Lead Mining in Derbyshire, in The Victoria History of the County of Derby, volume 2, pp. 323-349.

LAWSON, J.	1968	Index to the Mining Records in the Bagshawe Collection in the John Rylands Library, Manchester. Bull PDMHS, vol. 3, no. 6 and vol. 4, no 1, pp. 305-312 and 353-356.
LISTER, M.	1673	On a Subterraneous Fungus. Phil. Trans. Royal Soc. no. 100, p.120.
MANLOVE, E.	1653	The Liberties and Customs of the Lead Mines in the Wapentake of Wirksworth. London. (often known as *The Rhymed Chronicle*).
MATKIN, R. B.	1980	An Account of a Visit by John Rennie to Peak Cavern. Bull PDMHS, vol. 7, no. 6, pp. 333-334.
MAWE, J.	1802	The Mineralogy and Geology of Derbyshire. London. pp. 211.
MEDLICOTT, I. R.	1999	John Curr; 1756-1823; Mining Engineer and Viewer. Aspects of Sheffield, No.2. Wharncliffe Publishing Ltd.
PENNEY, D.	1985	Peakshole Sough. Bull PDMHS, vol. 9, no. 3, pp.171-185
PILKINGTON, J.	1789	A View of the Present State of Derbyshire. Derby. 2 volumes.
PORTER, L. and ROBEY, J.	2000	The Copper and Lead Mines around the Manifold Valley. Landmark, Ashbourne, 269 pp.
RIEUWERTS, J. H.	1981	A Technological History of the Drainage of the Derbyshire Lead Mines. Unpub. Ph.D. thesis. University of Leicester, 591 pp.
RIEUWERTS, J. H.	1983	Cromford Sough and the early use of gunpowder. Bull PDMHS, vol. 8, no. 5, pp. 315-329.
RIEUWERTS, J. H.	1987	A History and Gazetteer of the Lead Mine Soughs of Derbyshire. The author, Sheffield. 1st edn. 143 pp.
RIEUWERTS, J. H.	1991	An early Barmote Court dispute and some facts relating to Flots, Floats, Flats and Pipes. Bull PDMHS, vol. 11, no. 3, pp. 145-147.
RIEUWERTS, J. H.	1993	Elias Pedley, a Castleton Lead Miner and his Contribution to Early Geological Thought. Bull PDMHS, vol. 12, no. 2, pp. 57-59.
RIEUWERTS, J. H.	1994	Lead Mining within the Royal Forest of the Peak during the 13th Century. Bull PDMHS, vol. 12, no. 3, pp. 60-61.
RIEUWERTS, J. H.	1998	Glossary of Derbyshire Lead Mining Terms. PDMHS, Matlock Bath, 192 pp.
RIEUWERTS, J. H.	2004	The Lead Mines within the Lordship or Liberty of Ashford Northside. Private report commissioned by the Peak District National Park Authority.

RIEUWERTS, J. H.	2005	The Mines within the Lordships or Liberties of Calver, Hassop and Rowland. Private report commissioned by the Peak District National Park Authority.
RIEUWERTS, J. H. and FORD, T. D.	1976	Odin Mine, Castleton, Derbyshire. Bull PDMHS, vol. 6, no. 4, pp. 1-54.
RIEUWERTS, J. H. and FORD, T. D.	1985	Mining History of the Speedwell Mine or Oakden Level, Castleton. Bull PDMHS, vol. 9, no. 3, pp. 129-170
ROBERTS, J. F. and LEACH, J. R.	1985	The Coal Mines of Buxton. Scarthin Books, 94 pp.
ROBEY, J.	1964	Discovery of a Cavern on Crosslow Rake, Foolow. Bull PDMHS, vol. 2, no. 3, pp. 151-152.
ROLT, L. T. C. and ALLEN, J. S.	1997	The Steam Engine of Thomas Newcomen. Landmark Publishing, 2nd edn, pp. 160.
ROYSE, J.	1943	Ancient Castleton Caves. The author, Castleton. 76 pp.
SHORT, T.	1734	The History of the Mineral Waters of Derbyshire, Lincolnshire and Yorkshire. London. 359 pp.
STEER, G.	1734	Compleat Mineral Laws of Derbyshire. Sheffield.
STOKES, A. H.	1878-79	Economic geology of Derbyshire. Trans. Chesterfield and Derbys. Inst. of Mining, Civil and Mech. Engineers, volume 6.
STOKES, A. H.	1880-81	Lead and Lead Mining in Derbyshire. Trans. Chesterfield and Derbys. Inst. of Mining, Civil and Mech. Engineers. Contained in volumes 8, 9 and 11.
THOMPSON, S.	1969	Some notes on the Pindale Sough. Journal of the Sheffield University Speleological Society, vol. 1, no. 5.
THORNHILL, R.	1962	The Seedlow Lead Mine, 1764-1771. Bull PDMHS, vol. 1, no. 6, pp. 24-28.
THORNHILL, R.	1965	Lead Mining near Calver. Derbyshire Miscellany. Bull. Local History Section, Derbys. Arch. Soc., pp. 588-596.
THORNHILL, R.	1967	Some Accounts of an 18th century Lead Mining Agent in Great Longstone. Bull PDMHS, vol. 3, no. 4, pp. 219-232
STRAHAN, A.	1887	On Explosive Slickensides. Geological Magazine, Decade 3, vol. 4, pp. 400-408.
WALTERS, S.	1981	A Review of the Distribution and Correlation of Igneous Rocks in Derbyshire. Mercian Geologist, vol. 8, no. 2.

WALTERS, S. and INESON, R.	1981	Mineralisation within the Igneous Rocks of the South Pennine Orefield. Bull PDMHS, vol. 7, no. 6, pp. 315-325
WATSON, W.	1811	A Delineation of the Strata of Derbyshire. Sheffield. pp.76
WATSON, W.	1813	A Section of the Strata … in the Vicinity of Matlock Bath. Chesterfield. 19 pp.
WHITEHURST, J.	1778	An Inquiry into the Original State and Formation of the Earth. 2nd edition, 1786.
WILLIES, L. and FLETCHER, G.	1975	Brightside Mine, Hassop. Bull PDMHS, vol. 6, no. 1, pp. 33-39.
WILLIES, L.	1976	John Taylor in Derbyshire, 1839-1851. Part 1. Bull PDMHS, vol. 6, no. 3, pp. 146-160.
WILLIES, L.	1982	John Fairburn – Stationer and Mining Entrepreneur. Bull PDMHS, vol. 8, no. 3, pp. 159-165.
WILLIES, L.	1983	The Barker Family and Wyatt Lead Mining Businesses. Bull PDMHS, vol. 8, no. 6, pp. 331-368.
WOOD, W.	1859	History of Eyam. London and Derby. 3rd edn, 187 pp.
WRIGHT, G. T.	1906	Longstone Records. Bakewell. 389 pp.

MANUSCRIPT SOURCES;

Wherever possible full and detailed references to all manuscripts have been provided within the text. Exceptions and some anomalies are explained below.

Originally all manuscript collections held by Sheffield City Libraries were housed in the Central Library, Surrey Street. Some years ago they were transferred to a new building situated at Shoreham Street, initially called Sheffield Records Office thereafter to be called Sheffield Archives. However, during the preceding years hundreds of manuscripts had been referenced by the author as SCL = Sheffield City Libraries. To avoid confusion this has been retained. For example [SCL, Bag 546] refers to Bagshawe Collection, item 546 whereas more recent researchers would list the collections as SA = Sheffield Archives and reference the example quoted above as [SA, Bag 546].

A detailed calendar of the Duchy of Lancaster`s Barmaster Collection, held on loan at Chatsworth House, has been compiled by Mr. Roger Flindall. The numbering system is complex. Unfortunately, some items have been lost or are missing from the collection and readers should refer to the Calendar for full details.

The Devonshire mining collections at Chatsworth House are in a lengthy process of re-numbering and readers should refer to the interim indices prepared by the author and available to visiting researchers at Chatsworth House.

Belvoir Castle:
- Belvoir — Manuscripts relating to the lead mining interests of the Earls and Dukes of Rutland. The documents are not available for public consultation

British Geological Survey, Keyworth, near Nottingham.
- BGS — Field note books and maps of A.H. Green and A. Strahan.

British Library, London:
- Loan ms 16. — Minute Books of the Society of Mines Royal and the Company of Mineral and Battery Works. Three volumes, 1588 – 1713.
- Wolley — Additional Manuscripts volumes 6676 to 6686 relate to Derbyshire lead mining. A micro film of these volumes is available at the Derbyshire County Library, Matlock.

Cambridge University, Department of Manuscripts:
GB 0012 MS ADD 6304; Notebook of White Watson, Derbyshire geologist.

Chatsworth House:
- Bar Coll — Barmasters Collection, the property of the Duchy of Lancaster.
- Dev Coll — Devonshire Collection.
- Halifax — Papers of the Marquis of Halifax including his mining interests in Eyam and Stoney Middleton.
- Hardwick — Documents formerly housed at Hardwick Hall.

Derbyshire County Library, Matlock
- Wolley — Microfilm.

DerbyLocal Studies Library:
Acc No 8371; Scrapbook written and compiled by the Derbyshire geologist White Watson.

Derbyshire Record Office, Matlock:
- Br-T — D504; Brooke Taylor Collection.
- Br-T — uncatalogued refers to a series of presently un-numbered 17th century soughing agreements.
- BSA Coll — Seven large folio volumes, now lost. Photocopies in D.A. Nash private archive.
- D2090 — Barmasters Book, Eyam and Stoney Middleton, 1758-1829.
- Eyre — D598; 17th century mining papers, Calver, Hassop and Rowland.
- Eyre Deeds — D1836; 19th century papers concerning with lead mining in Litton, Peak Forest, Wheston, Brushfield etc.,
- Grant Papers — D2270 Micro-film, original documents housed at the Scottish Record Office.
- D3266 — Mining plans, formerly housed at the Mining Record Office, London.

D1763	Palmer Morewood of Alfreton Hall. Mining and soughing at Eyam, early 18th century.
PDMHS Coll	D2160; archives of the Peak District Mines Historical Society.
D394Z	Tideswell, Great Hucklow and Litton Deeds, 17th – 19th century.
Rieuwerts	1289B; Rieuwerts Collection.
Robinson	D3304; Eyam and Stoney Middleton Barmasters Book, 1714-1731.
Wright Papers	D5430; Papers of the Wright family, Eyam Hall.

John Goodchild, Central Library, Wakefield:

Goodchild	A private collection, including Derbyshire lead mining papers. On loan to Wakefield City Archives.

Guildhall Library, London:

Marples	Accounts and correspondence relating to Richard Marples` interests in Derbyshire mining.

Lichfield Record Office:

Lichfield R.O.	Papers relating to the will of Godfrey Haslehurst. They include correspondence and financial accounts concerning his mining and soughing venture at Stoney Middleton; 1692-1698.
BSA	1154G; records formerly held by the British Speleological Association, Settle.
Nash, D. Eyam	Photocopies of seven volumes now lost (see Derbyshire Record Office).

National Archive, Public Record Office, Kew, London:

C1	Early Chancery Proceedings.
C3	Chancery Proceedings Series II; Elizabeth I to Commonwealth.
C12	Six Clerks Series II, 1714-1758 and 1758-1800.
DL 1	Duchy of Lancaster, pleadings.
DL 4	Duchy of Lancaster, depositions and examinations.
DL 44	Special Commissions and Returns, 1558-1853.
E 112	Exchequer Bills and Answers.
E 134	Exchequer depositions.
STAC	Court of Star Chamber, 1485-1641.

Rieuwerts, private collection:

Papers, books, plans held at Torwood Drive, Sheffield.

Royal Society, London:

Boyle	Papers of Robert Boyle.

John Rylands Library, Manchester:
Bag   Bagshawe Collection.

Sheffield Archives, formerly Sheffield City Libraries, Local History Library:
(in the text all references are prefixed by SCL).
 Bag   Bagshawe Collection.
 Bowles   Bowles Deeds.
 Brooksbank
 Fairbank
 LD   Loan Deposits.
 OD   Oakes Deeds.
 Spencer Stanhope
 Tibbetts   Tibbetts Collection.
 WH   Wager Holmes Collection.

Surrey History Service, Records Office, Woking.
 Bray   Papers of the Bray family of Shere.

ACKNOWLEDGEMENTS

The author is indebted to those many individuals who have contributed toward production of this work by sharing their knowledge and expertise, often including loan, or copies of mining documents in their possession. Naming all of them is an almost impossible task, and for any glaring omissions I offer my profound apologies.

Interest in Derbyshire`s old mines was stimulated in the early 1950s by the late Nellie Kirkham (Mrs. J.H.D. Myatt). A glance at the bibliography herein will reveal the debt owed to her for her pioneering research. The following deserve special thanks; Messrs Stuart Band, Dr. John Beck, Roger Flindall, Dr. Trevor Ford, Doug Nash and Dr. Lynn Willies. Other friends and colleagues who have given freely of their time and knowledge include Dr. Christoph Bartels, Dr. Ivor Brown Graham Crisp, John Elkins, Dr. Peter Gstrein, Robin Hall, John Harrison, Dr. David Jefferson, Dr. David Kiernan, John Leach, John Peel, Dave Penney, Lindsey Porter, Derek Stables, Steve Thompson, Phil Wainwright, Dave Warriner, Dave Williams, John Wilmot and Terry Worthington.

Mr. Henry Walker of Bradwell allowed access, through the good offices of Mr. Chris Furness, to manuscripts relating to the Moss Rake and Hazlebadge mines.

Particular thanks are extended to my three walking companions, Dr. John Barnatt, Mr. Chris Heathcote and Mr. Phil Shaw who have accompanied me and made many useful comments and suggestions during excursions to both sough and mine sites throughout Derbyshire. Chris Heathcote has also shared with me much of his great knowledge of the Peak Forest and Castleton area mines.

Mr. Paul Deakin has not only supplied the majority of the magnificent photographs, but his knowledge of underground Derbyshire has solved many problems. Thanks also to Mrs Sheila Newton and Lindsey and Russell Newton, for permission to use Malcolm Newton's drawing of the Milldam Mine, Great Hucklow.

Archivists and librarians have given much time and energy to my many requests during innumerable visits or via telephone or postal requests. Sincere thanks are due to them and also for permission to quote from manuscripts in their safe keeping. Belvoir Castle, by permission of His Grace, the Duke of Rutland, and with particular thanks to Mr. A. Thompson and Mrs. D. Staveley; British Geological Survey, Keyworth; British Library, London; Chatsworth House, by permission of His Grace the Duke of Devonshire and the Trustees of the Chatsworth Settlement; Derbyshire Record Office, Matlock; Duchy of Lancaster Office, London, with particular thanks to Mr. Roy Smith; Mr. John Goodchild, Wakefield; Guildhall Library, London; Lichfield Record Office; National Archive, Public Record Office, Kew; John Rylands Library, Manchester; Sheffield Archives; Surrey History Service, Woking.

LEAD MINING IN DERBYSHIRE SUBSCRIBERS

Presentation copies to:

His Grace the Duke of Devonshire

Roger Wardle, High Sheriff of Derbyshire

Paul A. Clarke Chief Executive, Duchy of Lancaster

Roy A. Smith, Duchy of Lancaster

Henry Stephenson, Lord of the Field; Calver, Hassop and Rowland

Michael Cockerton, Steward of the Derbyshire Barmote Courts

Edward T. Tennant, Barmaster of the Derbyshire Barmote Courts

Adlam-Stiles, M. & N., Winster
Ambler, J., Wisborough Green
Ashmore, E.A., Youlgreave
Bade, R., Morden, Surrey
Baldwin, J.A., Rawtenstall
Barr, T.A., Mitcham, Surrey
Bell, D., Allestree, Derby
Black, M.C., Ware, Herts
Bonson, A., Congleton
Botham, A., Stoke-on-Trent
Bowden, C., Great Hallingbury
Brassington, N.J., Holymoorside
Brownson, I., Duffield, Derby
Burns, N.R., Bristol
Burt, Prof. R., University of Exeter
Buxton, G., Ilkeston
Challis, P.J., Wirral
Clark, R., Tonbridge
Clifford, J.G., Eyama
Cousins, P.J., Chesterfield
Cork, R, Kniveton
Crowther, D., Derby
Dalrymple-Smith, D., Baslow

Dixon, E.M., Belper
Elsegood, A.D., Middleton by Wirksworth
Eyam Museum, Eyam
Farlow, S.A., Bridgnorth
Froggatt, J., Basingstoke
Gill, M.C., Keighley
Goodman, M., Butterton, Nr. Leek
Gough, D., Seagrave, Leicestershire
Greaves, P., Bonsall
Gregory, D.V., Norwich
Gunn, J., Marsden
Hancock, E., Cheadle
Heathcote, C.D., Chapel-en-le-Frith
Henstock, A., Bingham, Nottingham
Higginson, M., Ilkeston
Higton, J.S., Draycott
Hollingworth, M., Dulnain Bridge
Hollis, D.B., Paisley, Scotland
Hossack, A.C.E., Leicester
Howard, M.L., Park Gate, Fareham
Jackson, P., Billingham
Jacques, J.K., Barnsley
Jefferson, D.P., Melton Mowbray
Kitto-Smith, D., Harwich
Knight, J.A., Shirland
Kyle, J.M., Birmingham
Lansdell, C.C., Norwich
Larimore, T.J., Chaddesden, Derby
Lawson, J., Castle Douglas, Scotland
Lewes, S.P., New Mills
Maddison, B., Sheffield
Makin, K., Todmorden
Mason, W.J., Eccleston
McGrory, P., Whaley Bridge
Mottram, P., London
Munro, M.P., Barry